D1246759

THE COMMUNIST PARTY
OF INDONESIA

Issued under the auspices of the
Department of Asian Studies,
University of British Columbia

THE
COMMUNIST PARTY
OF INDONESIA

ITS HISTORY, PROGRAM AND TACTICS

by

JUSTUS M. VAN DER KROEF

University of Bridgeport

PUBLICATIONS CENTRE
UNIVERSITY OF BRITISH COLUMBIA
Vancouver, Canada
1965

Printed in Hong Kong by
CATHAY PRESS
31 Wong Chuk Hang Road, Aberdeen

PREFACE

CONSIDERING its age and importance in national politics the Indonesian Communist Party has suffered from a comparative lack of attention by students of Southeast Asian affairs. Few up-to-date histories and even fewer comprehensive accounts of the organization of the party exist, while the monograph material about Indonesian Communism that has appeared since World War II is frequently too fragmentary and specialized to provide a clear picture of the party's overall operations. Especially the role of the party since the advent of the *Sajap Leninis* (Leninist Wing) in it has received but little attention, although under the influence of 'the Leninists' the Indonesian Communists have reached their greatest prominence thus far.

The following pages offer a brief account of the history of the Indonesian Communist Party, along with an analysis of its theoretical principles, organizational structure and present place in Indonesian political life. An attempt has been made to focus particularly on the events of the last decade or so, and on the re-emergence of the party as a major power center on the national scene. For some of the data in this volume I have drawn on previously published articles, particularly on: 'Agrarian Reform and the Indonesian Communist Party', *Far Eastern Survey*, January, 1960; 'Indonesian Communist Policy and the Sixth Party Congress', *Pacific Affairs*, September, 1960; 'Lenin, Mao and Aidit', *The China Quarterly*, April–June, 1962; 'Dilemmas of Indonesian Communism', *Pacific Affairs*, Summer, 1962, and 'Peasant and Land Reform in Indonesian Communism', *Journal of Southeast Asian History*, March, 1963. I am grateful to the editors concerned for permission to reproduce material that originally appeared in these journals. Although this book appears under the auspices of the Department of Asian Studies, University of British Columbia, responsibility for opinions expressed rests with me.

This book is for S.O., *puteri mas.*

JUSTUS M. VAN DER KROEF

University of Bridgeport
Bridgeport, Connecticut.
October, 1964.

TABLE OF CONTENTS

PART I

HISTORY OF THE INDONESIAN COMMUNIST PARTY

CHAPTER I

FROM SEMARANG TO MADIUN

T HE EMERGENCE and growth of Indonesian Communism is an aspect of a general Asian revival that has occurred since the beginning of the present century, and in a narrower sense it is a by-product of the Indonesian nationalist awakening and reaction to the pattern of Dutch colonial control as it gradually emerged in the East Indian archipelago since the seventeenth century. Since the beginning of that century the Dutch East India Company had slowly but inexorably become the principal political power in the Indies imposing, often with reluctance, on the various Indonesian peoples a colonial administrative framework established in the interests of the commercial monopoly, which the Company always zealously pursued. The Company's trade hegemony in the Indies, the principal focus of its Asian and European operations, tended to seal the Indonesian world off from the outside, and to make its indigenous political entities and systems of production mere subsidiaries of the Company's own over-arching pattern of control. But with the end of the Company in 1800 a new 'international' era was to emerge once more for the Indies as the Company's Indonesian possessions became part of the Kingdom of the Netherlands, as concepts of public responsibility gradually entered into the principles of colonial statecraft (expressed, for example, in increasing concern for education, health and other government-sponsored social services), as Indonesian land and labor increasingly became investment objects for international capital and thus of general concern to the world market, and as the spread and consolidation of Dutch power throughout the Indonesian islands created the image of an emergent national entity upon the international scene.

The revolution in Indonesian society gradually accelerated during the nineteenth century and contributed to the forces of the developing Indonesian national renascence.[1] A steady expansion of the Indonesian population (between 1815 and 1940 Java's Indonesian population grew from about 4 to 44 million) further disrupted the structure of the village-centered peasant society, while the proletarianization of the rural populace was further encouraged by the operations of the big Western estates and trading corporations, and by the expansion of government services (e.g. in the transportation field) and of small-scale and cottage industry. The slow emergence of an Indonesian élite of educated commoners and aristocracy, chafing under the political, economic and racial restrictions of the colonial system, gave impetus to new political aspirations that crystallized in a wide range of partisan ideological movements to which modernist currents in Islam made an important contribution. By the beginning of the twentieth century there emerged the image of a modern national Indonesian personality influencing, and in varying degrees expressed by, the younger aristocracy and the rising group of urban traders, by the Indonesian layers of the colonial bureaucracy, by younger Muslim and more secularly oriented intellectuals, and by the budding trade union movement, although potent and exclusivist ethnic and regional traditions were always present just beneath the surface.

The history of the Indonesian Communist Party can be divided into five principal phases: (1) the years from 1920–1927, during which the party rapidly reached a highwater mark of agitation but also almost destroyed itself by an ill-planned insurrection; (2) the period 1927–1945 during which the PKI was largely confined to underground activity; (3) a brief span of resurgence from 1945 to 1948 culminating in the party's disastrous coup at Madiun; (4) the years from 1948 to 1952, marked initially by a divided leadership and tactical conflict which gave way to a new 'Leninist' direction in the party under D. N. Aidit; and (5) the period of the PKI's greatest growth and influence, beginning with the National Party Conference of 1952 and marked by the uncontested leadership of Aidit as secretary-general and as party chairman up to the present. It is only in this last period that the PKI emerges as a truly Leninist party with a developed organization and revolutionary theory. To appreciate the party's position today and its achievements in the past decade it is necessary to describe the earlier periods in the party's history in some detail. The present chapter will be concerned with the first three periods in PKI history, the second chapter with the era of resurgence of the party from 1948 until after the general elections of 1955, while the third chapter will deal with events leading to the establishment of 'guided democracy'.

1920–1927. The founding of the PKI on May 23, 1920, was a culmination of the more radical Marxist currents which had been stirring colonial Indonesian society for more than a decade and which attained a new urgency as a result of the political upheavals in various parts of the world following the First World War. Since the turn of the century Dutch radicals, some of whom had developed their Marxist outlook during their student days at the Technical College in Delft, and others who also were members of the Dutch Social Democratic Labor Party or had been active in the Dutch trade union movement, had come to Indonesia, most frequently employed by various government services. One or two of this group almost at once attempted to steer the budding Indonesian nationalist and trade union movements in a revolutionary direction. The redoubtable Dutch communist H. J. Sneevliet (who under the name of 'Maring' was to play a fateful role as the Comintern's agent in the early period of the Chinese revolution in the 1920's[2]) took the initiative in the founding (in Semarang, Central Java) of an 'Indian Social Democratic Association' in 1914, which six years later on May 23, 1920, at its Seventh Congress in Semarang, changed its name to the 'Indian Communist Party' (*Perserikatan Kommunist di India*, or PKI).[3] This PKI, of which the youthful Javanese Semaoen was elected chairman (the Dutch colonial government had already, in December 1918, barred Sneevliet from further residence in the Netherlands East Indies), almost at once affiliated itself as a section of the Comintern. Its leaders found themselves in an atmosphere of rapid political change, occasioned by the turbulence of radical Socialists in the Netherlands, which was widely expected to have consequences in Indonesia, by the effects of the establishment in Indonesia of an embryo parliament (the so-called People's Council or *Volksraad*, in 1918) and by government promises and plans to revise the constitutional structure of the colonial Indonesian government in the direction of greater autonomy. The impact of rapidly developing, though heterogeneous, nationalist groups, and the increasingly radical temper pervading the recently formed trade unions, all reflected the advent of a new political consciousness which was ready for Communist exploitation.

Very shortly, however, the PKI was to demonstrate its inability to utilize this new spirit of political self-awareness in the country. In the 'Theses and Statutes' of the Third International, largely drafted by Lenin, and adopted by the Comintern's Second Congress meeting in Moscow in July and August, 1920 (the exiled Sneevliet acted at this Congress as the more or less official representative of Indonesia), it had been decided: that 'all Communist parties must give active support to the revolutionary movements of liberation' in the colonial countries; that Communist parties should 'establish temporary relations and even unions with the revolutionary movements in the colonies and backward countries, without, however, amalgamating with them'; that it was 'of special importance to support the peasant movements in backward countries against the landowners and all feudal survivals', holding out the promise of 'the distribution of the large holdings' among land-hungry tenants; and that in view of the importance of volatile national prejudices 'the class-conscious proletariat of all countries' had 'the duty of exercising special caution and care with regard to these national sentiments'. Although these theses also noted the eventual and widening divergence between 'the bourgeois democratic nationalist movement' on the one hand, and 'the mass action of the poor and ignorant peasants and workers' on the other, they particularly stressed that 'for the overthrow of foreign capitalism, which is the first step toward revolution in the colonies the cooperation of the bourgeois nationalist revolutionary elements is useful'. 'The revolution in the colonies is not going to be a Communist revolution in its first stages', the theses pointed out, 'but from the outset the leadership is in the hands of the Communist vanguard'. The task of the Communist parties in such colonial areas as Indonesia was to lead the 'revolutionary masses . . . through the successive periods of development of revolutionary experience'. In spite of these directives, however the PKI, despite some spectacular strike ventures and insurrectionary outbursts, managed within a few years virtually to isolate itself from the rest of the Indonesian nationalist 'liberation' movement, had given the strong impression that it believed a Communist society could quickly be stamped out of the ground in Indonesia, had been unable to effect the necessary 'cooperation' with the 'bourgeois nationalist revolutionary sentiments', had shown little success in mobilizing the peasantry, and had generally failed effectively to exploit the not inconsiderable reservoir of the new political consciousness that was present in Indonesia at the time of its founding. There were several reasons for this compound failure, mostly, though not entirely, attributable to the PKI strategy itself.

First of all, the PKI leaders were by background and education removed from the mass of Indonesians and generally lacked the training for leadership of a revolutionary front organization. Both the PKI chairman, Semaun, and the vice-chairman, Raden Darsono, belonged to the lesser Javanese nobility and had had an education far above that of the average Indonesian. Tan Malaka, one of the most important figures in party history, was the son of a high native official in West Sumatra and had been schooled in Europe. Muso, the party's principal organizer in the nineteenthirties, had been a school teacher. Alimin, a chief party leader in the Indonesian Revolution after World War II was the adopted son of a high Dutch official.[4] The élitist and doctrinaire character of this first generation of PKI leaders was woefully unsuited to the task of laboriously creating an organizational network among heterogeneous population groups and divergent class interests. To all of them applied in some degree the characterization once made of A. Baars (an early PKI leader) by an old Dutch Socialist and Indonesia hand: 'a chairborne Marxist'.[5] Even the more radical Dutch Socialists in Indonesia felt estranged from the dogmatic extremism which the early PKI leadership usually displayed.

As one Dutch Socialist in Indonesia, acquainted with Baars and his cohorts and describing their outlook, put it: 'That in the Netherlands Indies, which as yet stood at the very beginning of capitalist development there could be no question of complete Socialist action, and that to make propaganda to that end could only create confusion, was not understood . . . and the Socialist who did not share this opinion was in their eyes a bad Socialist, if not a renegade'.[6] It was this extremist tendency of the PKI leadership which Stalin was to criticize in a speech before the students of the University of the Peoples of the East in May 1925, during which he accused party leaders of isolating the Indonesian party from the masses and of turning it into a sect. As Aidit in his recent history of the PKI has echoed: 'The disease of left wing Communism with which the Party was afflicted did indeed transform it into a sect'.[7]

Even lesser leaders of the party stood by virtue of their educational background apart from the populace, and there is little doubt that even such limited schooling as some of them might have had created a status-conscious sense of superiority that made identification with mass action in a revolutionary 'movement of liberation' difficult.[8] In the early nineteen-twenties about 95 per cent of the then more than 48 million Indonesians were illiterate and popular education was only just beginning to accelerate. Even with limited or primary school education the second and third echelon of PKI leadership gravitated to petty bourgeois minor clerical and bureaucratic positions, where 'white collar' status reenforced their pretensions of élitism and semi-intellectualism. An analysis of Communist activists who were apprehended and confined by the colonial government after the abortive Communist revolt of 1926–1927 revealed the unusually high percentage of literacy, completion of some kind of primary school training, and of positions held in the lower echelons of government service among them.[9] This élite orientation, essentially urban-focused, also tended toward greater PKI action among the industrial proletariat of the towns, rather than toward work among the peasantry.

Indeed, despite the Comintern's emphasis on the importance of peasant movements, the PKI's work in the agrarian society was haphazard, with the possible exception of the party activities among some groups of workers on Western estates. However, the failure of the party to mobilize the peasantry may have stemmed not only from a certain aversion toward the untutored *tani*[10] (peasant) but also from ignorance of actual peasant conditions. The village world tended to be seen in the light of an almost idyllic, tradition-bound communalism, characterized by collective village control over the land and by far-reaching patterns of mutual assistance among the villagers. To a great extent this picture was correct but important, socially individuating and disruptive, tendencies had also long been evident in Indonesian rural society, creating tensions well suited to the propagation of the Marxist interpretation of class conflict. But to these changes the PKI seemed largely oblivious. For example, at the party's organizational meeting in May 1920 it was decided that the Comintern's advocacy of 'distribution' of land among the landless peasantry was not applicable to Indonesia, because Indonesia was held to be an area 'where large landownership in fact does not exist and collective village ownership predominates'.[11] Yet, even then, in many areas in Java concentration of landownership and growing numbers of landless villagers could have been observed. A special colonial government commission, formed at the beginning of the twentieth century to inquire into Java's diminishing living standards, reported in 1914 that there were villages where 30 to 50 per cent of the population was altogether landless.[12] These landless villagers increasingly reflected the general proletarianization of the indigenous society and the monetization of its economy, aggravated by the seemingly inexorable population growth. The landless tended to sink into what has been called 'a scavenger economy',[13] making a precarious living from a great variety of temporary forms of employment, such as grass-cutting, wood-cutting and gathering, a little trade, labor on the land of wealthier peasants or in nearby government construction projects, in cottage industry, and so on. The 1920 'Theses and Statutes' of the Comintern had described as 'the fundamental task of the Communist parties in all countries' the conducting of 'an energetic propaganda' among the 'agricultural proletariat, the hired laborers (by the year, by the day, by the job)' and the winning of this proletariat for the 'side of Soviet Power'. But the early PKI's concern for the agricultural proletariat was small and unfocused, except for its largely unsuccessful effort at capturing control of a few trade unions of estate workers.

As for the 'large landownership', which PKI leaders in fact believed to be non-existent, the same government report mentioned that it 'has reached a considerable extent in a number of regions in Java'.[14] One Dutch Marxist, analyzing the data of this report, states that at the beginning of the first World War 72 per cent of the landowners individually owned less than 1·72 acres on the average, while together they held about 36 per cent of the total area. At the same time less than 1 per cent of the population held more than 15 acres individually and together 7·6 per cent of the total area.[15] In some parts of West Java large landownership had in fact been the rule for many decades. The failure of the PKI to exploit these conditions was the more noteworthy because the early years of the party's history coincided with a period of serious recession in Indonesia's agricultural export economy, with sharply diminished employment opportunities for Indonesians and with new and burdensome taxes. In many layers of Indonesian society, including the rural sector, considerable economic misery was ready for political mobilization. A former president of the central bank of issue in Indonesia has given telling examples of declining popular living standards during these years: the sharp decrease in the consumption of such relative 'luxuries' as salt and in the extent of travel, the disappearance of the larger silver coins from popular use, the sharp increase in business of the government pawnshops, and so on.[16] The retrenchment of government welfare services also seriously affected many Indonesians. In the poorer villages of Java, according to an analysis in 1924 by one of the country's ablest Indonesian civil servants, thousands were compelled for months to limit themselves to one meager meal a day,[17] and with it all, as shown in a 1926 survey of the tax burden on the Indonesian population of Java and Madura, Indonesians were being heavily taxed: Indonesians with an average annual cash income of 225 florins paid the same 10 per cent in taxes as Europeans with an income of 9,000 to 10,000 a year.[18] One of colonial Indonesia's leading economists noted that in Java villagers were leaving their land because taxes on it were too high, and that despite the ancient social bonds uniting the peasant with his village and his land, landownership itself was no longer desired, and land was being rented out for less than the land rent tax.[19]

In a sense the PKI's comparative ignorance of this state of affairs is understandable, because with all its economic hardships village society in Indonesia as a whole showed considerable resiliency and traditional communal supports and absorptive capacity prevented utter disaster. The evils of the decline were apparent primarily in many scattered localities and a uniform rural *verelendung* process would have been difficult to substantiate. In the years from 1913 to 1924 a government survey found that there had even been some expansion of the area of arable land, theoretically sufficient to accommodate the growing population in such a way as to make at least the same amount of land available on a per capita basis in 1924 as about a decade before.[20] In contrast, as this survey pointed out, parts of the urban sector of the economy appeared to be much more seriously affected, and the decline in employment particularly affected various lower government service personnel and the budding Indonesian white-collar group of semi-intellectuals in the towns. The potential threat to the government of an unemployed intellectual proletariat was made explicit in the observation in the same report that precisely because of the prevailing unemployment the more educated element among the Indonesians were making increasing use of the public lending libraries at this time.[21] The eventual pre-occupation of the PKI with the urban proletariat and with white-collar intellectual elements is perhaps also understandable in the light of the comparative social isolation in which the village world of Indonesia still, though decreasingly, existed. But whatever the reason, there is little question that the party's class tactics had a strong tendency to deprive it of significant support from the growing political consciousness in many rural areas.

Equally responsible for the PKI's lack of success was its policy toward the Indonesian nationalist parties, which in the Comintern's view were part of the 'revolutionary movements of liberation', and toward bourgeois nationalist elements, which at the time constituted perhaps the most important segment of the nationalist movement. A number of prominent Indonesian Communists, among them Semaun, as well as many lesser fry, had come to the party via membership in another nationalist organization, namely, the *Sarekat Islam* (Islamic Association or SI), founded in 1912 and the first real nationalist mass organization in Indonesian history. Even after the founding of the PKI, prominent Communists retained their SI membership, undoubtedly with a view to utilizing the SI for Communist ends. But the SI conservative petty-bourgeois and bourgeois elements, strongly influenced by the new puritanism and orthodoxy of reformist Islam, and reflecting the resurgent power of indigenous traders and small-scale industrialists, came into increasing conflict with the PKI group, not least because of the Comintern's avowed opposition to the Pan-Islamic movements of the time. The Second Congress of the Comintern in 1920, as well as the Fourth Comintern Congress in 1922, condemned Pan-Islamic movements on the grounds that these movements were really used by 'European and American imperialism' to destroy the national liberation movement. But by this policy the Comintern left the PKI in an extremely difficult position, because in Indonesia Pan-Islamic sentiments had been propagated for some time and were generally appreciated as part of the Islamic modernist revival by those reform-minded Indonesian Muslims who looked toward the SI for leadership.[22] In September 1918 the SI had branded capitalism as 'sinful', but it soon became apparent that this epithet was to be applied primarily to foreign, especially to Dutch, capital in the country; Tjokroaminoto, one of the principal SI leaders, declared, 'We first must fight against foreign domination . . . later we shall see if we are Socialistic'.[23]

Faithful to Comintern directives, the PKI in 1920 had agreed to oppose Pan-Islamism, but this had created bitter opposition in many

Muslim circles generally, and in S.I. ranks in particular—a bitterness which was not eliminated when the PKI in its periodical attempted to show that the Russian Bolshevists were 'extremely tolerant' of religious beliefs.[24] Behind the Pan-Islam issue really loomed the basic question of Communist collaboration with the budding bourgeois-entrepreneurial class, whose nationalism was to a large extent determined (not only in Indonesia but in all African, Asiatic and Near and Middle Eastern countries where Islam had made significant inroads) by the ideological context of reformist Islamic movements. As Tan Malaka, one of the ablest theoreticians in PKI history pointed out at the Fourth Comintern Congress in 1922, Pan-Islamism meant for practical purposes nothing more than a fight for national freedom.[25] On that basis Communists could not very well avoid seeking a rapprochement with the entire movement of Islamic modernism, certainly if collaboration with the indigenous national bourgeoisie in a colonial country was held to be 'useful'. But the Fourth Comintern Congress not only reiterated its opposition to Pan-Islamism but also declined to indicate where and how collaboration with the non-proletarian elements of the native society was to be effected. Although Semaun and his associates at first tried to temporize in the inevitable conflict between the PKI and the SI, this eventually proved impossible, not only because the SI shortly made membership in itself irreconcilable with membership in any other party, but also because PKI leaders became increasingly dissatisfied with the ambiguities of SI-PKI cooperation, demanding a frontal assault on capitalism of all kinds, including the Muslim Indonesian variety. When, in the interests of party discipline, SI leaders insisted on the exclusive membership of their organization, Semaun, Tan Malaka and other PKI leaders formally gave up their SI membership, followed by SI sections that sympathized with them.

By the end of 1921 the PKI had decided to affiliate those sections of the SI that might be described as Communist with a new secessionist SI central body which would take a stand against the rest of the SI. A series of major strikes, which subsequently broke out in Java and in which Communist figures played a prominent part, strengthened the dogmatic position which the PKI leadership increasingly seemed to be adopting. At a PKI congress attended by about 2,000 persons in March 1923, 16 PKI sections, 14 Communist former SI sections, and a number of trade unions heard Darsono declare that he and the PKI membership were Bolshevists, led by Moscow, and the party announced a massive propagandistic action against the 'capitalistic' *Sarekat Islam*.[26]

Considered in retrospect, the breach with the main body of the SI was fatal for the early PKI, although admittedly to avoid such a breach would have been extremely difficult for the party leadership. But the party leaders thereupon aggravated the tactical dangers of the breach by an even stronger, uncompromising dogmatism and ideological inflexibility (an almost classical case of that 'left-wing deviation' in Communist party tactics which Lenin had termed 'an infantile disorder'), taking up the cudgels not only against 'capitalism' but also against virtually all existing Indonesian nationalist organizations of any significance, such as *Budi Utomo* ('Noble Endeavor', a moderate nationalist group, founded in 1908, of Javanese intellectuals and modern minded aristocrats), *Muhammadiyah* (a focal point of Islamic modernism, founded in 1912), and the SI. In Europe the PKI found some support among the members of the *Perhimpunan Indonesia* (Indonesian Association), a group mainly composed of young Indonesian students. But in Indonesia itself students and intellectuals, united in various 'study clubs', acted apart from the PKI, although more radical clubs, such as the one in Bandung, undoubtedly were sympathetic to Marxism. On the whole, however, the PKI in this period was unable to lead younger intellectuals in Indonesia, and when it showed any inclination to do so its efforts were spasmodic.

Throughout 1923 and 1924 the PKI attempted to reorganize itself on a narrower, more compact basis, first using the former SI sections that were under Communist direction (collectively referred to now as *Sarekat Rakjat*, or people's organizations) as a kind of infra-structure with the PKI proper acting as a kind of élite. A new political action program was adopted, noteworthy for its radical insistence on class war and on the necessity of revolutionary action. Beyond Java PKI activists organized party branches in West and Central Sumatra. For a while new and special efforts were made throughout the organization to win over the school-age youth by means of special Communist schools in which pupils 'learned to sing the International and marched in red-colored clothing'. But such efforts were of little immediate value to the party in adding significant strength and the party leadership seemed ever more inclined to narrow its social operational base: at a party congress in December 1924 the *Sarekat Rakjat* were even described as a liability to the party because of the 'petty bourgeois, local-nationalistic' elements within these organizations, and throughout 1925 party tactics began to de-emphasize mass organization, gradually transferring *Sarekat Rakjat* members either to reliable trade unions, or into party cells, or else simply allowing *Sarekat Rakjat* sections to disintegrate. Party action, the PKI leadership decided, would have to be focused principally on revolutionary trade union agitation, especially on strikes, and party leaders now spent almost all their time on capturing and directing the developing Indonesian labor movement.[27]

In this effort they were initially not without success. From its inception the indigenous labor movement had a political orientation.[28] Thus one of the more important trade unions, that of workers in government pawnshops (the so-called PPPB, founded in 1916), had begun to move almost at once in a revolutionary direction; its chairman proposed in 1919 that all native trade unions be federated for the purpose of agitating on behalf of self-government for the country 'along with the transformation of capitalistic society into a socialistic one'.[29] Later in the year such a federation, consisting of 22 unions with a nominal membership of 72,000, was in fact formed and subsequently placed under the leadership of Semaun. But here too the breach between Communists and SI manifested itself, and by June 1921, Semaun had formed his own 'Revolutionary Trade Union Central Organization' with which a number of important trade organizations affiliated, e.g. the railroad workers union. After 1921 the PKI threw itself with increasing vigor into the labor movement, organizing and reorganizing central federated bodies, directing or urging strikes (e.g. among government pawnshop workers in 1922 and among railroad workers in 1923) and seeking to extend the trade union movement outside Java. Primarily as a result of his labor agitation Semaun was arrested but permitted to leave the country (Tan Malaka had left earlier upon a similar threat of government internment). Despite the departure of these party leaders PKI influence in the labor organizations increased and 1925 saw serious strikes, especially in Semarang, among harbor and dock workers, and in Surabaya among various categories of industrial employees. Especially significant was the Communist effort to capture control of the labor organization of sugar-mill and sugar-estate workers, among whom wages, even in the opinion of government spokesmen, were far too low.[30] Although the sugar-estate companies made some effort to meet workers' demands, agitation continued and for a while it seemed as if the PKI might yet become a political force in those rural areas where the inroads of Western sugar production had led to grave stagnation and social unrest in the Indonesian village economy.[31] But the precipitate Communist insurrection of 1926–1927 abruptly cut this development short.

Beyond Java the PKI in these years was principally active in parts of West and Central Sumatra. Here the party became involved in a complex pattern of religio-cultural cross currents, all of them with political aspects that reflected the onrush of modernizing influences, especially in the Menangkabau area. Secular nationalism, defenders of the traditional *adat* (custom and folkways), Islam, and Communism presented a crazy quilt of ideologies which could not, except with considerable difficulty, be fitted into the Marxist interpretations of class conflict. Originally basing its strength on the *Sarekat Rakjats* the PKI in West Sumatra moved, in the course of 1925, slowly to dissolve these bases of mass organization in compliance with the decisions taken at the PKI congress in December 1924. SR members were to be incorporated as prospective PKI members in the party's subsections and there receive instruction in party fundamentals. But the more than 600 members which the SR had originally had (mostly unemployed government workers and small traders who had originally felt attracted to the Marxist *verelendung* theory) showed little interest in the finer points of theory and party organization, and by the end of 1925 'the movement had as good as faded out everywhere on the West Coast',[32] although a number of professional activists remained in the area, providing the nucleus for insurrectionary outbursts two years later.

By the beginning of 1926 the PKI found itself in an ambiguous position. The party had about 40 branches throughout the country, and in addition to a hard core of a few thousand had about 33,000 fellow-traveling supporters, mostly in Java. But party organization and training of cadres were most inadequate, and perhaps a majority of the members were so in name only—persons who for reasons of social and economic discontent broadly shared the party's aim to aid the empoverished but otherwise had little knowledge of theory and organization. The close contact with the labor movement and the direction of strikes gave the PKI great influence but evoked little or no rapport in the peasant society. Moreover, PKI leadership of such strikes usually weakened the party in the end, since leading Communists involved in the labor unrest were frequently arrested, confined for long periods or else required to leave the country. Semaun, while in exile, had attended the sixth extended plenum of the Comintern in Moscow in March and April, 1925, and tried to defend the PKI's policy of virtual non-cooperation with the Indonesian nationalist movement, but apparently with little success, for the Comintern plenum decided that 'the Indonesian Communist Party had not as yet become a truly proletarian party'.[33] As early as the PKI's December 1924 conference the PKI had decided to intensify its campaign of violence by attracting terrorists and criminal elements to its ranks, and throughout 1925–1926 there were attempts at murder, arson, bombings and various acts of intimidation throughout Java, instigated or perpetuated by Communists. This did not endear the party to moderates in the nationalist movement and in the end probably weakened the party, since Indonesians were usually the victims of these crimes. While trade unions remained the principal organizational target, the party in 1925, doubtless in response to Comintern criticism, rather suddenly adopted a different attitude towards the nationalist groups and the intellectuals, seeking to draw them into its intensifying campaign against the colonial government. But this new appeal, largely confined to a few overtures and sympathetic gestures in the Communist press, was to prove largely fruitless, mainly because it conflicted with the élitist view of the party taken by many of its leaders, and their lack of appreciation of united front tactics. Yet the Comintern had for some time been concerned about the character of PKI tactics and had remonstrated with its leaders. A letter from Moscow, reflecting Comintern thinking and dated May 4, 1925, prescribed for the PKI the task of broadening mass support and emphasized that nowhere in the world the proletarian cause could succeed 'without the active support of the majority of the peasantry'. But since the peasantry had its own interests, the directive went on, it could be used only if the PKI acted in defense of peasant interests. The *Sarekat Rakjat*, according to the Moscow instruction, should be reactivated and made into a separate parallel revolutionary organization under PKI direction and draw mass support from all layers of society. Indeed, so concerned was the Comintern about the significance of the peasantry in Indonesia, that at one point around this time it even expressed its fears that the new political movement among Indonesian peasants might altogether bypass the PKI.[34]

It does not appear that this Comintern directive was significantly heeded, largely because communication between scattered PKI leaders was difficult, and also because many would have been unable to appreciate its significance in terms of Leninist theory, in which few, if any, cadres were reasonably proficient. But the fault was not all due to the PKI leadership. The Comintern itself during various congresses and executive conferences tended to stress variable tactics, and for their prevailing policy of concentrating on the urban labor movement PKI leaders could have found impressive backing in Comintern pronouncements. Leninist theory itself suggested a measure of pragmatism, and the PKI leaders, thousands of miles away from Moscow, might well have felt justified in ignoring some of the Comintern's strictures and advice.

But perhaps the greatest danger to the party came from the atmosphere of tactical extremism and political unreality in the higher echelons. By 1926 most of the original principal PKI figures were either in exile or in confinement. In Singapore, where a number of PKI leaders (among them Alimin Prawirodirdjo and Muso) resided, a secret central organization had been established for the purpose of linking the PKI sections in Java closer to the Comintern and subsequently other Asian Communists labored to establish a central revolutionary federation for the Far East which, among other objectives, would launch a mass assault on the Dutch colonial regime and seek to establish a 'Federal Indonesian Republic'. These moves, and especially the party's agitation in the Indonesian labor movement, were undoubtedly in accord with the decisions of the Communist international labor federation *(Profintern)* and with the Comintern's Fifth Congress held in Moscow in June and July, 1924; but they betrayed a woeful ignorance of the degree of support which the party believed it could muster in an open insurrectionary campaign. Doubtless some party leaders mistook the turbulence which they had been able to create with their various strike ventures and campaign of terrorism for an aroused nation ready to break the bonds of colonialism. Toward the end of 1925 PKI and Communist labor leaders, meeting in the Prambanan temple near Surakarta, Central Java, decided to initiate revolutionary action in the immediate future, beginning in West Sumatra and intended to spread to Java; financial aid from Moscow for this purpose was expected. This Prambanan decision led to a serious rift between Tan Malaka and Alimin; the latter, having led the Prambanan meeting, defended the decision. The former maintained that precipitate revolutionary action would be folly; that not money but a determined display of mass action—as evidenced by an unending chain of strikes and demonstrations—was first necessary; that much closer rapport with local leaders was required in order to gauge accurately the extent of popular support for the party; and that in any event Moscow would be disinclined to finance the insurrection unless it had reasonable assurance of success. As will be indicated in Chapter IV, Malaka's views were far more solidly grounded in Leninist theory than those of his cohorts whose 'left-wing' dilettantism always seemed to suggest that the PKI by itself could create a soviet society in Indonesia almost overnight. Semaun, in Moscow, acting as the PKI representative at Comintern meetings, admitted early in 1926 before the Comintern executive committee that the party had become isolated from the masses, pointing out that hundreds of activists had been arrested in the strike waves and expressed his hopes for greater support from the Communist party in the Netherlands, but his opinions elicited little interest.[35] All the while lesser PKI leaders may well have been unduly encouraged in their dreams of mass support by the opening of party branches in various parts of Indonesia, such as those on the island of Ternate in Eastern Indonesia, on the East Coast of Sumatra, and even in Pontianak in Borneo.

The Communist revolts that eventually broke out between November 1926, and January 1927, showed clearly the lack of effective mass organization, the shallowness of such a 'front' as presumably existed, and the confusion of party leadership.[36] Malaka's worst fears were fully confirmed. Beginning in Bantam, West Java, and in the capital city of Batavia on November 12, 1926 (where the telephone exchange was briefly occupied and a vain effort was made to break open the municipal prison), the insurrection spread throughout West Java province and then moved into Surakarta, Central Java. In other sections of Central Java, where preparations to join the revolt had been made, the government was able to nip resistance in the bud by swiftly arresting the principal leaders. In Batavia within a few days, and in most of Bantam and Surakarta within a few weeks, the revolt had been brought under control, and the insurrection which broke out in West Sumatra the following January was also largely stillborn as the government quickly arrested PKI cadres and their followers. A repeated rebel effort to capture Sawah Lunto (the headquarters of the Ombilin coal fields in West Sumatra) was a failure, and the scattered instances of revolutionary discontent in various parts of Padang and Padang Pandjang districts of West Sumatra never became coordinated in a unified front. Throughout Indonesia some 13,000 persons were arrested, of whom about half were subsequently released; about 4,500 were given prison terms and an additional 1,300 were confined for indefinite periods. Four principal leaders were executed. With the failure of the revolt, with increased police vigilance over all political meetings and publications, and because of the lack of coordination between the scattered and now underground remnants of the party, the PKI went into a steep decline from which it was not to recover until nearly two decades later.

The reasons for the failure of the 1926–1927 Communist uprising, as well as the causes of the revolt itself, deserve passing attention, because of their significance for party strategy. The revolts, according to PKI theory today, showed the dangers of the absence of unity in party leadership, the failure to make adequate preparations to protect party activists, the lack of training of party cadres in Marxist-Leninist theory, the poor coordination between the cities and the rural areas and between the various parts of the country where the revolt had broken out, and so on.[37] The revolt was perhaps a valuable lesson to the party, but, as we shall see, the party had to learn much of the same lesson again after the disastrous Madiun revolt of 1948. The question also arises as to whether the Comintern could have prevented the 1926–1927 rebellions. The theses on 'Communism and the International Situation', unanimously passed by the Comintern's Sixth Congress on August 29, 1928, described the 'rebellion in Indonesia' as part of the 'most striking expression' of 'the general crisis of the world capitalist system', but privately the Comintern executive was probably less enthusiastic. There had been repeated criticism of the PKI leadership in the past, and it is not clear whether Muso and Alimin Prawirodirdjo, who travelled to Moscow shortly before the November 1926 outbreak to urge Comintern support for the intended revolt, obtained any more than lukewarm assent. Whatever benefit Indonesian Communists might have obtained from this Moscow mission was nullified in any event by the arrest of Muso and Alimin by the British in Johore, in Malaya, on December 18, 1926, as they were returning to Indonesia. By this time the insurrection had already turned into a disaster for the PKI and the subsequent release of Muso and Alimin came too late to salvage much of the party's position. Moreover the Comintern was not, in all likelihood, sufficiently informed of the situation in Indonesia to be able to decide between the conflicting arguments of Tan Malaka on the one hand, and Muso and Alimin on the other. And also it was probably more concerned with the situation in China. Toward the close of 1927 the Comintern Executive Committee, in an evaluation of the task of Communists in Indonesia, again criticized the PKI for its inability to mobilize the Indonesian masses, its lack of organization and its doctrinaire anti-imperialist sloganizing. At the Sixth Comintern Congress in 1928 (attended by Muso, Semaun, and Tan Malaka) the Comintern refused to take further serious notice of the failure of the rebellion; it certainly did not disavow those who had urged the uprising, although an Indonesian delegate at the Congress sharply criticized the Comintern for not having given the insurrection more support by calling on its sections abroad. There certainly was a lack of coordination between the various PKI branches and activists in Indonesia itself, but this defect also existed in the relationship between the Comintern and the PKI.

A Dutch colonial government report considered the insurrection in Bantam primarily as the work of agitators capitalizing on an enlarged but hazy consciousness of grievances and utopian aspirations of some segments of the populace; economic (and specifically agrarian) grievances were held to be of minor or no importance, and the rebels were said to come from all segments of society, poor as well as relatively well-to-do.[38] There is much truth in this. Certainly among the rank and file of the supporters of the rebellion, including many who later found themselves confined in the Upper Digul concentration camp in West New Guinea, there were chronic malcontents, with *déclassé*, employment, or personal grievances; they must also be considered in the context of Messianic influences which have always been an important psycho-cultural factor in Javanese popular aspirations.[39] The Indonesian nationalist leader Sutan Sjahrir, speaking of the Digul Communist internees, whom he briefly joined in confinement in the nineteen thirties, declared that most of them 'did not know precisely' what they wanted from the insurrection, and that some had 'vague, broadly religious ideas', while others probably looked perhaps for more 'directly economic advantages'.[40] All this cannot be denied, but the minimizing of the economic factors in the Bantam rebellion leads to a somewhat oversimplified conception of it, not far removed from the typical arch-conservative colonial's reaction to all such incidents: 'everything is fine here, except for a few agitators'.[41] In Bantam, at any rate, some attention should be given to the economic factor; for this was one of the poorest sections of the country, and had that reputation at least since the middle of the 19th century when the great Dutch writer Multatuli made his experiences in Bantam the basis for an impassioned plea for reform of the colonial system.[42] Later observers have not contradicted Multatuli on the misery of Bantam.[43] One noted Dutch authority on modern Indonesia indicates that in a recent journey to Java he had not seen any signs of extreme want until he came to Northern Bantam, where he saw something of the 'grey poverty' which he had observed in India, and compared to which Java was a 'paradise on earth'.[44] It was precisely the exploitation—that it was ineffective we will leave aside for the moment—of this 'grey poverty' and above all of the dawning 'politicalized' consciousness of it among admittedly quite heterogenous elements of society that provided PKI cadres with any chance at all. That Bantam somehow escaped the effects of the economic depression and unemployment of the early 1920's, of the ever increasing shortage of arable land evident throughout Java, and of the sharp increases in taxes in the period 1921–26 must, in any case, be doubted.[45]

The role of disruptive economic factors should also be considered in the insurrection in West Sumatra. The penetration of Western administrative and economic influences created an agrarian revolution, destroyed traditional social relationships and concepts of land tenure, introduced a monetization of all aspects of economic life, along with new and sometimes oppressive taxes, and brought about a new political awareness also in the context of conflicting religious, nationalistic and Marxist ideologies. In response to the Prambanan decision of December 1925, PKI leaders reactivated their dormant organization by indiscriminately exploiting all popular grievances resulting from the socio-economic and ideological revolution of West Sumatran society and by proceeding with a campaign of terror and intimidation wherever feasible, hoping thereby to encourage a spirit of popular restlessness and resistance in anticipation of the coming revolt. Dissension among the leadership in West Sumatra and lack of coordination between PKI headquarters in Java and the

Sumatran cadres was conspicuous (the conflict over the Prambanan decision also influenced the situation in West Sumatra), and the government, alerted by the events in Java, placed a number of suspected cadres early under preventive arrest. Nevertheless the turmoil which the remaining activists were able to create, including the attacks on the dwellings of government officials and on the Ombilin coal fields indicated the relative effectiveness of the slogan 'kemerdekaan!' (freedom!) which the party popularized wherever possible as an incitement to riot, as a proletarian war-cry, and as a slogan for the mounting sense of revolutionary estrangement from a despised political system that motivated considerable numbers in the West Sumatra region.[46]

But in the last analysis no obstacle to the PKI's early growth was so formidable as the Dutch colonial government and its police authority. At no time in the turbulent twenties was the government ever in real danger from the Communists. Beginning with the administration (1921–1926) of the conservative Governor-General Dirk Fock the colonial government broadened and intensified its security regulations, including the placing of all political activity (including political meetings) under increased surveillance, the arresting, or driving into exile, or interning, of all whom it regarded as dangerous to 'peace and order', the further curtailing of the press and the placing under close supervision of public communications facilities, the mails and the import of all printed matter. PKI membership was forbidden for all government officials, including Indonesians, and even to be known as a Communist made arrest likely. Under Fock's successors—A.C. de Graeff (1926–1931) and B.C. de Jonge (1931–1936)—the repressive policy was even extended. Neither in the *Volksraad* (where conservative influences from the Dutch colonial community grew in strength after 1927) nor in the States-General in the Netherlands (where the Communists were a negligible minority and the Socialists, though waxing in influence, had lost much of their post World War I zeal) could the PKI count on support. Socialist experts on Indonesia in the Dutch parliament like C. G. Cramer, when talking about the 1926–1927 rebellion, declared that 'what has happened in West Java we disapprove of and it is understandable that the government has immediately repressed those insurrections',[47] although he was not pleased with the alleged brutality with which the repression of the rebellion had taken place, nor with the fact that the government instigated a policy which made free political expression impossible. The same equivocation toward the rebellion, according to the Indonesian Communists, existed in the badly split leadership of the Dutch Communist Party, which was accused of not having given the proper support at the time of the insurrection. The Indonesian Communist Rustam Effendi, who was elected to the lower house of the Dutch parliament on the Dutch Communist slate in 1933, might urge consideration for 'our comrades in Upper Digul',[48] but the Indonesian Communist movement could hardly acquire a new lease on life through his efforts or through those of his party alone. Dutch Socialists generally, however sympathetic they might otherwise have been to the Indonesian nationalist movement, were not likely to abandon their anti-Bolshevist outlook in order to aid or speak in favor of the PKI's resurrection.

1927–1945. The scattered remnants of the PKI after the debacle of 1926–1927 gravitated toward the numerous new radical left-wing parties which emerged in this period. For some years radical nationalist Indonesian students and intellectuals in the Netherlands, united in the *Perhimpunan Indonesia* (Indonesian Association, or PI), had sympathized with the PKI and had sought a working relationship with the Comintern and with the Communist 'League Against Colonial Oppression'. In 1926 some PI circles planned the establishment of a revolutionary party (in Bandung) of both nationalists and Communists, and in December, 1926, Semaun and Mohammad Hatta (a principal leader of the PI, who as late as 1929, still was to describe the Digul internees as 'martyrs of the idea of freedom'[49]) had signed an agreement in which the PI agreed to lead the revolutionary movement in Indonesia and in which the PKI recognized the leadership of the PI.[50] Semaun had undoubtedly been led to sign this agreement because of Comintern pressure that the PKI seek closer collaboration with the Indonesian nationalist movement, but the actual subservience of the PKI to a nationalist organization seemed too much for the Comintern executive and on orders from Moscow Semaun soon repudiated the protocol. The collapse of the PKI organization which had meanwhile taken place as a result of the repressive government measures taken in the wake of the 1926–1927 rebellions made the planned formation of a joint revolutionary nationalist-Communist party also impossible. Radical left-wing elements did enter such new nationalist parties as the National Indonesian Party *(Partai Nasional Indonesia,* PNI), founded in 1927, the *Partindo (Partai Indonesia,* Indonesian Party) founded in 1931 after the PNI dissolved itself, and the *Gerindo (Gerakan Rakjat Indonesia,* Indonesian People's Organization), founded in 1937. All these parties, unlike some other nationalist groups of these years, attempted to be mass parties. They did manage to attract many of the former PKI rank and file; one of the *Gerindo's* principal leaders, Amir Sjarifuddin, later declared that he had been a Communist since the middle of the nineteen thirties, and another, Wikana, was one of the main figures in the Communist underground movement in the thirties. It would be incorrect to see these parties as mere Communist fronts, however, since the non-Communist element was usually stronger. *Gerindo* did reflect the anti-Fascist Popular Front policy as the Comintern developed it from the middle of the nineteen thirties, but not to the point of ignoring the Indonesian struggle for independence (expressed in the slogan of this period: *Indonesia berparlemèn!*—a parliament for Indonesia!). With the increasing amalgamation of nationalist groups in federative organizations many Indonesian radicals did not abandon the contention that the struggle against Fascism had its corollary in the anti-colonialist struggle as well. Underground Communist elements continued their efforts to control the Indonesian labor movement. In July 1928, a new labor federation, the Indonesian Labor Association *(Sarekat Kaum Buruh Indonesia*, SKBI) was founded, and in it a number of former PKI cadres were active from the start. The federation's aim was the establishment of the' dictatorship of the proletariat' and soon the organization sought affiliation with the Communist 'League against Imperialism'. On the East Coast of Sumatra Communist propaganda was being disseminated in trade union sections by Iwa Kusumasumantri (later to become Indonesian Minister of Defense) who had studied in Moscow, and other Indonesians had for some time been receiving instruction there at the 'University of the Peoples of the East'. Again the government blocked the Communist activities in the labor movement by arresting and confining the principal SKBI leaders. But the underground PKI was able to continue its agitation in part because of the aid now extended by the Dutch Communist Party. In 1934 a 'Foreign Bureau of the PKI' *(Biro Luar Negeri PKI)*, a branch of the Comintern, was founded in Holland in which the earlier mentioned Indonesian Communist, Rustam Effendi, acquired a seat. Acting as a propaganda center the 'Foreign Bureau' sent its publications to Indonesia, especially to women's, youth and labor groups. The Bureau also sought connections with all 'Indonesian proletarians' abroad in order to fight for an independent 'Soviet Indonesian state'.[51] As the effects of the economic depression of the nineteen-thirties made the Indonesian masses receptive to such propaganda, local Communist cadres endeavoured to strengthen their popular contacts by forming so-called 'committees of unity' (i.e. cells in business enterprises, political organizations and even among the peasantry) in order to unify the revolutionary potentials of the country. In July, 1932, these 'committees of unity' agitated on behalf of the following 18-point program:[52]

1. Complete independence for Indonesia and establishment of a government of workers and peasants.

2. Immediate release of all political prisoners and internees. Abolition of the Upper Digul concentration camp and return of exiles.

3. Freedom to organize political actions, strikes and demonstrations by revolutionary organizations. Complete freedom of movement of workers and peasants.

4. 'Not a cent and not a soldier' for the repression of Indonesia.

5. Abolition of all public debts to 'the capitalists'.

6. A maximum 8-hour work day for laborers, introduction of complete social welfare legislation to be financed by the state and private enterprise, and abolition of fines and corporal punishment (presumably of laborers).

7. Equal pay for equal work for Dutch and Indonesian workers, and for male and female workers.

8. Resistance to wage decreases, organization of action to raise wages everywhere.

9. Introduction of one paid day of rest per week, and regular payment of weekly wages under trade union supervision.

10. Introduction of unemployment compensation for workers and coolies at the expense of the government and private enterprise.

11. Combatting of illiteracy; introduction of free education, including vocational education, in the native languages, at the expense of the government and private enterprise.

12. Immediate abolition of all penal sanctions of laborers.

13. Abolition of personal labor taxes and unpaid services rendered to the village.

14. Land for the peasants; confiscation of land which belongs to usurers, 'feudal lords' and 'imperialists'.

15. Cancellation of all back taxes of laborers, peasants and the urban poor.

16. Abolition of all contracts with penal sanction clauses for plantation laborers.

17. Immediate cancellation of all debts, incurred through tenancy or because of usury, of the peasants.

18. Opposition to 'preparation for a new imperialistic war by the Dutch imperialists and to their aid in preparing for an intervention against the USSR and Soviet China'.

These demands undoubtedly helped to articulate the misery which the depression of the early 1930's visited on virtually all levels of Indonesian society, including the urban workers, lower government personnel, and in the rural areas of Java where 'thousands and again thousands of peasants . . . were forced to pawn away their land for years for practically nothing'.[53] The misery undoubtedly increased because of the fiscal policies of the colonial government which placed extraordinarily high and even discriminatory levies on peasants and smallholders, especially in Sumatra.[54] The disorganization of the agrarian society proceeded apace, and in Java the reserve land that could be used to accommodate the inexorably expanding population virtually reached its limits in the nineteen-thirties. In 1922 the average holding subject to the land-rent tax was 1·15 hectares; in 1930 this figure had dropped to 0·9 hectares, while in 1940 it was 0·84 hectares. From 1930 to 1940 the total arable area of Java increased by 3·7 per cent, but the population by 15 per cent.[55] All the evils of the 'scavenger economy', with its stunted estate export production and commercial ancillaries in which the Indonesian primarily fulfilled the role of the hewer of wood or the drawer of water, tended to become accentuated in the era 1930–1940. The one-sided effect on the indigenous Indonesian socio-economy exerted by foreign capital in the country made, in the well known phrase of one Dutch economic expert on Indonesia, 'the native population into a nation of wage-earners and with it made of Indonesia a wage-earner among the nations'.[56] These proletarianization processes, in the long run, could only strengthen the appeal of the Communist party, and while in the 1930's there were no spectacular outbursts that could be attributed to the works of the 'committees of unity' or to the activities of underground party cadres, there was undoubtedly a broadening of political consciousness in Indonesian society that was ready for exploitation at a later date. In 1933 sailors on the Dutch naval vessel *Zeven Provincien* mutinied briefly, seized command of the ship and attempted to sail it to a Russian port, until a bomb attack by a Dutch naval plane put an end to these plans. The mutiny, though apparently instigated by a Socialist trade union and by nationalists, was not without effect on developing Indonesian political opinion, despite its ignominious end. The present writer, who was in Indonesia at the time, heard in many Dutch circles that the Communists were really responsible for the mutiny, and it is noteworthy that the Communists in the Netherlands espoused the cause of the mutineers.[57]

From outside the country Indonesian Communists continued their efforts to direct various radical movements. Tan Malaka, who shortly after the abortive 1926 coup had fallen out with the rest of the PKI leadership, now began to operate as an 'independent' Communist. He had, by this time, also fallen out with Stalin, and was beginning to be branded as a 'Trotskyist'. Tactical differences were at the root of this controversy also, for Tan Malaka had little use for Stalin's 'Socialism in One Country' strategy. In 1927 Tan Malaka withdrew (or was expelled) from the PKI, depending on whether one believes Tan Malaka's or the PKI's version of the matter, and established in Bangkok a new organization, the PARI *(Partai Republik Indonesia)*, together with his two associates Tamin and Subakat.[58] In Bangkok PARI organized and trained underground cadres for Indonesia and for a projected international 'proletarian revolutionary' movement called ASLIA. For a while Adam Malik and Sukarni were leaders of the underground organized by Tan Malaka and Tamin, but this underground action soon came to naught as the government arrested the participants. In 1935 Muso, the Kremlin's emissary, surreptitiously entered Indonesia and stayed nearly a year in Surabaya. He had come with the specific task of developing the new anti-Fascist line in the Communist underground. The rise to power of the Nazis in Germany in March, 1933, produced a major turn in Communist strategy, explicitly formulated at the Seventeenth Congress of the Comintern in August, 1935. The new Communist policy of forming 'united fronts' against Fascism meant, as PKI theory today has it, that 'greater cooperation between Communists and bourgeois democratic elements' would be necessary.[59] As we have seen, Communists joined with other nationalists in such mass organizations as *Gerindo* and later participated in various federative nationalist fronts such as the *Gapi (Gabungan Politik Indonesia*, Indonesian Political Federation) and *Frani (Fraksi Nasional Indonesia*, National Indonesian Faction). However, zig-zags in Communist policy occasioned by the Nazi-Soviet pact and by the subsequent German invasion of the Soviet Union were not noticeably reflected in the policy of the Indonesian radical left as the third decade of the present century drew to a close. Along with their continued anti-Fascism most nationalists, as well as the Communists, reiterated their demands for a full-fledged parliament for Indonesia and showed little inclination to compromise with the colonial government because of the exigencies of war. Party history today sees this period as one in which the Communist party still 'had not yet drawn the conclusions of its experiences'[60] during the first period of intensive party activity (1920–1927), and thus Communist efforts were held to be again doomed to failure:[61]

Widespread collaboration between the leaders of parties and organizations, which was not, however, supported by the broad masses of people, resulted in failure of the movement around the demand for a parliament and in the failure of the movement of the people to force the Dutch government to participate actively in the anti-Fascist struggle together with the Indonesian people. This happened because the Indonesian Communist Party was not yet a party thoroughly grounded in the masses, able to bring together and quicken the broad masses of the people, above all, the workers and the peasants. The resolutions of the Gapi and the Indonesian People's Assembly (another federation of nationalist organizations in this period—vdK) were never translated into mass actions in the form of demonstrations or other actions which could exert meaningful pressure on the Dutch colonial government.

As a consequence of the fact that the anti-Fascist movement in Indonesia was not strong enough the Japanese were able to occupy the country without any resistance, not only without any resistance from the Dutch army, but also without any resistance from the movement of the people. Both in a material and a moral sense the people were inadequately prepared to face Japanese fascism. The result was that, in the early phases, the Indonesian Communist Party was in an isolated position in its fight against Japanese Fascism.

The collapse of the Dutch colonial administration of Indonesia in the Second World War and the effects of the Japanese occupation of most of the country (1942–1945) fall outside the scope of these pages except for noting two factors of indirect long-range benefit to the PKI. The first was the psychological effect of the ignominious collapse of Dutch colonial power on the mass of Indonesians, a collapse which destroyed the image of Dutch invincibility and gave new life, at least in the long run, to the hope of successful political action by Indonesians themselves. The second factor is the organizational and ideological revolution brought by the Japanese: the mass indoctrination campaigns, the intense politicalization of all phases of public life, the mobilization through new organizational devices of popular opinion and action, the propagation of a new, anti-Western, 'Asiatic' consciousness even in remote areas, and so on. These revolutionary changes in Indonesian social life created the possibility of mass and front actions by people increasingly accustomed to think in terms of modern ideological conflict, on a scale hitherto not thought possible. In this sense the Japanese occupation advanced the long-range 'educational' interests of the PKI: it destroyed the image of a superior colonialism, it greatly expanded political self-awareness and it indoctrinated large segments in ideological terminologies to which many turned for support in the turmoil created by the destruction of the traditional order. And all this was made possible during a period when Communists were supposedly in opposition to the 'Fascist' Japanese regime.

The extent of anti-Japanese resistance by Communists—as well as by nationalists—has thus far not been fully revealed, probably in part because of its relative insignificance and in part because it would create further embarrassment in view of the collaboration (rather than the resistance) of many Indonesian nationalist leaders with the Japanese—

including leaders like Sukarno who play an essential role in current PKI strategy. Aidit claims that 'at the beginning of the Japanese occupation many members of the Central Committee and important cadres were arrested by the Japanese and some were executed', and it is true that there was some kind of Communist underground.[62] But the degree to which nationalists were prepared to collaborate with the Japanese made effective PKI resistance initially difficult. For many nationalists of course believed that their aspirations for an independent Indonesia could eventually be realized via collaboration, and when the war drew to a close they became increasingly anxious for official Japanese approval of their independence movement. At the same time, however, the accelerating collapse of the Japanese Greater Asia Co-Prosperity Sphere and the gradually developing popular discontent with Japanese occupation policies also augmented resistance tendencies in other sections of society, and the Communists on the whole attempted to identify themselves with these as time went by. Party history today claims the emergence of many Communist-led anti-Fascist organizations with a developed organizational network among transport workers, youth and even among the 'armed forces of the enemy'. Organizations like *Djojobojo* (operating supposedly with Japanese approval but actually concealed Communist fronts) were established, and through them it was possible to coordinate various kinds of sabotage operations. According to present party history Japanese spies infiltrated the Communist-led 'people's movements' and for this purpose the Japanese employed 'Trotskyites'. This may perhaps help explain why the Japanese in 1944 allowed the return of Tan Malaka to Indonesia, although it is still unclear to what extent he allowed himself to be used by them.[63] Japanese efforts to counter Communist underground action were almost completely successful, according to party history; increasingly numbers of cadres were arrested, tortured and decapitated, but even in prison the party claims to have set up an organization to foment resistance. 'Inspired by the heroic example of the Soviet Red Army', the official party history today states, underground action groups of the party, like *Menara Merah* (Red Army) participated in, or even led, various popular outbursts against the Japanese in Sumatra, as well as in Java, and such party leaders as Pamudji Widarta, Sukajat and Kadiman are singled out for their heroic resistance efforts. These scattered anti-Japanese organizations led by Communists are said to have proliferated particularly during the last year and a half of the war. They include, among others, the *Geraf (Gerakan Anti-Fasis*, Anti-Fascist Movement) led by Widarta, *Gerindom (Gerakan Indonesia Merdeka*, Indonesian Freedom Movement) led by the two most important PKI leaders today, D. N. Aidit, and M.

H. Lukman, and the GIB *(Gerakan Indonesia Baru,* New Indonesia Movement) led by Wikana.[64]

But from the point of view of Communist class theory the Japanese occupation created important social imbalances that would have to be reckoned with in Communist strategy also after the war. As the Fifth National Congress of the PKI in March, 1954, described it in its historical perspective of this period, the original anti-Fascist front had been able to bring together the 'national bourgeoisie' (the more or less independent native middle class of merchants and professionals) and part of the 'compradore bourgeoisie' (i.e. middle class traders and professionals associated with foreign 'imperialists' capital in Indonesia) as well as petty bourgeois, workers and peasants, although the front was, from the point of view of party history today, weak and ineffective. After the Japanese occupation, however, most of the national and all of the compradore bourgeoisie collaborated with the Japanese, the cooperation of the former being dictated by the fact that 'they saw that the people's strength in resisting the Japanese was not very great', while they 'also had the illusion that the Japanese would give freedom to Indonesia'.[65] In other words the aim of nationalist collaboration was Japanese support for an eventual bourgeois revolution in Indonesia which would make a return to Dutch colonialism impossible but which essentially bypassed or ignored Communist aims. Thus, according to Aidit, the Indonesian independence proclamation of 1945 placed the party in great difficulties, because the party leadership had not 'objectively' examined the lessons of the preceding years in terms of united front strategy (e.g. proper utilization of the bourgeoisie in party tactics, as Lenin had outlined since 1905, and described in particular in the Comintern's 1920 'Theses and Statutes'); it therefore, had no clear conception of the role and development of the party.[66] Moreover, according to Aidit, the 'party also had no experience in armed struggle—which is very necessary in a period of revolution'. Ignoring the degree of rationalization which historical hindsight provides in these and other Communist explanations of a new impending party defeat (the Madiun fiasco of 1948), it remains true that such rapport as the party had with the non-Communist nationalist movement in the early days of the anti-Fascist fronts was dissipated by the collaboration of the nationalists with the Japanese—which placed Communists in a dilemma. Avowed and open collaboration with the Japanese, in the manner of Sukarno and his associates, was generally out of the question given the ideological polarization of the war. Opposing such collaboration would endanger the party's future in a new Indonesia. Occasional and more or less isolated anti-Japanese activity, combined with some kind of covert collaboration, seemed the wisest course for the party. Moreover, the occupation itself prevented effective reconstruction of the party, not to speak of a united front, and the Communists confronted the independence declaration of August 17, 1945, without the organizational or ideological means to control its implications.

1945–1948. The *Partai Komunis Indonesia* was not formally reestablished until October 21, 1945, and its initial position was extremely dubious. Its reactivator, Muhammad Yusuf, head of the *Djojobojo* organization which had collaborated with the Japanese, had had but little contact with the underground PKI cadres or with the older PKI leadership and it soon appeared that he was in fact a follower of Tan Malaka, the now sharply anti-Stalinist propagator of a novel brand of Communism who soon was to compete with Sukarno and his associates for the leadership of the Indonesian Revolution. As a result party history today has tended to treat Yusuf's PKI as 'illegal' and sees the formal postwar reestablishment of the party as beginning with the organizational efforts of other Communists who supplanted Yusuf soon after they returned from Holland and Australia where they had spent the war. Tan Malaka could make considerable headway because a number of Indonesian Communists abroad, especially in Holland, reflected the views of their Dutch comrades that Sukarno and Hatta were fascist collaborators and that the newly proclaimed Republic of Indonesia was of Japanese manufacture. Yusuf himself did not share this view, which was but a continuation of the 1935 anti-Fascist 'Dimitrov doctrine', but it did impede the party's development. The open collaboration of Yusuf with Tan Malaka, who ceaselessly labored to seize control of the revolution, led eventually to strong opposition among other PKI activists and at the party Congress in Djokjakarta in early March 1946, Yusuf's policy was condemned. By the end of April 1946, an old PKI veteran of the 1926 uprising, Sardjono (who until 1942 had been confined in Digul) had become chairman and, with the return from China of Alimin Prawiradirdja in August, the confusion in party leadership and strategy began to clear somewhat. Under the leadership of Alimin and Sardjono the party stressed the necessity of the anti-Fascist struggle against the Dutch, and by its moderate approach sought to curry favor primarily with the leadership of non-Communist nationalist parties. This approach was affirmed at the party's Fourth National Congress in January 1947, during which the party asserted its readiness to cooperate with all anti-colonial groups and states and declared itself in favor of vaguely worded resolutions stressing democratic freedoms and social reforms. Though still bound by the Dimitrov line the PKI now began to support the revolutionary Sukarno-Sjahrir regime.

The work of the revived PKI had been extremely ineffective thus far, and Yusuf had in fact managed to compromise the party gravely in the eyes of party supporters of Sukarno. During 1945 the party under Yusuf, for example, sought to capitalize on the discontent of tenant farmers in North Central Java, who rose against their absentee landlords and creditors and indirectly against the revolutionary republican government whose officials they believed were in league with the landlords. The peasants' insurrection had the 'sovietization' of the land as its aim, but lack of effective leadership, the corrective policies of the republic, and the larger issue of anti-Dutch resistance soon brought the movement to naught. Equally disastrous was the party's involvement in the schemes of Tan Malaka who especially since early 1946 had sought the backing of armed bands for his radical nationalist and ultra-leftist 'Fighting Front' (in which the PKI, under Yusuf's guidance, participated). Although Tan Malaka was arrested in March 1946, he was soon released, and, the forces which he had unleashed continued to exert enormous pressure on the republic's domestic political development in the weeks ahead, culminating in the attempt virtually to wrest control of the government from Sukarno and in the kidnapping of the republican premier Sjahrir, both in July 1946. The Sukarno government blocked the coup, however, and Malaka was again arrested. But by this time the PKI had acquired a new leadership and a more pronounced anti-Malaka orientation, and partly because of PKI support for Sukarno the latter was able to counter the coup of Malaka and the radical left.[67]

The party now rapidly gained in influence, bolstered for tactical reasons by Sukarno. In the Republic's proto-parliament, the KNIP (*Komité Nasional Indonesia Pusat*, Central Indonesian National Committee), Communist and fellow-travelling representation (from Communist-dominated labor and peasant groups) rose greatly as a result of a decree by Sukarno, which, after initial opposition, was ratified early in 1947. A vaguely defined but still relatively effective united front 'from above', the *Sajap Kiri* (Left Wing), comprising the PKI, the Socialist and Labor parties, and fellow-travelling youth organizations, had come into being in the closing months of 1946, mainly in order to support the so-called Linggadjati Agreement (between the Dutch and Indonesian governments, for the eventual creation of an independent federal Indonesian Republic). Powerful Indonesian political forces opposed the agreement, however, and the Sukarno regime in those days leaned heavily on the left.

The tide was to change soon. In accordance with the Cominform's new intransigeant Zhdanov line, announced in September 1947, the PKI went into the opposition. Tactically, a complete PKI disavowal of the revolutionary government would not have been necessary. The Zhdanov line divided the world into two hostile camps to be sure—one Socialist, the other imperialist—and indicated the developing opposition between them, but in the Indonesian setting a radical confrontation of the government would only have been possible with a developed party and united front; in the absence of these the strategy of the PKI and *Sajap Kiri* could, according to Communist theory, only be to accelerate the national war of liberation and not to seek the establishment of a socialist society by violence now, when the bourgeois-democratic phase of the revolution had not as yet run its course. It is still a matter of speculation as to how far the PKI leadership at this time had a clear picture of the consequences which a radical confrontation of the Indonesian revolution would bring with it; there are strong indications that open rebellion was not the aim of the party's principal leaders, mainly because it seemed unnecessary.

The new cabinet of the revolutionary Indonesian Republic formed on July 3, 1947, was headed by the mercurial Amir Sjarifuddin; he was a crypto-Communist, as was the vice-premier Setiadjit, who as chairman of the Labor Party had helped to bring the important Indonesian labor federation, the SOBSI (*Sentral Organisasi Buruh Seluruh Indonesia*, All Indonesian Central Labor Organization) under Communist domination. Wikana, another Communist, became Minister of State for Youth, and still another State Minister, Maruto Darusman, was a member of the PKI's executive. The fact that the Communist sympathies of Sjarifuddin and Setiadjit were not generally known at the time (they were to announce them in August 1948) could only have worked to the party's advantage, for Djokjakarta, the capital of the revolutionary Republic, was in the view of one authoritative writer 'blinded' to PKI activity.[68] Undoubtedly one reason for this was that a sharp demarcation between Socialists and Communists did not exist in the early years of the Indonesian Revolution; both collaborated, for example, in the formation of youth organizations and in the foundation of Marxist institutes.[69] An open confrontation of the revolutionary republic would also have gravely undermined the party's future development of a united front strategy.

It is clear that in the half year or so of Sjarifuddin's premiership the gains made by the party and its organizational ancillaries were lost to a considerable extent. On July 20, 1947, the Dutch launched a military attack (it is doubtful if Sjarifuddin could have prevented this, even if he had wanted to). Although the revolutionary Indonesian Republic retained, in much weakened form, its position as the vanguard of the nationalist resurgence in the country, after the intervention of the United Nations the Indonesia case became an element in the developing Cold War struggle between the Soviet Union and the U.S., and Sjarifuddin saw the future in terms of closer reliance upon the Soviet bloc. This, as well as his avowed radical Marxist orientation, also generally increased the opposition against him. Sukarno and Hatta, who remained the dominant political figures in the Republic, could hardly have been unaware that Sjarifuddin was strengthening his hold on the Republic's armed forces and its auxiliaries by appointing his followers to key positions.

On January 23, 1948, his cabinet fell (a major tactical blunder on Sjarifuddin's part, according to party history today), and within three weeks there was unmistakable evidence that the united front strategy, never very well developed, had been further gravely harmed. On February 11, 1948, the Socialist Party (in which Communists and Socialists had long found a common meeting ground) split and the anti-Stalinist Socialists established a new party. Sjarifuddin retained control over the original Socialist party, and the PKI and Setiadjit's labor party formed a new front with it—the Democratic People's Front (*Front Demokrasi Rakjat*, FDR) with which the *Pesindo* (*Pemuda Sosialis Indonesia*, Indonesian Socialist Youth), the principal fellow-travelling youth organization led by Wikana, and SOBSI also affiliated. For practical purposes the FDR was a continuation on a more radical footing of the *Sajap Kiri*, and within a few weeks it began to advocate a program that demanded rejection of the so-called Renville Agreement with the Dutch, abandonment of any further negotiations with the Dutch, and nationalization of all foreign enterprises. Component units of the FDR urged closer cooperation with the Soviet bloc, a purge of all untrustworthy officials, the giving of 'land to those that cultivate it', etc.—all in all a mélange of radical demands that reflected not so much a well coordinated program as an extremist temper. The revolutionary government, now under the premiership of Mohammad Hatta, proceeded with a 'rationalization' (demobilization of excess troops and better training for the remainder) of the Republic's armed forces, which had the effect of weakening the para-military elements in league with the FDR as well as of other political movements. The Communist confrontation of the Indonesian Revolution now accelerated as the FDR began to resist Hatta's army rationalization program, as strikes and a new restlessness began to stir the trade unions affiliated with SOBSI, and as FDR leaders worked for the removal of Hatta and accused him of being too favorable to the U.S.[70]

The final breach between the Communists and the Sukarno-Hatta government was probably hastened by the return of Muso, who on August 11, 1948, arrived in Djokjakarta from Moscow. Very shortly this veteran of the party became in effect its principal leader and largely at his insistence a PKI party conference was held within a few days after his return. Here Muso's ideas found crystallization and approval in the important resolution called 'New Road for the Indonesian Republic' *(Djalan Baru Untuk Indonesia)*. This outlined the Leninist principle of the multi-stage (or two-stage) revolution, stressed the Zhdanov two-camp doctrine of total confrontation of the 'imperialists', described the Leninist class dynamics of the 'bourgeois democratic' phase of the Indonesian struggle in terms also of the appeal which had to be made to various groups of the peasantry and the middle class, and reoriented the organizational role of the party. Tactically, acceptance of the resolution meant an uncompromising fight against the Dutch and against those Indonesian politicians who might be seeking any kind of diplomatic rapprochement with them.

The new resolution, according to party history today, found particular favour with younger PKI leaders, e.g. D. N. Aidit, M. H. Lukman, Peris Pardede and Njoto, who formed the *Sajap Leninis* (Leninist wing), in the party, and led to an organizational tightening under which the pro-PKI Socialist and Labor parties merged with the PKI in the closing days of August 1948. A new Politburo was announced in which representatives of the *Sajap Leninis* held a few executive responsibilities, but in which Muso and former Socialist Party leader, Tan Ling Djie (who had spent several years in Moscow, had been active in the PKI underground in the nineteen thirties, and who, like Sjarifuddin and Setiadjit had formally announced in August 1948, that he had long been a Communist) were the principal members of the General Secretariat. Alimin, accused by Muso of bearing responsibility for earlier party failures, was relegated to a relatively minor Politburo position. This organizational fusion, which met with considerable opposition from various branches of the Labor and Socialist parties and was therefore never effectively consummated, was tactically part of an intended test of strength with the Sukarno-Hatta government, during which the FDR hoped to bring so much pressure to bear that Hatta would lay down his premiership. A new cabinet, responsible to the Republic's proto parliament, could then be formed in which the FDR would occupy key posts and thus Communist aims would be realized. This was the essence of what came to be known as Muso's 'Gottwald' Plan, a Communist seizure of power through the incorporation of Communists in a national coalition government, just as had recently happened in Czechoslovakia.

Through the years this concept of coalition government was to continue to exert influence on party strategy. Muso and the other FDR leaders in effect hoped for a repeat performance of the Sjarifuddin regime, but this time without a surrender of the executive mandate. However, the opposition to all these schemes was formidable. Sukarno and Hatta retained their immense prestige, Muslims and anti-Stalinist left-wing groups effectively worked together to block the FDR in many ways. Moreover, Sukarno, always mindful of the balance of power, in August and September, 1948, released from prison Tan Malaka and other leaders of his 'Fighting Front'. The pro-Malaka radical left, usually branded as Trotskyites by their Stalinist opponents, despite the incarceration of its leaders had been able to maintain itself and in June, 1948, had formed a political federation of its own (including a paramilitary auxiliary) and strenuously agitated in favor of the Hatta regime.

While all this opposition was in itself bad enough, PKI membership under Muso again acquired something of the élitist character that had characterized the party in the period 1920–1927. Thus, after the merger of the PKI with the Labor and Socialist parties late in August 1948, it was decided to incorporate only about half of the membership of the latter two parties with the Communist party. This was a major theoretical and strategic error, for while in the context of an effective united front the selective, vanguard role of the party must be preserved, organizational tactics dictate less selectivity in party membership when the front has a comparatively narrow base, as was the case with the FDR (e.g. the national bourgeoisie did not significantly participate in the front). In a significant sense the FDR had become a repetition of the 'left' deviation that had debilitated the party in the nineteen-twenties. There is some evidence that Muso ultimately realized the danger of this organizational and tactical deviation, for on September 9 he made overtures in the direction of the Masjumi (Muslim federation) and the PNI (National Indonesian Party), both strongholds of the developing middle class and both, of course, essentially non-Communist if not anti-Communist in outlook. Muso wanted the Masjumi and the PNI to cooperate with the PKI (after all, both had been able to collaborate with the PKI, then under Yusuf, in Tan Malaka's radical 'Fighting Front' early in 1946), but Muso apparently underestimated the polarization of political ideologies and did not see that a new appeal to the national bourgeoisie could only be effected if the radical program of the FDR was considerably mitigated and if, indeed, much of the deliberate 'confrontation' of the revolution and of the Sukarno-Hatta leadership of that revolution was abandoned by the party.

Conflicts between pro- and anti-PKI military units now became more frequent and PKI sympathizers in the army were often kidnapped. In the complicated maneuvering a Communist army unit made the mistake of attempting an attack on the city of Surakarta on September 17, 1948, apparently without the foreknowledge of the PKI's Politburo. A few lesser PKI leaders, subsequently seeing this attack on Surakarta repulsed, began to fear that the defeat would be the beginning of a systematic government offensive against the PKI and its army supporters; hence they believed that there was no other alternative but to broaden the Communist attack.[71] It should be noted that these PKI leaders were probably aware of the results of the Communist-sponsored Southeast Asia Youth Conference at Calcutta early in 1948, and of the resurgence of violent Communist action in many Southeast Asian countries following that Conference; indeed the timing of Muso's return suggests that a Communist insurrection in Indonesia had been planned by the Cominform and was therefore but a matter of time.[72] At least the lower party echelons felt themselves ready, although the Politburo had not given the signal, and in the tense and confused situation occasioned by the conflict between pro- and anti-PKI army auxiliaries and by the current army rationalization scheme it may well have seemed to local PKI activists in East and Central Java that the time was now or never.

In any event, under Sumarsono, a local party leader who lived near the city of Madiun, and who had played a leading role in the *Zeven Provincien* mutiny of 1933, the PKI seized control of that city on September 18. Local military commanders in the area between Surakarta and Madiun, as well as some in the direction of Surabaya, declared their adherence to the new Communist regime in Madiun. The news of the coup brought the immediate arrest of PKI leaders who happened to be in Djokjakarta (e.g. Alimin and Tan Ling Djie) and some of these made it known that they were against the insurrection. Other PKI leaders (among them Muso, Setiadjit, Sjarifuddin and Wikana) arrived in Madiun on September 19, but their initial attempt to parley with Sukarno and induce him to form a new FDR-led government failed, as Sukarno in a radio broadcast demanded that his nation chose between him and Muso. Muso now declared himself the head of a 'National Front Government' and he found still more sympathizers among military commanders in North Central Java. Communist bands meanwhile unleashed a holocaust of violence and destruction in the countryside, attacking all those believed to be enemies, including the more orthodox

Muslims. However, the national Indonesian army units loyal to the Sukarno-Hatta government needed but little time to go into action against the rebels. Despite heavy resistance Madiun fell to the Sukarno forces on September 30, and Muso and his 'government' fled, Muso himself being killed in a skirmish on November 1. Systematically the national army cleared the remaining pockets of Communist resistance; the scattered units of the 'national front', lacking all effective organization, soon were dispersed into small bands and thus decimated. Sjarifuddin and some of his associates were captured by December 1, and executed by the army on December 19.

With these events the PKI, now perhaps more gravely compromised than at any other time in its history, went into a new period of decline. The FDR and the united front lay in ruins, party organization was shattered as cadres were arrested, went underground or (like Aidit) left the country. The prestige of Communism generally had suffered a grievous blow in virtually all segments of articulate opinion. The Sukarno-Hatta government never proscribed the party as such during the Madiun rebellion; thus, experienced PKI leaders like Alimin (who was soon released, protesting that the whole affair had been Muso's doing) were still available, but the job of reconstruction would be arduous.

It is difficult to say in retrospect if the party's Madiun disaster—or a disaster like it—could have been avoided. It is not unlikely that the Cominform at or around the time of the Calcutta Conference in February 1948, instructed the PKI to resort to violence and open rebellion in the near future, although direct evidence upon this point is lacking— which is not surprising considering Communist planning of such matters. And it is also likely that few PKI leaders would have been willing openly to resist Muso who clearly had come to Indonesia as Moscow's agent with the new party strategy. Even so, the PKI leadership made costly and possibly avoidable errors. Party organization remained weak, a fact all the more dangerous to the PKI in view of the tensions and confusions surrounding the army 'rationalization' program which increased the possibility of precipitate action by undisciplined cadres. The party leadership was far from united: Muso may or may not have had organizational ability, but it is certain that in asserting his position as the voice of Moscow he denigrated Alimin too much, and caused dissatisfaction among those loyal to the latter in the higher party echelons. Sukarno may well have realized this since, during the rebellion, he constantly spoke of the 'PKI-Muso' as if to indicate that the party was divided and that the rebellion was but the work of a particular faction. The united front was woefully undeveloped, and because of the failure to draw the bourgeoisie in effectively (although the tactical significance of bourgeois support had received explicit recognition in the 'New Road' resolution fathered by Muso), the party's base remained much too narrow. Had the front been allowed to develop itself (necessitating a less intransigeant party line, to be sure) an eventual coup might have presented a much greater danger to the revolutionary Indonesian government. Considering the polarization of political opinion in the revolutionary Indonesian republic in Java, it would undoubtedly have been difficult, though not impossible, to broaden the class founda-tion of the FDR. Muso may have realized all this since it is probable that he did not approve of the timing of the insurrection, though he attempted to direct it after it had broken out. Finally, after the rebellion had erupted, tactical errors were made. The gravity of the failure to occupy Surakarta, for example, was not sufficiently understood and little effort was subsequently made to concentrate on control of that city.[73]

It is of interest to consider the 1945–1948 era and the events leading up to the Madiun insurrection from the point of view of current party history.[74] The party today is at pains to stress the important role it played in this period in mobilizing the Indonesian people in their revolutionary struggle against the Dutch. SOBSI, the BTI (*Barisan Tani Indonesia*, Indonesian Peasants Front), youth groups like *Pesindo* and the BKPRI (*Badan Kongres Pemuda Republik Indonesia*, Indonesian Republic Youth Congress Organization), para-military units like the *Lasjkar Merah* (Red Troops) and the *Lasjkar Rakjat dan Tentara Peladjar* (Students Army and People's Troops) are all described as PKI-organized units participating in the war against the Dutch. But all through the revolution there were grave organizational weaknesses and tactical errors. The speed with which revolutionary resistance spread exceeded the party's ability to channel and supervise it. Party cadres had to do double and sometimes triple duty and 'this dispersal of strength had a bad influence on the internal life of the party' and in the confusion 'Trotskyite and right-wing leftists' influenced 'the masses by using the mask of Marxism'. There was little understanding of theory, although a few publications by the *Sajap Leninis* provided the rank and file with a measure of insight into Leninist party concepts. A real under-standing of Marxist-Leninist principles, as applied to the realities of the Indonesian condition, was lacking, however, and the Fourth National PKI Congress (January, 1947) showed the serious organiza-tional and ideological weaknesses of the party so that some of this Congress' decisions, like the one supporting the Linggadjati Agreement, 'had the character of capitulating to the Dutch imperialists'. Particularly dangerous from the point of view of party history today was the comparative lack of attention to the work of a united front, and the organizational gap between workers and peasants in such a front.

Party history sees Muso's arrival and the adoption of the 'New Road' resolution as events of major significance, because they 'facilitated the relations which had been established by the Leninist wing' in the party's executive. In its review of PKI strategy during the Indonesian Revolution the 'New Road' resolution described the party as having made two errors: (1) 'that the PKI did not understand the revolutionary teaching "that the national anti-imperialist revolution of the present time has become a part of the world proletarian revolution", and that "the national revolution in Indonesia must have firm relations with other anti-imperialist forces in the world..."; ' and (2) 'that the PKI did not completely understand the balance of strength between the Soviet Union and British-USA imperialism after the Soviet Union speedily occupied all of Manchuria. At that time it was clear that the position of the Soviet Union was very strong on the continent of Asia, and this counter-balanced the military strength of U.S., British, and Australian imperialism, thus offering a good opportunity to the Indonesian people to begin their revolution. At that moment the Indonesian Communists exaggerated the strength of the Dutch and other imperialists and reduced the energy of the Indonesian revolution, together with other anti-imperialist groups'. In addition, the 'New Road' resolution criticized the weaknesses of the front strategy of the Party ('the Communists neglected the establishment of a national front as a weapon of the national revolution against imperialism. Although they later became conscious of this national front, they did not properly understand the technique of its creation. Various forms of national fronts have been set up during the past three years, but they always remained only on paper, they just consisted of agreements between organizations or between leaders, so that as soon as there was any dispute between the leaders the national front broke up'). It also counselled closer attention to party work in the armed forces (army ranks, it was urged, 'must be given special education in keeping with the tasks of the army . . . the army must unite with and be loved by the people. The army must be led by progressive cadres. Obviously, and above all, among its cadres, the army must be cleansed of reactionary and counter-revolutionary elements'.) The importance of more training in Marxism-Leninism for all party members was also stressed.

Much of this criticism, it may be remarked, was a critique of the Dimitrov line, and the PKI was in effect accused of not anticipating the Zhdanov 'two-camp' doctrine. The Leninist concepts (applied with success by Mao) that the 'national liberation' movement against imperialism is part of the proletarian world revolution, and that, therefore, it must be under the guidance of the party, and that the bourgeois-democratic phase of the revolution must be consistently directed toward the Socialist phase—all this was accentuated by the Zhdanov line. Its implementation meant a widening of the national front 'from below' so as to include the national bourgeoisie as a class, not just national bourgeois political leaders (the tactic of the national front 'from above'). From a theoretical standpoint the 'New Road' resolution thus was consistent in urging both the leadership of the national liberation movement as a whole and a widened national front on the party at the same time. But the criticism that the PKI had exaggerated the strength of the Dutch imperialists and that it had failed to understand the meaning of Soviet strength in Manchuria can only be interpreted as a justification in advance of the more violent course which the party would take soon after the adoption of the 'New Road' resolution. To some extent this second criticism strengthens the first, in that the party is charged with not being aggressive enough in seizing leadership of the national liberation movement which it presumably could have done, on the grounds that the Soviet Union was showing its power in Manchuria! Needless to say, the implications of the Dimitrov line which continued to form the basis of much party activity throughout 1946 and 1947 are rather easily glossed over in this second criticism.

For Aidit, the 'New Road' resolution made possible 'the development of a new upward trend in the Indonesian Revolution' and the new line was 'enthusiastically welcomed' by the masses, after 'tens and hundreds of thousands of people' had the party's program explained to them. According to the party history, this very evidence of popular support caused 'Dutch and American imperialism and its Indonesian hirelings' to attempt to smash the party, e.g. by murdering and kidnapping PKI sympathizers in the army, by illegal occupation of Pesindo and trade union offices, and ultimately by what the party now consistently calls the 'Madiun provocation'. The party's view now is that the whole Madiun affair was really engineered by the 'reactionary' Hatta government. As Aidit has put it:[75]

In the middle of September 1948, an incident occurred in the army in Madiun between the group which agreed to the then government's reactionary and provocative policy and the group which remained faithful to the revolution. This event was maneuvred by the Hatta government and it was said that in Madiun the Communists had carried out a seizure of power and that they had established a Soviet state. On the basis of this lie the government called on its entire apparatus to hunt down, arrest and murder members and sympathizers of the PKI. . . . The Madiun provocation was a preparation for the new Dutch colonial war which took place in December 1948, and all this was in preparation for forcing Indonesia to make further capitulations to Dutch imperialism.

In November 1954, Aidit was haled into court in Djakarta, as the person responsible for a statement of the PKI Central Committee (published on September 14, 1953) which, in a commemoration of the Madiun affair, strongly endorsed the party line of 'provocation' and pointed to Mohammad Hatta as the villain of the whole incident. This attack on Hatta was deemed defamatory and resulted in the court action. During his defense plea, on February 24, 1955, Aidit elaborated on the provocation theme, stressing the kidnapping and murders of PKI sympathizers in the revolutionary army in the weeks preceding the coup, and noting the fighting between army units in and about Surakarta. 'During this confused situation', Aidit declared, the deputy mayor of Madiun (a PKI sympathizer named Supardi) assumed leadership of the city administration (the mayor being too ill at the time and the Resident Commissioner of Madiun being away from the city), having been urged to do so by 'left-wing parties and organizations', since he seemed willing 'to come forward and take control of the situation'. The central republican government, though informed of the events in Madiun by the Madiun regional government and requested to send instructions, 'magnified' the problem and chose to regard Supardi's assumption of power as an attack on the authority of the central government, as a plot to establish 'Soviet power', and so on. Once the government took this line there was no turning back and the Communists had to defend themselves against those in the Sukarno-Hatta government who wished to 'magnify' the Madiun event in order to crush the PKI. Aidit does not explain how the tense and 'confused' situation around Surakarta necessarily affected affairs in Madiun, nor the initiatives taken and the role played by Sumarsono, nor the raising of the red flag in Madiun after the Communists had seized control, nor the appeal to surrounding army commanders to come to the aid of the rebels. Instead, Aidit holds—as does the party line today—that 'the bloody Madiun Affair would never have taken place if a mountain had not been made out of a molehill, if the good intentions of the left-wing groups had not deliberately been wrongly taken by the Central Government as something which, by chance, gave it an excuse to blacken the good name of the Communists', and thus provided 'a "reason" to mobilize all the forces of the state to hunt them down and exterminate them'. Even the fact that the PKI lost the struggle is understandable, Aidit has argued, because 'we had really no intention of waging war on the government of the Republic of Indonesia'.[76]

This last interpretation is particularly relevant to the party line today because it is made to lend support to the contention that the PKI is not a party of 'coup-ists',[77] as Aidit has frequently said, since its whole strategy since the 'New Road' revolution has been different. As Aidit put it in his earlier mentioned defense plea of February, 1955:[78]

It is quite impossible for the PKI to have carried out a coup d'état and set up a Soviet in Madiun, not only because these two steps are contrary to Communist theory but also because they are contrary to the proposal made by Comrade Muso after he returned home from abroad. . . . I still remember the PKI conference in August 1948, which was led by Comrade Muso himself. This conference endorsed a resolution entitled 'A New Road for the Republic of Indonesia', a copy of which I attach to this speech. Everybody can know that this resolution did not draw up a program for a coup d'état or for the establishment of a Soviet government.

It is difficult to reconcile the above assertion with some of the conclusions which Aidit and party historians today drew from the 1945–1948 era. Aidit has stressed that during the early revolutionary years the PKI was in no position to duplicate the guerilla warfare technique and the utilization of a 'people's liberation army' in the manner of the Chinese Communists. The insular nature of Indonesia and the absence of a friendly neighboring country (in the case of the Chinese Communists this was the Soviet Union) in the rear, which could prevent encirclement by the enemy, dictated different tactics. But Aidit also indicates that guerilla warfare 'is one of the correct forms of struggle to achieve national independence' and in principle guerilla warfare could certainly have been used in Indonesia. Not only that, but Aidit appears to suggest that the PKI could have won a victory in the revolution if such warfare had been properly applied by it:[79]

During the Revolution, the Party had armed forces, but the Party was not able to dominate. There was no arrangement made for Party cadres to study military science and the science of revolutionary warfare. . . . But in order to make guerilla warfare more effective in the situation prevailing in Indonesia, it was necessary to combine guerilla warfare with revolutionary actions of laborers in the cites occupied by the enemy, and with general economic and political strikes. . . . Work in Dutch occupied regions, which was to organize labor and lead extreme labor actions did not receive the attention of the Communists. . . . Besides . . . the PKI did not conduct intensive work in the ranks of the Dutch armed forces, not a few of whom were composed of peasant and labor youths who could have been drawn to the side of the revolution.

It is not readily apparent how an effective and coordinated action between the PKI's 'armed forces' and a revolutionary strike action, though presumably primarily directed against the Dutch, it is true, could have failed to generate also a policy of aggressive action within the revolutionary Republic's and against its internal policies and thereby make a Communist effort to seize the government of the Republic equally likely. As far as Aidit is concerned the 'August Revolution 1945–1948' (i.e. the period of the Indonesian Revolution during which the PKI was active) failed, mainly because the PKI had 'not yet drawn the conclusions from its experiences' with, among other, 'the questions of armed struggle'. And, as Aidit was to emphasize again in his *Peladjaran Dari Sedjarah PKI* ('Lessons from the History of the PKI'), 'in a revolution, armed struggle is the most important form of struggle'. Seen also in the context of violent Communist action in Asia following the Calcutta conference and the Cominform's connection with such action, Aidit's stress on the proper use of guerilla warfare and on armed struggle implies a contradiction of his avowal that it was 'quite impossible' for the party to have carried out a coup d'état.

In retrospect it would seem that even the party's 'armed struggle' strategy would have met with formidable, if not insurmountable, obstacles in the Republic itself, especially so since the PKI's focus remained Java. To be sure, a Communist offensive of sorts began in Tapunuli and in the Asahan region of Sumatra early in September 1948, but here the action was primarily that of terrorists, escaped criminals and opportunists in army auxiliary units, marching under the Communist banner, and it remained wholly ineffective. The FDR branches in Sumatra (and indeed a few in Java) refused to join the Madiun uprising. In Eastern Indonesia Communist influence was negligible.

Certainly by the beginning of 1947 a gradual polarization of political and ideological life was beginning to take place, in which the PKI and its Labor Party and Socialist fellow-travellers came slowly but inexorably to be arrayed against virtually all sections of the Muslim political movement, against leading segments of middle class secular nationalism, against anti-Stalinist Socialists, nationally oriented Communists (branded as Trotskyites by the PKI) and Christian confessional groupings in the fledgling Indonesian Republic. In terms of Communist class analysis much of this opposition—of course by no means all—reflected bourgeois or petty bourgeois interests. Party theory today never wearies of pointing out that the revolutionary period, and even the Madiun debacle, provided the PKI with 'important experiences concerning the wavering nature of the national bourgeoisie'. The national bourgeoisie, as Lenin and Stalin indicated early in the Comintern's history, and as Mao was to agree, can under certain circumstances participate in the revolution, while at other times 'it can waver and betray'—and the Indonesian Revolution as studied by party cadres and neophytes today presumably provides an illustration of this dual nature of the national bourgeoisie and lights up the essential problems in organizing the party and the united front so as to use, direct and not be 'betrayed' by the non-proletarian forces in an anti-imperialist movement.[80]

And so the PKI entered the last year of the Indonesian revolution and the subsequent early months of national independence (formally attained at the Round Table Conference at The Hague in December 1949) with the view that Indonesia was in the hands of a clique of bourgeois reactionaries and traitors who had prepared a sell-out of the Indonesian people to the Dutch and American imperialists. This view was echoed in Moscow, though the Soviet Union had unreservedly come to the aid of Sukarno and the Republic shortly after the Madiun Affair when the Dutch had launched a second 'police action' against the much battered and truncated Republic in December 1948. By 1949 Soviet views on Indonesian events reflected the criticism of the PKI which Muso had already formulated in the 'New Road' resolution the year before: the party was upbraided for its 'soft' line support of the Linggadjati agreement, for failing to press for an expansion of Communist power when Sjarifuddin was premier (as the 'New Road' resolution had stated, Sjarifuddin's voluntary resignation wholly ignored Leninist exhortations on the proper use of power in the revolution and thus 'opened the way to compradore bourgeois elements to seize control of the leadership of the government'), for failing to counteract the influence of rightwing nationalism, and so on. These errors, in Soviet opinion, did not begin to be corrected until the reorganization of the party in the middle of 1948.[81] It is of interest to note this indirect Soviet approval of 'The New Road' resolution, because this resolution remains in Indonesian Communist thought today perhaps the most tangible gain of the Indonesian revolution for the PKI: 'the resolution was the first important step towards creating a bolshevised Party, which is nation-wide in scale, has close ties with the masses, and is consolidated ideologically, politically and organizationally'.[82] The rehabilitation of the party after 1952 was to be achieved largely in terms of the 'New Road' resolution.

CHAPTER II

REORGANIZATION AND RESURGENCE

1 *948–1952*. The period 1948–52 in party history was marked by disorganization and factional disputes, gradually giving way to greater firmness and clarity of purpose as the Leninist wing of the party gained control, bringing with it new strength. Following the Madiun disaster many party cadres went more or less underground for a while; younger party leaders such as Aidit and Lukman left the country and travelled in China and in North Viet Nam. Whatever influence the PKI once had in the armed forces and para-military organizations was now shattered, and when the Hatta government announced the end of the Madiun uprising on December 7, 1949, over 30,000 people (a majority probably being members of para-military units that had been Communist-infiltrated) were under arrest. The government was careful to indicate that it did not oppose the Communist party as such, but only those who had resorted to violence, and a judicial hearing was necessary for those who had supported the rebellion and applied for government positions.[1] The Madiun coup had caught many FDR activists off guard and for some months after the coup many cadres and, indeed, top leaders like Alimin, certainly encouraged the notion that the rebellion had not reflected the views of the party at all, and that most of the party had in fact opposed it. The Hatta government largely chose to accept this view, and it even allowed PKI members who had not participated in the rebellion to hold seats in the provisional parliament of the Republic. But despite the opportunity afforded by this moderate policy of the government, the PKI's resurgence in the subsequent months proved far from easy and for months the party seemed to flounder ineffectually in the backwash of its defeat.

There were several reasons for this. For one thing, the popular image of the party was seriously tarnished: at a critical moment (i.e. when the Dutch were preparing a new offensive against the Republic) the party had stabbed the government in the back, so it was believed. The party's duplicity as a mere tool of Moscow was stressed by those who had studied the pattern of Communist insurrections in Asia all through 1948 and who regarded the nearly simultaneous occurrence of these insurrections, including the one in Madiun, as more than accidental. For another thing, even in defeat and at a time when it was greatly weakened, the party had to follow a policy of extreme opposition to the Sukarno-Hatta government and ultimately to the Round Table Conference Agreements by which Indonesia formally attained its independence. Especially after the second Dutch 'police' action against the Republic in December 1948, popular support for Sukarno and Hatta had grown, even in the areas beyond Java, where under Dutch sponsorship separate Indonesian states had been established. And while the RTC Agreements left a satisfactory settlement of a number of important issues in abeyance, even radicals could find cause for celebration that these Agreements did make Indonesia formally independent at last. But to the PKI Sukarno and Hatta remained tools of the reactionaries and the RTC a compromise with imperialism. The time was to come when these views, at least insofar as Hatta and the RTC Agreements were concerned, would find broader sympathy in Indonesian life, but that time was not yet and in the meantime the party found itself out of step with majority opinion.

Then there was the serious rift in tactics and organization policies. After Madiun the party once again came under the leadership of Alimın and also of Tan Ling Djie; neither had participated in the Madiun rebellion (having been arrested in Djokjakarta by the Republican government at the time of the outbreak of the revolt), and they gave it out that the rebellion had been the work of Muso and his cohorts. Increasingly opposed to Alimin and Tan was a group of younger leaders, among them Aidit and Lukman, who in the party history today are described as 'Leninists' to distinguish them from the 'opportunists'. The conflict between these two factions probably did not begin until the middle of 1950, well after the return of leading 'Leninists' from their visit to China. It is also clear that personal jealousies and mutual recriminations had much to do with the struggle between the two factions, but it is necessary to stress the genuine and important differences between them. The Alimin-Tan faction wished to keep the PKI as such more or less out of the limelight for some time, and in any event keep the party small and élite-structured. From this point of view Communists should work within and through other parties, e.g. strengthen the *Partai Sosialis* (one of the groups that had fused with the PKI in August, 1948, and not to be confused with the anti-Stalinist *Partai Sosialis Indonesia* led by former premier Sutan Sjahrir), making it a genuine 'working class party' *(Partai Klas Buruh)*, and use it as its principal front, especially among the urban proletariat, and among those with radical Marxist sympathies but reluctant to join the PKI formally. It is not true that the Alimin-Tan group completely foreswore the 'New Road' technique, and its stress upon an ideological and organizational strengthening of the party, and on building a broad united front, including the national bourgeoisie and the peasantry, but the group did seem to believe that the times were not propitious for a new, more or less open, organizational campaign directly under PKI auspices. Nor did the Alimin-Tan faction in principle abandon the approach of Muso's 'Gottwald Plan', though the party's role was to be much more indirect in fostering the idea of a coalition. Considering the times, the faction believed that the party might make better headway by concentrating first on victories in parliament rather than by a new campaign among the masses. With this position the group around Aidit took sharp issue.[2] The party, they argued, should remain the principal concern of Communists; it should be active among the masses in order to rebuild a broad united front and not just confine itself to parliamentary politics. The party should not submerge itself, or retreat or de-emphasize its role in the revolution, nor should it concentrate merely on new tactical alliances with other parties, but should have its own 'front' groups. At the same time the party should, however, be prepared to prove its constitutionality by parliamentary participation, and by its concern for national interests. Above all, the Aidit group wished for the full implementation of the 'New Road' resolution and it accused the Alimin-Tan faction of having no regard for the necessity of party reorganization and of wishing to leave the party organizationally defenseless in an essentially hostile environment, where the PKI's known opposition to Sukarno and Hatta and to the RTC Agreements might well lead to new 'provocations'.

The turning point in the factional struggle came in September 1950, when upon the initiative of the Surakarta section committee of the party the bodies of the eleven PKI leaders (among them Amir Sjarifuddin) who had been shot by the Republican government in December 1948, after the failure of the Madiun uprising were re-buried by the party faithful. The Alimin-Tan faction had cautioned against this demonstration and the government also originally placed all manner of obstacles in the way, but the ceremony, attended by 'tens of thousands of members, lovers of the PKI, and people from the Surakarta and other regions', as the party history today puts it, did take place. The ceremony, according to this same source, 'ended the atmosphere of panic among Party members';[3] whether it actually did so is difficult to say, but it is clear that the re-burial ceremony ended the more or less underground phase of the party's post-Madiun history and gave a measure of prestige and confidence to party leaders, especially to the 'Leninists'. Help to the party may also have come from another quarter: on August 14, 1950, Red China's ambassador presented his credentials to President Sukarno and according to a number of Indonesian sources the Peking government's embassy in Djakarta actively began to assist the PKI with money and printed matter.[4] Aidit has, however, excoriated these reports of

Communist Chinese assistance as slanderous, and has stressed that the party raised itself by its own strength.[5]

Meanwhile the breach between the two factions in the party's leadership had become irreparable and a new incident was to set the stage for the eventual eclipse of the Alimin-Tan faction. On December 2, 1950, Alimin and Tan Ling Djie, in the name of the party's Central Committee, issued a statement on the party's policy toward West New Guinea, the one area formerly part of the Netherlands East Indies which had not been transferred to the Indonesian government at the Round Table Conference in December 1949. The Indonesian government claimed West New Guinea (*Irian Barat*, as Indonesians call it) as its own but both Alimin and Tan Ling Djie essentially opposed this claim, in conformity with the stand of the Dutch Communist Party and with the PKI's general opposition to the policies of Sukarno, Hatta and Masjumi premier Mohammad Natsir (who had succeeded Hatta as prime minister by October, 1950). The December 2, 1950, statement issued for the party ('the Secretariat of the Central Committee of the PKI was in Djakarta and knew nothing about it', according to the party history today) favored the creation of a 'Republic of West New Guinea' loosely joined with Indonesia in a dual State federation but wholly free from Dutch control. This view seemed to undercut the official position that West New Guinea, far from becoming a republic, should be brought completely under national Indonesian control. The issue took on added meaning because during the first half of 1950 the sixteen component states of the original federal Indonesian Republic that had come into being at the conclusion of the Round Table Conference at the Hague in December 1949, had concluded a merger with the original revolutionary Republic of Indonesia, then merely confined to a part of Java. But this process of unification, carried out in a number of areas by means of questionable legality, had produced sharp political antagonism in the country and had even led to armed rebellion in East Indonesia against the new unitary national government in Djakarta. The December 2 statement issued by the Alimin-Tan faction not only attacked the government's policy on an issue which was to wax in emotional and political significance for Indonesians in years to come, but it also seemed to indicate opposition to the unification of all parts of the country under a single central government. The Aidit faction cried 'sabotage' and in a statement of its own declared that the December 2 statement had not been issued by the Central Committee of the party at all. Mainly in order to repair this breach a plenary session of the Central Committee convened in January 1951; this session not only decided that 'a policy error' had been committed in the issuance of the West New Guinea statement, but it reviewed the entire existing conflict in party tactics and decided ultimately in favor of the Aidit-Lukman faction and the 'Leninist' approach. Further efforts to develop the Socialist Party were halted. A new Politbureau composed of Alimin, Lukman, Aidit, Njoto, and Sudisman was elected by the Central Committee Plenum. Tan Ling Djie was essentially made the scapegoat in the whole tactical conflict and of the December 2 statement in particular, but he was allowed to retain his membership in the Central Committee for the time being. The 'Leninists' regarded a too drastic break with him as inopportune, but for all practical purposes Tan's influence had come to an end. Alimin too, was now surrounded by his party opponents in the Politbureau and thus effectively neutralized. Shortly thereafter the party's principal theoretical journal, *Bintang Merah* (Red Star) and newspaper *Harian Rakjat* (People's Daily) reappeared with new editorial staffs largely composed of members of the *Sajap Leninis;* Peris Pardede, Lukman and Aidit became editors of *Bintang Merah*, and Njoto became the main figure on the editorial board of *Harian Rakjat*. In April 1951, another plenary session of the Central Committee gave birth to a draft party constitution and this development according to Aidit, became 'a great incentive for the development of the Party throughout Indonesia'. The new constitution, declared to be thoroughly 'Marxist-Leninist' in character and providing for a 'bolshevized' party organization and the building of a united front, was accompanied by a new party program of 12 articles, which elaborated the 'New Road' resolution and served the party as principal documentary base until the Fifth National Congress of the party in March 1954.[6] Significantly this program echoed the concept of a 'national coalition' as Muso's 'Gottwald Plan' had already outlined it, and it made a united front approach, also in parliamentary politics and in the cabinet, indispensable.

Welding the scattered and still poorly organized branches of the party together proved no easy task, but there is evidence that from May through July 1951, considerable headway was made. Party discipline was enforced, considerable selectivity began to be practised in regard to membership and party branches were told to report on the reaction to and implementation of the new party constitution in their local areas, so that the constitution could be revised at a forthcoming National Conference of the Party. So-called Central Committee Commissariats were established in many parts of the country, in conformity with the constitutional directive and in order to effect tighter local organization on the basis of 'democratic centralism'.[7] Followers of the Alimin-Tan faction were 'reoriented' and former Socialist and Labor Party members who wished to join the PKI were subjected to considerable scrutiny.

At least a skeleton of an organizational structure began to emerge; Section, Sub-Section, and Resort Committees were established in provinces, residencies, districts, and towns. Finding considerable support still among various categories of the urban proletariat and among the workers on foreign-owned estates, party cadres throughout 1951 had been stirring up labor unrest by encouraging raids by terrorists, by former members of army auxiliaries, and by plain criminals on sugar plantations in East Java. Partially because of this the anti-Communist Masjumi premier, Sukiman, whose cabinet had come to power in April 1951, felt justified in starting a mass arrest of Communists and suspected Communists in August 1951, as charges that the PKI was planning another coup against the state filled the air. The immediate cause of the arrests was an attack by dissident harbor workers and local Communist agitators on a police post in Tandjong Priok, the port of Djakarta; probably with the agreement of President Sukarno, some 2,000 Communists and party sympathizers were subsequently confined. While the evidence is not clear, the belief that the party leadership was in fact planning a coup seems unfounded, and the Tandjong Priok affair seems to have been primarily the work of local hotheads. Though kept behind bars for many months all prisoners were subsequently released 'without it having been possible to bring a single person up before a court'.[8]

The mass arrests did not significantly slow the rebuilding of the party; in retrospect the Sukiman cabinet itself does not appear to have been wholly united in further implementing anti-Communist measures. Even then the party's renewed national front approach, its willingness to collaborate with other 'anti-imperialist' groups in completing what it called the 'bourgeois democratic' phase of the Revolution (part and parcel of the two-stage or multi-stage revolutionary concept which PKI theory stressed), and its presence in the Republic's provisional parliament, were beginning to have effect on the political life of the young Indonesian Republic. Sukiman's arrest of PKI parliamentary deputies created adverse reactions also in non-Communist circles. Aidit stressed the connection between the forces making for the 'provocation' in Madiun in 1948 and those responsible for the August arrests, and branded them tools of the fascist-imperialist camp in the world, while he urged that during this new assault on the party as much party discipline be maintained as possible.[9] Early in 1952 a National Party Conference was held which took the position that 'the party's political line which placed the center of gravity of the party's task on building a united national front against the ultra-reactionary Sukiman government, could only be carried out if the most important organizational question of the time were solved, namely the expansion of Party membership and Party organization'.[10]

According to Aidit, the number of party members and candidate members at this time was 7,910, and cadres were over-extending themselves, having to fill many different functions simultaneously. At the National Party Conference the decision was therefore reached to broaden the party's base and according to the party, PKI membership after a six months' campaign had increased to over 126,000.[11] A further ideological stiffening of the membership, by placing increased emphasis on theoretical training, was agreed upon at this National Party Conference in order to root out the 'sectarianism, capitulationism and adventurism, which still persisted in the party'. The new Politburo began to insist on regular reports from lower level committees, pushed through an indoctrination program at all party levels everywhere, enormously increased the volume of printed materials (especially inexpensive tracts by Lenin, Stalin, Aidit and the 'New Road' resolution), rationalized party finances, encouraged 'criticism and self-criticism' sessions, and above all, endeavored to remove the conspiratorial and 'coup-ist' aura which the party had acquired in the popular mind after Madiun. After the National Party Conference little or no opposition to the 'Leninist' group remained and the subsequent rapid rise of the party has occurred on the basis of Aidit's strategy.

There are certain aspects of the ascendancy of the *Sajap Leninis* and its defeat of the Tan Ling Djie and Alimin faction which will probably not be cleared up for some time to come. While it is evident, for example, that by January 1951, and the plenary meeting of the Party's Central Committee, the power of the Tan-Alimin faction had largely been broken it was not until October 1953 and the plenary meeting of the Central Committee of that date that both Tan and Alimin were removed (or 'resigned') from the Central Committee. One reason may have been simple caution on the part of Aidit and his cohorts not to bring about too abrupt a change. Another, and perhaps more likely reason was that early in 1953 Aidit had journeyed to Prague to attend the Czechoslovak Communist Party Congress and met not only leading European Communists for the first time, but also became familiar with the details of the decisions of the Nineteenth Congress of the Soviet Communist Party held the previous October 1952. Reportedly, Aidit returned from Prague with money and instructions for the regeneration of the PKI and shortly thereafter detailed the new strategy to the Central Committee and to the Fifth PKI Party Congress (March 1954). By that time 'Tan Ling Djie-ism' had become the accepted scapegoat and justification for Aidit's own strategy.

Before considering the years since 1952 it seems wise to indicate the broad lines of the strategy of Aidit and his associates as it emerged in this period.[12] The dual task of building the national front and building the party meant the necessity of simultaneous appeals to four classes— workers, peasants, petty and national bourgeoisie. Each of these was seen as suffering from the effects of 'imperialism' and feudalism, and to each the 'completion' of the anti-imperialist revolution could bring significant advantages. To the peasants it would bring the abolishment of exploitation by foreign estates, by landlords and by usurers; to the national bourgeoisie it promised the end of the repressive controls still exercised by foreign, especially Dutch, capital in the country. In a tactical sense this meant that the party more than ever before would have to increase its work among the peasantry by articulating its griev- ances, politicalizing its outlook on a fast changing world, and arousing its class consciousness. With increasing vigor therefore, the party has sought a following in the rural Indonesian society since Aidit's accession to power in the party's central committee in 1951. As far as the bour- geoisie was concerned, the party faced a different problem. Relatively speaking, the bourgeoisie was more politically conscious than the peasantry and its grievances and uncertainties stemmed from its position in a national economy which retained much of its traditional colonial structure, especially insofar as the role of Dutch capital in export agriculture, industry and the import-export economy was concerned. Bourgeois political adhesion was divided among a number of parties, but especially between the anti-Communist Masjumi, where a Reform Islamic ideology prevailed, and the non-Communist PNI (National Indonesian Party, Sukarno's old stronghold) where a nativistic kind of 'populism' called *marhaenism*[13] provided a vague rationale for action. The Masjumi and the PNI had collaborated reasonably effectively in the early years of national independence, but rivalry between them for political control was mounting steadily. The PKI in its appeal to the national bourgeoisie was gradually able to drive a wedge between the Masjumi and the PNI, thus, in the parlance of party theory, drawing the bourgeoisie to the left. It is necessary to emphasize that this tactic with one or two exceptions could be made, and was made, to harmonize with the party's earlier opposition to the RTC agreements, and with opposition to those whom the party blamed for these agreements. The national bourgeoisie was 'suffering' from imperialism, so it was argued; the Dutch were still in control of the economy because the anti-imperialist revolution was 'incomplete'. The party's opposition to imperialism thus was accompanied by the promise that 'national' industry, and indeed the 'national capitalists', would enjoy the protection of the PKI. The non-party politician Hatta along with Natsir, Sukiman and other Masjumi leaders, remained the PKI's implacable enemies, but Sukarno, the embodiment of the nativistic populist mystique which served the PNI as its party program, as well as of the more volatile elements in Indonesian nationalism generally, was a potential ally. Thus the PKI hoped to gain support in the bourgeoisie via a kind of endorsement of the brand of nationalistic and nativistic temper which Sukarno reflects, as well as by its campaign against the evils of lingering 'imperialism'. The success of this strategy, certainly insofar as Sukarno was concerned, depended on a number of then relatively imponderable factors, of which an expectation of worsening of Dutch-Indonesian relations was certainly one. By allying itself with a strongly nationalist approach to many problems (e.g. in the matter of Indonesia's claim on West New Guinea) the PKI under Aidit hoped for, and was for some years largely successful in establishing a new rapprochement with important elements of the bourgeoisie.

The proletariat in this strategy was, and is, the principal dynamic element of the revolution, and the SOBSI as well as the SARBUPRI (Union of Plantation Workers), two of the major Communist-dominated, though nominally independent labor federations, were to provide the party with much of its strength. One rough estimate, made in June 1952, by an American trade union expert, put the number of SOBSI members at over 800,000 and the number of SARBUPRI followers at over 350,000, out of a total of two million organized workers.[14] SOBSI's great strength partly derived from the fact that it dominated labor in essential sectors of the economy, such as the petroleum industry, and that it virtually controlled all dockworkers. In line with the organizational tightening of the party, SOBSI also reorganized its leadership structure according a new Constitution (1952). Njono, an early follower of Aidit, could, as Secretary-General of SOBSI, be counted upon to steer its tactics in the approved direction. SOBSI's new 1952 constitution declared that the federation regarded the class struggle as the basis of its program and also accepted the two-stage revolution concept, basic to PKI strategy, under which SOBSI declared it would collaborate with all other groups in the fight against imperialism and feudalism.[15] As for the petty bourgeoisie, the PKI was faced with an almost novel organizational campaign. Petty bourgeois had always provided the party with a large proportion of its cadres but the party had rarely been effective in acquiring a following among the petty bourgeois as such. In Aidit's maturing united front strategy such groups as independent workers, fishermen, intellectuals and white-collar workers were to be the targets of new organizational drives, though the ambivalent outlook of some petty bourgeois would, in Aidit's view, always have to be considered a danger to the party. From the point of view of strategy, the benefits which the advancing anti-imperialist and anti-fedual revolution could bring to some petty bourgeois groups would have to be 'intellectualized' to a considerably greater degree than those for the workers and peasants, and hence the establishment and organization of youth fronts and students leagues was to attain ever more significance in party tactics.

On the Indonesian political scene the implementation of this four-class front strategy necessitated front activity both 'from below' (mobilization of the masses and direct organizational contact with, or control over, disparate population groups and organizations) as well as 'from above' (political alliances primarily with the leadership of various parties). An example of the latter was the formation in February 1951, of the BPP *(Badan Permusjawaratan Partai-Partai*, Consultative Organization of Parties), a loose federation of the PKI with a number of lesser parties, including labor, peasant, and some smaller Muslim and nationalist parties. The PKI envisaged the BPP's value primarily in the parliamentary sphere and the federation's conveniently broad program (with its demand for nationalization of industries, for the distribution of land to the landless peasantry, the abrogation of the Round Table Conference Agreements with the Netherlands, the acquisition of West New Guinea, and for greater political freedoms) provided an ideal basis for a political front in the 'anti-imperialist, bourgeois democratic phase' of the revolution. The practical influence of the BPP was relatively small, although it continued to be useful to the PKI in mobilizing opposition to the Masjumi, especially in the closing days of the Sukiman cabinet. Although the PNI refused to join the BPP and although during the Sukiman and Wilopo cabinets both Masjumi and PNI members were in the government, the strain between the two groups was steadily growing. Despite the difficulties the PKI was to have in wooing the PNI and in attracting 'national bourgeois' support, the BPP also served the party well in reorienting domestic political thinking in such a way as to help in the creation of a new image of the party in radical nationalist terms that could find an acceptable place in the partisan ideological vocabulary of the time.

1952–1955. Thus directed by the decisions of the National Party Conference of 1952 and under the leadership of youthful, self-styled 'Leninists', the PKI was to experience in the next decade the greatest advances in its history. It may be desirable to sketch the antecedents of these leaders. Dipa Nusantara Aidit, probably of Arab descent, was born in Medan, Sumatra (though other reports say on Banka island near Sumatra) in 1923, had a secondary commercial education and later followed the nationalistic 'New Generation' courses taught by Indonesian nationalist leaders during the Japanese occupation. Subsequently, he is said to have been active in the anti-Japanese underground, particularly in the 'semi-illegal' *Pemuda Angkatan Baru* (New Generation Youth). Arrested briefly by the Japanese toward the end of the occupation, he was subsequently turned over to the Dutch and the British and released in 1946. During the revolution he served in the Republic's provisional parliament and was active in the FDR, becoming a member of the Agitprop (agitation and propaganda) section of the PKI's new Politburo on September 1, 1948. The extent of his involvement in the Madiun coup is uncertain, but it is definite that shortly after the Madiun affair he, and M. H. Lukman, traveled through the Communist sector of China and also visited Ho Chi Minh. In 1949, Aidit returned to Indonesia as a stowaway, was briefly arrested again by the Dutch, and after his release concentrated his efforts on the development of party publications and on youth work. Elected First Secretary of the Central Committee in 1951, he was subsequently chosen as Secretary-General at the Central Committee's Plenum in October 1953, and confirmed in that post at the Fifth National Party Congress in 1954. In 1959 he became Chairman of the Central Committee of the PKI, and since 1951 has been the party's principal theoretician and tactician.

Next to Aidit Mohammed H. Lukman became perhaps the principal PKI leader. Born in Tegal, Java, in 1920, Lukman joined the *Pemuda Angkatan Baru* organization during the Japanese occupation and later was the principal propagandist of the *Barisan Banteng*, a semi-military youth group. He is described as one of the founders of the *Gerindom-Gerakan Indonesia Merdeka* (Free Indonesia Movement), an 'anti-Fascist' front in which Aidit also had been active; like Aidit, he was briefly arrested by the Japanese toward the close of the occupation. Since 1946 he has been formally a member of the PKI, rising to deputy secretary-general in 1953. He was originally regarded as Aidit's alter ego, but a strain developed between the two over tactical differences in the period after 1957, Lukman urging usually a more militant and intransigeant approach toward the Indonesian government.

The third most prominent figure in the party is Njoto, born in Djember, East Java, in 1925. Active primarily in radical youth groups, he participated in revolutionary actions against the Dutch and British in Surabaya, Bangil and Djember, heading the PKI branch in the last-named city. With Aidit he joined in lower echelon leadership of the FDR, was briefly arrested by the Dutch during the revolution but escaped, and became an editor of *Bintang Merah*, the party's theoretical journal in 1949, and a deputy Secretary General in October 1953. *Harian Rakjat*, the party's daily, has been his principal concern. Mention may also be made of second-string figures like Sakirman, a former Socialist Party leader, who has been the PKI's principal economic expert in parliament; Njono, who has directed labor affairs; B.O. Hutapea, an editor of *Bintang Merah* and a prolific writer; Peris Pardede, the principal leader of the Djakarta branch of the party; and Asmu, the party's agrarian reform specialist.

The year 1952 began well for the PKI. The Sukiman cabinet fell on February 23 over its handling of the Mutual Security Agreement with the United States, which was widely interpreted as threatening Indonesia's independent foreign policy.[16] Certainly a factor in Sukiman's ultimate fall was the machinations of the Communist-led BPP, the party's principal parliamentary front weapon to split the Nationalists and the Masjumi. As on the occasion of the fall of the Natsir cabinet, the party worked after the fall of the Sukiman regime to exclude the Masjumi from the government, at first insisting that the cabinet be based primarily on the BPP, the Socialist Party of Indonesia and the PNI, but gradually moderating its demands and indicating that it would support the new cabinet of PNI premier Wilopo (sworn in on April 4, 1952) in which Masjumi was represented, so long as the cabinet's program remained 'progressive and national'. Through PKI influence labor radicalism was minimized somewhat, and the party strongly identified itself with the symbols of nationalism, including the growing demand in radical circles for the immediate return of West New Guinea. The success of the PKI's strategy by the middle of 1952 was evident from the fact that:[17]

On August 17, the seventh anniversary of the proclamation of the Republic the PKI had positions of great influence in celebration committees throughout the archipelago. Just twelve months earlier the PKI leaders had been arrested on the grounds that they were planning to overthrow the State!

An important factor in this process of acquiring new respectability for the PKI was provided by the developing pattern of domestic party politics, in which the PNI, for political as well as religio-cultural reasons, found itself more and more opposing the Masjumi. To a large extent the PNI reflected the traditional, nativistic value-system of the village world and its aristocratic superstructure. The party had always been strong among the *pamong pradja* (civil service), traditionally drawn from the aristocracy but slowly being democratized, and its nationalistic outlook sought to combine a specific view of traditional Indonesian culture with modern radical populism centering around the *marhaen* or common man. As such the PNI could draw strength from a major cultural dimension in Indonesian (especially Javanese) life. namely the so-called *abangan*, the term usually given to the Indonesian who is not strict in his observance of Muslim religious belief and practice, venerates pre-Muslim animistic forces, and is obedient to his ancient custom *(adat)*. Customarily seen in antithesis to the *abangan* orientation is that of the *santri* (the term designating Islamic orthodoxy, strict obedience to Muslim precept in all aspects of life, including such fields as education, politics, and family and social relations). In the Masjumi a great many nuances on the *santri* theme had found an organizational haven, ranging from a modernistic reformist Islam with Socialistic tendencies and cosmopolitan in orientation that attracted younger intellectuals to a more conservative and more nationalistic bourgeois commercial outlook that saw little salvation in a neutralist foreign policy and opted for closer ties with the West in the Cold War. The *abangan-santri* antithesis has deep roots in Indonesian life and in the past it has occasionally erupted in violence and persecution.

The *abangan-santri* antithesis as such, however, was not an important factor in bringing the PNI and the PKI closer together. Rather in the pattern of domestic Indonesian politics this antithesis, always dormant, was heavily accentuated and thus derived significance from the rivalry for political power in the various organs of the young Republic between the PNI and Masjumi, the two principal political parties. As this rivalry developed, particularly in the forthcoming first national parliamentary elections, the PNI searched for allies and found the PKI ready and willing. In both parties there were reservations about a rapprochement and an awareness of its dangers; nor must it be thought that a formal political alliance was concluded between the two groups. It was rather that the two parties could share a policy of opposition to Masjumi on the basis of a radical nationalism and populism, combining an appeal to the interests of the national bourgeoisie and the *rakjat djelata* or common man.

The middle-class nationalistic elements in the PNI, the native business and professional groups in particular, could find much to approve in the Communist program of support for the national bourgeoisie and its attacks on the lingering control of Dutch 'imperialist' capital over the Indonesian economy. The Masjumi-led cabinets of Natsir and Sukiman, and the PNI-led cabinet of Wilopo, while certainly undertaking to assist the indigenous entrepreneurial groups, especially in the industrial and importing fields, nevertheless tended to follow a policy of accommodating foreign capital, and of adjusting to the structural controls imposed by that capital. This, along with the retrenchment in government spending initiated by the Wilopo cabinet and necessitated by the drop in income following the decline of the post-Korean war raw materials market, placed particular burdens on Indonesian bourgeois entrepreneurial groups. Having little control over the capital market and over the influx of capital for further investment and development of the economy, many of these groups and their allies in the civil service, the professions and the lower socio-economic levels, were apt to be more 'consumption-minded' than production-conscious, and strict financial rationalization policies geared to national development (which had characterized the thinking of most ministers of Finance and Economic Affairs up till then) were not particularly advantageous to these groups.[18] Rightly or not, significant sections of the burgeoning middle-class entrepreneurial groups, already assisted by the government through loans and market privileges, came to feel that further measures against foreign capital were clearly indicated. Since independence the power of Dutch capital had been conspicious, and after all:

In 1952 it was estimated that 50 per cent of all consumer imports were still being handled by four Dutch firms, and 60 per cent of exports by eight firms. The bank of issue was a largely Dutch-owned corporation, controlled by Dutch officers. Private banking was largely in the hands of seven foreign banks, three of which were Dutch.[19]

Thus the PKI found that its agitation against the Round Table Conference Agreements of December 1949, which had given Indonesia its political freedom but which had also assured the position of Dutch capital in the country, was beginning to find supporters among the middle-class followers of other parties. The nationalization of the bank of issue, carried out under the Sukiman cabinet, seemed a mere palliative; drastic reorganization of the economy was necessary. At the Sixth PNI Congress in December 1952, a new party program, notably leftist in tone, was approved. It included demands for the nationalization of vital enterprises and for restrictions on foreign capital, while at the same time further assistance to 'national' businessmen was demanded, e.g. in the form of protection from foreign enterprises.[20] The new program breathed a spirit decidedly different from that which PNI premier Wilopo had presented to the Indonesian parliament at the time he assumed office, and which, while generally favoring a 'national' economy, had stressed the necessity of affording opportunities and security to foreign business and foreign capital. The new PNI program indicated a shift of emphasis in economic policy that heralded a breach between Wilopo and his followers, and the left wing of his own party, as well as other policy dissensions which were soon to bring the cabinet down. From December 1952, some major PNI policies, certainly in the economic field, began to run parallel to those of the PKI. In its 12-point program of 1951 the PKI had also demanded the nationalization of important enterprises, the revocation of all agreements with 'alien monopoly capital' which were harmful to the economy, and the granting of special assistance to 'small' and 'medium' private enterprises of benefit to the people. This was to remain the party's line in the coming years. In 1952, in its directives to the labor movement, the PKI again noted the protection to which national businessmen, suffering from the continued hold of foreign capital in the country, were entitled.[21] The plight of the people in a semi-feudal country dominated by 'imperialist' capital, and the importance of building unity between the proletariat and the national bourgeosie, were themes which Aidit was to stress again and again in important policy addresses in 1953 and 1954.[22]

In the meantime the split in the PNI between Wilopo and the more radical wing was growing. Wilopo represented a trend in the PNI which on a number of essential policy points was quite close to the position of the Masjumi and of Masjumi's principal ally, the anti-Stalinist Socialist Party of Indonesia (PSI), led by former premier Sutan Sjahrir. Pragmatic, interested in systematic development and efficient public administration and less inclined to manipulate the symbols of radical nationalism, the Wilopo group in the PNI stood apart, not only from the PNI radical nationalist faction (whose followers were generally not intellectuals and who, influenced by Japanese ideology, had primarily risen to positions of power during the Japanese occupation and the Revolution as leaders of mass organizations and military auxiliary units) but also from an older generation of PNI leaders, among whom Sukarno still figured prominently, but who also numbered many in the aristocratic civil-servant corps among their followers, and who also had gained some prominence during the Japanese occupation and were in some respects as devoted to radical nationalistic mystiques as the first group. As we have noted, the economic policies of the Wilopo government particularly conflicted with the interests of national business elements usually associated with the second and third divisions of the PNI, but they also tended to undermine the prominence of the party in other arms of the state such as the officers corps of the army. For Wilopo concurred with his Masjumi and Socialist colleagues in a fairly drastic program of army reorganization and rationalization which had as its aim the elimination of radical nationalist auxiliaries and a strengthening of top army officers (many of whom were sympathetic to the PSI and Masjumi) and of the Defense Ministry. This would have had the effect of minimizing and counter-balancing the influence of Sukarno, while various transfers and promotions approved by the cabinet definitely undermined PNI power in the higher echelons of the army leadership.

Finally, Wilopo and his associates appeared much more vigorous than their predecessors in moving toward the holding of the long-awaited first national elections for parliament (the existing provisional parliament, largely composed of the provisional parliaments of the revolutionary and federal periods had a party representation determined by Sukarno in consultation with party leaders); this caused considerable anxiety in PNI circles, which felt that the party would not emerge victoriously from the elections, and indeed, might take a fearful drubbing at the hands of the Masjumi and the PSI. Most PNI leaders knew that elections were inevitable, but they wanted time to use their available political power to build up party strength.[23]

All these factors enabled the PKI to drive a wedge between the Wilopo faction and the other two PNI divisions, thereby in effect preventing a further collaboration between Masjumi and the PSI, and the PNI. Be it noted that this tactic could probably not have worked if Sukarno hand not to some extent approved of it. His sympathies lay with the radical nationalist wing of the party he had founded and with the populist mystique, called *marhaenism* or 'Indonesian Socialism', with which the PKI found it easy to identify itself. The Sukarno who could write a brochure entitled 'Capitalism Creates Poverty'[24] and who has been the principal exponent of the view that the Indonesian Revolution is 'not yet finished', was an ideal symbol of the new marriage of radical nationalism and Communism. Thus the PKI abandoned its criticisms of Sukarno, no longer identified him with Hatta and the hated Masjumi, and ceased describing him as a stooge of American-Dutch imperialism who had betrayed Indonesia at the Round Table Conference. Instead the PKI began to develop a new image of Sukarno—as the national rallying point of all true anti-imperialistic forces in the first, or bourgeois-democratic, phase of the revolution, a kind of symbol of the PKI's own multi-structured united front. This cultivation began around August 1952, and has not been changed since; there can be little question that it has served the party (and Sukarno) well.

The liaison which the PKI thus gradually established with the PNI has puzzled many students of Communist theory, not least because it is interpreted as a deviation from traditional national front policy. In such a policy the Communist party must traditionally have uncontested leadership of the front, while in contrast the PNI-PKI relationship was more of an informal political alliance of convenience, and the PNI could certainly not be said to be under the hegemony of the PKI in a united front. While one must admit the importance of the relative flexibility in the PKI-PNI relationship, the question of Communist hegemony in front tactics should not be over-stressed. As long ago as

1938 Mao Tse-tung had emphasized the tactical necessity of the 'independence of parties and classes, that is their independence within the united front' at the time of the war against Japan.[25] This meant not a tightly organized united front under Communist domination, but a tactical alliance directed against 'imperialism' (the target of the first phase of the revolution) which is particularly appropriate for that phase. Not only other parties, but the Communist party too must preserve 'independence' within the united front—a point Aidit again stressed at the PKI national congress in March 1954.[26] Mao, in dealing with the question of independence within the united front, had fitted this front into the concept of a 'national struggle' of the Chinese people against the Japanese invaders and Aidit was to do the same when he translated PKI united front strategy into the federative movements that had existed among Indonesian nationalist parties in their 'national struggle' during the colonial and Japanese periods.[27] Absolute Communist hegemony is then inappropriate in such a phase, for the party should simultaneously follow a front policy 'from above' and 'from below', and whatever weaknesses may result from one approach will be corrected by the other. Thus the tactical collaboration with the PNI *as a party* in a front of comparative equals is to be seen as a front 'from above'. The advantages of such a front 'from above' can far outweigh its disadvantages. Such disadvantages as it has can be corrected by direct ideological appeals and organizational efforts among the various social classes and their individual members, i.e. by a front policy 'from below'.

The party was, therefore, not just concerned with a tactical alliance with the PNI, but also with the mobilization of the mass movement, and Aidit continuously urged formation of fronts among the youth and women of the land, peasants and laborers, and intellectuals and national entrepreneurs.[28] The practical application of this dual-front policy lay in the formation of a national coalition government as the party's Politburo had indicated when it formulated its program of 12 articles in April 1951, and as Muso had expounded it earlier in his 'Gottwald Plan'. The same relative flexibility was to be advocated by the party during the 1955 elections when the concept of a national coalition government was particularly stressed again, even to the point of suggesting a conflict with other party aims.

Its alliance with the PNI not only afforded the party a chance to redraw its popular image from that of a conspiratorial clique and tool of Moscow to a legitimate radical nationalist group with strong Marxist leanings (there were a considerable number of political groups with such leanings at the time, and though small, they did afford the PKI a kind of protective coloration), but also to retain its freedom of movement.

The Madiun affair and the Sukiman arrests of 1951 threatened to fix an image of the party as an always convenient whipping boy, the target of whatever political anti-Communist agitation might from time to time be generated.[29] To remove the taint of implied illegality and to assure the organizational expansion and ideological indoctrination to which the Aidit faction had pledged itself, freedom of action was essential. The PKI, by leaning on the PNI, could assure itself that both cabinet and parliament would have to think twice before initiating another anti-Communist drive.

All during the history of the Wilopo cabinet the effects of the PKI-PNI alliance were to make themselves felt. The economic policies of the cabinet, especially the new prepayment regulations for importers announced in August 1952, and the general retrenchment on spending necessitating the reorganization and rationalization of many government services, including the armed forces—all these had a tendency to augment the opposition to Wilopo, especially from within his own party where the radical nationalist wing, closely supported in its parliamentary machinations by the PKI, progressively debilitated the government's position. The focal point of the anti-Wilopo forces was the parliament, as yet a provisional body, whose members held no clear mandate from the people (no national election was held until the close of 1955) and who had been appointed by the President in consultation with party leaders. A new high of the opposition was the political crisis of October 17, 1952, over the organization of the army, during which army leaders (sympathetic to the PSI and Masjumi and to the cabinet's rationalization schemes generally) unsuccessfully attempted to bring pressure to bear on Sukarno to dissolve parliament, where opposition to Wilopo's policies seemed to nullify the systematic development of the country that these army officers and their political associates desired. The 'October 17 affair', as it is generally known, brought significant evidence of the strength of the PNI-PKI alliance, and of the indirect backing for this alliance by Sukarno. From that time the Wilopo government was largely at the mercy of the radical nationalist factions in the PNI and in parliament. The Communist issue was also injected directly into the factional crisis of the PNI and into the developing hostility between the Masjumi and the PNI when the parliament, on April 9, 1953, passed (after repeated postponements of voting) the so-called Rondonuwu motion demanding the creation of an Indonesian embassy in Moscow before the end of 1953. The Masjumi led the opposition to this motion, capitalizing on popular fears of seemingly closer ties with the center of world Communism, while the PKI and the radical nationalist faction of the PNI spearheaded the drive for approval.

The passage of the motion demonstrated again not only the effectiveness of the PNI-PKI alliance but also the growing polarization between this alliance and the Masjumi, and thereby the impending fall of the cabinet. For already the Wilopo government was embroiled in the aftermath of the Tandjong Morawa incident which ultimately was to be its doom. All during the Japanese occupation and revolutionary periods peasants had begun to squat illegally on land leased to foreign estates in North Sumatra, and both because of the Round Table Conference agreements and because various Indonesian cabinets had become convinced that the estate economy needed to be restored and foreign capital be assured, these peasant squatters needed to be removed. In the Tandjong Morawa sub-district in North Sumatra, on March 16, 1953, local police forcibly tried to remove the squatters, using tractors to plough up and raze their lands. This was not a matter of local initiative but a part of the Wilopo cabinet's policy. Fighting broke out between the squatters and the police and in the end an Indonesian and four Chinese squatters lay dead. A furore followed, in which the PKI fully exploited the 'tractors of death'. There can be little question that for some time the local PKI sub-section had inflamed squatters' indignation against the government policies, and according to one police report local PKI cadres were in fact to blame for the whole affair. It was clear that the cabinet could not survive the ensuing crisis. Disavowed by much of his own party, the premier returned his mandate on June 2, 1953, and the door was opened to the accession to power of nationalist radicals in the PNI, assisted by various splinter groups, and not least by the PKI.

Still, its increasingly anti-Wilopo policy had been quite risky to the PKI, because the government's fall might yet precipitate a political crisis from which the Masjumi and the Socialist Party (PSI) might emerge in control of a new government and thus the position of the Communists would again be threatened. The two months of complicated maneuvering which followed Wilopo's fall revealed that this danger was not altogether imaginary, and it was again Sukarno's influence in the rivalry between the PNI and the Masjumi which probably proved decisive in the appointment of Ali Sastroamidjojo of the PNI as premier of a cabinet which excluded the Masjumi and the PSI.[30] The new government relied heavily on minor nationalist parties and on the Nahdatul Ulama (Moslem Scholars Party, NU), an important grouping of conservative Muslims which, in July 1952, had broken off from the Masjumi. The PKI aided the cabinet in parliament and out, and in the early months of the new government made a point of stressing its support on a number of public occasions. Thus, early in September 1953, the PKI organized a mass demonstration of several thousand members of peasant associations and trade unions in Medan, North Sumatra, which thanked the government for rescinding the squatter policy of Wilopo and for 'stopping the tractors of death'. Unceasingly too, the party followed the nationalist line. The PKI, declared Aidit late in October 1953, would always defend the red-white national Indonesian flag and the 'Indonesia Raya' as the national anthem. Moreover, the PKI would strongly resist every effort to make a satellite of Indonesia, whether of the USA or of the USSR. As far as the Soviet Union was concerned, stated Aidit, Moscow certainly did not wish to make a satellite out of Indonesia.[31] Throughout the closing months of 1953 he pointed out that the PKI program could be realized through the Ali cabinet. But the one exception to this, he also emphasized, was the cancellation of the RTC Agreements with the Netherlands; he did not believe this could be accomplished unless a genuine popular front was formed. Increasingly the denunciation of the RTC Agreements became a popular topic in the party literature,[32] even after Indonesia and the Netherlands signed a protocol on August 10, 1954, agreeing to the dissolution of the Netherlands-Indonesian Union. This protocol provided the PKI with new ammunition, since much of the original financial and economic provisions of the Union agreements remained in effect and Dutch capital interests in Indonesia were not greatly affected. For various reasons the protocol was never ratified by the Indonesian parliament (not until February 1956, did the Indonesian government unilaterally abrogate all provisions of the Union agreement), and meanwhile the PKI continued all through 1954–1955 to attack Dutch 'imperialist' capital and to demand that the Union agreement be abrogated, since because of the Union Indonesia still did not have 'sovereignty in her own hands', as Aidit put it in a speech in Palembang early in September 1954. The continued strength of the PNI-PKI axis was also evidenced again at the PNI party conference for West Java in September 1953, during which Dahlan Rivai of the PKI, who had been invited to attend, also spoke and expressed the appropriate national front line:[33]

The task of Indonesian patriots in these times is enormously heavy. For in these times there are many provocations and acts of intimidation directed against the PNI and PKI which at this moment are engaged in removing the undesirable conditions in the state. The PNI and the PKI must eliminate the provocations and intimidations which originate from certain leaders of the Masjumi. . . . It is now no longer a question of controversy between Communists and Muslims or between nationalists and Muslims; there is only a question of a struggle between those who wish to meet the needs of the people and those who labor, consciously or unconsciously, on behalf of foreign capitalism.

But with the passing months the PKI, feeling its new won strength, also become more aggressive. Despite strike restrictions and compulsory arbitration provisions, SARBUPRI and SOBSI (the Communist-dominated labor organizations) staged repeated walkouts ('to encourage the government') and exhibited continuous restlessness. Toward the the end of 1954 and all during the first half of 1955, the PKI pressed for an improvement in the living and working conditions of the tenants and landless agricultural workers especially in West Java. Party pronouncements also urged the government to confiscate the land of West Java landlords who had been collaborating with the *Darul Islam* ('Islamic State'—a term indicating marauding gangs of Muslim fanatics seeking the establishment of an Islamic State in Indonesia). Local PKI leaders made headlines by inflammatory accusations and by a bold defense of the PKI's role during the Madiun affair. Clearly the party now saw virtue in a muscular display of its views and in being as open and as aggressive as the law allowed. Thus the PKI section secretary of Malang, East Java, accused Hatta and the Masjumi leader Mohammad Rum, in October 1953, of having received $56 million from the U.S. in order to liquidate the communists in the Madiun uprising;[34] the libel suit which this charge brought in its wake was a regional *cause célèbre* that kept the PKI on the front pages of newspapers for many weeks. On the fifth anniversary of the Madiun uprising in September 1953, the PKI proposed a 'national day of mourning' and issued a 'White Book' on the insurrection which charged the 'rightist liquidationist régime' of Hatta and Masjumi leader Sjafruddin Prawiranegara of having been responsible for the whole affair. To accusations that the PKI was a Muscovite Fifth Column, parliamentary party spokesman Sakirman declared that 'the PKI follows a national policy which represents the interests of the country and the people', and that such charges were therefore preposterous. All the while the Ali government, which within half a year after its formation had become considerably discredited because of its corruption and its ineffectual handling of economic problems and regional discontent, provided the ideal political climate for this new PKI aggressiveness; the government's very weakness gave the PKI a chance to deploy its strength.

The opportunity to display its growing power was not an unmixed blessing to the party, however, for it rendered imposition of party discipline more difficult, especially in connection with semi-military action groups and bands of plain terrorists and criminals operating under the party banner. Some of these organizations dated from revolutionary days and had retained a semi-official status as units of the loosely organized army in the years following independence. Badly disciplined, they were often a burden to PKI leaders attempting to reform the party after Madiun. In 1951 the depradations of the bands had provided some justification for the Sukiman actions against the party. During 1952, after their release from confinement, Communist terrorists began to operate from a new base in Central Java (between Mounts Merapi and Merbabu), providing intensive political and military training to youths from various Javanese cities, raiding the countryside and battling vigorously against government troops. These 'Merapi Merbabu Complex' (MMC) bands in time provided cadres for other armed Communist gangs, notably the *Gerakan Kaum Merah* (Movement of Red People, GKM) with headquarters in Madiun. Shortly after the formation of the Ali Sastroamidjojo cabinet MMC and GKM terrorism markedly subsided. It is not clear whether this happened primarily in response to pressure from the PKI leadership which wished to cement good relations with the Ali government and the PNI, but in any event the lull was only temporary. During 1954, the provincial governor of Central Java, a prominent PSI member, undertook a new military campaign against the MMC bands, acting almost certainly contrary to the policies of Ali's Defense Minister, Iwa Kusumasumantri. The latter, of markedly radical views certainly in earlier years and widely suspected to be sympathetic to the Communists, had shown no hurry to reorganize the army and rid it of various auxiliary units. On the contrary, Iwa was soon rumored to be suggesting the arming of a Communist-controlled veterans' organization in order to aid the army in its operations against the Muslim extremists of the *Darul Islam* movement in West Java.

In the beginning of 1955, the MMC bands again suddenly became active,[35] seeking new contact with the GKM and with other Communist bands, semi-military units and associations of 'village guards', of which the *Bambu Runtjing* (Pointed Spear), particularly active in West Java, was of special importance. The *Bambu Runtjing* became in effect a new organizational home for many former MMC members. In view of the outcry against the MMC marauders, PKI leaders appear, in fact, to have encouraged a 'transfer' of MMC members to the *Bambu Runtjing* during 1954–1955, and sought to emphasize the more 'respectable' role of the latter organization as the protector of villages against the attacks of the *Darul Islam*. How successful these PKI efforts were is difficult to say. Realizing the asset which all these units could be to party tactics, but also well aware of the liability of being constantly charged in the Indonesian press with maintaining private terrorist bands, the PKI by the end of 1954 even began to urge the legalization of the *Bambu Runtjing* and other groups in the struggle against the *Darul Islam*, by suggesting official government approval of their status. But this effort, despite Iwa's sympathies, had little success. In the end even Iwa felt apparently not strong enough to overcome the almost solid opposition from leading army officers to the PKI's 'legalization' schemes.

The PKI became more and more convinced that, unless the para-military groups and just plain gangs claiming Communist allegiance were somehow legalized, the united front policy and the new national image which the party was trying to develop would seriously suffer. This became particularly true after the activities of the so-called 'Night PKI' or 'PKI-B' in Central Java were revealed in the press. In Central Java, according to these press reports (which were, however, denied by the PKI), the Communists operated at three levels. There was the legitimate PKI or 'PKI-A', which was the small formal and largely innocuous party organization. Then there was the 'PKI-B', the larger, dynamic underground section, which had as its task to terrorize the countryside at night and to recruit new members, also for Communist fronts. Thirdly there was the 'PKI-C', which consisted of the various 'regular' or 'full-time' gangs of the MMC and which were regarded as the 'army of liberation', particularly in the event the PKI did not reach its objectives in the forthcoming national elections. According to these reports the 'PKI-B' had several sections (e.g. for youth, peasants, women, for neighborhood associations, and a section for the combatting of illiteracy) and appears to have been the more or less secret division of militants and active cadres of the party, as distinct from the legal organizational façade and from the more professional MMC terrorists. Conviction of a number of 'PKI-B' elements in Temanggung, Central Java, in January 1955,[36] and the publicity which followed this, seriously embarrassed the party. After 1955, one hardly heard of the Com-munist bands anymore, perhaps less because of army action against them (the army battled the *Darul Islam* in West Java for many years with little success) but more because of strong pressure of the party leader-ship. In time the government did legalize many village guard units under army supervision and those bandits who ultimately lost their semi-military status found new associational havens—some organized by the PKI—such as youth, veterans, labor, peasants' and other fronts.

Another consequence of the party's new vitality was the growing apprehension of those political parties which in parliament usually looked to the PNI for support. PKI support for the cabinet and the PNI-PKI alliance were subjects of increasingly critical speculation in the press, and the editorial view of one newspaper surveying the position of the Ali cabinet at the close of 1954 to the effect that 'Only if the Communists would turn against the cabinet . . . would any real danger exist to its continuance',[37] reflected common appreciation of, and also concern over, the PKI's pivotal position. Pronouncements by cabinet spokesmen seeking to allay this apprehension—such as one cabinet minister's statement in November 1954, that the PKI had no influence on the cabinet, but that the cabinet was rather influencing the PKI in view of the latter's acceptance of the cabinet's outlook—were not very convincing. The Nahdatul Ulama, which was one of the principal supporters of the cabinet and whose leaders even more than other party leaders, often appeared to be opportunistically guiding their party by the exigencies of the existing power interplay than by any clear ideology (even Islamic ideology), repeatedly urged early in 1954 that the Communists be outlawed.[38] Even in the radical nationalist wing of the PNI there were beginning to be some misgivings. PNI parliamentary deputy Manai Sofian, a leader of the radical nationalists, at a three-day PNI party conference in Tjurup in the spring of 1954, warned against the 'Communist danger which is attempting to widen its offensive over the entire world and therefore also toward Indonesia'. By June 1954, premier Ali Sastroamidjojo was explaining that his cabinet was 'neither Communist nor *kafir*' (*kafir* is the Muslim term for unbeliever).[39]

All these pronouncements should be seen against a backdrop of increasing inter-party rivalry in conection with the long awaited national elections. This rivalry also had a tendency to augment itself as the many weaknesses of the government became more and more apparent and thus the further viability of the cabinet became increasingly doubtful. In October and November, 1954, a serious cabinet crisis was precipitated by the resignation of three ministers belonging to the *Persatuan Indonesia Raya* (Greater Indonesia Party, PIR) and primarily caused by the widespread discontent with the economic deterioration of the country and with the policies of the Economic Affairs Minister, Iskaq Tjokrohadisurjo of the PNI.[40] Iskaq's policies of preferential treatment for indigenous Indonesian businessmen, especially importers, was wholly in conformity with the demands of the radical nationalist wing of his party, but the corruption in the government because of this policy reached unprecedented proportions (even vice-premier Wongsonegoro of the PIR admitted in April 1954, that 'corruption in Indonesia increases daily'),[41] and there was a widespread feeling that the new import licensing system had also enriched the PNI party treasury to an unconscionable extent. The cabinet survived the crisis (Iskaq resigned), partly because of Sukarno's personal interventions, but the government was, if anything, even weaker, and the PKI's support even more essential. Government parties, with considerable reluctance, realized the significance of this support. Noteworthy was the position of the NU during and after the cabinet crisis. It came out of the October-November 1954, political crisis with its position considerably strengthened in the cabinet, and though only a few months before it had demanded that the Communists be outlawed, it now intimated that cooperation between the NU and the PKI on the basis of 'common interest' was possible, for as a spokesman declared, the NU only refuses to cooperate with the *kafir habir* (the unbeliever who actively fights against Islam).[42] Since the PKI had not officially attacked and did not attack Islam as such (indeed a number of Muslim clerics were and are members of the PKI, and the party has always capitalized on this fact to prove that it is not against religion)[43] the NU thus indicated the manner in which it would be prepared to accept continued PKI support for the revised cabinet. But promptly after the cabinet crisis the PKI indicated the price of further support. On January 2, 1955, Njoto stated that if the Ali cabinet wished to retain the support of the PKI, the government would immediately have to repeal emergency law No. 16/1951, which provided for compulsory arbitration of labor disputes and limited the right to strike. Shortly thereafter the Communist-dominated SOBSI labor federation urged the government to allow wage increases, gratuities and social benefits for civil servants and other workers, and demanded that Indonesia's 'one-sided orientation on the U.S. and Western Europe' be replaced by normal trade relations with 'all countries'.[44] The PKI also began to repeat with increasing vehemence its earlier demands formulated in the party program approved by the PKI's Fifth National Congress in March 1954. In the six months of life which the Ali cabinet had left these demands were not significantly met, although in January 1955, parliament did begin consideration of a law to replace emergency law No. 16/1951 (the new labor law was not to be promulgated until 1957), and strike activity reached its highest peak since 1951. The important new role of the PKI continued to arouse hostility and the tendency toward 'mutual destruction' *(saling banting membanting)* in the higher levels of government, as the Information Minister put it in March 1955, also persisted. In the often confusing pattern of political feuding the PKI proved to be a formidable opponent.

At the same time significant developments were taking place within the party. In October 1953, the PKI Central Committee held a plenary session in preparation for a forthcoming national party congress. For the last time Tan Ling Djie, then still a member of the Central Committee, tried to rally opposition to Aidit's policies, but in vain; since the Central Committee's plenary session in 1951 and the Party Conference a year later Aidit's postion had become impregnable. Aidit, Lukman and Njoto were elected secretary-general, and first and second deputy secretary-general respectively. Alimin 'resigned' from the Politburo

'due to ill health' and Tan Ling Djie 'resigned' from the Central Committee.[45] The new Politburo was now composed of Aidit, Lukman, Njoto,
Sudisman and Sakirman. The plenum approved a new program for
the party and a new party constitution and condemned the policy of
'liquidationism' of Tan Ling Djie; by this was meant: (1) the idea that
a 'working class party' should be formed for those who were sympathetic
to Communism, but 'not brave enough' to join the PKI; (2) the idea
that the party should stay out of the limelight and be as circumspect in
public affairs as possible; and (3) the idea that the party should concentrate on a parliamentary struggle rather than on a mobilization of the
masses. Instead, the plenum endorsed the principle of the 'open',
aggressive, and 'bolshevised' party that Aidit had been implementing
since January 1951. From March 16 to 20, 1954, the party's Fifth
National Congress took place and the decisions and proposals of the
Central Committee's plenary session the previous October were all
approved.[46] Among the most important actions taken by the Fifth
Party Congress were the following:

1. Approval of the formation of a new Central Committee, consisting
of Achmad Sumadi, D. N. Aidit, Bachtaruddin, Djokosudjono, Jusuf
Adjitorop, M. H. Lukman, Njoto, Nursuhud, Peris Pardede, Sakirman,
Sudisman, Karel Supit, and M. Zaelani.

2. Approval of a new program for the party (replacing but also
incorporating most of the '12-point program' of 1951), which began
by noting that 'the tasks of national liberation and democratic reforms
in Indonesia have not yet been carried out' since the RTC agreements
make Indonesia a victim of continuing Dutch imperialism.[47] The
program emphasized the 'semi-starvation' among the people, the misery
of the workers and the peasantry (the latter suffering from 'feudal
exploitation'), the lack of opportunity of the national bourgeosie to
'broaden its activities and build new industrial enterprises' because of
foreign competitors, and the general conditions of 'backwardness' and
'inequality'. The program therefore, demanded the formation of a
'People's Democratic Government' based on the masses and having the
character of a 'united national front' of peasants and workers, led by the
working class. Such a government would *not* be a government of the
dictatorship of the proletariat, but rather 'a government of the dictatorship of the people'. This government would not effect 'Socialist' but
'democratic' reforms, namely, giving land to the peasants, defending
'national industry and trade against foreign competition', improving the
conditions of the workers and abolishing unemployment, and so on The
concept of the 'People's Democratic Government' seemed to supplant

the idea of the 'national coalition government' as the party had accepted it in its program of April 1951, but events around election time were to show that the idea of 'national coalition' had by no means been replaced by 'people's democracy'.

Specifically, the 1954 party program advocated Indonesia's immediate withdrawal from the Indonesian-Dutch Union and abrogation of all RTC agreements; the 'maintenance' of West New Guinea as a territory of Indonesia; the holding of parliamentary elections with the franchise to be exercised by 'all citizens who have reached the age of 18'; protection of civil freedoms such as those of press, speech, assembly, and religion; institution of compulsory free education of all children up to the age of 12; confiscation of the land of landlords and redistribution of this land among the landless peasants and small peasants on the basis of 'private peasant ownership of land; development of the national industry along with the fixing of a minimum wage for workers; protection for the development of trade unions and establishment of strict control over commodity prices; and, in the area of foreign affairs, implementation of a 'consistent policy' of 'peace and cooperation with all the peace loving countries with the object of preserving peace', and of opposition to 'the propaganda of war'.

Describing party tactics the program went on to state that 'the parliamentary struggle alone is not enough to achieve the aim of establishing a people's democratic government', and that while the party is by no means indifferent to parliamentary activity, indeed, treats it with 'utmost seriousness', such activity is 'not the main work of the party'. The main tactic is to cause a shift in 'the balance of forces between the imperialists, landlord class and compradore bourgeoisie on the one hand, and the people on the other'. Such a shift can be created by mobilizing the masses, 'above all the workers and peasants'. The working class must head the united national front and the struggle of 'the whole people' and in this struggle the peasantry, the intelligentsia, the petty bourgeoisie can all join, but not the 'compradore bourgeoisie who are linked by a thousand threads to the imperialists' and whose interests merge with the interests of the colonizers. (As will be indicated presently Aidit has on occasion a different appreciation of the compradores.)

Finally, the program presented a brief review of past Indonesian political history and a list of demands to the Ali Sastroamidjojo government. After the 'reactionary' Sukiman government, the Wilopo government, it was stated, was able early in its existence to carry out 'certain democratic measures'. But soon, as a result of the 'inadequate strength of the democratic elements within this government and as a result of the policies of the ministers from the reactionary anti-people's and anti-national parties, the Wilopo government was leaning over to the right'. It was the 'pressure of the people' which brought about the formation of the Ali Sastroamidjojo cabinet and this cabinet had 'the necessary conditions' to act much more vigorously than the Wilopo government. Specifically, the PKI demanded that the Ali cabinet: (1) assure 'the broadest democratic liberties' to the people and their organizations and the annulment of all laws (including martial law) that restricted these liberties; (2) hold elections for a Constituent Assembly in the near future; (3) affirm the rights of workers and annul laws prohibiting strikes; (4) improve the condition of the peasantry by forcing landlords to lower their rents and reduce the interest of peasant loans and by other measures; (5) 'suppress and uproot' the Darul Islam and other terrorist organizations; (6) 'democratize' local and rural organs of government; (7) reform the national bureaucracy by making it more democratic, dismissing 'reactionaries', embezzlers, grafters and traitors; (8) improve the economy of the country by cutting down 'somewhat' on cultivation of rubber and other exports and to replace these with food crops for the people and by protecting national industry; (9) increase and improve the schools and their facilities; (10) bring about Indonesia's withdrawal from the Dutch-Indonesian Union, establish regular bilateral diplomatic relations with the Netherlands, recall the Dutch military mission, and insist on 'the maintenance' of West New Guinea as Indonesian territory; (11) refuse to recognize the San Francisco treaty with Japan, demand reparations from Japan and protest against the remilitarization of Japan; and (12) follow a 'consistent peace policy' by refusing to be drawn into any bloc, to cancel the aid agreements with the U.S. and protest against 'giving military bases in Indonesia to other states'.

3. Approval of a general party program for the forthcoming national elections called 'Manifesto for the General Elections of the PKI' *(Manifes Pemilihan Umum*, MPU) wich primarily recapitulated the principal objectives of the party program (sub. 3 above), including the party's general aim of establishing a 'dictatorship of the people', and listing specific objectives, mostly those that had been enumerated as the party's demands on the Ali Sastroamidjojo government and mentioned above. The MPU appears to have caused gradual disquiet in the higher echelons of the party because it seemed too 'radical' in stating the party's objective as being a people's 'dictatorship'. Election tactics seemed to demand a more moderate tone and in June 1955 the party's Politburo in effect disavowed the MPU, at least for the period of the election.

4. Approval of a new party constitution—actually the first such document in the party's history fully and publicly to spell out the details

of internal party organization, the party's ideological bases and training program, the role of party functionaries, members and the hierarchy of committees (from 'resort committees' and 'sub-section committees' to section and provincial committees and to the Central Committee) and the election of delegates to the various committee conferences, the function of special departments, of the national party congress, the plenary session of the Central Committee, and of the control commissions, and to describe the requirements of discipline and the relationship of the PKI to other parties. (Details of the 1954 PKI constitution as compared to the current PKI constitution are given below in chapter V.)

5. Approval of Aidit's 'General Report on the Political and Organizational Situation' delivered by Aidit in his capacity as Secretary-General of the party. This report, entitled 'The Road to People's Democracy for Indonesia', ranks among the most important documents in PKI history, and as an authoritative source for party strategy it replaced the 'New Road' resolution of 1948, which after 1953 was not reprinted. Aidit's report is also a kind of summation and elaboration of the ideas which had been developed in his principal previous addresses and essays since 1951. It opens with an analysis of the international situation and a description of the fundamental antagonisms between the 'camp of imperialism and war' on the one hand, and 'the democratic world' with its 'peace-loving policy' on the other. The internal contradictions and tensions between the capitalist countries express themselves in 'exploitation, oppression, antagonism, destruction, and war', whereas in the Socialist bloc is unmistakable (e.g. in Korea 'the world peace-loving forces' achieved a 'brilliant victory'), and Aidit draws freely on utterances of Malenkov to make his point. He also excoriates 'Tito in Yugoslavia, Rajk in Hungary, Slansky in Czechoslovakia, Gomulka in Poland, Kostov in Bulgaria' as being 'American imperialist agents' and as perpetrators of 'sadistic and foul actions'. (This particular passage has been deleted in later versions of the report, doubtlessly in deference to the changing Moscow line which, for example, restored Gomulka as a member in good standing of the world Communist leadership.) In the conflict between the 'imperialist' and the Socialist power blocs there can be no 'neutrality', for a neutral or 'independent' attitude is either a ruse of imperialist agents, like the Masjumi, or an expression of mystical naiveté. Therefore, a true peace policy opposes Japanese remilitarization, advocates the unification of Korea and Viet Nam, supports national movements for independence everywhere, and so on.

The second part of the report, which examines the 'internal situation in Indonesia', begins with a description of the country's economic crisis, its lagging development, and the evil effects of the RTC agreements. Only a 'united national front, which unites the Communists with all other patriots' can bring improvement, but in order to make the front as broadly effective as possible 'the primary task' of the party is to bring the peasantry into the national front and to recognize that 'the agrarian revolution' is 'the essence of the People's Democratic revolution in Indonesia', i.e. of the first stage of the multi-stage revolutionary development as Lenin and Mao outlined it. (See chapter IV below.) But this emphasis on the peasantry must in no way lead to neglect of the workers, the intelligentsia, the petty or the national bourgeoisie. Also, since the primary target of the revolution is Dutch imperialism, it is against that objective that all energies should be coordinated and directed; Aidit cautions against attempting to liquidate 'all foreign imperialisms in Indonesia at the same time'. The expulsion of the Dutch, the annulment of the RTC agreements, the withdrawal of Indonesia from the Netherlands-Indonesian Union, and the expropriation of Dutch holdings are the immediate objectives; only in the event of American and other imperialist support for the Dutch must the struggle be directed against all imperialisms at once. Though the party does not regard the Ali cabinet as 'a truly progressive government' or as a 'united national front government', it would be 'adventurism' if the PKI were to withhold its support from the cabinet, for the party will give 'any government' the chance to work provided it allows 'the people's movement' to develop. In this respect the Ali government shows 'promise', and along with implementing party work among the masses, and defending parliamentary democracy and civil liberties, the party should give the Ali cabinet its support.

The third and last part of the report is concerned with the building of the party. Aidit begins with reviewing the problems encountered in rebuilding the party since the plenary session of the Central Committee in January 1951. The building of the anti-imperialist united national front based on 'the anti-feudal alliance of workers and peasants' and the development of a 'bolshevized', nationwide and mass party are said to be two 'extremely urgent' tasks in this connection. Reviewing the various phases in the development of the national front Aidit notes that in the present period (since 1951) the party must resolutely oppose 'the right deviation which gives exaggerated significance to unity with the national bourgeoisie', as well as the 'left deviation' which attaches no importance to front unity with the national bourgeoisie. In apparent contrast to the party program he states that it is not only the national bourgeoisie which can be an ally in the anti-imperialist struggle, but under specific circumstances, when the party's policy 'is only directed against one particular imperialism', even '*a part of the compradore bourgeoisie can also be an additional force in the struggle against that particular imperialism*'.[48] It may be observed incidentally that the possibility of such support from a section of the compradores existed, at that moment because, the party's primary target (so long as West New Guinea had not been acquired) was Dutch imperialism, not 'all foreign imperialisms in Indonesia at the same time'. Again Aidit in this section stresses the important role of the peasantry and, as was also indicated earlier, urges the party to preserve its independence within the united national front even though it is cooperating with other parties and social groups. Finally, emphasis is placed on the importance of ideological training ('Without the theory of Marxism-Leninism' it is not possible to have a revolutionary party 'of the Lenin type') and 'raising the ideological level' of party members should be of primary concern. For Indonesia is 'a petty bourgeois country' where the party is particularly exposed to the usual twin petty bourgeois subjectivist 'diseases', 'empiricism' and 'dogmatism', the former a failure of theoretical understanding, the latter an excessive concern with 'books alone' and with 'isolated dogmas'.

So much for the decisions of the Fifth Party Congress. During the remainder of the Ali cabinet's tenure of office it was especially the national front policy and the identification of the party with national symbols that dictated PKI policy. Masjumi leaders might call Communism a dangerous and gigantic octopus, but Aidit would insist that the PKI could even collaborate with Masjumi. Thus during a mass meeting late in September 1954, Aidit urged Masjumi leaders to be 'realistic and not to act like a Don Quixote' with their anti-Communist attitude, for the only enemy of the PKI was 'imperialism' and in the fight against this, Aidit declared further, 'we appeal to the Masjumi to collaborate with us in order to create a strong national unity. We appeal to the entire Indonesian people, to all political parties and people's organizations: let us be united in the struggle against imperialism!'[49] The necessity of tactical cooperation with the bourgeoisie continued to be stressed in party journals, and party leaders in 1954 hailed the appearance (in an Indonesian translation) and strongly commended the reading of Lenin's *Left-Wing Communism: An Infantile Disorder*, precisely the treatise by Lenin most concerned with describing the dangers of failure to appreciate bourgeois revolutionary movement as forerunners of the proletarian revolution, while the applicability of Leninist theory to Indonesian conditions came to be generally expounded in party organs.[50] It was this approach too which caused the PKI to wax enthusiastically over the Conference of Asian-African nations in Bandung, West Java in April 1955. The decisions of the conference and especially the pronouncements of Communist China's Foreign Minister, Chou En-lai—whose appearance at the conference was designed to convince the Asian world of Peking's peaceful intentions—were given extensive publicity by the party.[51] But the PKI's tactic of seeking entry into mass movements generally was not free from occasional troublesome tactical errors. A case in point was the party's attempt to let its hammer and sickle symbol not only represent the PKI but also 'those without party affiliation' in the electioneering and voting for the forthcoming national elections. The party thus hoped to strengthen its contingent of fellow-travelling candidates, but parliamentary pressures became so great that in January 1955, the PKI was compelled to eliminate the offending words from its election posters and banners. The government's national election commission agreed however, that this decision should not be interpreted as affecting the 'original intent' of the PKI, namely to advance the cause 'of those partyless candidates who support the PKI program'.[52] The press and parliamentary furore that arose over the affair, however, did the PKI's national front approach no particular good.

In the first half of 1955 a military policy crisis developed which ultimately was to bring the Ali cabinet down.[53] In this crisis the issue of Communism was indirectly a factor. The same tensions that had arisen over the army rationalization program during the tenure of the Wilopo cabinet were responsible for serious rifts in the Defense Department and in the army's officer corps, which the hapless Army Chief-of-Staff, General Bambang Sugeng, proved powerless to repair. Defense Minister Iwa Kusumasumantri appeared unable or unwilling to meet serious grievances of leading field and staff officers with respect to the maintenance, organization and payment of army units, and when Sugeng finally resigned, late in the spring of 1955, and Iwa attempted to foist the appointment of a compliant follower, Colonel Bambang Utoyo, on the army, the stage was set for a new army cabal. Leader of the resistance to Iwa was the assistant and acting Army Chief-of-Staff, Colonel Zulkifli Lubis, devout Muslim and fanatical anti-Communist, who had long been critical of Iwa in view of the latter's alleged Communist sympathies. Lubis and his associates refused to recognize Utoyo's appointment and installation, and when Iwa attempted to dismiss Lubis from his post, the latter refused to accept his dismissal and declared that the new Army Chief-of-Staff would have to resign. When it became apparent that Lubis enjoyed the support of powerful army territorial commanders, the Ali cabinet first attempted to reach a compromise by sacrificing Iwa, who promptly resigned and immediately accompanied President Sukarno on a pilgrimage to Mecca in the midst of the governmental crisis. Even Ali's willingness to have Utoyo resign and have the army officers agree on a successor was ignored by the adamant Lubis, whose opposition, it now seems, was not directed against Defense policies alone, but also against the entire policy of the Ali cabinet in which PKI support for the PNI and the cabinet was by no means a negligible factor.

On July 24, 1955, premier Ali returned his mandate to Vice-President Hatta. In retrospect it seems clear that even in the ranks of the government parties there was weariness with the ineffectual policies of the cabinet, though the PKI, ever mindful of what it would mean to the party's safety if Lubis and his associates were to be allowed to dictate government policy, had urged the cabinet to be forceful in settling the army dispute and to back Iwa. The circumstances of the cabinet's fall, like those which had brought the Wilopo government down two years before, suggested the existence of a political temper, which if allowed to crystallize itself in a new cabinet, might well be dangerous to the party. There were, for example, currents in the Masjumi, the PSI, and other parties favoring formation of a 'presidential' or 'national extra-parliamentary' cabinet which would not be responsible to parliament and its pressures, and thus might take autocratic measures which the PKI might find difficult to handle. Hatta proceeded cautiously in forming a new government, sounding out the opinions of party leaders, including those of the PKI. In its statement to Hatta the PKI declared that it favored a 'parliamentary cabinet' which would continue the 'positive side' of the Ali cabinet and 'liquidate' its 'negative sides'. The PKI strongly opposed the formation of a 'presidential' or an 'extra-parliamentary' cabinet, because with the formation of such cabinets 'one enters into adventures and one brings the Indonesian people even further into the mire of economic crisis and divisiveness'.[54]

The PKI was to be reassured about its major fears, however. Hatta's attempt to bring about a new coalition cabinet of the PNI and the Masjumi failed. In the end Burhanudin Harahap of the Masjumi was sworn in as premier of a government (August 12, 1955) which excluded the PNI, relied heavily on lesser nationalist parties and the PSI, and was initially also supported by the enigmatic NU which held the Interior Affairs portfolio in the cabinet. The PNI and the PKI now formed the principal parliamentary opposition. High on the cabinet's program was the holding of the first national parliamentary elections, as well as the restoration of the 'moral authority' of the government, especially as regards the armed forces, and of sound economic conditions. Though it was to be in office only about 8 months, the Harahap cabinet went far in realizing its objectives. For one thing, in little over a month after the inauguration of the cabinet, the national elections were held and three months later the elections for a Constituent Assembly. In

Masjumi and PSI circles there had long been the belief that the Ali government and the PNI generally had been dawdling in holding the elections, in order to advance their own partisan interests. Because it did not wish to have its own following weakened by further delays, the Masjumi wanted elections as soon as possible. This very fact, however, gave the Harahap cabinet a kind of caretaker and temporary quality. If the PKI feared a return to the repressive days of the Masjumi-led cabinet of Sukiman, its anxiety was soon shown to be groundless. The PKI's new strength and standing within the framework of national political life would have made a determined anti-Communist policy now impossible, unless the PKI was foolish enough to attempt a new coup. But the party's new line of winning respectability precluded a coup and at the same time strengthened its position with other organizations. In any event the Harahap cabinet soon showed that it had other aims. It immediately undertook vigorous economic reforms and managed to steal the thunder from its opposition by severing all RTC agreements with the Netherlands in February 1956 (the abrogation of the Nether-lands-Indonesian Union had been hanging fire since August 1954). The PKI had been in the forefront of those demanding total abrogation of all Union agreements (the August 1954 protocol had left Dutch capital largely undisturbed) and the Harahap government's decision deprived the PKI of a hitherto always convenient issue.

In the elections the PKI followed a policy which was puzzling to many observers. Its position in the election campaign had originally been laid down in the MPU or 'PKI General Elections Manifesto', of March 1954, which included essentially a restatement of the party program of 1954. But on June 24, 1955, the Politburo suddenly issued a resolution which declared that 'By means of the forthcoming general elections a National Coalition Government will be established'. 'National Coalition' according to this resolution, referred not to a 'dictatorship of the people', not even to a 'People's Democracy', as the 1954 party program had specifically declared the Communist objective to be. Rather, 'the program of the National Coalition Government which is desired by the PKI . . . is fundamentally the same as the PKI aims in the government of Ali Sastroamidjojo'. The Politburo thus recommitted the party to the policy of its April 1951 program, which had also stressed national coalition government as the PKI's main political objective. Party history today recognizes the disparity between the aims of the party as formulated at the Fifth Party Congress, and as formulated by the Politburo elections resolution and terms the latter 'a correction' of the former, which was duly, if retroactively, approved by the next (Sixth Party Congress) in 1959.[55] The effectiveness of this corrective maneuver, however, must be doubted. The party's 1954 program had been given wide publicity and the concept of the 'People's Democracy' as a necessary preliminary phase of the Socialist revolution and as an immediate goal of the party was in line with Communist strategy elsewhere in Asia. The attempt in the resolution of June 24, 1955, to water the program down was obviously a bid to win support from the PNI and radical nationalist groups, voters and candidates and thus widen the party's 'national appeal'. The PKI presented itself as interested in participating in a national coalition in order merely to realize specific aims such as more permissive labor legislation, abrogation of all RTC agreements, more vigorous action against the *Darul Islam*, improvements in the living conditions of peasants and workers; the Communist theory of the multi-stage revolution and the important role played in it by the concepts of 'People's Democracy' and of the new national or bourgeois democratic order was deliberately ignored. Whether many voters were persuaded to cast their ballots for the party because of this announced attenuation of the PKI program, whether additional independent candidates with radical leftist leanings but with no formal party affiliation were now willing to run for office with PKI backing, or whether among the politically tutored there was anyone who really believed that the PKI had now foresworn its long-range aims in favor of its 'national coalition' program, may all be doubted.

Aidit admitted that the June 24, 1955, resolution could give rise to a feeling that the MPU had now been contradicted, but he was at pains to stress that the resolution in fact conformed to the decisions of the Fifth Party Congress the year before, provided the general context of the PKI program as decided at that congress were considered.[56] The program, said Aidit, had indicated that the 'way out' of the situation in which reactionaries are powerful lies in 'shifting the balance of forces' between the imperialists and landlords on the one hand and 'the people' on the other, and that the 'parliamentary struggle' was not enough to achieve the people's democratic society. National coalition government, Aidit seemed to imply, was as a tactic in the framework of the election campaign better suited to the party's aims. Thus the Politburo resolution of June 24, 1955, did not deny the decisions of the Fifth Party Congress, but according to Aidit, provided a correction to the MPU inasmuch as the MPU was not in harmony with the program of the party. Anticipating those who might wonder why the decision to change the MPU was not brought before a party congress, Aidit declared that the question would certainly be considered by a party congress in the future. But in the meantime one could not let an issue such as this remain unresolved. The party was not retrogressing, Aidit added further, for to correct mistakes is progress. He reaffirmed the objective of 'People's Democratic Government' since such a government would be more concerned with the people's interests than a national coalition government. However, in confronting the general elections the party should have a 'concrete' program which could be immediately carried out and to this end the national coalition tactic was addressed. Seeking 'concrete' action the party's election slogan should therefore be the formation of a national coalition government, and not the MPU. This, however, did not mean that the MPU was now completely valueless, for the document could still be used to 'explain' the concept of people's democratic government to new members. *Inter alia* it may be noted that after the elections, and in any event by June 1956, the PKI reaffirmed the 1954 party program objective of establishing a 'People's Democratic Government' (see below, pp. 85–86).

In the weeks of campaigning the party proceeded with great vigor in mobilizing mass support and obtaining financial contributions. Indeed, the source of these contributions became a recurrent item of speculation in the press and even in parliament. It is likely that significant sums were received from wealthy Chinese interests in Indonesia and possibly also from Communist governments via their legations in Indonesia. The party's solicitation of funds among the Indonesian masses was extremely well organized, even in the remoter areas of the country. Local cadres organized popular drives for the collection of refuse, empty bottles, wood, leaves, frogs, legs, and even 'the sand of the rivers', which were all sold to strengthen the party's campaign chest.[57] The party's promotional campaign was ingenious and effective. As one observer has described it:[58]

The Communist Party was tremendously active in the displaying of its symbol, establishing an early overall lead over the other parties in this technique and then maintaining this throughout the campaign. Furthermore, while its billboards were to be found in very large numbers in every city and town, it did not by any means neglect village areas. Very many of its billboards were pieces of sheet iron of one size and marked, identically-factory-produced clearly. Yet the party was second to none in the imaginative use it made of everything from children's kites to the decor of village theatre for the advertising of its symbol.

In its appeal to the voters the party always endeavored to present the same image, namely, that of a genuinely national organization (not the tool of Moscow and Peking, as the Masjumi kept on claiming), alert to the problems of an anxious to win support from all indigenous classes and population groups, except, of course, those in rebellion against the government like the *Darul Islam* (with which Masjumi was in league as the PKI saw it), dedicated to a truly free and self-reliant nation no longer in the clutches of Dutch big business interests which were still exploiting the people, far more concerned with the social welfare of the common man than any other party, and committed to the defense of civil liberties for all, including freedom of religion. The latter position meant that the party opposed any concept of an Islamic State in Indonesia, an objective to which virtually all Muslim political organizations in varying degrees were dedicated, and this in turn meant that the PKI, broadly speaking, sought its support from the *abangan* cultural stream in Indonesian national life, especially in Java. This in a sense strengthened the party, because it allowed identification with an important traditional dimension in Indonesian experience and thus further clarified the national image which the party was trying to present. But at the same time this position brought the PKI in collision with other, secularly nationalist, *abangan*-oriented organizations, particularly the PNI.

As the election results were to show, the PNI and the PKI drew their principal support to a considerable extent from the same geographic and relatively culturally distinct areas. To a greater degree than most other parties the PKI used the election campaign to strengthen its membership, or rather, to identify and enlarge its following within the context of a national front. The renewed emphasis on a 'national coalition' in the election program of the party, as has been indicated, was made as free from any distinctive Communist implications as possible, and the party labored strongly to effect vote-pooling arrangements with independent candidates of radical persuasion. As a matter of election strategy, PKI membership classification was widened and not only included members and candidate-members, but also a third category of 'supporters' *(anggauta-pentjinta)* whose position was much less formal and disciplined than that of the first two categories and of whom little more than a vote for the PKI at election time was actually expected. PKI peasant and youth fronts were particularly active in enrolling these 'supporters'.

The results of the elections for the new national parliament which began on September 29, 1955, and for the Constituent Assembly which began on December 15, 1955, showed the PKI to be among the principal four parties in the country, receiving a total of 6,176,914 votes or 16·4 per cent of the total votes cast.[59] The PKI finished fourth, behind the PNI, the Masjumi and the NU, and it became entitled to 39 seats out of the 257 elected seats in the new parliament (it had held 17 seats in the provisional parliament). The party fell about 600 votes short of an additional 40th seat. It showed its greatest strength in the electoral districts of East and Central Java, from which it obtained 14 and 15 seats respectively. From other electoral districts the PKI received the following seats: 5 from West Java, 1 from the Greater Djakarta Area, 1 from South Sumatra, 1 from Central Sumatra, and 2 from North Sumatra.[60] In a number of important cities, e.g. Semarang and Surabaya, the PKI obtained impressive majorities, and it also became the strongest party in such residencies as Djokjakarta and Surakarta in Central Java province, and in Madiun and Kediri residencies. In East Java province these residencies, together with the surrounding East and Central Javanese provincial areas, form the ancient heartland of traditional pre-Islamic Javanese culture, and PKI strength here showed to some extent how successful the party had been in appealing to traditional and nativistic Javanese currents of thought and expectations and to the radical nationalistic mystiques with which this nativism is frequently blended these days.[61] Here, as in various parts of Sumatra, the party found support among the rural uprooted, among estate and peasant laborers and the landless, among the urban poor, and organized labor and among the youth, both in city and countryside.

Unquestionably PKI emphasis on the economic plight of the country and on the misery of estate laborers and small or landless peasants proved extremely effective. Finally, the influence of village and other government officials, directing or guiding the citizenry under them by gentle, and sometimes not so gentle, pressures to vote for the party, should not be overlooked. The extent of these administrative hierarchical pressures by officials and civil servants and their ability to influence the voting in favor of a particular party (not necessarily the PKI alone) are still matters of conjecture, but probably explain in part why the NU and the PNI as well as the PKI all drew most of their support from Central and East Java provinces.[62]

CHAPTER III

TOWARD 'GUIDED DEMOCRACY'

1 *955–1960.* The PKI by the beginning of 1956 had won increased legitimacy and had seen its strength, only seven years after the Madiun debacle, widely demonstrated and recognized. Doubtless the party's strong showing in the September 1955 elections had contributed to the fact that two months later in the elections for the Constituent Assembly, in December 1955, the PKI gained more than 55,000 votes over the total it had received in September.[1] In general the party was pleased with the elections, which according to its official history today, 'were manifestations of the victory of democracy'. The PKI's only real political setback—rather an indirect one—in the remaining weeks of the Harahap cabinet's term was the cabinet's unilateral abrogation of all RTC agreements on February 14 and 21, 1956. The fact that this abrogation, long one of the PKI's much propagandized political objectives, was accomplished by a Masjumi-led cabinet was particularly galling to the party, although the fact that West New Guinea remained in Dutch hands provided the PKI with the old allegation that 'Dutch imperialism' was still threatening the country.

On the whole the party benefitted from the political furore occasioned by President Sukarno's charges early in November 1955, that he was in possession of 'secret documents' proving that certain elements were using the general elections to lead the Indonesian Republic to disaster by means of sabotage. Sukarno also mentioned documents which showed that the *Darul Islam* was maintaining relations with 'foreign imperialism', and he castigated 'provincialism, federalism and intellectualism', as well as 'poverty and illiteracy' as causes of the disunity in the nation.[2] The President never publicly revealed the details of the plot against the republic, but it would appear that the charges, like similar ones he had made about a year before,[3] had the effect of primarily embarassing the Masjumi and thereby the Harahap cabinet. This fact may have contributed to the loss by the Masjumi of more than 114,000 votes in the December 1955 elections for the Constituent Assembly. The rumored sympathy of some prominent figures in Masjumi for the Darul Islam—a rumor on which the PKI had long capitalized—could now be made to link up with an official charge of 'foreign imperialism'.

Another event that embarrassed the Harahap regime the PKI attempted to exploit. Harahap had been able to solve the army crisis by taking the Defense Ministry portfolio himself, by persuading the Army Chief-of-Staff, Bambang Utoyo (Iwa Kusumasumantri's appointee, it will be recalled) to resign, and by appointing Col. A. H. Nasution in his place. Nasution had resigned as Army Staff Chief in the aftermath of the October 17, 1952 affair, and his return to the army's top post occurred with the approval of the Republic's powerful army territorial commanders, whose opinion Harahap had been careful to solicit in advance. But if peace now had returned to the army leadership for a while (partly because of Harahap's personal popularity with those army officers favoring a modernization and rationalization of the defense establishment), trouble was to break out in another branch of the service—the air force. Its chief-of-staff, Vice-Marshal Suryadarma (long rumored to have far leftist leanings), had been at odds for personal reasons, as well as because of an intra-organizational conflict, with one of his principal subordinates, Vice-Commodore H. Suyono. Suyono and a few of his fellow officers had resigned during the Ali cabinet and a military court, which had tried Suyono on various vague charges, had subsequently cleared him.

Despite Suryadarma's objections Harahap intended to rehabilitate Suyono (perhaps for the same reason which had led him to help in the rehabilitation of Nasution), but when on December 14, 1955, Suyono was to be reinstated as Suryadarma's second in command in a public ceremony attended by the premier himself, a group of recalcitrant personnel of the air force prevented the oath-taking and trained their Sten guns on the premier. The latter, however, prevented an incident by walking away. Sukarno refused to accept Suryadarma's resignation and because of this and the change of cabinets shortly thereafter, the affair was never really resolved. The PKI criticized the premier's airforce policy and expressed cautious sympathy for Suryadarma; in this it found itself in a minority, since much of the press endorsed Harahap's stand, expressing dissatisfaction with the antics of 'a cowboy state' as one irate editorial termed the incident. But PKI support for Suryadarma (whose personal ideological outlook was and is known to be close to that of Sukarno) was certainly a significant element in the developing pattern of increasing Communist support for Sukarno personally, and for those armed forces leaders who shared the President's temper.

With the intended installation of the new elected parliament the Harahap cabinet resigned and Communist efforts to obtain a seat in the new government were redoubled. M. H. Lukman argued that the collaboration between the political parties for a stable government should not be based on ideology, but on a common political program acceptable to all. (Aidit was away at the time, attending the Twentieth

Congress of the Soviet Communist Party.) Lukman's approach was, of course, the concept of national coalition government writ large. The common program envisaged by the party as basis of a coalition included 'anti-colonialism, national independence, domestic democracy and world peace'. Lukman declared that his party was ready to collaborate in the formation of a 'national unity' cabinet or a 'national peace' cabinet in which the PNI, NU, Masjumi and PKI would participate. No consistent anti-colonial cabinet seemed possible, Lukman further argued, unless the PKI, 'which represents 20 per cent of the Indonesian electorate', participated in it, but the Masjumi, according to Lukman, rejected such PKI participation in the new government. Additional points which the PKI advanced as bases for a national coalition were: (1) granting of the greatest degree of autonomy to the various regions and the recognition of the regions' right to manage their own cultural and economic affairs, but with obedience of all regional population groups to the central government; (2) protection of the civil rights of state employees and other workers, including the right to organize, and to the unemployed and prohibition of arbitrary dismissals; (3) abolition of the double citizenship provision for Chinese in Indonesia, as agreed upon between the Indonesian and People's China's governments in 1955;[4] (4) granting the right to peasants to defend themselves against the Darul Islam and 'other terrorist bands'; (5) progressive restriction of foreign capital in the country; (6) a foreign policy based on the decisions of the Asian-African Conference in Bandung; and (7) mobilization of the domestic potential to compel the Netherlands to give Irian back to Indonesia.[5]

When it became apparent that the PKI's offer of a national coalition fell on deaf ears (e.g. PNI leader S. Mangunsarkoro had declared as early as January 1956, that it 'will be difficult for the PKI to participate in the new government'),[6] Communist pressures increased. On March 8, 1956, Sukarno had designated former premier Ali Sastroamidjojo of the PNI to form a new cabinet (since the PNI had emerged as the strongest party from the elections) and Ali's efforts at a coalition included Masjumi and NU, but not the PKI. When eight days later Ali had succeeded in forming a tentative list of participants in the new cabinet and it became known that the PKI was to be excluded, Sukarno was reported to have been flooded by resolutions and demands that the PKI enter the government. Most of the resolutions came from Communist-led labor, youth and veterans' groups in the Djakarta area. When on March 18, 1956, Sukarno returned to Djakarta from a trip to East Java, he was met at the airport by a crowd of demonstrators demanding Communist participation in the government.[7] Sukarno appears to have been in favor of a minor seat in the cabinet for a radical but partyless figure in the particularly good graces of the PKI (such as a new ministry of state for 'parliamentary relations'), but the Masjumi, backed by the Catholic Party which had also agreed to participate in the cabinet, were adamant. The growing political influence of a number of anti-Communist army commanders probably also prevented such a move. Thus the second Ali Sastroamidjojo cabinet, installed on March 24, not only excluded the PKI, but also any representative from the non-Communist radical left. 'Considering the composition and personnel of the cabinet', Lukman declared, 'it is certain that the greater part of the Indonesian people will be disappointed'.[8] However, despite its strong reservations, the party again decided 'to give the cabinet an opportunity to work', and it announced that it would support those policies of the government which it deemed 'progressive'.

The first few weeks following the formation of the Ali cabinet were marked by a minor crisis in the PKI leadership. Whatever benefits the 'national coalition' program may have brought the party in the elections, it was clear that as a device to get the PKI into the cabinet it had wholly failed. Hardly had the Ali cabinet been installed when Alimin began his attack on Aidit and on the 'class collaboration policies' of the party (cf. chapter II, note 45). While Alimin by now lacked any significant following in the higher echeons of the PKI, in a few local party sections his accusations did strike a responsive chord. Further tension arose with the news of Khrushchev's denunciation of Stalin in his February 24, 1956, address before the Soviet Communist Party's Twentieth Congress. The ensuing 'de-Stalinization', which was to be only very mildly echoed by the PKI leadership in coming months, nevertheless seemed—when considered in conjunction with the party's watered-down program of 'national coalition'—a kind of general abandonment of hallowed Communist principles and strategy. The dissension in the party occasioned by all these developments never reached significant proportions, however, not least because a plenary session of the PKI Central Committee was convened in June 1956, which, in effect, reaffirmed in militant tones the basic strategy of the 1954 party program without abandoning altogether the idea of 'national coalition' government. With his usual dialectical skill, Aidit was able to bring about a new shift of emphasis in party strategy by synthesizing the apparent antitheses between the party's 1954 program and the 'national coalition government' program used in the elections. With the conclusion of the elections, as Aidit put it in his report to the plenum, three principal political forces, roughly balancing each other in strength, can now be discerned in Indonesia. First there are the 'progressives', consisting of workers, peasants, petty bourgeoisie and revolutionary intellectuals; secondly, there are the 'middle-of-the-road' forces, consisting of the national bourgeoisie and all other anti-colonial patriots, including leftist landlords; and finally, there are the 'die-hards', the 'feudalist and compradores' in league with the imperialists. The last group wished Indonesia to be free in appearance only, while in reality it would be a country under the control of 'the great foreign capitalists'. The middle group was in conflict with the imperialists and seeks to make changes that are in its own interests and in the interests of 'national capitalism'. The 'progressives' also resolutely oppose the economic, political and cultural interests of the imperialists and advance the slogan 'land for the peasants' so as to end 'feudal ownership of land'. The policy of the PKI must be to actively develop the 'progressive' forces, to seek alliances with the middle of the road forces and to weaken the die-hards.

Basing himself now almost entirely on certain pronouncements of Sukarno, Aidit urged the 'completion' of the 'August Revolution' (i.e. the revolution of the Indonesians against the Dutch which began with the independence proclamation of August, 1945)—that is, the completion of the 'bourgeois democratic' revolution in Indonesia. The aim of the party was the establishment of 'People's Democracy', i.e. a democracy 'of a new type' based on the unity of, and recognizing the common interests of, the progressive and middle-of-the-road forces directed against imperialism and feudalism and expressed through a united national front. Fulfilling the national 'August Revolution' thus meant fulfilling the national democratic or bourgeois democratic phase of the Indonesian revolution, preparatory to the establishment of a new 'People's Democratic Government' as the 1954 program, to which Aidit repeatedly referred, had already outlined.[9] In line with the policy of fulfilling the 'August Revolution' the Central Committee's Fourth Plenum also approved a 'Three-Year Plan for Organization and Training', which set up specific quotas for branches in their enrolling of new members, coordinated indoctrination and intensified publication of party literature and tightened party discipline and central control. This first Three Year Plan was formally inaugurated in August 1956 and its first fruits were to be the noteworthy election gains of the PKI in the middle of 1957, to be described presently.

Thus the specific points that made up the 'national coalition' program were not abandoned by the party, but rather incorporated into the overall strategy of 'fulfilling' the bourgeois democratic revolution, now equated with the 'August revolution'. The development of the national front was to be focused on both class and party; the technique of simultaneous front formation 'from above' and 'from below', which had been employed by the party since 1952, was again endorsed. A 'national coalition government' was still desired but it was realized that such a government depended on a greater mobilization of popular support than had been accomplished thus far, and the presence of Masjumi in the second Ali cabinet was given as evidence of the present strength of the reactionary forces supporting imperialism and feudalism in the country. Here we see a favorite PKI formulation—the alleged bourgeois tendency to vacillate and turn periodically to the right, away from the 'anti-imperialist' front. The apparent fear in PNI circles that the PKI might obtain a cabinet seat and the willingness of the PNI to collaborate again with the Masjumi in a new cabinet were both seen by the PKI as evidence of the ambivalent nature of the national bourgeoisie. In fact it is doubtful that the Masjumi-PNI collaboration pleased all sections of the two parties, although it would appear that national bourgeois elements in both believed that a rapprochement was possible, particularly after the policies of the Harahap cabinet which had placed severe restrictions on the national importers and thus blocked the relatively easy road to wealth for the Indonesian businessman available under the first Ali cabinet.[10] The bourgeois vacillation required a redress of the tactical balance of PKI strength, and for Aidit this meant redoubled efforts to win followers among the peasantry, as he had indicated in a *Bintang Merah* article in 1954. The party realized that it could use its strength in a number of cities in Central and East Java to influence the composition of local and regional government councils, and in the middle of 1956 parliamentary deputies of the PNI, Masjumi and NU expressed their anxiety that the PKI would play a major role in local councils in such a way as to oppose the policies of the central government.[11] Indeed, in Surabaya and Semarang, Communist influence in municipal affairs was increasingly shown in minor clashes with the police and in labor unrest.

The development of the PKI now came to be intertwined with the military crisis of the second Ali cabinet. The return of Ali as premier could hardly please his old enemies among leading army officers, chief of whom was Col. Lubis, Assistant Chief-of-Staff of the Army, whose opposition to the policies of Defense Minister Iwa Kusumasumantri, it will be recalled, had been chiefly responsible for bringing the first Ali cabinet down. In August 1956, Foreign Minister Ruslan Abdulgani was arrested by the military, on charges of bribery and other corrupt practices, and although a government commission initially cleared him of any malversations, he was subsequently indicted. Lubis, who was probably the principal power behind the arrest, appears to have felt that even stronger action was necessary after Ruslan was initially cleared, and on November 16 and 19 he attempted to stage a coup d'état with the assistance of an army unit in West Java. The coup failed; Lubis fled and a wave of arrests of leading army officers began, which in turn aroused the anger of leading army territorial commanders in sympathy with the fugitive Lubis. Lubis' intentions became clearer when the Djakarta press, on December 14, 1956, published an 'open letter' allegedly written by him, in which he termed the present governmental structure unsound and called for a strong extra-parliamentary 'business' (i.e. non-political) cabinet led by vice-president Hatta and Hamengku Buwono, the Sultan of Djokjakarta (who had had to resign as Defense Minister in the aftermath of the October 17, 1952 affair). The political dissatisfaction of army officers with the Ali cabinet was further complicated by the freewheeling economic policies of army commanders in their territories and the smuggling in which they engaged in order to defray maintenance costs of their units. The Harahap government had already attempted to curb army smuggling, but with little success. The second Ali cabinet, in the face of this army dissension, followed a wavering policy, dogmatically proclaiming the principle of civilian control over the military, while at the same time showing extraordinary leniency to those officers who had engaged in smuggling. On December 22, 1956, Col. Simbolon, territorial commander in North Sumatra and a friend of Lubis, announced that he had 'severed' connections with the Djakarta government and no longer recognized its authority; two days before, an officers' junta of a demobilized army division, led by Lt. Col. Ahmad Husein, took over all civil authority in Central Sumatra and in effect constituted itself an independent government. Thus, within nine months after Ali had become premier again, the country was on the brink of civil war.[12]

While criticizing 'irresponsible army officers' and strongly endorsing the Ali cabinet's stand of civilian control over the military establishment, the PKI ever mindful of its own security needs and freedom of action, moved cautiously in the first few months of the renewed outbreak of army unrest. In part this was because the resistance against Djakarta seemed to be spreading and the PKI's future began to look uncertain. For example, on December 24, 1956, the governor of South Sumatra, under local army pressure, decided to assume vastly increased economic and fiscal provincial autonomy and in March 1957, a military junta essentially opposed to the Ali government took control over the area. In March 1957, too, a 'revolutionary' junta was formed and took authority in Eastern Indonesia. All these juntas were led by men who in various degrees were opposed to the PKI. Thus, taking power in Central Sumatra the Husein junta arrested local and regional Communist leaders. Further evidence that the issue of Communism was involved in the regional rebellions was made clear with the counter-coup led by Lt. Col. Djamin Gintings against the Simbolon junta on December 27, 1956—the only success that the hapless Ali regime could register in this period. Gintings, loyal to Ali and Sukarno, used Communist estate labor and squatters' organizations in North Sumatra, armed them, and thus gave them quasi-military status. Subsequently, Gintings even armed units of the Communist-led SOBSI labor federation in the area and by February 1957, formed a 'civic guard' of SOBSI elements. Simbolon, who had to flee the North Sumatran region, had clearly miscalculated the strength of the PKI among the labor and peasant groups there, and Communist veterans' groups like PERBEPSI and other fronts showered Gintings with congratulatory messages after his successful counter-coup and promised to support him. Aidit himself hailed Ginting's action as a 'great victory for the people of Indonesia at the close of 1956'.[13] The support of the Communists was a considerable factor in preventing the tottering Ali cabinet from collapsing at this time.

Ali and the PNI were not ungrateful. The possibility of a 'national coalition' government which would include the PKI came again under active consideration. On December 26, 1956, Dahlan Ibrahim, Minister of Veterans Affairs and a representative of IPKI (a minor party with strong following among moderately conservative military) left the cabinet and went into opposition. Shortly afterwards Mangunsarkoro, leader of the PNI's radical nationalist wing, declared that if the PKI now wished for seats in the cabinet, such a request would be considered, since the support of the Communists 'would certainly be welcome'.[14] Again Sukarno at this time appears to have urged an 'opening to the left' by the inclusion in the government of a radical figure or figures acceptable to all of the far left parties. Soon thereafter, in his well known *konsepsi* (concept) of February 21, 1957, Sukarno urged creation of a new government which would include representatives of all parties, including the Communists. But NU and Catholic party leaders warned that such an inclusion would widen the gulf between the Ali government and the dissident regional leaders and their juntas. Dissension in the cabinet over the issue of PKI inclusion further undermined the government. Although the upshot was that the Communists again were excluded, this did not prevent the further spread of the army revolt, first to East Indonesia, and thence to Kalimantan where the formation of yet another junta was taking place; even in East Java the cry of secessionism was heard. Faced with determined anti-PNI and anti-PKI hostility in many areas, divided within itself and besieged with insistent demands for money to aid overdue regional development of the outlying provinces, the Ali cabinet returned its mandate on March 13, 1957. President Sukarno proclaimed a general 'state of war and siege' throughout the country and invited regional rebel leaders to Djakarta for consultations.

As early as February 21, 1957, Sukarno in his *konsepsi* had openly endorsed Communist participation in the government. Declaring that Western principles of parliamentary democracy had failed in Indonesia, Sukarno suggested instead a system of what he had earlier called 'guided democracy',[15] which would be 'in harmony with the soul of the Indonesian people'. In it the cabinet would be revised so as to include representatives of all parties, including the PKI; second, a National Advisory Council would be established to be composed of representatives from 'the functional groups of society' (e.g. labor, youth, national businessmen, women, peasants, religious groups, and so on) which 'will give the cabinet advice, whether it wants it or not.' The President emphasized that his *konsepsi* was not intended to 'draw the cabinet toward the left', but rather to promote national unity.[16] However, the PKI and the PNI were the only major parties completely to support the *konsepsi;* the Communists declared that it was 'just, democratic and . . . a guarantee of unity and resistance to fragmentation'.[17] On February 28, representatives of the Masjumi, NU, the Christian (Protestant) and Catholic parties visited Sukarno in order to tell him that they would not approve of Communist participation in the government and had grave doubts about the constitutionality of the *konsepsi.* On March 1, 1957, the information bureau of the Masjumi circulated an article written by Mohammad Natsir in which it was argued that religion and Communism could never be mixed, and Muslim clerics throughout the country also expressed their opposition.

But all these negative reactions and developments encountered an open and determined PKI campaign in favor of the *konsepsi*, during which American and British embassies in Djakarta were painted with anti-Western slogans (e.g. 'Beware of foreign subversion') and the PKI formed 'encouragement teams' at the entrance of Sukarno's residence whenever political leaders were scheduled to discuss the *konsepsi* with him. There is little doubt that the *konsepsi* was generally agreeable to the PKI's national coalition strategy and the opposition to the PKI, after the fall of the second Ali cabinet, rallied around the principle of a presidential cabinet, specifically excluding the Communists. The latter idea found particular favor in the provinces where the name of Hatta as head of such a presidential cabinet was being increasingly suggested. Nasution and other leading army officers reportedly also favored a presidential cabinet led by Hatta and excluding the PKI. Opposition from potent elements in the PNI, NU and lesser parties and from the entire PKI made such a Hatta led cabinet virtually impossible, however, while Sukarno himself was smarting from a variety of criticisms of his 'concept' and was reported to be reworking it.

On March 16, 1957, in the midst of the negotiations for a new cabinet, Sukarno announced his 'thoroughly boiled' (i.e. final) 'concept' in which he in effect abandoned the idea of a *gotong royong* (mutual cooperation) cabinet that would include representatives of all the parties, although he reaffirmed his idea of a National Advisory Council. But the deadlock in the formation of a new government worsened, and as PNI chairman Suwirjo, whom Sukarno had designated as the new cabinet former, reported failure, the President moved boldly forward and appointed himself, 'citizen Sukarno', as cabinet-former in the presence of some 150 political and military leaders. On April 9, Sukarno announced formation of a new 'extra-parliamentary cabinet of experts', headed by the partyless planning expert, Djuanda Kartawidjaja. The PKI again had no representatives in this cabinet, but it could certainly take comfort from the fact that such well-known leftists as the Stalin Peace Prize winner, Professor Pryono (who obtained the Education and Culture portfolio), the new Agriculture Minister, Sadjarwo, and A. M. Hanafi, secretary-general of the radical People's Congress (who became Minister for 'Mobilization of People's Energy') were now members of the government. The PKI had undoubtedly expected to have a measure of influence in the new government, for, encouraged by Sukarno's original support of Communist inclusion in the cabinet, the party had strongly emphasized its 'national coalition' line and on March 21, 1956, the Communist-led SOBSI labor federation had warned Suwirjo, then still attempting to put together a new cabinet, that if a new government included the Masjumi but excluded the PKI, a general strike might be called throughout Indonesia. The Djuanda cabinet contained two recently 'unaffiliated' Masjumi figures (one of whom was expelled from his party the day after the cabinet was announced, the other, after a prolonged squabble, resigned from the party just prior to his appointment) and their dubious position apparently satisfied the PKI, for on April 18, D. N. Aidit announced that although the Djuanda cabinet was not the beginning of 'guided democracy' for Indonesia, it was 'good enough' for the Communists to be able to support it.[18]

The initial months of the Djuanda cabinet saw a marked overall strengthening of the PKI. Party leadership praised Djuanda's pronouncement that, though his cabinet was characterized as 'extra-parliamentary', the government would still be responsible to parliament. A renewed effort was made on April 25 to bring the dissension in the provinces to an end by holding yet another conference of the restive military commanders in Djakarta (the first had been held on March 15 in Djakarta, but had largely been ineffective), and this meeting appears to have given the Djuanda government some confidence in dealing with the regional and army crisis. On May 8, 1957, in the midst of the state visit to Indonesia of USSR President Voroshilov, a new emergency law announced the formation of a National Council such as Sukarno had outlined earlier. The party could be pleased that its influence, via radical representatives from the labor, artists' and youth 'functional groups' represented in the Council, could now be brought to bear directly on the cabinet. The Council, to be sure, could only give 'advice' to the government, and it was heavily dominated by Sukarno, but for the PKI the creation of the Council meant another step toward 'national coalition'. To those (e.g. many Masjumi members) who questioned the constitutionality of the National Council, Njoto of the PKI replied that the rebellious military councils in the various provinces were 'also illegal' and that hence the creation of the National Council could hardly be criticized by those who sympathized with the provincial rebellions.[19] In parliament the PKI was assuming an ever more militant attitude toward the dissident military leaders, denouncing 'regional adventurers' as puppets of the 'diehard' reactionary and imperialist forces, and according to party history today, taking 'a firm attitude which was stated by Comrade D. N. Aidit in Parliament as "the confrontation of the Madiun and Sumatra Incidents".'[20] This line meant in effect that the PKI was blaming the Sumatran army revolts on the same groups which had been responsible for the Madiun provocation in 1948. At the PKI Central Committee's fifth plenary meeting in July 1957, Aidit reaffirmed the party's endorsement of Sukarno's concept as a means of combatting the 'warlords' in the rebellious provinces and urged further implementation of the party's 'Three Year Plan'.[21] The PKI's aggressiveness and the unquestioned evidence that the central government regarded the party as an important source of support, however, also tended to aggravate intra-parliamentary and partisan political tensions in Djakarta and strengthened the conviction of secessionist-minded military commanders that the central government was far too much under Communist influence to be able to deal with.

These tensions and suspicions were certainly augmented by the results of the municipal, district and provincial elections in Java, held from June through August 1957. In virtually all of these elections the PKI scored notable successes. In the Djakarta municipal elections the Masjumi narrowly retained the lead it had first established in the national elections in 1955, but the PKI ran a close second (in 1955 it had finished fourth in Djakarta), ahead of the PNI and NU. In Semarang the PKI won a great victory, greatly widening its 1955 majority and accumulating nearly as many votes as all other parties combined. The same voting results appeared on the whole, throughout Central Java province, especially in the elections for the provincial council, in which the strength of the PKI nearly balanced the combined strength of PNI, NU, and Masjumi. (In 1955 the PKI had been second here, running behind the PNI). Equally spectacular was the party's increasing strength in Surabaya (a city already won for the PKI in 1955) while in the East Java provincial elections the PKI won over 600,000 votes more than its nearest rival, the NU, which finished in second place. In 1955, the NU had largely been dominant in East Java. Even in West Java, where in 1955 the PKI had only obtained 5 parliamentary seats to the Masjumi's 13 and had finished a poor fourth, the PKI now increased its strength by about 25 per cent, although the Masjumi retained its lead; in West Java the PKI registered a particularly impressive victory in the Bandung municipal council elections.[22]

The election successes of the Communists—the PKI daily *Harian Rakjat* boasted that with the total of 7 million votes which the PKI had obtained in the elections the party had now become the largest in Java—were due to a variety of factors, among which were the deteriorating economic conditions, the falling prestige of the PNI (PKI gains in many areas seemed to have been made particularly at the expense of the PNI) and the continuing drive and discipline of the PKI party and front organizations. The relative lack of interest in the elections by other parties probably also played a role. The new Communist strength not only alarmed anti-Communist military and provincial leaders but many of the other, essentially Java-based, political parties as well. NU spokesmen suddenly resumed their cry that the PKI be outlawed and on August 12, 1957, Ida Bagus Putra Manuaba, a leading PNI executive, declared that PNI ideology had always been different from the PKI's and that the PNI was quite willing to collaborate with the Masjumi and NU in an anti-Communist front. Manuaba's words were echoed in other PNI circles, and early in September 1957, the PNI executive committee for Central Java openly came out against any collaboration with the PKI; if such collaboration existed, declared the Committee, it existed without its knowledge or approval. Incensed over the aggressiveness of some PKI tactics during the regional elections and over PKI counter charges that the PNI was 'ambivalent' in its policies, other PNI foremen, like Kosasih and Subagio Reksodipuro, attacked the 'two-faced' character of the PKI leaders, half of whom 'are in Moscow and half of them are in Indonesia'.

Despite all this critical talk many PNI leaders remained mindful of the importance of PKI support for the Djuanda government (in which the PNI was importantly represented, holding, among other portfolios, the first vice-premiership). At a conference of PNI leaders on August 23, 1957, the PNI general chairman, Suwirjo, flatly declared that a collaboration between PNI and Masjumi was impossible, chiefly because the PNI supported Sukarno's 'concept' of 'guided democracy' and the Masjumi did not. Recent PNI election losses, according to Suwirjo, were mainly due to a certain party 'passivity'. This was to be a fateful decision, for the rejection by the PNI of the chance to form an anti-Communist ideological or political front with the Masjumi and NU, which both—though in different degrees—would have been willing to consider, would lead to a further polarization of partisan political interests, strengthen the suspicions of dissident provincial and army leaders and contribute to a deepening of the regional rebellions in the coming months.[23]

Yet anti-Communist undercurrents in Java were running more strongly, one of them emanating from Sundanese regional nationalist feelings in West Java, allied with anti-Djakarta and pro-regional autonomy convictions among intellectuals, bureaucrats and army officers in a number of regions outside Java, and with intensely anti-Communist, ultra-orthodox Islamic trends of opinion evident as much in North Sumatra, in Southern Celebes as in the *Darul Islam* movement of West Java. In Java a number of army officers, sympathizers of the still fugitive Lubis, appeared to be in league with bands of revolutionary terrorist organizations having the kidnapping and even the assassination of leading government officials in view. There could, in fact, be little question that terrorist and counter-terrorist organizations were widely operating in Djakarta. Between July 4 and August 15, 1957, four separate grenade attacks were made in the capital. The first, in the night of July 4, was made on PKI and SOBSI headquarters and on August 15 PKI headquarters was again attacked. Army officers were involved in these attacks. On July 30 grenade attacks took place at five different locations in the city at once, and on August 9 a grenade was thrown at the home of a prominent Masjumi member, Prawoto Mangkusasmito. On November 30, 1957, an attempt was made on President Sukarno's life at Tjikini in Djakarta, as a result of which 11 died and scores were wounded.

An atmosphere of rumor, high tension and lawlessness began to pervade the seat of government. Intimidations, arbitrary detentions, and house searches of those suspected to be in opposition to the government, especially of Masjumi leaders, became the order of the day. Tension in the capital was heightened and at the same time found a target in the renewed campaign to obtain control over West New Guinea. When on November 29, 1957, the United Nations General Assembly again failed to muster the necessary votes for the Indonesian resolution on West New Guinea, there was a wave of strikes against Dutch business establishments and seizures by workers of Dutch shops, offices and plants. The PKI prided itself in being in the vanguard of these 'spontaneous' workers' actions, during which Dutch enterprises were declared to be 'property' of the Indonesian Republic or adorned with a hammer and sickle in red paint. As the PKI Politburo put it in a statement of December 8, 1957, on the anti-Dutch action:[24]

It now depends on the Dutch government: negotiate for the surrender of West Irian to the Republic of Indonesia with the hope of being able to get compensation, or continue being stubborn, with the result that all big Dutch capitalist enterprises will be confiscated by the Republic of Indonesia. The Indonesian people are ready to take either one of these two courses! . . .

At the present moment, when we must wage a struggle to paralyse all the economic forces of the Dutch colonialists and to turn these economic resources into the economic strength of the Republic of Indonesia, it is very necessary for us to recall to mind our experiences during the first days of the August 1945 Revolution. The spirit of the August Revolution must become the spirit of today, our courage in those days must inspire us today. . . .

Thus the PKI continued to hew closely to its line of 'completion' of the August 1945 revolution as a national democratic revolution against imperialism and feudalism, and of the anti-Dutch action as being part of the 'completion' process. The economy worsened because of the precipitate action against the Dutch and a collapse of inter-island trade and the foreign commerce related to it stared the government in the face. By personally visiting the rebellious areas, by staging still more conferences with military commanders, and even by holding on September 10, 1957, a 'National Conference' *(Musjawarah Nasional)* between central and regional government leaders with a view to restoring the unity between Sukarno and Hatta, premier Dujanda had endeavored to bank the flames of civil war. But it was to little avail. New dissidents continued to concentrate in West Sumatra. In an open letter to President Sukarno, published in the Palembang daily *Batanghari Sembilan* on January 21, 1958, the Masjumi leader and Bank of Indonesia Governor, Sjafruddin Prawiranegara, declared that he had fled from Java and that he did not wish 'to die for nothing or to become the victim of wild beasts in human form'. Urging Sukarno to return to his constitutional position Sjafruddin stated that 'all Indonesian patriots must stand ready to prevent a repetition in Indonesia of the Hungarian tragedy and to safeguard Indonesia from becoming a Soviet satellite'.

Another Masjumi leader and sympathizer with the rebels, former premier Mohammad Natsir, shortly thereafter accused 'the regime of President Sukarno' of exploiting the general economic deterioration and the West Irian crisis in order to 'seek an alliance with the Russian bloc'. As more and more dissident army and political leaders found their way to the West Sumatra camp of Lt. Col. Husein the Djuanda government was first presented on February 10, 1958, with a demand from the rebels that it resign in favor of a government headed by Hatta or by the Sultan of Djokjakarta, Hamengku Buwono, and that Sukarno return to his constitutional position and dissolve such extra-constitutional bodies as the National Council. When Djuanda and Sukarno refused, Husein on February 15, 1958, proclaimed a new 'Revolutionary Government of the Indonesian Republic' (Pemerintah Revolusionèr Republik Indonesia—PRRI), with Sjafruddin Prawiranegara as premier. A civil war, in which the question of Communist influence in the central government and in the country generally had become a major factor, was now added to Indonesia's many problems.[25]

That Communism was an issue in the outbreak of this civil war seems quite evident. From the point of the PKI's regional election gains in the middle of 1957 onward, widespread fear of steadily advancing Communist influence became a major dimension of Indonesian public life, even in the ranks of the PKI's erstwhile ally, the PNI. Anti-Communist terrorism and counter-terrorism, further cabals in the ranks of army officers, campaigns of intimidation and arrest of political leaders in the capital in the closing months of 1957 were all fruits of this fear. Communist endorsement of Sukarno's 'concept' and of 'guided democracy' generally, increased the anxiety in responsible political quarters. By the beginning of 1958 former premier Sutan Sjahrir, in an interview with an Indian newspaper, was reported to have predicted that 'if the present trend' continued 'the Communist might attempt to seize Indonesian leadership with unpredictable consequences'.[26] Though Sjahir denied the interview, D. N. Aidit branded him a 'daydreaming adventurer', and stated that an attempt to seize power would be 'treason' and that Sjahrir seemed to need the PKI as a 'black sheep'.[27] Whether Sjahrir ever made the accusation or not, there is little doubt that his views reflected those of a considerable segment of non- and anti-Communist opinion. As we have seen, at about the same time such Masjumi leaders as Sjafruddin and Natsir expressed their concern over Communist influence. During the trial of the perpetrators of the attempt on Sukarno's life at Tjikini it was revealed that army officers were not only involved in the Tjikini incident, but were also directly responsible for the earlier grenade attacks on PKI headquarters in July and August 1957. During the

Tjikini trial, according to a press report, the following exchange took place between the judge and defendant Lt. Col. Raden Achmad Nasuhi:[28]

(Judge): What is your reason for issuing the bombing (of PKI headquarters) order?

(Nasuhi): We are of the view that the Indonesian Communist Party (PKI) is the main source of the present difficulties and troubles in the country.

(Judge): So the PKI has to be liquidated, isn't it so?

(Nasuhi): Yes, that's right, because the PKI up to now is still washing its hands of any problem of the country.

(Judge): Why did you order the bombing of PKI headquarters and not the Communists themselves?

(Nasuhi): It is enough with just bombing the headquarters in order to warn the government and the Army Chief of Staff of the situation in the capital, which indeed was already in danger, and not to merely accuse the insurgent provinces which have risen up following the mismanagement of the central government itself.

Under the circumstances it would be difficult to determine the degree of rationalization, if any, in the anti-Communist pronouncements of Husein, Sjafruddin and other PRRI leaders. Along with several Djakarta press analyses of the revolt at the time of its outbreak one might stress that the conflict between Djakarta and the *daerah* (provinces) originally involved the division of revenues produced by the sale of agricultural products raised in the provinces,[29] and by the feeling in the *daerah* that a parasitic Djakarta was getting too great a share of the wealth produced by the regions. Ancient inter-ethnic hostilities amplified these economic grievances, as well as a general dissatisfaction with the lack of meaningful local autonomy, and the weariness with the corruption in the capital. But the Communist issue was certainly not a mere afterthought to all these grievances; on the contrary, undue accommodation of Communist influence was from the start an important feature of the image which Sukarno and his government presented to many anti-Communist Muslim politicians, military commanders and regional leaders. In its own subsequent publications the PRRI was to stress the Communist danger to Indonesia and the ties of the PKI with foreign Communist powers such as People's China.[30]

For its part the PKI was vociferous in its opposition to the PRRI and its associates in Celebes, demanding strong action not only against them, but also against their alleged sympathizers in the government and in the Masjumi and Socialist parties. On September 19, 1958, it introduced, along with other leftist groups, a resolution in parliament demanding parliamentary condemnation of those parliamentary deputies 'who have openly sided or are involved with' the PRRI and its supporters in

Celebes. When premier Djuanda charged that pilots employed by the rebels were Americans (as well as nationalist Chinese), Aidit in a cable to the U.S. Ambassador in Djakarta declared that the PKI would urge economic measures against American interests in Indonesia if the US did not 'immediately stop the delivery, either overtly or covertly, or arms to the rebels'.[31] The party proved also unrelenting in its campaign against Dutch capital. In July SOBSI charged the government with 'passivity' in its policies toward the taken over Dutch enterprises, and demanded: (1) that government supervision be extended to those Dutch enterprises which 'have not yet been taken over up to now'; (2) that the government set up advsiory boards for the management of the taken over enterprises, with organized labor to have representation in these boards; and (3) that the government resist 'attempts by liberal groups' to convert the government-supervised enterprises into privately-run enterprises. Both SOBSI and PKI in coming years were to repeat the substance of these charges, especially reiterating the need for a kind of anarcho-syndicalist control by boards or committees of workers over the enterprises taken over from the Dutch and subsequently nationalized, in a manner somewhat similar to the pattern of workers' control over some Dutch enterprises during the Indonesian revolution.[32] In a further statement on the former Dutch enterprises in November 1958, the PKI urged that no compensation be paid to the Dutch owners until West New Guinea was handed over to the Indonesian government, and that Dutch capital in mixed (i.e. partially Dutch) enterprises also be expropriated; it again demanded that labor and peasant representatives be seated in the bodies supervising the expropriated enterprises and that the management of these be chosen from 'patriotic' people.

But throughout its campaign against 'imperialist' capital the PKI in 1958 was also concerned to portray itself as the common man's friend and as the champion of those political liberties which safeguarded its own security. Thus it sought to attach amendments to the government's draft budget bill for 1959 which would increase the basic wage of government servants and reduce the price of medicine. In March 1958, party spokesmen urged drastic revision in the export certificate system, which they charged had led to soaring prices in such basic necessities as rice and textiles. The organizational and production problems of the Indonesian economy were far more complex than the palliatives suggested here by the PKI, but the party unquestionably proved itself popular by these proposals. Fully realizing its growing electoral strength, also in such areas beyond Java as South Sumatra, the island of Riau, and even in Central Borneo,[33] the party at its national conference in July 1958, sent a telegram to premier Djuanda and other cabinet ministers demanding that new parliamentary elections be held, since postponement of the second general election 'would mean violation of the people's fundamental rights'.[34] The minor reshuffle of the Djuanda cabinet, carried out in June 1958, met with PKI approval, mainly because a radical nationalist, Muhammad Yamin, was added to the cabinet as Minister of State, but the party also continued to urge a *gotong royong* (mutual cooperation) cabinet, in which all parties including the PKI would be included, and in November 1958, demanded another cabinet reshuffle to that end. It might be noted *inter alia* that the PKI increasingly came to use the term *gotong royong* and, later, the term NASAKOM to express its continuing demand for a national coalition government.

Meanwhile, in the Constituent Assembly, which had held its first session on November 10, 1956, the polarization of partisan opinion, especially between the PKI and Masjumi, prevented any significant progress in drafting the Constitution. Here the issue came to be the ideological character of the state; Muslim groups demanded that recognition be given to Islam as the foundation of the nation's fundamental law, whereas secular nationalist and Marxist parties opposed this and adhered to the Pantjasila. (Formulated by Sukarno, Pantjasila, the official Indonesian ideology, includes five principles, i.e. belief in God, nationalism, democracy, social justice, and humanism or internationalism.) The PKI which had earlier expressed its approval of Pantjasila, urged incorporation of it in the Constitution,[35] thereby further underscoring its opposition to Muslim groups some of whose members regarded Pantjasila as a mere 'man-made' ideology of heretical implications. The stalemate was aggravated by the hostility between the Masjumi and the PNI, between certain leaders in the PNI and the PKI,[36] and by the split in PNI ranks which in August 1958, led to the establishment (or perhaps one should say re-establishment) of the *Partai Indonesia (Partindo)* by disgruntled PNI leaders.[37] All this discord made Constituent Assembly decisions on any but minor matters virtually impossible, and in his Independence Day message on August 17, 1958, Sukarno criticized the Assembly's 'endless' discussions. As if on cue the PKI four days later also criticized the slowness of the Assembly's work, proposed changes in the working methods, and also declared that it was even contemplating a resolution asking for the dissolution of the Assembly. Although the PKI criticism prodded the Assembly to greater action, the Islamic state issue continued to divide the membership of the body and ultimately contributed to its dissolution by Sukarno the next year.

The year 1958 saw two important plenary sessions of the PKI Central Committee and a party national conference. At the first of these plenary meetings (held from March 31 to April 3, 1958), M. H. Lukman, the PKI's deputy secretary-general, surveyed its successes in the recent regional elections, indicating that the party had polled more than 7·7 million votes and that 'it can definitely be stated that our party has jumped from fourth place in the parliamentary elections to first place in the whole of Indonesia in the DPRD (i.e. regional) elections'. Lukman also noted however that party regional organization still left a good deal to be desired and that there were symptoms which pointed to disturbed relationships in the united front, due to a 'deterioration' of the strength of 'the moderate forces' and to 'excesses in the election campaign'. In what seemed a bid for renewed unity with the PNI (which came closest to what the PKI called the 'moderate' forces), Lukman emphasized that the party's power should be demonstrated by successes 'which can be experienced also by the moderate forces'.[38] In his general report to this plenum, Aidit too noted the party's surge of strength in the regional elections, declaring the PKI to be 'the first party throughout the whole country', and reiterating the party's line of developing the progressive' forces, uniting with the 'middle of the road' forces and isolating the 'diehard' forces. Implementation of this line, however, depended on 'the extent of the political freedom of the proletariat and the other working people', for only with such freedom could the party carry on its propaganda and organizational expansion and work for the '100 per cent implementation' of Sukarno's *konsepsi* and for the 'completion' of the August 1945 revolution. The necessity of cooperation between the people and the army, while opposing the anti-Communists, was something which the party needed also to understand more fully, Aidit went on. The present difficulties with the PNI Aidit ascribed, without alluding to the PNI as such, to the 'inconsistent nature' of the national bourgeoisie, an inconsistency which he said had already been revealed by Lenin in 1905. Aidit cautioned against the 'diehard bourgeois elements' and the 'right nationalist elements' who were concluding 'hawker's bargains' among themselves, and who were promoting such slogans as 'contain Communism' or 'save Java from the red danger'.

Another 'anti-democratic policy' of the moment, according to Aidit, was the demand in some quarters to dissolve the political parties. Aidit regarded such a dissolution to be 'diametrically opposed to the democratic President Sukarno concept', but the fact was, of course, that Sukarno had become by this time a principal critic of Indonesia's multi-party system and had at various times in the past spoken of a 'burial' or a 'simplification' of the parties. Thus, on October 28, 1956, during the developing crisis of the second Ali Sastroamidjojo cabinet, Sukarno had already proposed that the political parties be 'buried', but there had been vociferous opposition from all political quarters, and in time Sukarno came to suggest a 'simplification' of the party system—an idea that found particular favor in some military circles. Whether Sukarno meant a dissolution of all parties, or only elimination of smaller ones, or a new kind of organizational unity between the major parties, was by no means clear. But Aidit made it a point to express his opposition to any tampering with the party system, while being careful not to attack Sukarno personally, and in fact giving the impression that mergers or 'burials' of parties would even be contrary to Sukarno's views. More likely Aidit was really attacking those military circles which favored, in effect, a thinly veiled military dictatorship. 'The policy of dissolving the parties cannot be interpreted as anything else but paving the way to brute force, to a fascist regime', Aidit declared, and although the people who advocate it 'say that their policy is based on "learning the lessons of the situation in Egypt",' the lessons of Egypt (where a military junta had recently replaced the Farouk monarchy) were in fact quite different. 'The Indonesian Communists and people stand firmly by their conviction that however bad democracy may be in practice, it is much better than fascism'.[39]

Two other points in this report by Aidit to the March-April, 1958, Central Committee Plenum deserve brief mention. One is the renewed emphasis on the danger of various 'middle-of-the-roaders' as well as some reactionaries, who were attempting to obtain private control over the enterprises taken over from the Dutch. 'The radical steps taken by the workers' when they took over these Dutch enterprises in December 1957, were allegedly being reversed by 'restraining' measures carried out by the government and these measures, according to Aidit, were 'welcomed by the reactionaries'. He urged full control by the government of the expropriated Dutch industrial establishments and estates, for only in this way could production be significantly increased to the benefit of all.[40]

One might remark here that the Indonesian government at this time was under considerable pressure from national bourgeois elements to allow seized Dutch business concerns of various types to pass into the hands of Indonesian private enterpreneurs, and the government had in fact been 'legalizing' quick and sometimes fictitious sales of such concerns by their former Dutch owners to Indonesian businessmen. This usually involved the smaller enterprises, but the PKI could, of course, see no reason why the economic and operational base of the indigenous capitalist element in Indonesia would necessarily have to benefit in any way from what the party conceived as a 'spontaneous anti-imperialist action by the workers'. Aidit's criticism of government policy toward the expropriated enterprises is worth stressing, because it was to become an increasingly important issue between the PKI and the government in subsequent years, especially after the military had begun to acquire a leading role in the management of these nationalized estates and plants.

The second matter to be noted in Aidit's report is the section in which continuing emphasis was placed on the party's 'Three-Year Plan' of organizational development and training. To bring the party 'in line with the fast developing revolutionary situation' required, according to Aidit, a 'strengthening' of the party's ties 'with the masses', which in its organizational application meant first of all an increased centralization of leadership and, secondly, establishment of additional levels of intermediate leadership in the party hierarchy. Declaring that the Secretariat of the Central Committee was in fact overworked, Aidit suggested 'electing an Executive Committee of the Political Bureau, a body which would carry out leadership during the times between Political Bureau meetings'. This would allow the Central Committee Secretariat to confine itself to 'daily routine work' and give the Politburo's executive committee day-to-day executive responsibility. Such a Politburo executive committee (consisting of Aidit, Lukman, Njoto and Sudisman) was approved by the plenum. Another 'question', stated Aidit, 'is that of making the contact between the Central Committee and the committees immediately beneath it closer'. To this end it was decided by the Politburo to set up 'Island Bureaus' and 'Island Committees' of the PKI to strengthen and coordinate the relationships between local branches in one island and between these branches and the Central Committee. Increased centralized control was apparently Aidit's aim in these proposals (which were formally ratified by the Party Congress in 1959); as he put it: 'The contact "from above down and from below up" must be carried out with the emphasis on the contact "from above down".'[41]

Solidification of party control in the regions, especially in the context of the civil war and provincial secessionist movements, was the PKI's principal organizational and tactical problem during the year and the Party Conference held from June 25 to July 3, 1958, had as its main task the 'discussion of the work of the Party in the regions'.[42] Attended by members of the Politburo, the Central Committee, and the Provincial, regional and the newly created Island committees, the Conference operated under the belief that new parliamentary elections would still be held in the future, and the various delegates gave reports on party strength in their respective regions to this purpose. The Conference was chaired by M. H. Lukman (Aidit was again in Europe to attend, among other gatherings, the Eleventh Congress of the Czechoslovak Communist Party), who touched on familiar subjects in his opening address: increased 'reactionary' activity to destroy the united front, the losses suffered by the middle-of-the-road groups and the 'diehard forces in the election' and the resulting fear in moderate ranks, and the anti-Communist campaign. The middle-of-the-road forces, declared Lukman, were showing a tendency 'to lean to the right' and this was due also to imperialist machinations which—now that the Masjumi and the PSI were discredited because of their leaders' involvement in the rebellions —had to look for other potential allies. Thus the party might find itself attacked by 'the nationalists' (a clear reference to the PNI) but in facing such attacks 'we have to determine which of those attacks should be firmly repulsed, considering the limits to which such things should be allowed to go'. Clearly the PKI intended to continue to show forbearance to the disgruntled elements of the PNI.

It was also significant that the final session of the Conference was devoted to a discussion of Mao Tse-tung's *On the Correct Handling of the Contradictions among the People,* and the decision of the Conference to study this treatise was 'enthusiastically welcomed' by cadres, according to one of *Harian Rakjat's* editors.[43] The Conference adopted some half dozen resolutions, of which the most important were: one expressing 'gratitude to the armed forces and the people' in their struggle against the secessionists and rebels; one called 'smoothing the preparations for a second parliamentary election', which urged the speedy staging of new national elections and the taking of 'firm steps' by the government against those who were allegedly sabotaging the elections; and one which demanded intensification of the study of Marxism-Leninism and specifically of Mao's essay on contradictions.

The resolutions by this Conference urging the holding of the second parliamentary elections deserves comment. On September 22, 1958, the Djuanda government announced that the next general elections, originally scheduled to be held in September 1959 (four years after the last elections as prescribed by the provisional constitution), would be postponed for not more than one year. This was a blow to the PKI, which, encouraged by the results of the recent regional elections, was confident that in the next general election it would emerge as the dominant party. As reason for the postponement the cabinet statement mentioned communications difficulties and the 'continued disorders' prevailing in various parts of the country. On September 24, 1958, the PKI Politburo issued a statement on the postponement, declaring that in view of the party's consistent demand that elections be held on schedule, the PKI 'can only understand the decision of the Djuanda cabinet to postpone the elections if it is genuinely aimed at securing order throughout the entire country within the period of at the most one year'. If this were not the case, the statement went on, the postponement could only be to the advantage of 'the imperialists and the right-wing parties' now supporting the rebel movements such as the PRRI and the Darul Islam. But by September 1960 (the deadline of Djuanda's postponement), the political situation had become even more unstable, and elections had been postponed again. The elections issue gave the PKI the opportunity to agitate in defense of democratic liberties, however, and while always acquiescing in the inevitable, it never abandoned its stand in the coming years of standing for the regular exercise of the people's franchise.

On November 19, 1958, when it had become quite clear that the central government was not going to collapse because of the PRRI revolt, when central government forces had in fact been making noteworthy successes, and when the power of the military in national political affairs was visibly increasing, another expanded plenary session of the PKI Central Committee was held in Djakarta. Its immediate purpose was to develop proposals to be presented to the party's sixth national congress next year, including revisions of the party program and constitution. In his principal address to this plenary session, Aidit showed that he had absorbed Mao's concepts of 'contradictions' as domestic and world wide political forces,[44] and had applied them to Indonesian conditions. The Indonesian people and the PKI, he declared, are confronting two 'basic contradictions', one between the nation and imperialism, the other between the peasantry and the landlords. The former was 'the most basic', being primarily a contradiction between the people and their enemies. Obtaining West Irian, combatting Dutch and American imperialist policies, and demanding that land belonging to landlords who have sided with the PRRI or *Darul Islam* be confiscated and given to the peasants, were all part of this 'most basic' struggle. However, there were also contradictions between the people themselves, e.g. between the workers and the national capitalists, between the peasants and anti-*Darul Islam* and anti-PRRI landlords and between 'the progressive forces and the middle of the road forces'. The latter contradictions were 'not basic' and must be settled by 'peaceful means', and unity among 'the people' must in the end prevail. The party must, therefore, continue to advance the cause of unity and prevent the establishment of fascist regimes, for 'democracy, even liberal democracy' is better than colonialism or Fascism, even though, Aidit added, liberal democracy was in a bankrupt condition in Indonesia. However, the conditions for a 'new' or 'people's' democracy were not yet ripe in Indonesia and therefore the party must work for the realization of President Sukarno's concept of 'guided' or Indonesian democracy, which is an advance over liberal democracy. (As Aidit had said earlier, in a statement to the press on October 24, 1958, the PKI 'accepts guided democracy on the understanding that what we are accepting is democracy and a democracy which is not liberal. The positive side of guided democracy lies in the fact that it is on the one hand against military dictatorship, and one-man dictatorship, while on the other hand being against liberalism'.) 'Guided democracy' should have as its goal, however, 'the guarantee of a political life for the people that is democratic and healthy'.

As for the Djuanda cabinet, the PKI's support had been a qualified one: the cabinet's progressive policies were endorsed by the party, and policies injurious to the people were opposed. Aidit still demanded a reshuffled cabinet and a program that ranged from 'enthusiastic support' of the country's economic rehabilitation and continuation of the struggle to regain West New Guinea to 'normalization' of conditions in the Republic of Indonesia and creation of a National Security Council (a body which presumably would direct national defense and in which the PKI hoped to be represented). Aidit also urged that the war against the PRRI rebels be made more 'popular', i.e. by putting into 'practice the principle of mobilizing the people in a great effort to wipe out the counter-revolutionary insurgents'. Presumably this meant the creation of a quasi-military bands of the people to help the army—something the army high command had already opposed. But organization of 'people's' resistance to the rebels nevertheless remained a part of the party's program in coming months.[45]

Above all, Aidit urged the 'extension of the political liberties of the people', an end to army-imposed suspension of political activity in some areas, and a lifting of the prohibition on strikes. Aidit reiterated the need to place the enterprises and industries taken from the Dutch under national control and under 'patriotic leadership', and to have 'all of the labor groups' participating 'in the planning of production and in the controlling of its administration'.[46]

In approving Aidit's report, the November 1958 plenum stressed that the party's policy must be '*dwitunggal*' (dual unity) between the army and the people, 'or in other words, the line of "the People help the Army" and "the Army helps the People",' as well as unity 'along the path of guided democracy' toward the '100 per cent implementation of the President Sukarno Concept'.[47] PKI strategy thus called for a balancing of growing army power by (1) unqualified endorsement of Sukarno,

(2) 'popular' participation by means of para-military groups in the army's struggle against the provincial rebels, (3) creation of a national security organ to direct overall policy composed of individuals endorsed by the party, and (4) insistent demands that 'political liberties' be restored or expanded. There is little question that the relative success of the Indonesian army (and of many of its commanders with known anti-Communist views) against the rebels, and the resulting prestige of the army generally, was causing considerable concern in PKI leadership. Aidit's November 1958 speech at the Central Committee Plenum in fact contains an anti-army strategy. As early as the end of March 1958, the Indonesian army had recaptured the Riau mainland on East Sumatra for the government and after an amphibious landing and assault on the West coast of Sumatra, the rebel capital of Bukittinggi fell on May 4. In June the army intensified its attacks in East Indonesia, especially in the northern part of Sulawesi, and by June 26 the city of Menado, a principal stronghold of rebels in league with the PRRI, was occupied. In subsequent months the advance slowed and intense guerilla activity followed. By the end of 1958 the rebels were operating in scattered units and the army controlled most of the principal cities in rebel territory. By that time the popularity of the army had never been higher and the pressure that it should assume a more commanding role in public affairs was never greater.

The issue of the army's power came to be closely interwoven with the problem of implementing Sukarno's concept of 'guided democracy'. The first few months of 1959 witnessed a good deal of public confusion over the implementation of Sukarno's schemes and the press carried reports of ceaseless conferences and wrangling in high places. It was primarily President Sukarno, using the National Advisory Council as a kind of forum to test his ideas of political reform, who provided the principal drive behind contemplated governmental reorganization. A change in parliamentary membership, including the addition of army officers to that membership, alteration of the party system, greater control by the executive—these were some of the many notions stirring public life. The PKI promptly reacted to many of these ideas. In his 1959 New Year's speech, Aidit—borrowing another phrase from Mao Tse-tung—branded as a 'paper tiger' the idea advanced by some in the country that a military dictatorship be established and the parties be dissolved.[48] On January 11, 1959, after a conversation with Sukarno, Aidit stated that the PKI favored 'guided democracy' and the inclusion of 'functional groups' in the Indonesian parliament, but had not yet considered the exact number of such functional representatives to be included.[49] Behind Aidit's statement lay the party's fear (shared by other political groups at the time) that too many functional representatives might diminish the party's influence in parliament. Thus the PKI, while endorsing 'guided democracy' generally, came to urge partisan control over functional parliamentary membership. In line with other parties, the PKI also appears to have been opposed to reserving as much as 50 per cent of parliamentary membership for functional deputies.

The PKI's hesitation inevitably became a political target for some of its enemies. On January 20, the editors of *Merdeka* (one of the nation's biggest dailies, nominally without party affiliation, but having close ties with certain PNI elements and national business interest groups) openly attacked the PKI. The attack was in a sense a reply to earlier, more veiled Communist criticism of *Merdeka* and the subsequent exchange revealed the continuing disenchantment of the PNI and national bourgeois elements over the PKI's growing strength. According to *Merdeka*, the PKI had been making a show of patience because the worsening political and economic conditions of the country under recent cabinets, supported by the PKI, strengthened the party's appeal among the masses. *Merdeka* also asserted that the PKI rejected the notion (recently advanced, under Sukarno's prodding, by the National Advisory Council) that half the seats in parliament be given to members from functional groups; instead the PKI was only willing to let the 'functionals' have one-third of the seats, 'for if in the next elections the PKI gets 50 per cent of the seats in parliament the 1/3 of the functional groupings has no meaning whatsoever. And this will ultimately bring victory for the PKI'. On January 22, 1959, *Harian Rakjat* replied, condemning *Merdeka* for its tactics of alleged intimidation, and two days later *Merdeka* returned to the attack by declaring that the PKI was hiding behind 'guided democracy' but was in reality secretly opposed to it. The battle of words was continued into February, with *Merdeka* charging that the PKI really wished to continue the existing system of 'liberal democracy' because under it the country was sinking into poverty and ruins on which the PKI wished to build its own power, and with *Harian Rakjat* charging that *Merdeka* was trying to play off Sukarno, the National Council and the Djuanda cabinet on the one hand, against the PKI on the other, notwithstanding the fact that the PKI was 'in full agreement' with 'guided democracy'.

The effects of this minor press war are difficult to gauge. Late in November 1958, the PNI chairman (Suwirjo) had suggested formation of a 'Pantjasila front' to realize Sukarno's 'guided democracy'. The NU categorically rejected the suggestion because of its anti-Islamic State implications, while the PKI organ *Harian Rakjat*, editorially wondered on December 4, 1958, if the front was not intended to be anti-Communist in character, since some of Suwirjo's explanatory remarks (e.g. his denunciation of the Madiun Affair) seemed to indicate that he did not wish the PKI to join the front. If Suwirjo hoped to increase the PNI's sagging prestige, he was, in any case, disappointed. It is not clear whether *Merdeka's* attack expressed PNI disappointment or even reflected a bid for Masjumi support. Undoubtedly the PKI looked with concern upon the inclusion of a large number of functional representatives, especially of representatives from the military, but the party was reservedly in favor of the 'guided democracy' principle (in line with its general strategy of the 'multi-stage revolution' for Indonesia, discussed below in Chapter IV) and it had generally supported the 'functional' National Advisory Council, where it had its own followers.[50] Moreover, the exact apportionment of functional representatives was a topic of contention in other parties, including the PNI, where such figures as former premier Wilopo (who also presided over the Constituent Assembly) complained of the vagueness of the guided democracy idea, of the constitutional function of the National Advisory Council, and of the idea of 'functional' parliamentary representation.[51]

The real nature of the PKI's concern over the next step in the development of 'guided democracy' was again revealed in a statement by M. H. Lukman in January 1959; he declared that the PKI strongly opposed the seating of army officers in parliament, unless they were elected to their posts by the people, especially by the voters among the armed forces membership. He also rejected again any idea of dissolution of the parties.[52] The PKI was, as ever, concerned about its organizational identity and freedom of action and expansion.

In all this the PKI seemed in effect to be arraying itself against Sukarno, for whom a 'merger' or 'simplification' of parties, as well as the inclusion by presidential appointment of army officers in the 'functional' segment of a reorganized parliament, were ideas really no longer subject to debate. But the PKI was careful never to attack Sukarno personally and in general the party took protective cover from the general and often confused public discussion of Sukarno's plans. On February 21, Sukarno announced that he had accepted a cabinet proposal to bring about a return of the 1945 Constitution, and that this would provide the necessary legal framework of 'guided democracy'. Sukarno also declared that he would ask the cabinet to draft a law simplifying the party system and a new election law. The 1945 Constitution provided for a Presidential cabinet and greatly increased executive authority. In deference to the wishes of political parties, it was originally decided that 'the political parties should fill every second name on their electoral lists with functional group representatives', which 'ensures proper representation for these groups but in a way which does not side step the political parties', as a PKI publication described it,[53] but this decision was soon to prove a dead letter, since elections had to be postponed. In any event, half the parliamentary deputies were to come from the functional groups, and 35 seats would be given to members of the armed forces by appointment, not by election as the PKI had wanted.[54]

It cannot be said that these February 21 decisions found generally enthusiastic approval among the parties, partly because they were in a sense arrogations of the functions of the Constituent Assembly. Although it was reported that the President and cabinet would officially request the Assembly to approve the return to the 1945 Constitution, there was a growing feeling in the country that such a request was but a formality and that the chief executive intended to have his 'guided democracy' and 1945 Constitution one way or another.[55] The PKI was well aware of this and after Sukarno's February 21 announcement it followed a policy of cautious endorsement of his plan, which after all—by recognizing party control over the electoral lists of functional group candidates for parliament, except the military—to a considerable extent met PKI interests. In any event the party decided not to fight the procedure of appointment of the military to the new parliament. In a statement on February 24 the PKI Politburo declared that 'returning to the 1945 Constitution opens the fullest opportunity in a constitutional way for the President to exercise direct leadership in the legislative as well as executive fields. . . . Since the very outset the PKI has determined its stand in supporting the President's concept and his guided democracy idea'.[56] But the same statement noticeably equivocated on PKI support by declaring that the idea of returning to the 1945 Constitution was only acceptable to the PKI if it was aimed at realizing 'for 100 per cent' the President's concept of guided democracy. The rumor that the PKI was lukewarm to the return to the 1945 Constitution thus had some grounds, and on March 20, the PKI second deputy secretary-general, Njoto, found it necessary to denounce 'certain people' who had been 'spreading the slander' that the PKI 'does not give its full support to guided democracy within the framework of the return to the 1945 Constitution'. The real aim of these people, declared Njoto, was 'to monopolize guided democracy, to become the sole owner of guided democracy'. 'As one of the democratic parties', Njoto went on, the PKI 'has full confidence in democracy in general and in guided democracy in particular' and he stressed 'the general elections as one of the prime democratic methods'.[57] It is clear that the party's support for Sukarno's schemes still hinged to a considerable degree on the expectation of a forthcoming general election in which functional candidates would appear on party electoral lists.

But this expectation was dashed by the events flowing from the subsequent deadlock in the Constituent Assembly over acceptance of the 1945 Constitution as the nation's fundamental law. On April 22, Sukarno addressed the Assembly with an impassioned plea to restore the 1945 Constitution which 'harmonizes best with the Indonesian atmosphere.' In the Constituent Assembly, however, principal Moslem parties (notably the Masjumi and the NU) held out for the inclusion in the preamble of the 1945 Constitution of the so-called 'Djakarta Charter', a document dating from June 1945 (preceding the original August 17, 1945 independence declaration) which stipulated that those who followed the Islamic faith had the obligation to abide by Islamic law. Other parties, including the PKI, opposed any explicit constitutional warrant for a particular religious belief, even though Sukarno and other government leaders anxious to resolve the deadlock were willing to accord official recognition to the 'historic influence' of the Djakarta charter on the 1945 Constitution.

No compromise over this issue, which had plagued the constitutional development of Indonesia since it became a state, was possible, and in the end the Constituent Assembly failed three successive times to pass Sukarno's April 22 proposals with the requisite majority and to accept the 1945 Constitution. But the President was ready. Already on June 2 General Nasution had issued a military decree banning all political activities in Indonesia in order to avoid the danger 'that political differences and fanaticism continue to drag on and on indefinitely' in connection with the discussion before the Constituent Assembly on the return to the 1945 Constitution. After the Assembly's failure to approve the return to the 1945 Constitution, Sukarno, on July 5, declared the Assembly dissolved and proclaimed 'the re-enactment of the 1945 Constitution for the whole Indonesian People and the whole Indonesian Fatherland'. On July 6 the Djuanda cabinet returned its mandate and within four days a new cabinet, called the *karya* or 'work' cabinet, had been formed. It was sworn in on July 10, now with Sukarno as concurrent President and Premier and with Djuanda as 'First Minister'. The cabinet's program pledged the meeting of the people's food and clothing needs, the establishment of security in the country and a fight against 'imperialism' (specifically to attain control over West New Guinea). A large number of army officers were among the new ministers and deputy ministers, although such fellow-travellers and radicals pleasing to the PKI as Professor Pryono, Sadjarwo and Professor Muhammad Yamin also returned, though in less important posts. With the ban on party activity the PKI and other parties felt they had to move warily, although Communist publications greeted the new cabinet with the well known line of support for 'progressive' policies and criticism of 'reactionary' measures. Realizing that the cabinet as such was headed by Sukarno and therefore as a body could not be attacked, the PKI increasingly was to follow the tactic of blaming a particular minister for a cabinet decision of which it disapproved.

This tactic became evident in the protests which arose in September and October 1959 over the promulgation of the so-called Presidential Ordinance No. 6/1959, which shifted authority from regional executive councils and vested it largely in regional heads appointed by the President and the Interior Minister.[58] The PKI, mindful of its growing influence in local government councils as demonstrated in the last regional elections, was most vociferous in opposing the measure, and the party newspaper *Harian Rakjat* was suspended for a week by the military because of its reporting of the opposition to the ordinance. The Supreme Advisory Council (formerly the National Advisory Council) deliberated upon the measure again on October 20, and the day after, when the Council had not been able to reach a decision, the PKI's Politburo issued a statement summarizing 'the very strong reactions of the people' against the ordinance and declaring that if the President decided to repeal the ordinance, this would be 'most conforming to the hopes of the people', and that the PKI 'will give its fullest support to this decision'.[59] In parliament the PKI deputy Nguntjik led the opposition to the measure. The party line was not only opposition to the decree as such, but against the threat of military power in conjunction with it and against the limitations on partisan political activity enforced by the military, particularly in former areas held by the rebels. As the PKI daily, *Harian Rakjat*, put it:[60]

In a situation when the people are so weighed down by difficult living conditions as they are today, it is really hard to understand that in some regions they are forbidden by the authorities to discuss the Presidential Ordinance No. 6/1959. The government has appealed to the people to support it in the realization of its program. . . . How will the people be able to support the government if they are not free to express their constructive opinions, and when the results of their struggle are abolished, merely to satisfy a handful of profiteers of the revolution?

Despite protests against the ordinance, no significant modifications were made in it, and central government authority in the conduct of the executive branch of regional and local government was decisively established; making a virtue out of necessity the PKI in the end acquiesced and a party publication claimed that the ordinance had really been 'a glorious victory for the party' since Communists were appointed as deputy heads in three out of the five primary level autonomous regions

in Java and seven Communists became heads of secondary-level
autonomous areas on the island.[61] But in view of its demonstrable
partisan strength in the regions the central government's assertion of
its powers continued to cause concern in the PKI, particularly so because
it became quite apparent in the months after the return to the 1945
Constitution that Sukarno and his cabinet were determined to minimize
the role of political parties generally in all levels of government. By
ministerial regulation the members of regional government executive
councils were to be free from party affiliation, government officials
having so-called F-class first-echelon rank or higher were prohibited
from holding any political party membership. Almost at the same time
the members of the Veterans' Legion, the principal veterans' organization in the country, were prohibited from conducting political activities
not in conformity with policy set by the government. Meanwhile the
army moved decisively to bring youth, labor, peasants' and women's
organizations in 'cooperative bodies' with the army, so as to allow the
army to exercise greater supervisory control over them. This measure
was especially a threat to the PKI and its front policy. Although the
ban on political activity, imposed on June 2, was lifted on August 1,
1959 (except for a number of areas 'recently liberated' from the rebels),
expression of partisan opinion and political life generally was increasingly
restricted.

The new parliament, convened after the return to the 1945 Constitution, had taken an oath to support that constitution, but then parliament
had been sent into recess, not to reconvene until October 1, while
Sukarno kept issuing decrees in considerable profusion. Even after
parliament returned, the decree issuing continued and when protests
arose Sukarno declared that he reserved the right to govern Indonesia
by decree 'even though this may not be the procedure stipulated in the
1945 Constitution', and that he intended to do so until the People's
Congress (the principal source of public power under the 1945 Constitution charged with the drafting of broad outlines of state policy) had been
convened.[62] Sukarno's justification was that if he was right and had the
power to re-enact the 1945 Constitution, he was also empowered to
regulate 'everything inherent in and closely related to' the decree that
established that constitution. On December 17 he replaced the state-of-
emergency decree of 1957 by a new state-of-war decree, whereby he
himself became the supreme 'state-of-war administrator', a position
which under the 1957 law had been shared by the heads of the three
military services.

Yet another important Presidential Decree (No. 7/1959) was
promulgated on January 11, 1960. This was the long heralded party

'simplification' decree. Among other provisions, it required parties to subscribe to the 1945 Constitution and the state ideology of *Pantjasila*, to follow only peaceful and democratic procedures, prohibited acceptance of foreign assistance, and demanded that parties must possess a minimum number of branches at various levels of local government throughout Indonesia in order to exist. The President was empowered to ban parties that did not satisfy these conditions or ban those parties whose leaders had participated in rebellions against the state unless these leaders had been specifically expelled from the party. Finally, on January 13, 1960, the President announced the formation of a National Front which would unite all 'revolutionary forces', including the political parties, for the completion of the national revolution 'through close cooperation with the government and other state institutions'.

The PKI was hostile to most of these developments but expressed its opposition cautiously. With reference to the simplification of the party system decree, M. H. Lukman declared that a general election was the appropriate way of reducing the number of parties, but he emphasized carefully that the PKI was not opposed *per se* to the government's intent to simplify the parties. Rather, Lukman stated, the existing election law could be amended so as to set a minimum percentage of votes which a political party would have to obtain in an election in order to provide it with official parliamentary representation. The PKI's ultimate stand toward the simplification decree, according to Lukman, would depend on the manner in which the decree was being implemented, particularly whether or not it restricted the rights of citizens 'to organize' themselves.[63] The PKI, as well as other parties, strongly disapproved of the government's decision to prohibit high government officials from holding party membership, and the PKI along with the Masjumi, NU and PNI supported a fruitless effort in parliament to get the government to reconsider the party ban decree for high officials.

In general the climate of 'guided democracy' in the months after the restoration of the 1945 Constitution seemed to become more threatening to the PKI. The announced formation of the National Front (which supplanted the National Front for the Liberation of West Irian, created as a public control device by the army) and the restriction on the political activities of the Veterans' Legion appeared to the PKI as a further threat to its organizational liberty, while the increasing vigilance being exercised by the military over the press and the suspension of *Harian Rakjat*, the PKI newspaper (a suspension which was to become monotonously frequent in the coming months), could only fill the party leadership with foreboding. The government's decision to 're-tool' the press, forcing it to subscribe to a definite state ideology and urging it to aid in 'creating calmness among the population', as Djuanda put it,[64] was a danger sign which no political party in Indonesia (where many parties used to have their own newspapers) could ignore.

In all this the strong hand of the army high command could be discerned, as well as Sukarno's skill in playing one center of power against the other. But well before 1959 came to an end it had become clear that executive and legislative branches of the government were now on a collision course. In the early months of 1960 the principal parties, including the PKI, moved to battle the executive on well chosen ground, namely the budget for 1960. It is clear that this common opposition to the government on the budget issue was inspired by the general dissatisfaction in parliament over the profusion of decrees which the President had been issuing. With almost complete unanimity the PKI, Masjumi and PNI opposed the government's intention to promulgate a budget in which expenses far outran revenues and insisted that the government was not to take on deficits and borrow without explicit parliamentary approval. PKI parliamentary deputies, Hutomo Supardan, Tjoo Tik Tjun, and J. Piry, sharply criticized the tremendous increases in state expenditure, the government's fiscal policy which would 'seriously intensify the burdens being borne by the people', the issuance of 14 new tax decrees 'without the consent of parliament', and the threat of 'continuous inflation' which would further nullify budget estimates and would mean that the actual deficit would be even larger than the government now indicated.[65] But government spokesmen in parliament proved adamant, and it became clear that parliament would reject the budget for the first time in Indonesia's national history.

Again Sukarno acted swiftly: on March 5, 1960, he issued a new decree stopping 'the present members of parliament . . . from carrying on their tasks', since existing 'cooperation between the Government and parliament . . . does not fulfill my hope'. Sukarno indicated that the composition of parliament would shortly be 'refreshed', and local military administrators explained to the press that this did not mean that parliament was 'dissolved', but only that it was 'frozen'. Protest from various quarters to the Presidential move was almost a formality; perhaps sharpest was the criticism of the PKI, although even now the Communist still voiced their general approval of *gotong royong* government as a convenient expression of its own 'national coalition' line and also as embodying the substance of 'guided democracy' as the party saw it. In a telegram to Sukarno or March 7, 1960, Aidit declared:[66]

Every patriot who upholds basic democratic principles very seriously regrets the action taken to put an end to the task and activities of the members of the People's Legislative Assembly (Parliament), an Assembly which was elected by the people and which has already been brought into conformity with the 1945 Constitution.

The Indonesian Communists regard this event as being one which seriously endangers democratic life in our country because it can be utilized by elements who are indeed deliberately trying to establish an anti-democratic and anti-people's regime, something which we think that you too do not favor.

Therefore, on behalf of the Central Committee and the entire membership of the Communist Party of Indonesia I submit two proposals to you: Firstly, that general elections for parliament be held during the course of this year, in keeping with the pledge once made by the government. Secondly, that the composition of Parliament be immediately renewed, based on the feelings of justice of the people, that is, in conformity with the balance of forces among the people, in conformity with the *gotong royong* spirit, and that this reconstituted Parliament should truly be only temporary in character, remaining in office only up to the time a Parliament is formed as a result of general elections held during the course of this year.

The President was not wholly to accede to these criticisms and requests; indeed, soon thereafter First Minister Djuanda declared that the next general elections would not take place until 1962. When on March 9, an Indonesian Airforce Mig-17 machine-gunned Sukarno's palaces in Djakarta and Bogor, and subsequently the government revealed the existence of a subversive organization which had the assassination of Sukarno and Nasution as its aim, public opinion seemed ready to accept further drastic government action. After consultations with party leaders Sukarno on March 27, 1960, announced a new *gotong royong* parliament, originally consisting of 261 members (130 from political parties and 131 from functional groups) all appointed by him. The Masjumi and PSI—the old enemies of the Communists—were excluded from membership in the new parliament on the grounds that they had not disavowed some of their leaders who were still heading the PRRI rebellion, and in his Independence Day address to the nation on August 17, 1960, Sukarno ordered the two parties to dissolve themselves within one month. A number of lesser organizations also disappeared from the roster of deputies. The PNI had 44 seats, the NU 36 and the PKI 30, but, as was evident from a look at the list of 'functional' members, Communist influence if not control extended itself also to at least 25 to 30 functionals, so that with about 55 to 60 followers the PKI had become one of the largest, if not the largest, party bloc in parliament.

Aidit, in a press interview on April 1, declared that the new parliament 'was better than having no parliament at all', that the PKI was still of the opinion that a parliament elected in democratic elections would be better and that these elections should be held that year (1960) as the government had previously promised. But he also called on 'the

Indonesian people' to defend the new parliament as an 'anti-PRRI' parliament, though he declared that if elections were held the PKI would have a larger number of seats than the 30 allotted in the new parliament. He admitted that the party would have the support of 20 members of the functional group, so that the PKI would command 50 votes in parliament.[67]

The size of the Communist bloc in the new parliament, the absence of the leading anti-Communist groups, and the ease with which Aidit and other PKI leaders continued to identify Communist aims with newly promulgated ideological rationales for national development, such as Sukarno's 'guided democracy' and the more recent 'Political Manifesto' (Manipol),[68] all increased the alarm in the ranks of Muslim groups, especially in the NU, among army officers and in the Protestant and Catholic confessional parties (which had been given six and five seats in the new parliament respectively). Opposition crystallized in the formation of a 'Democratic League' which questioned the constitutionality of Sukarno's new hand-picked parliament and the influence of the PKI in it.[69] Though the government first denounced and ultimately banned the League, Sukarno was wise enough to heed the clamor and on June 17, 1960, he enlarged the membership of the new parliament from 261 to 283, the new additions coming primarily from anti-Communist religious circles.

In a sense Sukarno's June 17 decision was a fateful one for shortly thereafter, as a result of its famous 'evaluation' of the Djuanda government published on July 8, an open rupture developed between the PKI and the army, and the Communist party entered on a new and critical phase in dealing with its political enemies. (Various aspects of this are described in chapter VI, below.) For the time being, however, the PKI could congratulate itself that it had stayed on the right side of the government in a period of rapid political changes, and, while maintaining its programmatic independence, had become an accepted part of the agencies of an increasingly monolithic and autocratic state. The party was, or was soon to be, prominently represented in the Supreme Advisory Council (in which Aidit and Njoto held seats), in the new parliament (where such party stalwarts as Aidit, Lukman, Njoto, and Njono had seats), in the presidium of the Provisional People's Congress, in the National Planning Council (in which Sakirman was a vice-chairman), in the leadership of the new National Front and in most levels of local government. While it had no member in the cabinet, it had its fellow-travellers there.

All this could not have been accomplished without the aid of Sukarno, who increasingly after 1959, and in the implementation of his concept of 'guided democracy' dexterously balanced the Communists against the anti-Communist army high command, now seeming to favor one then the other.[70] At the same time party leaders increasingly realized after the return to the 1945 Constitution that the PKI was becoming a bird in a gilded cage, that despite all official recognition of its influence and position the party was more and more being circumscribed by policy decisions which either originated in or were implemented by, the party's enemies in the army high command and that independence of action was becoming more and more illusory. Thus the party had achieved increased power by its identification with nationalistic and Socialistic ideas in 'guided democracy' but having thus marched in lockstep fashion with the new authoritarian and collectivist tenor of Indonesian political developments, the PKI found by the middle of 1960 that it had in a real sense also become the prisoner of these developments.

Illustrative was the party's position toward Presidential Decree No. 10/1959, dated November 16, 1959, which provided that as of January 1, 1960, Chinese retailers, distributors and middlemen would be banned from the rural areas of Indonesia with compensation to be paid for their properties. The operations of these Chinese were to be taken over by Indonesian cooperatives. This measure, taken in line with the ongoing 'Indonesianization' of the national economy, and reflecting longstanding dislike of the Chinese traders and moneylenders in Indonesia, created serious diplomatic tensions with the Peking government and led to various incidents of violence, as Chinese traders, egged on by Red Chinese diplomatic officials from Djakarta, refused to depart from their rural business establishments. The Presidential decree merely confirmed a similar measure promulgated by Trade Minister Rachjat Muljomiseno in May 1959, which had led to a spate of orders in July and August by local army commanders requiring Chinese to quit their former residences and closing certain areas to them. These orders had created great resentment among Chinese.

The subsequent wave of anti-Peking feeling in the national press greatly embarrassed the PKI and it had to steer a cautious course in its criticism of decree No. 10/1959, always being careful to place the necessity of continuing friendship between Djakarta and Peking in the foreground of the argument. A Politburo statement of November 22, 1959, recognized that the Indonesian government 'is fully entitled to introduce a regulation concerning foreigners', while at the same time 'the government of a friendly state, in this case the Chinese People's Republic, is fully entitled to request that the reasonable rights of its citizens in Indonesia be protected . . . '.[71] The Politburo statement went on to attack not the government, but first of all the implementation of the decree by certain military authorities and the 'anti-Chinese sentiments and demagoguery about Socialism' spread by Masjumi and PSI party newspapers. Following its usual line of being more nationalists than the nationalists the Politburo statement then criticized the decree for not specifying how the business enterprises left by the departing Chinese traders could be successfully integrated into the national production process so as to benefit all the nation, while the departing traders themselves were being rendered unproductive, having been told by the government 'to go and live without any definite means of livelihood'. The Politburo also criticized the fact that under the decree the military were not prevented from removing foreigners at will 'for reasons for security'.

As the press campaign against Peking and the Chinese traders increased in intensity in the closing weeks of 1959 (a campaign, it may be noted, left virtually free from any interference by the military censor), the PKI too became the target of sharp attacks for attempting to defend the Chinese point of view. Anti-Communist papers published an alleged secret PKI 'Special Instruction on the Fate of Chinese Comrades' which presumably urged cadres to sabotage decree No. 10. M. H. Lukman, in a statement on December 1, 1959, repudiated the authenticity of the 'special instruction,' excoriated the 'right-wing papers' for publishing 'slanders' about the PKI, affirmed the party's role in opposing 'foreign investment' (mentioning in this connection Stanvac, Caltex and other foreign-owned petroleum companies, but not Chinese capital in Indonesia), and announced that the PKI would take 'those newspapers spreading falsifications to court'.[72] The press war against the PKI continued, however, and party organs returned again and again to the line that the 'misguided and dangerous chauvinism and racialism against foreigners of Chinese origin' reflected the influence of 'U.S. imperialists' aided by certain national business interests anxious to displace the Chinese.

Early in January 1960, in a lengthy oration in parliament, PKI deputy Thaher Thajib defended the small Chinese traders and their capital which, in his opinion, the government should consider as a 'progressive potential' in the development of the country and suggested devising means of channelling this capital to the field of cottage and middle industry. Thajib pointed out that although the PKI was aware that the purpose of decree No. 10 was to strike 'at the progressive groups', his party did not oppose the measure since proper implementation of the decree could render it useful to the industrial growth of the nation. However, there were a number of cabinet members who 'appeared to like to hit at small capital', declared Thajib, that is at capital which is not at all an enemy 'instead of hitting or sweeping clean big foreign capital investment', which has been openly behind the PRRI insurrection.[73] Several weeks later the PKI deputy and Central Committee member, Jusuf Adjitorop, reiterated this view in parliament, stating that the PKI did not oppose decree No. 10 if it was really intended to reserve the retail trade for Indonesian cooperatives in the rural areas, but that instead the government had not been 'serious' in implementing the decree and was only seeking an opportunity to get the Chinese to leave the country 'without it having to spend any money'.[74]

Throughout 1960 hundreds of Chinese left Indonesia for the Chinese People's Republic and their departure seriously dislocated the distributing trade in a number of areas not only in Java, but also in Kalimantan (Borneo), thus giving substance to the PKI's warnings about the improprieties in the implementation of decree No. 10. During the first months of 1960 the diplomatic tension between Djakarta and Peking was high and the *Peking Review* of July 12, 1960, detailed how Chinese in West Java had been wounded, beaten up and intimidated by Indonesian military acting 'at the instigation of certain influential Indonesian circles'. However, after initial difficulties, Peking and Djakarta resumed their diplomatic review of the entire position of Chinese in Indonesia in the latter half of 1960, in light of the previous treaty between the two governments on dual citizenship. By the end of the year further agreement had been reached on the implementation of the dual nationality treaty, and this was followed by a formal treaty of friendship and cultural exchange between the two countries on April 1, 1961.[75] During this diplomatic review the PKI continued to take up the cudgels for the 'citizens of Chinese origin', insisting on 'the principle of equal rights for all citizens regardless of origin'.[76]

The controversy over decree No. 10 showed the typical dilemma the PKI has been in since the ascendancy of 'guided democracy'. To oppose the decree outright was out of the question since (1) it had been a matter of party strategy always to endorse, as much as possible, government policy in principle, especially its nationalistic approach in economic matters and in foreign affairs; and (2) it might open the possibility of a direct conflict with Sukarno. At the same time the party felt bound to attack the anti-Chinese character of the decree, especially when the Peking government, ever mindful of the strategic importance of the 'overseas Chinese' in Southeast Asia, decided to denounce it. The PKI could hardly disavow the Chinese Communist regime on political and ideological grounds, quite apart from the fact that the party was deeply indebted to People's China for its assistance to Indonesian Communism in the difficult days following the Madiun insurrection and during the

1955 national election. Within the context of its approval of guided democracy the party could not criticize the intent of the decree to 'Indonesianize' the national economy and to oppose the role of foreign capital; yet it realized that Peking expected it to speak out on behalf of the Chinese traders and their financial interests.

In balancing these conflicting demands the party essentially followed a policy that had been consistently typical since the second Ali Sastro-amidjojo cabinet: it approved the decree in principle, but attacked its implementation; it voiced general support for the government, but criticized the conduct of a cabinet minister or ministers and army officers; and it always tried to place the larger issue of international amity and preservation of democratic rights in the foreground when discussing any controversy. In criticizing not the government as such but rather individual ministers the PKI also reenforced its 'national coalition' line, suggesting that effective implementation of the government's policies could only occur if ministers who truly had the 'confidence of the people' (i.e. ministers who were PKI members or otherwise followed the party's program) were in the cabinet. Despite a heavy barrage of criticism from many political quarters and from much of the press, the PKI kept on trying to stress the importance of good relations with Peking and the rights of the Chinese traders and Chinese citizens in the country, and when at last Peking proved more amenable and a new agreement on the dual nationality question was reached, the party's position—in the midst of a sudden new aura of friendship between the two countries—seemed in no small measure to have been vindicated. But the incident did show how severely circumscribed PKI policy had now become by the very nationalistic and authoritarian political climate in the country in which the party had been able to grow.

The PKI was soon to experience further restriction in an area where it had been quite free with its advice and criticisms—the field of economic policy. The effects of the political instability, of the provincial rebellions and of the doctrinaire, collectivistic philosophy of economic development with its proliferation of state controls had come to call the future viability of the Indonesian economy ever more into question.[77] Stagnation in production, mismanagement of distribution, a nefarious fiscal policy, a rampant inflation, and an ever-rising cost of living marked by recurrent shortages of such basic necessities as rice, textiles and kerosene all gave ample opportunity to the PKI to demand reforms. For the party the whole context of Indonesia's economic crisis was, of course, the hold of 'imperialists' and landlords on the national economy ('the target of the struggle of the Indonesian people today is the imperialists and the landlords and not the Indian, Arab and Chinese shopkeepers', as Aidit had put it in May 1959). The party's general line was that 'the vast majority of the Indonesian people have not enjoyed . . . an improvement in living conditions as a result of the August 1945 Revolution'.[78] To meet the basic needs of food and clothing for the people, the party made various suggestions to raise agricultural production ('plough deeply, plant closely, more fertilizers, better seeds and better irrigation') and output of textiles ('all textile factories must be operated at full capacity, on a two or three-shift system, morning and night'), declaring that the latter could be accomplished 'if the textile workers are drawn into negotiations' and 'if they are invited to join in taking responsibility for maintaining output and for preserving the enterprises' (it may be noted again that establishment of 'workers' councils' and worker participation in the management of enterprises, especially the larger state controlled enterprises, always was a party panacea).[79]

In its New Year Message issued on December 30, 1959, the Politburo complained that 'there have as yet been no signs that the Government will take concrete, correct measures to reduce the burdens pressing down upon the people's living conditions'.[80] The Politburo statement specifically criticized the monetary devaluation in August 1959, which had halved the value of 500 Rupiah and 1000 Rupiah banknotes and froze bank deposits in excess of 25,000 Rupiah. Increasingly the party called attention to the landlord problem, especially in Java ('The peasants cannot possibly be called upon to work the land really intensively so long as the land is not their own possession'),[81] and published surveys revealing the extent of the concentration of ownership of land in the hands of a few. In April 1959, the party had held a 'national peasants' conference' to formulate a specific program for land reform which it urged with increasing insistence on the government in the following months. In January 1960, M. H. Lukman again questioned the government's ability to fulfill its announced program of meeting the basic needs of the masses, doing so with the party's usual 'approve the principle, attack the implementation' line:[82]

Although the program of the *carya* cabinet is a good one, namely to supply food and clothing to the people in the shortest possible time, to establish security for the people and the State, and to continue the struggle against economic imperialism and political imperialism, the people have in fact, right from the start, had their doubts as to the ability of the present Cabinet to implement this program, in view of the composition of the ministers who are the President's assistants, consisting in the main of persons whom the people do not know and whom the people do not directly support.

Lukman went on to criticize the sharp increases in kerosene and transportation costs which would only benefit the 'foreign imperialists' (i.e. the foreign oil companies), the increase in the number of taxes, and the excessively high amount (nearly 38 per cent) allocated in the 1960 state budget for security and defense needs. Lukman singled out the Ministers of Trade and of the Interior as particularly blameworthy, but concluded that 'the working cabinet has been in office for six months already, but during all this time there has been no sign that the Ministers in this cabinet are capable of implementing its programme'.

This was as sharp a critique as the PKI had ever levelled at a cabinet since 1955, but more was yet to come. On February 10, 1960, the Politburo issued another criticism of government economic policy, particularly calling the government to task for the steadily rising prices, for Presidential decree No. 10 (banning the Chinese traders from rural areas) which 'not only did not raise the level of production, but, on the contrary, caused stagnation and disturbed the flow of goods', and for raising transportation costs.[83] Once again the government's policies toward the enterprises taken over from the Dutch were criticized, for these enterprises, now under state control, 'were chasing after profits no less than private enterprise'. The main trouble, as the Politburo statement had it, was that 'the new orientation spoken of in the Political Manifesto had not yet been implemented' and that 'despite all the talk about having a "guided economy" liberalism was still holding sway over the economy and finances'. The party, therefore, urged the government to increase wages, lower taxes, initiate land reform, improve the distribution of goods, make proper use of all foreign earnings and assist the private national enterprises. In the following weeks party spokesmen elaborated on these and related themes.

When, therefore, on July 8, 1960, the Politburo published yet another 'evaluation' of the cabinet, again criticizing among other things, the government for not having met the people's food and clothing needs, and for allowing 'bureaucratic capitalists' imbued with the profit motive to control the state enterprises, including the enterprises taken over from the Dutch, it could hardly be said that the party was saying something new. But this time, as will be indicated more fully in chapter VI, the army had had enough of PKI attacks on the government and on its own policy toward the rebels (the July 8 statement had also criticized security policy). The measures taken by the army against the PKI made further criticism of government economic policy (or of any other aspect of policy) dangerous and seemingly impossible in the future. Thus, by the middle of 1960, the party saw yet another problem area of national life where it had spoken out freely in the past (and where, in view of the stagnating if not deteriorating economy, it had managed to make quite an impression on public opinion) limited as future to discussion. From now on only cautious generalities seemed permissible as local army commanders appeared to work overtime to scrutinize party statements and publications.

It is perhaps ironic that this turning point in the party's history came so shortly after it had managed to reach the apogee of its strength thus far. In a real sense the Sixth National Congress of the party (September 7 to 14, 1959) marked that apogee. Carefully prepared by another plenum of the Central Committee,[84] and enlivened by the presence of Sukarno who had personally intervened with the military to let the affair be held,[85] the Sixth Congress approved a new party program and constitution (discussed in greater detail in chapter V below), heard Aidit declare[86] that there were now 1·5 million party members (as compared to a little over 165,000 at the time of the fifth congress in 1954) and listened to congratulatory messages from Australian, Bulgarian, Hungarian and East German, Italian, and Cuban Communist party delegates. Aidit, Lukman and Njoto, were elected chairman, first and second Vice-Chairman of the Central Committee, respectively. Elected to the Politburo were Aidit, Lukman, Njoto, Sakirman and Sudisman (who constituted the Politburo's executive committee), along with Jusuf Adjitorop (perhaps the fastest rising PKI leader today) and Njono as Politburo candidate-members. Elected to the Secretariat of the Central Committee were all the principal second echelon party leaders, including Adjitorop, Anwarkadir, Amir Anwar Sanusi, Djokosudjono, Peris Pardede, Siswojo, Sudisman and Karel Supit. Sudisman and Adjitorop were named head and deputy head of the Secretariat of the Central Committee.[87] According to the official party history today, 'all forces of Indonesian Communists took part in the congress', listing them as follows:[88]

The 'force of 1926' is one which established the party in 1920 and which staged the first national rebellion under Communist leadership in 1926; the 'force of 1935' is one which reestablished the party after the failure of the 1926 rebellion; the 'anti-Japanese Force'; 'the force of the August, 1945 Revolution'; and the 'Force of 1951' or the force which reconstituted the party after the raging 'white terror' of the 'Madiun incident' of 1948 and the 'August Razzia' of 1951. As was completely explained by Comrade D. N. Aidit: 'Indonesian Communists name this Congress the 'Congress of Glorious Unity' because this Congress definitely demonstrated the great unity of Communists and the working people of Indonesia.

It was undoubtedly the largest congress ever staged by the PKI and the one that received the greatest attention from the Communist movement outside Indonesia. In the resolutions approved by the Congress a strong international note was heard. There was, for example, a demand for the dissolution of SEATO; a condemnation of the murder of the Iranian agitator Ali Olowi and of the firing of Iranian workers; a demand for the release of Fajarullah Helou, 'Hero of Lebanon', for the release of Manolis Glezos and of Alvaro Cunha (General Secretary of the Communist Party of Portugal); as well as a resolution urging support for 'the Algerian people' in their 'struggle'.[89] More 'national' resolutions included condemnation of the Dutch for their continued occupation of West New Guinea, demands for reductions in prices, land reform, the smashing 'of the remnants' of the PRRI and the confiscation of property of 'Kuomintang persons', and support for Sukarno's 'Political Manifesto' (which must be made 'the basis' for assisting and supporting the *karya* cabinet).[90] In his official report on the Congress Aidit noted how the people had prepared for the congress by means of participating in numerous public works projects, resulting in the recovering and constructing of '3,249 km of roads, 985 km of drains, improving and constructing 2,280 houses, 80 school buildings . . . 5,119 public lavatories' and in the killing of 186,698 field mice.[91]

In the report Aidit outlined again the theoretical and tactical position of the party. The people need democracy more than ever 'since it is under constant threat as is the case in many newly independent Asian-African countries' (an allusion to the military dictatorships that have been emerging in the new Asian-African nations). The national bourgeoisie has not been able to solve the pressing problems of development while at the same time 'the masses of people' increasingly demand advances in their living conditions. It is, therefore, imperative to prevent a 'sliding' into military and personal dictatorship and hence inclusion of the Communists in the cabinet is the only solution, although not necessarily a panacea:[92]

The demand for the formation of a 'gotong royong' cabinet now is the summing-up of the experiences of the Indonesian people themselves, who in spite of the frequent changes of cabinets have seen for themselves that no cabinet without Communists, not even a cabinet supported by the Communists, can succeed in bringing about a change in the life of the people. Indonesian Communists have always felt themselves responsible for this situation in Indonesia and on the basis of this they demand participation in the government. . . . Of course, participation of Communists in the government is not to be looked upon as infallible medicine . . . nevertheless to let Communists participate in the government is a positive sign, i.e. a sign that all democratic and patriotic groups are deeply aware of the gravity of the situation . . . a cabinet with Communists is sure to arouse new hopes, create new possibilities and fresh enthusiasm among broad masses of the people.

The nation must continue to combat imperialism and feudalism, urged Aidit, and the Sixth Congress declared Dutch and American imperialism to be the principal enemies, while in the fight against feudalism it stressed that the division of the crop between peasant cultivator and landlord (hitherto usually on a fifty-fifty basis) should be changed to a new ratio, 60 per cent going to the cultivator and 40 to the landlord. The economic crisis in the country reflects the continuing strangulation of the nation by foreign imperialist capital and in liberating the economy, indeed, in implementing the general party line the party's policy remains the same: develop the 'progressive' forces, unite with the 'middle-of-the-road' forces and isolate the diehards. The last named 'have greatly deteriorated', stated Aidit, while the progressives have grown stronger. The party must continue to support the 'Political Manifesto' of President Sukarno, and in the implementation of the Manifesto by the cabinet the party should encourage the cabinet's 'progressive' policies, and 'oppose those ministers whose policies are harmful to the people'.[93] To promote the expansion of the party a second 'Three-Year Plan' was approved by the Congress (the first had been adopted at the Central Committee's Plenum at the end of June 1956, it will be recalled, and inaugurated the following August) and the Congress affirmed that 'expanding membership can only be considered correct if it is obtained in the first place through mass action and if it is continuously being followed up by intensive education . . .' A further intensification of 'Marxist-Leninist' education is the best way to combat 'subjectivism', against which 'the Congress declared war'. In view of the rapid political changes the party must have organizational flexibility so that it can 'push the development of the situation forward'.[94]

So much for the decisions of the Sixth Party Congress. In the period since then, and particularly since the middle of 1960, the party frequently found it increasingly difficult to maintain itself, until the Malaysia issue in the course of 1962 provided it with a new momentum. Before dealing with the threats to the PKI position and with its place on the Indonesian scene in the past year or so (detailed in chapters VI and VII) it seems first desirable to probe a little more deeply into the theoretical founda-tions of the PKI and to examine its organizational structure.

PART II

*PARTY PROGRAM AND
ORGANIZATION*

CHAPTER IV

THEORETICAL FOUNDATIONS *

THE INTERNATIONAL ADVANCE of Communism in our time is in no small measure due to the apparent flexibility with which Marxist and Leninist concepts have been applied—often with startling selectivity—to the problems of the newly emergent and underdeveloped countries. While generally observing all strictures against 'revisionism' and 'subjectivism' Communist leaders in most of these new nations, Indonesia included, dip with ease into the reservoir of the thought of Marx and Lenin for a justification of their particular tactics, pointing out that Communist thought itself invites flexibility and adaptability. Stalin could quote with approval Lenin's dictum that 'We do not regard Marxist theory as something complete and inviolable; on the contrary, we are convinced that it has only laid the cornerstone of the science which Socialists *must* further advance in all directions if they wish to keep pace with life'.[1] The word 'creative', as applied to Marxism and Leninism, has in recent years received an unparallelled emphasis in Communist pronunciamentos. Thus, the 1960 Moscow Statement reiterated the principle of the 1957 Declaration and Peace Manifesto that 'Marxism-Leninism demands creative application of the general principles of socialist revolution and socialist construction, depending on the specific historical conditions in the countries concerned, and does not permit of a mechanical copying of the policies and tactics of the Communist Parties of other countries'. In his eulogy of Mao Tse-tung, on the publication of the fourth volume of Mao's *Selected Works*, Lin Piao, vice-chairman of the Chinese Communist Party's Central Committee, declared that 'Comrade Mao Tse-tung creatively applied and developed Marxism-Leninism' with 'the greatest ingenuity and dexterousness in the art of struggle. . . '.[2] The Indonesian Communist Party program, adopted at the party's Seventh Special National Congress in April 1962, echoes this emphasis on creative flexibility in the application of Communist theory: 'Every nation will take its own path to Socialism based on the development of the national situation and on the political, economic and cultural conditions'.[3] Whatever the significance for the world Communist movement of the present theoretical and tactical differences between Moscow and Peking, the operative

* This chapter is a revised and expanded version of my article 'Lenin, Mao and Aidit', *The China Quarterly*, April-June, 1962.

term 'creative application' has retained its value as a touchstone of successful Communist theory and strategy in various countries of the world today.

Since 1948 and since the more or less simultaneous promulgation of the PKI's 'New Road for the Indonesian Republic' resolution and the appearance of younger Communist leaders like Aidit and Lukman in the *Sajap Leninis*, the party has consistently articulated the same theoretical premises; indeed, it has generally had the same basic program and strategy. Prior to 1948, and especially prior to the outbreak of the Indonesian Revolution, ideological training of party members occurred haphazardly, if at all, and a lack of adequate theoretical insight characterized virtually all the Indonesian Communist leaders. The exception was Tan Malaka, whose ideas, as will be indicated below, displayed a strong Leninist influence and in a significant sense foreshadowed the principles by which the party has abided since 1948.[4] Aidit is undoubtedly correct when he remarks that prior to the outbreak of the Indonesian revolution in 1945 Indonesian Communists were virtually unacquainted with Lenin's works and that during the revolution itself Lenin was read only by those party leaders who had a command of English or Dutch— the only languages in which translations of Lenin's works were then available in Indonesia. To this fact Aidit contributes the 'failure' of Communist activity in the 1945–1948 period, and indeed, of the revolution as a whole, remarking that it was a 'revolution without Lenin'.[5] For Aidit, the lesson to be drawn from the past experiences of Indonesian Communists 'is the importance of revolutionary theory', for only if armed with correct theory can the party save itself from difficult circumstances and move steadily forward.[6]

Considering his emphasis on theory it is not surprising that the most important theoretician which the PKI has produced is Aidit himself. Building upon Muso's ideas and the 'New Road' resolution, Aidit has been the principal exponent and certainly the most prolific publicist on Marxism-Leninism in Indonesia. His ideas, though certainly influenced by the theoretical emphases and elaborations of Mao Tse-tung and of other Communist Chinese ideologues, are fundamentally Leninist in character. In this chapter three interlocking areas of Aidit's theory— areas which are the basis of the PKI program today—will be briefly examined, in the light of their Marxist-Leninist and Maoist antecedents. These are: (1) the concept of the two-stage or multi-stage revolution, and of the role of the bourgeoisie in that revolution; (2) the function of the peasantry; and (3) the role of the proletariat and of the party. Subsequently some consideration will be given to the question of revisionism in relation to the Sino-Soviet conflict and finally the current

PKI aims will be briefly analyzed in terms of the existing political-ideological order in Indonesia.

The Revolution and the Bourgeoisie. Since August 17, 1945, when Indonesians proclaimed their independence, Indonesia, according to Aidit has been in a two-stage revolution. The first stage, yet to be completed, is the 'bourgeois democratic' (now also called 'national democratic') revolution and involves the elimination of imperialism (i.e. the acquisition by Indonesia or West New Guinea, and more recently the 'crush Malaysia' campaign, destruction of 'counter-revolutionary' rebel movements in Indonesia, which the Dutch are accused of aiding, and the elimination of all 'imperialist' capital in the big foreign enterprises in Indonesia), of feudalism (i.e. promotion of land reform), and the establishment of democratic liberties (i.e. expression of partisan political opinion). The second or Socialist stage, which cannot be completed before the first stage is finished, will see the establishment of a 'just and prosperous' Socialist society in Indonesia. In mobilizing support for the completion of the first stage, the proletariat with the PKI in the vanguard, must seek the support of various non-proletarian groups, including the peasantry and the bourgeoisie, i.e. classes the richer strata of which are certainly capitalistic but which if carefully guided can collaborate with the proletariat and the PKI in a united front to complete the bourgeois-democratic phase of the revolution.[7]

Though party work among the peasantry must always be intensified since 'the essence of the Indonesian revolution is the agrarian revolution',[8] the bourgeoisie is of special importance in the first or 'bourgeois-democratic' phase of the revolution. Before describing Aidit's analysis of the bourgeoisie and its subdivisions it seems well to stress the long historic perspective of the potential revolutionary role of the bourgeoisie and of the concept of the two stage revolution in Communist thought.

Both Marx and Engels refer to the revolutionary potential of the bourgeoisie in conjunction with the proletariat. In his work, *The Class Struggles in France, 1848 to 1850*, Marx had described the 'petty bourgeois, the middle classes in general, stepping alongside the proletariat' in defense of 'democratic republican institutions', and shortly before, in the Communist Manifesto' Marx and Engels had already pointed out that the very dynamic of the class struggle forces the bourgeoisie to turn to the proletariat for help and indeed, 'a portion of the bourgeoisie goes over to the proletariat' as the process of disorganization in the ruling class of a capitalist society reaches its zenith. Engels, in *The Peasant War in Germany*, noted how the liberal bourgeoisie of Europe on the eve of the revolutions of 1848 'was still revolutionary,

called itself socialist and communist, and clamored for the emancipation
of the working class'. In describing the unrest in Algeria in 1848 for the
English Chartist newspaper *Northern Star*, Engels touched on a specific
dialectic basic to the concept of the two-stage revolution in underdeveloped countries today when he indicated that 'the modern bourgeois with civilization, industry, order and at least relative enlightenment
following him is preferable to the feudal lord or to the marauding robber
with the barbarian state of society to which they belong'.[9]

While Marx's disillusionment with the bourgeoisie tended to mount
over the years (his *Eighteenth Brumaire of Louis Bonaparte* and *The Civil
War in France* well express his disenchantment), the notion that the
bourgeoisie, or at least a portion of it, can be an ally of the proletariat,
that its dominance is preferable to the old feudal order, but that the
wavering of the bourgeoisie might again make it into a reactionary force
remained influential. Lenin explicitly adopted the course of bourgeois
revolution as 'precisely a revolution that most resolutely sweeps away
the survivals of the past, the remnants of serfdom (which include not
only autocracy but monarchy as well)', which is 'why a *bourgeois*
revolution is *in the highest degree advantageous to the proletariat*', indeed,
why '*in a certain sense* a bourgeois revolution is more *advantageous* to
the proletariat than to the bourgeoisie', since the very inconsistencies in
the position of the bourgeoisie even during its own bourgeois revolution
will become more clearly revealed.[10] 'That is why', wrote Lenin, 'the
more consistent the bourgeois revolution is in its democratic changes,
the less will it limit itself to what is of advantage exclusively to the
bourgeoisie.'[11] But on the other hand the inconsistent and the wavering
nature of the bourgeoisie will also reveal the more consistent democratic
position of the proletariat all the more fully. Thus, he argued, in a
sense the proletariat in its alliance with the bourgeoisie cannot lose:
a consistent championing of democratic principles by the bourgeoisie
can only benefit the proletariat directly, while if the bourgeoisie wavers
and becomes inconsistent the antagonistic position of the proletariat as
the only champion of true democratic principles more fully reveals itself.

As was indicated in chapter I, the policies of the Comintern reflected
these Leninist ideas. As early as 1920 the Comintern's theses, adopted
at its Second Congress, declared that 'For the overthrow of foreign
capitalism, which is the first step toward revolution in the colonies, the
cooperation of the bourgeois nationalist revolutionary element is useful'.
Hence, these theses went on, the revolutionary development in the
colonial areas would, 'in its first stages' not be Communist, although
leadership should be in the hands of the Communist vanguard; but the
revolutionary masses in the colonies would go through 'successive

periods of development of revolutionary experience'. Even after Lenin's death the concept of the multi-stage revolution and the place of the national bourgeoisie in that concept continued to be Comintern policy. Thus in the program adopted at its Sixth Congress on September 1, 1928, one reads that 'as a rule transition to the dictatorship of the proletariat in these countries (i.e. colonial and semi-colonial countries) will be possible ony through a series of preparatory stages, at the outcome of a whole period of the transformation of the bourgeois democratic revolution into socialist revolution. . . '.

Some early Indonesian Communists had tended to disparage this view. With the notable exception of Tan Malaka, whose appreciation of the importance of the non-proletarian and petty bourgeois elements in revolutionary development will be dealt with presently, Indonesian Communists around 1920 seemed to feel that a socialist state could be established directly in Indonesia. In back of this belief lay the conviction that the bourgeois elements in Indonesia were of foreign origin (i.e. Dutch and Chinese) and that, therefore, the Indonesian revolution should combine the processes of national liberation and the establishment of a proletarian order. Thus the Indonesian revolution was considered to be of a higher order than that of other Asian countries where an indigenous middle class of some size and importance did exist.[12] The Comintern condemned this 'left deviationism' of the early Indonesian Communists and today Aidit shows that he has taken the Comintern's strictures to heart. For the multi-stage revolutionary process, and above all, the role of the bourgeoisie in it, is a key element of his strategy which must be fully understood before one can appreciate the general line and policy of the PKI today. Otherwise one 'cannot possibly understand thoroughly why, for example, the nature of the Indonesian Revolution at the present time is not socialist but bourgeois democratic, why the PKI supports the "concept" of President Sukarno, why it supports the idea of "guided democracy" and the idea of "back to the 1945 Constitution" . . .'.[13] Aidit's manner of interpreting Sukarno in Leninist terms has now also extended to Sukarno's 'Political Manifesto' (Manipol), currently the official ideological foundation of Indonesian state policy. In this Manipol Sukarno divided his nation's objectives into so-called short-term and long-term objectives. The former are: to satisfy the basic needs of the people, to establish security and to struggle against imperialism (in short the program of the cabinet which took office with Djuanda as 'First Minister' in July, 1959). The latter are: to establish a just and prosperous society, eliminate imperialism everywhere and establish world peace. For Aidit the short and the long term objectives of the Manipol are in conformity with the stages of the

Leninist revolution, since the *Manipol* 'clearly states that the character of our revolution now is national and democratic' inasmuch as it seeks to liquidate imperialism and the vestiges of feudalism and 'because it is against military dictatorship and personal dictatorship'. But the future of the revolution according to Aidit's interpretation of *Manipol* is 'an Indonesian socialist society'.[14]

At this point a slight deviation in Aidit's thinking from the main stream of Leninism (including Maoism) may perhaps be noted. Leninism, especially as reflected in early Comintern decisions, holds that there are several stages, not just two, in the development toward socialism in colonial or semi-colonial countries;[15] but Aidit has thus far stressed a two-stage revolutionary course, consisting of a bourgeois-democratic or national democratic and a socialist phase. The deviation is not a major one—Lenin himself on occasion spoke of two basic stages in the revolutionary process—and is probably caused by the fact that for Aidit the first phase of the revolution is not yet finished in Indonesia and thus the possible sub-stages in the second or socialist phase—when the Communists have come to power—cannot be clearly envisaged. If Mao is a criterion then, as will be indicated shortly, the appearance of such sub-stages in the second phase of the revolution is likely to be allowed for in future Indonesian Communist theory. For Aidit all this is not a matter of immediate concern. Basic to his present two-stage concept of revolution is the belief that the establishment of socialism (the second stage) cannot be accomplished unless the reforms of the first phase have been completed. As he put it in his May 23, 1960 address, commemorating the 40th anniversary of the PKI: ' . . . we must complete our revolution, a revolution that is national and democratic in character. . . . To talk about socialism is a joke and deception of the people if action is not taken to completely eliminate the influences of imperialism and feudalism in economic, political, social and cultural affairs'.[16]

This position has, of course, its reference points in Marx and Lenin. Marx, in his *Contribution to the Critique of Political Economy*, asserted that 'no social order ever disappears before all the productive forces for which there is room in it have been developed, and new, higher relations of production never appear before the material conditions of their existence have matured in the womb of the old society'.[17] Lenin shared this view at one time when he excoriated those who were trying to leap at once from 'the eve of the collapse of capitalism' to the 'higher phase of Communism', without going through 'the first steps in the transition from Capitalism to Socialism, or the lower stage of Communism', and he equally upbraided those who refused to collaborate with the bourgeoisie in an attack on monarchical absolutism and feud-alism.[18] In collaborating with the bourgeoisie Lenin even urged this followers to soften their socialist demands for the sake of unity in the attack on autocratic institutions. That this meant a short-range tactical support by the proletariat of bourgeois capitalist interests, which would serve the double purpose of strengthening the forces seeking the over-throw of the old order, while at the same time ultimately drawing the future class antithesis between proletariat and bourgeoisie in starker colors, was clearly in Lenin's thought. But this tactical approach also meant a liberation of capitalism, however temporary, as the old feudal-order was overthrown. It is on this basis that Aidit has championed 'national' capitalism in Indonesia today, i.e. as part of the bourgeois democratic phase of the revolution which will see the end of imperialism and feudalism.[19]

But the liberation of bourgeois capitalism from the confines of feudal autocracy is not designed to create a traditional bourgeois capitalistic order, for the party and the proletariat must direct the anti-feudal and anti-imperialist revolution beyond this stage. It is this which gives the first or bourgeois-democratic phase of the two or multi stage revolution its peculiar character. Both Marx and Lenin commented extensively on the fact that a bourgeois liberal revolution may turn reactionary and contrary to proletarian interests once it has succeeded, and that is why the proletariat must guide and force the bourgeois-democratic process onward toward the Socialist phase. In the bourgeois-democratic phase proletarian interests must therefore predominate. Mao Tse-tung, basing himself on Stalin and Lenin, thus speaks of a 'new-type' bourgeois-democratic revolution to distinguish it from the old-type bourgeois revolutions in Europe which culminated in the establishment of a liberal capitalist order, and this new-type bourgeois-democratic revolu-tion is therefore part of the 'proletarian-socialist world revolution'.[20] Aidit explicitly follows this view: ' . . . the Indonesian bourgeois-democratic revolution of today . . . is no longer of the old out-dated type, but is something special, a new type. This new-type bourgeois-democratic revolution is a part of the world proletarian revolution which firmly opposes imperialism . . .'[21]

It was not Mao but Lenin who first called attention to the revolution-ary role of the bourgeoisie in underdeveloped countries, especially in the context of what since has come to be known as the 'national liberation' movement. In his article 'Democracy and Narodism in China', published in 1912, Lenin pointed to the fact that 'The Western bourgeoisie is in a state of decay; it is already confronted by its gravedigger—the prolet-ariat. In Asia in contrast there is *still* a bourgeoisie capable of championing sincere, militant, consistent democracy. . . '.[22] For Lenin Sun Yat-sen's program was essentially that of the dynamic bourgeois-democratic and capitalistic forces, which also agriculturally were seeking to demolish the medieval and feudal old order in China. Revolutionary bourgeois interests and the interests of the peasantry were thus brought together, argued Lenin.[23] This junction of forces in China is by definition anti-imperialistic, for it seeks to eliminate the hold of Western imperialism and capitalism on Chinese society. The liberation of indigenous bourgeois capitalistic forces thus parallels the political liberation of the nation from foreign control and hence the 'national liberation' movement in Asia partakes of the nature of the bourgeois-democratic phase of the two or multi stage world proletarian revolution. Lenin, commenting on 'The Junius pamphlet' in 1916, said: 'National wars *against* the imperialist powers are not only possible and probable; they are inevitable, *progressive* and *revolutionary*'. In his *Report of the Commission on the National and Colonial Questions* to the Second Congress of the Comintern in July, 1920, he again underscored the bourgeois and inherently capitalistic character of the national liberation movement: 'There need not be the slightest doubt that every national movement can only be a bourgeois-democratic movement, for the overwhelming mass of the population in backward countries consists of peasants who represent bourgeois capitalist relationships'.[24] Lenin regarded it as 'utopian' for proletarian parties to pursue Communist tactics in these underdeveloped countries without giving effective support to the peasant movement, i.e. without supporting the bourgeois capitalist relationships which the peasantry represent. To make sure that under these circumstances Communists would not end up by supporting pseudo reformers and reactionaries—the ever-present danger in the class dynamic of the bourgeoisie—Lenin recalled that the Comintern's Commission on the National and Colonial Question proposed that the term 'national revolutionary' be substituted for the term 'bourgeois-democratic' and that only 'genuinely revolutionary' bourgeois 'liberation' movements be supported 'in the colonies'.

Today Communist theoreticians in many countries have been wont to combine the two terms and use the terms 'national democratic' and 'national democracy' alongside with, or as automatic extensions of 'bourgeois democratic' and 'bourgeois democracy'.[25] In keeping with periodic condemnation of the bourgeois element and in order to stress the similarity of Communist aims and national liberation movements the concept of 'national democracy' is frequently used to the exclusion of the older term although the operational differences between the two terms seem rather minor. For Aidit bourgeois democratic strategy and national liberation strategy is particularly a feature of the emergence of the new countries in recent years:[26]

The victory of socialism in one country made it possible for the bourgeois democratic revolutions in the colonial and dependent countries to blend with the national revolution against imperialism. Under these conditions, the national liberation movement has become a broad anti-imperialist and anti-feudal movement for the establishment of people's rule as a stage leading to socialist society.

Lenin's concept of 'the people', so extensively used also by Mao, thus is the politico-sociological base of 'national democracy'. Those of the bourgeoisie capable of participating in the ongoing revolutionary process are also subsumed in 'the people', and it is in this way that Aidit and other Indonesian Communist writers see the bourgeois role. Bourgeois 'ambivalence' has always been regarded as troublesome to Communist strategy, nowhere more so that in the bourgeois democratic phase of the revolution. For Mao, as for Aidit, the bourgeoisie in their respective countries has never been free from a dualistic character (revolutionary at times, reactionary at others), as has indeed the peasantry, among whom feudal and capitalistic interests may also be present.[27] Yet even so, the proletariat led by the party can guide them effectively in a common anti-imperialist front. The unity of bourgeoisie, peasantry, and proletariat, forged and directed by the Communist Party is therefore not only essential to the bourgeois-democratic phase of the revolution, but is particularly indispensable to the success of the 'national liberation' movement—part and parcel of the bourgeois-democratic phase—in the underdeveloped, colonial or semi-colonial areas. For example, the principle of class unity under party guidance is basic to the tactics of the national liberation movement in Asia as described by Liu Shao-chi, to the Trade Union Conference of Asian Countries in Peking, in November 1949.

Class unity under party guidance will not only prevent the bourgeoisie from wavering and becoming reactionary, but will also insure the intimate linkage between the first and the second stage of the revolution. Stalin, in defending Lenin's version of the development of the revolution, condemned the leaders of the Second International for thinking that between the first and second phase there would be a period in which capitalism fully developed itself and the proletariat would gather strength for the final assault on the newly liberated bourgeoisie. Rather the 'bourgeois-democratic revolution, in a more or less developed country must . . . verge upon the proletarian revolution . . . the former must pass into the latter', and the proletariat (Stalin declared, citing Lenin) would 'immediately' take advantage of the liberation of the bourgeois from the Tsarist feudal order in Russia 'to bring about the socialist revolution in alliance with the proletarians of Europe'.[28] It is of interest that Chinese theoreticians have recently again stressed this intimate linkage between the two phases of the revolution.[29] But the degree of accommodation to be accorded to bourgeois capitalistic interests in the first stage of the two-stage revolution, and even more in the early period of the second stage, is a matter dictated by variable circumstances. At one point in *On New Democracy* Mao Tse-tung also speaks of 'several stages' (not apparently just two)[30] in the course of the revolution, and elsewhere emphasizes that 'contradictions still exist in a socialist society' (i.e. in the second phase of the revolution) and that 'contradictions' between the national bourgeoisie and the proletariat or even within the ranks of the national bourgeoisie must be considered as expected contradictions among 'the people' (i.e. are not of a fundamental or reactionary character).[31] The latter view is also shared by Aidit. This would suggest some room for expression of the capitalist orientation of the bourgeoisie even in the early periods of the second or Socialist phase of the revolution.

A related view appeared in the work of Tan Malaka, probably the most important Indonesian theoretician before Aidit. It was he who in the early nineteen-twenties introduced the essence of the multi-stage revolutionary concept in Indonesia.[32] He did not think it possible to establish Communism overnight in Indonesia, even after the national 'liberation' from colonial control had been accomplished. A preparatory phase was necessary, he maintained, during which non-proletarian elements in society would be brought under, and led by, the workers' movement and the party. Immediate establishment of a pure dictatorship of the proletariat would harm the economy, he contended, and would drive the non-proletarian majority into opposition to the numerically still small industrial working class in Indonesia. Therefore, it would be necessary to allow limited degrees of capitalist enterprises (though large-scale business establishments would have to be immediately nationalized) after liberation from colonial control, partly with a view to increasing production. For this reason Tan Malaka regarded the inauguration in the Soviet Union in 1921 of the so-called New Economic Policy, under which a limited degree of capitalist enterprise and private property were permitted, as being of signal importance for Indonesia. Though only touching on these important theoretical concepts in passing, he seems to indicate the need for recognizing bourgeois and petty bourgeois economic interests on the road to a Socialist society, even cautioning against a too hasty establishment of the dictatorship of the proletariat, although eventually, of course, these bourgeois remnants were expected to give way completely to the new political order of the workers. Obviously Tan Malaka's thought here closely parallels that of Bukharin, of the Comintern (particularly the Comintern's directives to the Chinese Communists during this period) and, in the last analysis, of Lenin.[33] He also had a clear appreciation of the concepts of the 'united front' and of 'the people'. He saw, for example, that the role of the Communists was 'to bring together all layers of the population who are dissatisfied with Dutch imperialism, and to lead them in all actions'[34] and to broaden the base of the PKI's support as much as possible. The party must be sure, however, that the 'national solidarity' which is desired, is and remains under the leadership of the proletariat as embodied by the PKI, for only the Communists can effectively lead the Indonesian revolution. All these ideas of Tan's remained essentially without fruit during the first period of PKI action in the nineteen-twenties, although they undoubtedly underlay much of Tan's policies during the early years of Indonesian Revolution after the Second World War. For the PKI today these ideas officially came to Indonesia for the first time with Muso and the 'New Road' resolution of 1948. That resolution, it may be recalled, also embodied a two-stage or multi-stage revolutionary concept, indicating that the Indonesian revolution was still in its bourgeois-democratic stage and that capitalism would have to be preserved, and though effectively controlled, even be stimulated, until the requisitive level of national economic strength had been attained.[35] In the 'New Road' resolution too, the united front of proletarian and non-proletarian elements of society led by the party as the representative of the workers is an important concept. For Aidit also accommodation of capitalist interests in the first phase of the revolution is an accepted fact, though as noted, he has had no reason thus far to comment on the extent of such accommodation in the early stages of the socialist phase.

For Mao as for Aidit the logic of the two- or multi-stage revolution is based upon a recognition of the semi-feudal or semi-colonial condition of their respective countries.[36] This recognition is not new with Mao, of course, for Lenin had already said as much, and in their acceptance of Lenin's premise Mao and Aidit also endorse the implications of the essentially anti-feudal and anti-imperialist character of the bourgeois-democratic phase of the revolution. The importance of the national bourgeoisie in China's economic reconstruction had been explicitly acknowledged by Mao ('Our present policy is to control, not to eliminate capitalism'),[37] and earlier he had declared that 'it would be sheer illusion to try to build Socialism on the ruins of the colonial, semi-colonial, and semi-feudal order' without, among other things, the development of 'private capitalist' enterprises, that is 'without pushing to its end the

the democratic revolution which is bourgeois in character. . . '.[38] In Aidit's writings, as in the present party program of the PKI, there is less explicit mention of the economic importance of the national bourgeoisie, but the protection and development of national capitalist enterprises and the concept of the participation of the national and petty bourgeoisie in the Communist-led united front of 'the people' are recurrent themes and are basic to PKI theory today.[39]

According to Aidit the bourgeoisie is divided into three groups: compradore, national, and petty bourgeois. The first 'serve the interests of the big foreign capitalists', e.g. they are representatives of the big foreign trading and mining companies and as stooges of imperialism they are major targets of the revolution. But even the compradore element can be an ally of the party under certain specific circumstances, e.g. 'when the party's policy at a given time is only directed against one particular imperialism'. Even so, the reactionary character of the compradore element makes it generally the enemy of the proletariat. The national bourgeoisie also has a dual character: on the one hand it too is a victim of imperialism and feudalism and so can be an integral element in the Communist-led united front; on the other hand the national bourgeoisie 'does not have the courage fundamentally to fight imperialism because economically and politically it is weak and it has class ties with imperialism and feudalism'. Thus the national bourgeoisie must be under constant scrutiny and guidance of the proletariat and communists must remember that 'it is not very difficult to pull this class to the left to make it stand firmly on the side of the revolution. . . '. But in dealing with the bourgeoisie the party should be flexible, and, as Sidartojo (a North Sumatran PKI leader) explained in the May 18, 1960, issue of the party newspaper *Harian Rakjat*, there are different phases in working with the bourgeoisie: the party must emphasize sometimes struggle, and sometimes support, and the party has come to learn 'how useful it is' in operating in alliance with, and in opposition to, the bourgeoisie. Finally, the petty bourgeoisie ('the urban poor, the intellectuals, the small traders, the handicraft workers, the fishermen, the independent workers') have a status, according to Aidit, almost the same as the 'middle' peasantry: they too 'suffer from the oppression of imperialism, feudalism and the big bourgeoisie' and therefore 'they are one of the forces pushing the revolution forward and are a reliable ally of the proletariat . . . they can only attain their freedom under the leadership of the proletariat'.[40]

In his application of this class analysis Aidit and the PKI pronouncements tend to be particularly concerned with the national bourgeoisie. It is 'the establishment of a united front with the national bourgeoisie' which 'opens up possibilities for the development and building of the Party', Aidit has said, and in the reconstruction of the PKI since the the disastrous Madiun coup, stress was especially placed, according to him, on indoctrinating cadres with Leninism, particularly with Lenin's *Left Wing Communism, an Infantile Disorder*, the treatise which emphasizes the necessity of the party's tactical cooperation with the bourgeoisie.[41] The PKI's Politburo has indicated that 'at the present stage it is in Indonesia's national interest to develop and raise the output of private national enterprises', and a policy of active support for private national enterprise, by providing technical and financial assistance and protection against competition from abroad, has been recommended by the PKI's 'National Economic Seminar'.[42]

The party recognizes the difficulty in winning adherents from among the national bourgeois capitalist class. First Deputy Chairman M. H. Lukman, in an analysis on party work among the national bourgeoisie, notes that while with respect to other classes the PKI learns to identify itself best if it actively seeks members from these classes, with regard to the bourgeoisie this tactic 'is not applicable' since the party, for obvious reasons, cannot give the impression that it is a party for the bourgeoisie in the same way that it attempts to portray itself as a party for the peasants and workers.[43] But the party can closely study the problems of the national bourgeoisie and render it all feasible assistance in presenting its own party program. 'We should start off with their own needs, not with our own desires', Lukman counsels, particularly the needs stemming from 'obstacles and difficulties caused by various government ordinances'. The PKI when addressing itself to the bourgeoisie should also bear in mind that the latter generally accepts intellectuals more readily as potential or actual leaders and the party should therefore make a special effort to bring the 'more progressive' intellectuals, who move within the circles of the national entrepreneurial segment of society, into unity with PKI aims.

But winning support in entrepreneurial ranks bisects other Communist policy considerations, and especially since the end of 1957 and since the rise of the military in politics a new problem confronts the PKI's policy toward the bourgeosie. With the transformation of large foreign-owned (many formerly Dutch-owned) big private enterprises into state enterprises—a policy which the PKI has strongly supported on principle—there has emerged the problem of 'bureaucratic capitalism' in the management of these state enterprises, i.e. the military and civil official managers are 'chasing after profits no less than private enterprise'[44] and the party alleges that these profits have benefited the managers to an unconscionable extent. Thus the emergent state capitalistic structure

—a continuation from the colonial era[45]—has presumably tempted the national bourgeoisie toward a reactionary direction and in its celebrated statement of July 8, 1960, on the performance of the government, as well as in many previous statements, the PKI's Politburo has excoriated this reactionary development. Yet the problem here confronting the PKI is not novel. Mao Tse-tung had already signalled the danger of the 'bureaucratic capitalists' as ancillaries of feudalism and imperialism, and the necessity of dealing with them in the context of an 'antagonistic contradiction'.[46] In the dilemma PKI theory has already had recourse to the tested old procedures of strata differentiation, distinguishing between managers of state enterprises and other private entrepreneurs. The two strata interlock at many points, however, particularly where class interest is concerned, and the simultaneous appeals to and criticisms of the national entrepreneurial element, whether in the public or the private sector of the economy, unavoidably continues to debilitate party strategy as a whole.

The position of what Marx and Engels called the 'intermediate' classes (e.g. the petty bourgeoisie) and their relationship to the proletariat has always been subject to considerable re-interpretation in Communist thought and even today the debate goes on.[47] For Aidit, as for Mao, the concept of the national bourgeoisie serves to enlarge the area of those intermediate classes which can be allies of the proletariat in its revolutionary struggle, i.e. the national bourgeoisie is by way of being an underdeveloped country's extension of the more orthodox Marxist concept of the petty bourgeoisie; indeed, the native small trader, shopkeeper or industrialist in a colony who would ordinarily have been designated as petty bourgeois, becomes (after the colony's political independence) a 'national' bourgeois concerned with the elimination of the remaining privileged positions of the big foreign-owned enterprises in his country. The revolutionary potentials of the petty bourgeoisie, especially of the petty traders, Marx acknowledged explicitly on a number of occasions (e.g. in *Germany: Revolution and Counter-Revolution*), and the modern application of this concept in underdeveloped countries today has immediately strengthened the preliminary base of operations of the Communist movement.

The Peasantry. Proletariat and bourgeoisie supply two elements of the *troika* of the national united front in the first stage of the Communist revolution. The third element comes from the agrarian society. Together these three constitute what Mao often calls 'the people', a concept invented not by Mao, however, but by Lenin. Aidit, like Mao, fully subscribes to

Lenin's detailed analysis of the 'advanced class', i.e. the proletariat fighting for the 'cause of the whole of the people' and being 'at the head of the whole of the people'.[48] The 'people' then, led by proletariat and Communist party, make up the national united front which is the dynamic force of the first phase of the revolution and of the 'national liberation' movements today. Since underdeveloped nations tend to be overwhelmingly agrarian, it follows that in those countries the rural mass is in the numerical majority in the national united front and the PKI has recently pointed with pride to the fact that most of its members today are from the peasantry, and has insisted that 'work among the peasants is the most important sphere of party activity'.[49] The agrarian character of the Chinese revolution was also stressed by the present leadership of the Chinese party, as in Mao's assertion in *On New Democracy* that 'the Chinese Revolution is virtually the peasants' revolution'.[50]

In applying the class structure of rural society to Communist action, however, it is Aidit who has been particularly flexible. But before we describe his views, those of earlier theorists should briefly be considered. Both Marx and Engels, while recognizing the conservative inclinations of the peasantry, had earlier acknowledged the revolutionary potentials of the peasantry, especially in the context of anti-feudal, bourgeois revolutions, and Engels' *The Peasant War in Germany* has served more than one Marxist historial and theoretician as an instrument with which to analyze other peasant insurrections in Europe. Despite his well known tactical vacillation—now rejecting the proprietary-capitalistic interests of the peasantry, then again explicitly catering to them by favoring a kind of nationalized system of land distribution among them— Lenin always recognized the importance of peasant support for the success of the revolution generally, and especially in the demolition of the feudal order. ('The agrarian question is the basis of the bourgeois revolution in Russia', he wrote, 'and determines the national peculiarity of this revolution. The essence of this question is the struggle the peasantry is waging to abolish landlordism and the remnants of serfdom in the agricultural system of Russia, and consequently, also in all her social and political institutions.')[51] But Lenin made plain in his article 'Socialism, Petty Bourgeois and Proletarian' (1905) that 'to the Marxist the peasant movement is not a socialist but a democratic movement', and that the revolution furthered by the peasant movement is not anti-bourgeois but anti-feudal in character.[52] In underdeveloped countries (especially those in Asia, where the peasantry had grown equally restive), the same appeal was to be made by Lenin and his associates to the peasant's proprietary bourgeois inclinations as was done in Lenin's agrarian program for Russia. The Comintern's Second

Congress' theses of 1920 deemed it to be 'of special importance' for Communist parties 'to support the peasant movements in backward countries against the landowners and all fedual survivals', and in order to win the peasantry over it would be necessary for the Communist movement 'to include many petty bourgeois reform clauses, such as division of land' in its program. The theses on the 'agrarian question' of the Fourth Comintern Congress of 1922 categorically asserted that 'the revolutionary movement in the backward countries of the East cannot be successful unless it is based on the action of the masses of the peasantry' and therefore revolutionary parties 'in all Eastern countries' should struggle for the elimination of feudalism and large landownership and should 'proclaim the radical reform on the basis of landownership' in order that 'the peasant masses may be drawn into active participation in the struggle for national liberation. . . '. And so, along with emphasis on the organizational unity of workers and peasants in the colonial or semi-colonial countries of Asia, a program of land distribution ('land to the peasant' as the Communist slogan has it) for the benefit of the small farmer, the tenant and sharecropper, was to become part of Communist policy in underdeveloped lands. In these lands the small size and the comparative weakness of an industrial proletariat rendered the strategic value of the peasantry all the greater, and in accordance with Leninist policy the significant characteristic of the Communist cadres is not their class origin but their Marxist political consciousness,[53] which translates itself as 'practice' into the ability effectively to mobilize the 'national liberation' movement. The concept of the peasantry as representing 'the main army of the national movement' (that is, as representing the chief force of the 'national democratic' or 'bourgeois democratic' revolution) was, of course, also accepted by Stalin.[54]

For Mao 'the strength of the peasants constitutes the principal force of the Chinese revolution'.[55] The path along which the agrarian sector of the anti-feudal bourgeois democratic revolution will develop in order to reach its culmination in the Socialist phase Mao has described thus:[56]

The agrarian revolution we have carried out is already and will be a process in which the landowning landlord class becomes a class deprived of its land, while the peasants, once deprived of their land, become small holders of land . . . 'Under socialism the peasants' private ownership will in turn become communal ownership in socialist agriculture; this has already taken place in the Soviet Union and will take place throughout the world.

Mao's principal views on the peasantry are derived from Marx and Lenin, as is apparent also from his attempt to identify the peasantry with the Marxist-Leninist class antithesis. Thus in Mao's essays on the classes of Chinese society the group of the 'middle' peasants (those who have sufficient land for their own needs and also till their own soil) are subsumed under the class of 'petty bourgeoisie', along with small traders, lower government officials, intellectuals, and so on, while the category of 'the semi-proletariat' for Mao includes 'the overwhelming majority of the semi-tenant peasants' and the 'poor peasants'. In addition Mao identifies a 'rural proletariat' of peasant laborers and a 'lumpen proletariat', consisting in part of peasants who have lost their land, and groups them with the proletariat generally. Moreover, he considers that 'the industrial proletariat is the leading force in our revolution', although 'all sections of the semi-proletariat and the petty bourgeoisie' (presumably including middle peasants, tenants, poor peasants and farm laborers) are 'our close friends'. For Mao landlords and compradores are generally the enemies of the revolution and represent the most backward and most reactionary elements in China hindering the development of her productive forces.[57] However, they are not undifferentiated, for among the landlords and the rich peasants are what Mao calls 'the enlightened gentry', who have 'democratic leanings' and who have 'contradictions' not only with 'bureaucratic capitalism' and imperialism but also with other feudal landlords and rich peasants.[58] These 'enlightened gentry' can join the united front of workers, peasants and sections of the bourgeoisie, in the revolution. Mao's approach here is typical of his theoretical flexibility: in 1948, for example, he was still advising party cadres to distinguish between landlords and rich peasants, between big, middle and small landlords, between those landlords and rich peasants 'who are local tryants and those who are not', and so on, and asserted that 'we should not decide on and give the same treatment to them all but should differentiate and vary the treatment according to varying conditions'.[59]

Aidit's thought is in this respect an elaboration on Mao's.[60] Agrarian production relationships according to Aidit, considered in their political setting, involve five categories (1) 'imperialist' landlords, (2) 'patriotic' landlords, (3) rich peasants, (4) middle peasants, (5) poor peasants and agricultural laborers. The predominantly rural character of Indonesian society dictates that the peasantry be the 'basic force' of the Indonesian revolution; indeed, he argues, 'Without the active participation of the peasants the Revolution cannot possibly succeed'. In order to enlist the support of the peasants (especially of the poor peasants and agricultural laborers who, before the contemplated agrarian revolution 'comprise the majority in the villages in our country') it is necessary to restore land to them. To insure the establishment of 'a peasant land-ownership system, or in other words, private ownership by the peasants of the land' (as stipulated by the current PKI party program)[61] land must therefore be taken from the landlords and given to the peasants. But not all landlord holdings are subject to redistribution, for of the two basic enemies confronting Indonesia (imperialism and feudalism), the former is the 'most basic', and in practice this means that only 'imperialist' landlords, i.e. those who support various subversive rebel movements in Indonesia, should suffer expropriation now. The 'patriotic' landlords (those who join in opposing the rebel movements supported by the imperialists) are not now confronted with expropriation, but only with a demand that the rent paid by their tenants be reduced from the traditional 50% to 40% of the crop. While the 'contradiction' between the 'imperialist' landlords and 'the people' is a 'basic' one, that can be resolved only by force, the 'contradiction' between the 'patriotic' landlords and 'the people' is not basic, but is a 'contradiction among the people', capable of being resolved 'by peaceful means, by democratic and mutually persuasive and mutually beneficial negotiations'.

In thus broadening the base of his united front, Aidit has not only managed to bring the compradores on the side of 'the people' in certain specific anti-imperialist frames of action as we have seen, but also a substantial number of the landlords. With respect to the latter tactic there is, as we have seen, a reference point in Mao's doctrines and in early Chinese Communist thought. In 1938, within the context of the new united front resistance to the Japanese invasion, Mao had urged that 'the landlords should reduce rent and interest, but at the same time the peasants should pay rent and interest and unite with the landlords against foreign aggression'.[62] It should also be noted that in distinguishing between 'imperialist' and 'patriotic' landlords, Aidit was elaborating on a theme which had been introduced by Muso as early as 1948 in 'The New Road' resolution. That resolution also had demanded that 'rich' peasants who had opposed the Indonesian resolution should have their land confiscated forthwith, while those 'rich' peasants who had supported the revolution would be allowed to keep enough land for their own use. Though on other occasions Aidit has emphasized that the struggle against imperialism and feudalism within the framework of the bourgeois-democratic revolution must be waged simultaneously,[63] it is equally clear that to him the anti-imperialist campaign is primary and that peasant victories on the anti-feudal front can come only 'one after the other', i.e. more gradually. Hence the apparent solicitude at present shown to the 'patriotic' landlords in PKI theory and tactics.

The 'rich' peasants generally have more than enough land for their own use, but tend to work it themselves. Some, however, also lease out their excess land, lend money and are 'by nature semi-feudal'. In a sense they stand in between the peasantry and the landlords, but their 'productive activities will continue to be utilized for a certain period to come', and that is why they too can participate in the anti-imperialist phase of the revolution and join the national united front. The 'middle' peasants are economically independent, do not lease out land or act as money-lenders, and like the 'poor' peasants often are victims of the grip of the landlords on the rural economy. Hence they not only can join the anti-imperialist phase of the revolution, but 'they can also accept Socialism', and are a reliable ally of the proletariat. Like Mao, Aidit equates the 'middle' peasants with the petty bourgeoisie of small traders, intellectuals, lesser officials, and so on. Aidit also emphasizes that the 'middle' peasantry is particularly important for the revolution, because after the agrarian revolution (that is, after the end of feudal relationships) the self-sufficient 'middle' peasants with their plots of land will 'comprise the majority in the countryside'. Before the agrarian revolution, however, the majority of the rural society is composed of 'poor' peasants and landless agricultural laborers, unable to make a living from their miniscule holdings or wages, exploited by money-lenders and through the feudal services they must perform for their landlords. Following Mao, Aidit characterizes the poor peasantry as the 'village semi-proletariat'; they are 'the largest force pushing the revolution forward', are 'the most reliable of the allies of the proletariat' but, like the 'middle' peasants, can only be liberated under the leadership of the proletariat.[64]

These three divisions of the peasantry are not based on exact definitions of the size of land holdings in each division, although recent PKI land reform proposals suggest that the borderline between 'middle' peasants and 'rich' peasants is a holding of about 12 acres of irrigated fields, or 18 acres of irregularly irrigated fields, or 24 acres of unirrigated fields.[65] Above this lies the category of 'rich' peasants and landlords, below it (sometimes far below) the category of the poor peasants begins. As part of its intensive campaign to win adherents among the peasantry the PKI under Aidit has carried on extensive research in land-tenure patterns in Indonesia; this has revealed very high concentrations of landownership in the hands of a few peasants and landlords in many areas.[66] These data confirm the analyses made by non-Communist investigators, at least in Java. Great stress continues to be placed by the PKI on improving the conditions of the peasantry. The party's organizational literature abounds with directions and programs to win peasant support,[67] and the abolition of 'feudalism' and inauguration of land reform are of constant concern to party leaders. In his report to the Central Committee's plenary meeting in December 1960, Aidit listed as one of the aims of national development the complete fulfillment of the land reform program 'and the liberation of the peasants from the bonds of feudal methods of production', while the unity of peasants and laborers and the bringing of 'more order' in the peasant ranks are paramount party objectives.[68] Though the party fully supports the government's land reform program, Aidit also declared that land reform could only succeed if the peasants in fact liberated themselves from their landlords —an assertion which can only be understood if it is remembered that implementation of the land registry and land redistribution program has thus far occurred slowly in Indonesia, partly because of the resistance of the wealthier peasants themselves.[69] Aidit now evidently hopes for a display of tenant aggressiveness against the landlord elements, but thus far he has been largely disappointed.

Finally, mention should be made of the special efforts made by the PKI to win a following among fishermen, whose living conditions closely parallel that of the peasantry, and whose support broadens the popular foundation of the united front.[70]

Proletariat and Party. 'The Indonesian Revolution will not succeed unless it is under the leadership of the Indonesian proletariat', Aidit has written,[71] and the united front of 'the people' requires a politically highly conscious proletarian party as its vanguard. Only rarely, if ever, may the popular base of the united front be narrowed; on the contrary, the party has the obligation always to seek to broaden mass support. As M. H. Lukman, the PKI's first vice-chairman, has put it, 'We must always remember the terms for attracting the moderate forces . . . we must also be able to prove our power and our arguments against imperialism and against the reactionary forces in the country with successes which can be experienced also by the moderate forces'.[72] The strengthening of the party involves development of political appeals also to non-proletarian quarters. (As Lenin had stated in *What is to be Done?* (1902), 'To bring political knowledge to the *workers* the Social-Democrats must *go among all classes of the population*, must dispatch units of their army in all directions . . .'.) Though the PKI has foresworn armed resistance to the government for the moment, the party would agree with Mao's directive at the time of the anti-Japanese war that 'the main task confronting the party of the Chinese proletariat has been to unite the largest possible number of allies'.[73] PKI support today for Sukarno's new National Front and for his concept of NASAKOM (meaning the unity of all the major political groups, including nationalists, religious groups and the Communists in the country) mirrors the PKI's policy of developing unity and maximum mass appeal in this anti-imperialist phase. 'The Party constantly reminds its members that without strengthening the National Front the contradiction between the Indonesian people and imperialism cannot be solved', and in the current situation in Indonesia, which according to the party is marked by a struggle between the supporters of Sukarno's Political Manifesto and its opponents, the PKI is 'in the vanguard of the former'.[74]

But as Aidit pointed out as early as 1954, 'in the struggle to create a united national front, both by cooperation with various political parties or by cooperation with people of various trends and ideologies, the Party must not become merged with them. The Party must preserve its political, ideological and organizational independence'.[75] This approach also closely reflects Mao's war-time policy of preserving 'independence within the united front' and of declaring a 'national' struggle (i.e. against the Japanese) to be a form of the class struggle. In opposing imperialism (which Aidit today never wearies of describing as Indonesia's 'most basic' enemy) the class struggle must be subordinate, Mao had argued, and hence the relative independence of parties and classes should be preserved in the first phase of the revolution.[76] With this tactic Aidit wholly agrees; he has opposed in Indonesia proposals of a complete merger or a total dissolution of the political parties at this time; he has urged freedom of partisan political expression and in general favored the independence of class interest and partisan movements within the united front. The prevailing state ideology at the moment would not tolerate articulation of avowed class war concepts and Aidit, ever careful to stay within the limits of this state ideology, has repeatedly asserted 'that the class struggle is placed below the national struggle' and class interests are placed 'below the national interest'. Of late Aidit and other PKI leaders seem to prefer not to mention the notion of class struggle at all, not least because of the great emphasis placed on national unity in the PKI's united front tactics.

The party has also been particularly anxious not to become swallowed up by Sukarno's National Front, and while it approves of the National Front as such, has also insisted that NASAKOM and the National Front allow for party independence. In turn Sukarno has sought to allay fears that Communism may take over through the NASAKOM concept and the National Front. Thus he rejected the request of the Independence Upholders Party (*Ikatan Pendukung Kemerdekaan Indonesia*—IPKI), a small anti-Communist organization, especially influential among army officers, that the term NASAKOM be abandoned in favor of the term POLKAR (from *politik karya* or 'work politics') to designate the unity of the parties. Sukarno stated that the 'revolutionary powers' should continue to be unified on the basis of NASAKOM and in his August 17, 1961, independence day address to the nation scoffed at those who feared the collaboration of nationalists, 'religionists' and Communists. 'We need not be afraid', declared Sukarno, 'of any trend at all, provided it is progressive-revolutionary. . . '.[77]

The principle of 'independence within the united front', as evidenced for example, in the July 7, 1937, agreement between Chiang Kai-shek and the Chinese Communists, reflects an experience of major importance to all Asian Communists today, namely the disaster which befell the Chinese Communists in the mid-nineteen-twenties, when on Stalin's orders they merged with the Kuomintang and were subsequently all but destroyed by Chiang. From the point of view of class theory what this merger meant was that the bourgeois democratic elements in the first stage of the revolution came to swallow up the revolutionary proletariat and its vanguard in the party. The memory of this experience undoubtedly still plays a role today in the current tactical and doctrinal tension between Moscow and Peking, in which the latter accuses the former of seeking to curtail the revolutionary proletarian forces in underdeveloped countries and of supporting unreliable bourgeois-nationalistic elements in favor of a policy of general peaceful co-existence, in which war is no longer considered necessary for the triumph of world Communism.[78] The lesson from the Chinese experience is that the party must always retain its identity in the national front and its militant aggressiveness, for only in that way can it provide the proper leadership to the bourgeoisie and other non-proletarian forces of that front. The potential 'vacillation' and 'treachery' of the bourgeoisie not only made a victim once of the Chinese Communists (in 1926–1927) but, as Aidit has argued, also of Indonesian Communists (for example, in the period between 1948 and 1951). In those years the PKI, demoralized and weakened by its unsuccessful coup in Madiun, sought to establish a new base of strength by trying to win indiscriminate favor in bourgeois-nationalist quarters, only to fall victim to the bourgeois Sukiman government in 1951. From an international point of view party independence means that Communist parties everywhere must continue to press for an aggressive confrontation with 'imperialism'. Just for the sake of 'peaceful co-existence' or of winning adherents in non-proletarian groups a muscular display of party independence and party criticism may never be abandoned. It is therefore perhaps hardly surprising that in the current ideological and strategic dispute between Moscow and Peking Aidit has unofficially tended to favor the latter.

Precisely because of this insistence on party independence the old question which long plagued early Communist theoreticians (when to employ revolutionary activity in a front 'from above', and when to employ such activity in a front 'from below') has lost much of its significance for Indonesian Communism since the Aidit era. For Aidit's technique (like Mao's), within the context of the multi-stage revolutionary concept, has been essentially to employ *both* approaches at the same time, to seek active collaboration also in parliament and other organs of government with other 'patriotic', 'anti-imperialist or 'anti-feudal' organizations for the purposes of developing and completing the 'national democratic' (not the Socialist) revolution—this being in effect the approach 'from above'—and at the same time to build up the Communist party as such along with its front groups, aggressively insisting on 'democratic liberties' which will allow the party to expand, staging campaigns to win popular support—all characteristic of the approach 'from below'. For example, by splitting the bourgeoisie and by stressing its 'vacillating' character, the party hopes to have the best of both worlds, for a segment of the bourgeoisie and its political organizations can under these conditions always collaborate with the party 'from above'—sometimes a larger segment, sometimes a smaller. At the same time mass action 'from below' can be continued against a definite target, i.e. that segment of the bourgeoisie which the party happens at the moment to regard as its enemy. The same technique can be applied to the landlords, some of whom (the 'patriotic' ones) are not confronted with confiscation and can even be allies of the party, while others (the 'imperialist' landlords) remain a target for mass action from 'below'. 'Independence' within the united front can give the party maneuverability and theoretical flexibility, although conflicts between the two simultaneous approaches cannot always be avoided.

Related to the above questions is the problem of the class origin of Communist party members. Both Mao and Aidit regard the peasantry as the basic force, and the agrarian uprising virtually the essence of the revolution. In the dark days of 1931, when the Chinese Communists were in serious crisis, Mao reiterated his belief, expressed even earlier, that 'it is also a mistake for any of our Party members to fear the development of the power of the peasants lest it become stronger than that of the workers and hence detrimental to the revolution'.[79] The revolution in 'semi-colonial' China, Mao went on, will never suffer just because the peasants become stronger than the workers, but will fail only if the workers cease to give leadership to the peasantry. The same approach is to be found in Aidit. Though the Indonesian industrial proletariat is small, it can readily lead the peasant mass, especially the mass of poor peasants and landless agricultural workers, because of their class identity. This stress on the identity between the industrial and the rural proletariat, and again between the petty bourgeoisie and the middle peasantry, is to be found in the class analysis of both Mao and Aidit and reflects the Leninist principle that it is less the class origin and more the degree of political consciousness of Communist party members and their allies which determines the success of the revolution. Proper ideological training enables anyone regardless of class to become a 'true' Marxist, indeed, according to one PKI editor, the 'greater part of the true Marxists in the party has always come from other than the working class'.[80] It is in the context of this emphasis on ideological training that the PKI also addresses itself to Indonesia's intellectuals. According to Aidit the intellectuals are not a separate class but their class position is determined by family origin. Even so the party seeks to win support from intellectuals in terms of their distinct position in society. As in the case of the national capitalist element the PKI seeks to identify with the needs of the group. As the report on party work among intellectuals, written by Central Committee member Jusuf Adjitorop and approved by the Central Committee on December 31, 1961, put it, the PKI must strengthen the professional organizations of the Indonesian intellectuals and to encourage their efforts to advance 'scientific learning' in combination with the struggle to fulfill revolutionary objectives. The nucleus of the academic groups in Indonesia, according to Adjitorop, are people who got their training before August, 1945, i.e. in the era of colonialism. In the last few years the number of progressive intellectuals has not been great but although this 'democratic' group is now growing it has not yet taken a decisive part in revolutionary activities. It is therefore essential that the party gain supporters from among the younger 'progressives'.[81]

In developing political consciousness proper theoretical training of cadres is the indispensible first step. 'A person who is flabby and shaky in questions of theory', Lenin said in *What is to be Done?*, 'is not a revolutionary but a wretched amateur', and in his historical description of the PKI Aidit has attributed the failure of party programs in the past to the lack of training in Marxist-Leninist fundamentals among cadres.[82] As has been indicated earlier, the advent of the *Sajap Leninis* (Leninist wing) in the party under Aidit has meant very great emphasis on theoretical training, and today, Aidit claims that 'The increased efforts in the matter of Merxist-Leninist education, and particularly the study of Marxist philosophy, have greatly strengthened the Party ideologically'. Aidit's advent has also meant a revision of the internal power structure of the PKI and an increasing emphasis on Leninist 'democratic centralism', party discipline, and the 'principle of criticism and self-criticism'. 'Centralism', as B. Hutapea (the editor of the party's principal theoretical journal) has put it, 'means the formation and the work of the party based on the one Party Constitution', acceptance of the decisions of one leading organ (the party congress) and in the intervals between party congresses the decision of the party's Central Committee. Discipline means acceptance of a common discipline for all party members, be they leaders of the party or just neophytes and candidate members. It also means 'subordination of lower committees to the higher committees' and of the minority to the majority and of all party levels to the Central Committee. Such subordination is not merely 'serfdom', however; there should be free discussion and criticism within the party in order to achieve unanimity of action, but after a decision has been accepted, 'all party members must act as if one man'. A consideration of Indonesian Communist party history reveals several periods in which 'the principles of the Lenin-type party', particularly of centralism and discipline, were not observed (e.g. during and after the 1926 uprising and in the period 1954–1948), but since 1951 these principles have been dominant and the party has risen with them.[83]

The development of the party can only take place if it is recognized that despite certain weaknesses the proletariat in Indonesia 'is nevertheless the basic force pushing the revolution forward'.[84] The proletariat in Indonesia as in other countries has certain basic advantages: their work is 'in the most advanced economic forms' which helps them give an understanding of the need of organization and discipline, and since they do not own any means of production, the proletariat is 'not individualistic by nature'. Unfortunately, the Indonesian proletariat is very small, still very young compared to the proletariat in the advanced capitalist countries, and it has a level of culture lower than that of the bourgeoisie. Even so the revolutionary movement cannot do without them, or rather without the revolutionary unity between various social groupings—a unity that must be built up by the proletariat. Hutapea has insisted that a working-class background is not in itself a guarantee of faithful party affiliation; this is a point of particular importance in Indonesia, where the industrial proletariat is still small, but it would be entirely wrong to delay the revolutionary movement until the proletariat has grown. Selectivity must be applied with respect to those workers who wish to join the party; only the 'most advanced' (those active in defending their class interests against their employers and those who have some minimum cultural level) should be invited to join, for these qualifications guarantee that they can benefit from the ideological training which the party gives them. But people from other classes, provided they have had the same kind of training, can also faithfully serve the party.[85]

The Problem of Revisionism and the Sino-Soviet Conflict. Applying these basic Marxist-Leninist principles to Indonesian conditions demands that the PKI steer a careful course between the extremes of dogmatic rigidity and heretical flexibility. Counsels by PKI leaders to avoid these extremes occur frequently in the party literature. As was noted at the beginning of this chapter, the current party program states that every nation will proceed along its own path to Socialism and in accordance with its national peculiarities. The 'uniqueness' of the historical situation in Indonesia has led Aidit to warn explicitly against a slavish adoption of Chinese Communist methods in Indonesia. For example, during the Indonesian Revolution against the Dutch 'one of the basic mistakes of the party' in studying the Chinese revolution according to Aidit, was that the party only tried to find the similarities between the Chinese and Indonesian revolutions, but did not discover the differences and the peculiar conditions in Indonesia.[86] Thus the geographic condition of Indonesia did not lend itself to waging successful guerilla warfare as in China. Lenin's dicta,[87] stressing the many and diverse stages through which the mass movement must pass on the road to freedom and Socialism, particularly in Eastern countries, the PKI under Aidit has made fully its own. But at the same time warnings against too much flexibility are heard. Jusuf Adjitorop, one of the fastest rising younger party leaders, declared in an address to a Communist training centre in Semarang in August 1961, that the 'socialism we want to create in Indonesia must not have specific characteristics', but that Socialism as a social system should be seen from its general characteristics in all Socialist countries.[88] In commenting on the Yugoslav situation, Njoto has been even more explicit:[89]

> The 'Program' of the Yugoslav Communist League which has come in for a great deal of criticism concludes with the following bombastic sentence: 'Nothing that has been created should be so sacred to us that it could not be transcended and give way to something still more progressive, freer and more human'. From the point of view of Marxist philosophy this key sentence in the Yugoslav Communist League's Program means injecting the existence of absolute truth. It is indeed true that absolute truth only exists because there are relative truths, but relative truths always contain within them a grain of absolute truth. Is it not an indisputable fact that Marxism is correct? Is it not indisputable that Communism is just? . . . Here in this philosophical sentence, lies, in my opinion, one of the sources of the revisionism of the leaders of the Yugoslav Communist League. If we are to stand by such a postulation then even Communism itself would not be so sacred as to be unable to give way to something said to be 'more progressive, freer and more human'. We should like to know what it is that is 'more progressive', than Communism, what it is that is 'freer' than Communism, and what it is that is 'more human' than Communism? . . . The leaders of the Yugoslav

Communist League always want their right to 'reach Socialism by another path to be recognized'. The reason they give is because 'each country has its own national peculiarities'. If we ignore these national peculiarities then, of course, we shall be committing big mistakes. But if people stress too much the 'national peculiarities' and do not recognize the general laws that have general validity, then they will certainly become national bourgeois.

For Njoto, and indeed for PKI theory today, Yugoslavia is a case of the 'bourgeoisation' of the revolution, a classic instance of the arrest and betrayal of the people's revolutionary forces. The Sixth National Congress of the PKI condemned 'the disgusting practices of the Tito clique of modern revisionists' and Aidit explained then that the PKI cannot remain passive in the fight against 'this dangerous deviation'.[90] But in attacking Tito the PKI is moving on dangerous ground from the point of view of national Indonesian policy, for Tito is much admired in official Indonesian circles. Sukarno's National Front bears a close resemblance to, and may indeed even have been modeled after, Yugoslavia's National Front, and according to several observers the Yugoslav development has been an example to Indonesia in other fields.[91] When, therefore, Aidit recently sent a letter to the 18th Congress of the Austrian Communist Party in which he again attacked Tito's revisionism, there was considerable furore in the Indonesian press because this was criticism of the head of a friendly state. It was pointed out that Aidit holds important official positions in the government (he is one of the vice-chairmen of the Provisional People's Congress and is a member of the Supreme Advisory Council) and that in attacking Tito he was really indirectly attacking the Indonesian government which has maintained such friendly relations with Belgrade.[92]

PKI opposition to Yugoslavia inevitably became part of the general question of the status of the Indonesian Communists in the rapidly developing Sino-Soviet conflict. Even though Sino-Soviet disagreements had become quite severe by the beginning of 1961 the PKI attempted initially to remain as aloof from them as possible. At the Twenty-Second Congress of the Communist Party of the Soviet Union in October, 1961, Aidit had been fulsome in his praise of the Soviet Union, noting that Soviet Indonesian relations were 'blossoming rapidly like flowers in spring', and declaring that neither anti-Soviet slander nor imperialist intrigue could disrupt the unity between the USSR and Indonesia.[93] But Aidit did not join in the condemnation of Albania at this Congress on the grounds, as he explained upon his return to Indonesia, that he had received no instruction from the Central Committee for such a purpose, that he was 'not convinced' that such a condemnation would make it 'any easier' to settle existing differences of opinion, and that

PKI members, having been educated 'in the spirit' of the 1960 Moscow Statement, 'would not have understood what I was doing'. Officially Aidit tried to keep the party neutral in the Sino-Soviet dispute. Again and again referring to the 1960 Moscow Statement he has stressed that the PKI is 'an independent Marxist-Leninist party, which has equal rights with other Communist parties, which is not led by any other party'.[94] This declaration of the independence of the PKI may well have been dictated by the domestic Indonesian requirement that Indonesian parties not receive any aid from foreign sources or be (in practice: even seem to be) under some kind of foreign control, yet in his report to the Third Plenum of the PKI Central Committee toward the close of December 1961, Aidit affirmed that 'there is only one vanguard of the world Communist movement, and let there be no doubt about it, that vanguard is the Communist Party of the Soviet Union'.[95] As for the Soviet downgrading of Stalin, Aidit has tried to keep the PKI equally 'independent'. 'It is the right of the Soviet Communists to do what they like with their former leader Stalin'; moreover the PKI supports the Soviet Communist Party in its criticism of Stalin in connection with the cult of the individual. But the services of Stalin to the Soviet Union will never be forgotten, and the PKI continues to appreciate Stalin's speeches and writings, 'such as those about the revolution in the countries of the East, including the Indonesian revolution. . . '.[96]

Overtly, the PKI has sought to maintain a placating tone in the Sino-Soviet conflict. In a message to the Sixth Congress of the German Socialist Union (Communist) Party in January 1963, Aidit declared that Indonesian Communists regarded 'as correct' Khrushchev's statement in his new year's message that 'differences in the international Communist movement are differences within the family'.[97] This position continued to be held.[98] Yet the attacks on the Yugoslavs and their 'revisionism' also continued without let-up, to the evident delight of Peking which widely advertised the Indonesian attacks in its own media. In his report to a Central Committee Plenary Meeting in February, 1963, Aidit repeated his critique of revisionism and described 'Yugoslav revisionism' as 'now dependent on U.S. imperialist "aid".'[99] Shortly afterwards the PKI daily extensively cited Aidit's February, 1963 report in rebuttal to an earlier attack made by a weekly of the League of Communists of Yugoslavia on Indonesia.[100] The *Harian Rakjat* reply was subsequently republished in *Peking Review*, which two months later accorded a similar honor to a speech of Njoto which also lashed out at Yugoslavia.[101]

By the middle of 1963 it was becoming quite evident that the PKI unofficially had not only begun to side with Peking, but that for various reasons, it was becoming one of Peking's major allies. In July 1963, Aidit visited Moscow where his reception could perhaps best be described as lacking in warmth. His stay in the Soviet Union was productive of no important developments in Soviet-Indonesian relations or in policy statements. On August 28, 1963, Aidit arrived in Peking, where he was greeted by Chou En-lai at the airport and soon found himself the recipient of honors and eulogies. In making Aidit an honorary member of the Chinese Academy of Sciences on September 6, 1963, Kuo Mo-Jo, President of the Academy, described Aidit as 'a respected revolutionary activist of the Indonesian people, a distinguished figure in the International Communist Movement, and a close friend of the Chinese People'. Significantly Aidit was also described as having made a great contribution to the 'Indonesianisation' of Marxism-Leninism and as having opposed both revisionism and dogmatism. Aidit duly reciprocated and in various addresses during his stay in People's China he branded Yugoslavia as 'a country serving the interests of the capitalist bloc', spoke of the need to 'eliminate the poison of revisionism', and condemned 'revisionists' who under cover of 'nationalising' Marxism-Leninism really were betraying it.[102] At a mass rally in Peking on September 4, 1963, Aidit spoke at length of the Indonesian Communists' experience, emphasizing the 'hard line' approach of militant struggle which was bound to please his hosts. He noted, for example, that armed struggle is the most important form of struggle in the conduct of revolution and declared that guerilla warfare and 'revolutionary struggle' by the workers in 1945 would have resulted in a Communist victory then. He did not fail to appeal to the national bourgeosie of Indonesia, however, to join with the PKI and urged the party to win adherents in bourgeois ranks.[103] During a brief sojourn in North Korea, Aidit repeated his attacks on Yugoslavia, now declaring that the 'Yugoslav revisionists' were supporting the 'imperialist scheme of Malaysia'. In Pyongyang, the North Korean captal, Aidit laid down this criterion for membership in the international Communist movement:[104]

To condemn or not to condemn the modern revisionist is the easiest way to test the purity of a Marxist-Leninist party and its faithfulness to Marxism-Leninism, proletarian internationalism, the 1955 declaration and the 1960 statement.

Upon his return from his journey abroad Aidit received the open endorsement of his statements by the PKI Central Committee, and by early October 1963 was reported to be ready to take the PKI formally into a Peking planned 'new Communist International', which would include, along with Indonesia, the Communist parties of North Korea,

North Viet Nam, Japan, Burma, New Zealand, Norway, Venezuela, Puerto Rico, Cameroon and Albania. Yet resentment within the ranks of the PKI over this seemingly increasingly overt drift toward Peking was also being reported. M. H. Lukman, believed to be pro-Soviet, appears to be arguing that the Sino-Soviet dispute is having very little effect on the PKI, whereas Njoto, reputedly pro-Peking, has argued for continuing revolutionary conflict in the world and has been as vociferous as Aidit in condemning 'revisionism'. Meanwhile there is little doubt that Peking claims the PKI as its own, giving continuous prominence to Indonesian Communist pronouncements which receive little or no mention in Indonesia itself. On October 16, 1963, Radio Peking announced, for example, that Aidit had made a speech in Bandung urging Indonesia to 'take the road of revolution against Malaysia' (neither Radio Djakarta nor Radio Moscow reported this speech) and shortly thereafter Radio Peking declared that the conclusions drawn from the 'Southeast Asia revolutions in particular' helped the Indonesian Communists 'to understand further their position, tasks and responsibilities in the framework of the world revolution, in opposing imperialism and new and old colonalism, and in striving for national independence of all nations, genuine democracy, socialism and world peace'.[105]

The reasons for the PKI's rapprochement with Peking are complex and since they involve also Indonesian political strategy in the Malaysia question they are best dealt with below (see chapter VII). From the theoretical point of view the militancy of the Peking approach not only serves the PKI's interests to maintain its independence as a party (as was indicated above) but today also suits Indonesia's efforts to foment revolution in the Borneo area of Malaysia, and by her 'confrontation' assist in the 'national liberation' of North Borneo. The Peking line, with its stress on revolutionary rather than evolutionary change in the colonial or newly independent areas of the world, happens to dovetail neatly with Indonesian policy considerations. This, too, has made Indonesia the ally of those Communist or Communist influenced Chinese, especially in Sarawak, who oppose Malaysia and who seek to turn the area into an overseas dependency of Peking.[106] Thus, despite the long record of tensions between Peking and Djakarta over the position of the Chinese in Indonesia and notwithstanding the anti-Chinese riots in various Javanese towns as recently as May 1963, during which 13 Chinese were killed and hundreds wounded, at present the forces making for a rapprochement appear to be stronger. Indonesia, for domestic reasons more than ever concerned with grandiose spectacles that will demonstrate her Afro-Asian leadership, has in the past year seemed more than ready to act as a kind of front for Peking in staging various Afro-Asian conferences, not to mention the 'Games of the New Emerging Forces' in November 1963, which were largely financed by Peking.[107]

Apart from these policy considerations and diplomatic ploys the fact remains that the 'hard line' of Peking, also for what it portends for the solution of domestic problems, is likely to have a greater appeal in Indonesia than the Soviet approach. Indonesia's chaotic economy, aggravated by her rapidly growing population seems, from a Communist theoretical point of view, more suited by far to Chinese than to Soviet methods, that is, in the terminology of Lowenthal, more to the Leninist than to the Marxist style of development.[108] But it would be dangerous to carry this theoretical affinity much beyond practical policy interests: it is not so long ago that Gomulka of Poland was described, along with Tito, as an American imperialist agent in the PKI literature.[109] The significance of the present unofficial entente between the PKI and the Chinese Communists should always be considered in the light of the *quid pro quo* arrangement under which a Chu Teh expresses 'firm support' for Indonesian opposition to Malaysia and Sukarno announces that Chinese language dailies are permitted to reappear in Indonesia and a leader of Indonesia's Chinese 'Baperki' association is given a minor cabinet post.

Party Theory and Indonesian State Ideology. The official ideological temper in Indonesia at present is expressed in such concepts (all devised by Sukarno) as *Manipol*, *Usdek*, NASAKOM and Pantjasila. The first of these refers to Sukarno's speech of August 17, 1959, which under the name of 'Political Manifesto' has become the official basis of Indonesia's broad policies today. *Usdek* is an acrostic formed by the first letters of five concepts which are: the Constitution of 1945, Indonesian Socialism, guided democracy, guided economy and Indonesian national identity. *Usdek* is considered the essence of *Manipol*. NASAKOM, as was already noted, is the ideological basis of Sukarno's new national front and means the cooperation between the three principal political currents in the country, *nasionalisme* (nationalism), *agama* (religion) and *komunisme* (communism). Occasionally this concept is broadened to NASAKOMIL, the last three letters referring to the military and their participation in the various phases of the process of government today. Pantjasila, which received major official attention as the state ideology before the more recent advent of *Manipol* and *Usdek*, comprises—it will be recalled— the following principles of the Indonesian state: belief in God, nationalism, democracy, social justice, and humanism (internationalism).[110]

Aidit and other PKI leaders have been at pains to identify Communist aims in terms of the official Indonesian state ideology, particularly in terms of *Manipol* and *Usdek*. *Manipol*, as the base of Indonesian state policy, has been described by Aidit as being in keeping, within certain limits, 'with the features of the national and democratic, the anti-imperialist and anti-feudal aspect of the Indonesian revolution',[111] i.e. as being in keeping with the PKI's own aims. The general Socialist objective of the Indonesian state, as announced by Sukarno, the PKI has, of course, also been able to endorse and, indeed, Aidit has made it a point to stress the similarities between the PKI program and the ideas of Sukarno as developed in the latter's major speeches in recent years.[112] In the popular brochures written for the PKI's 'People's Classes' *(Kursus Rakjat)* Indonesian Communist leaders endlessly elaborate on *Manipol* and NASAKOM and on Indonesian nationalism and proletarian internationalism.[113] To a more sophisticated audience, like that, for example, of the students and faculty of *Satya Watjana* Christian University, Aidit ranges from Plato's *Republic* to Engels' *Anti-Dühring* in order to establish the 'ethics and morality of Communism' within the context of the Indonesian state ideology.[114] In all these efforts PKI strategy is designed to effect a union between the charismatic and highly romantic nationalist ideology of Sukarno on the one hand, and the party's own chiliastic Leninism on the other. Sukarno's striving for grandeur, and his constant production of ideological baubles and slogans, creates an aura of limitless confidence in the therapeutic results of mass action, which wholly coincides with PKI policy. In this supercharged atmosphere Sukarno's call to the nation to *vivere pericoloso!* ('live dangerously') is readily echoed by Aidit,[115] for the very temper of grandiosity that it calls forth opens new and useful tactical avenues for the party. When Indonesian Foreign Minister Subandrio, evidently moved by the spirit of *vivere pericoloso*, declared on December 5, 1963, that Indonesia was deliberately neglecting her economy so that she could concentrate on 'regaining her national identity' and on 'reviving the iron spirit' of the people, PKI leaders found it possible to both praise and condemn this statement, since on the one hand it expressed the proper 'anti-imperialist' spirit, but on the other hand seemed to neglect the 'legitimate demands of the people for food and clothing'. It needs hardly to be pointed out that the atmosphere of 'living dangerously', particularly in the context of Indonesia's anti-Malaysia campaign, is also conducive to the growth of pro-Peking sympathies in the Sino-Soviet ideological conflict. China's 'hard line' toward national liberation movements, Sukarno's ritualistic and messianic nationalism and his anti-Malaysia policy, and the PKI's own 'bourgeois democratic' or 'national democratic' strategy thus reenforce each other in Indonesia today. At the same time the grave unbalancing effects of the policy of militancy, especially in the domestic Indonesian economy, provided new opportunities to win adherents, and the party, in the latter half of 1963, took the lead in publicizing the rising prices and scarcity of goods that followed in the wake of the very anti-Malaysia campaign that the PKI had helped to initiate.

Complete identification with the state ideology has been an asset as well as a source of occasional difficulty for the party. Thus the concept of NASAKOM makes Communism an accepted and integral part of the officially sponsored unification of political currents in the country and the PKI has been quick to capitalize on this fact. For example, a statement of the Politburo on September 4, 1960, quoted an utterance by Sukarno which stressed the need for unity and mutual assistance between the nationalists, the religious groups and the Communists as 'the most important political consequence for all supporters of the Political Manifesto and Usdek'; it went on to comment on this exhortation as follows: *'it is also clear that anti-Communist actions taken by anyone, whatever the form may be, are contrary to the broad lines of the State policy of the Republic of Indonesia, and are an act of hostility against one of the major groups of the Indonesian people'.*[116] From this vantage point NASAKOM has also increasingly proved useful to the PKI in pressing for a national coalition government, just as *gotong royong* has served such a purpose. But sometimes the PKI's support of nationalist ambitions runs ahead of state policy and opens the party to criticism. When, late in July 1959, Foreign Minister Subandrio announced that Indonesia would not seek to place the West New Guinea case on the agenda of the United Nations that year, the PKI launched a vigorous attack on this decision in line with its policy of all-out support for Indonesia's claim on the Dutch-held West New Guinea area. *Harian Rakjat*, in sharp tones, demanded that the issue be placed before the U.N. again, in order to arouse the 'enthusiasm' of the Indonesian people. Other papers accused the PKI of wanting to exploit the West New Guinea issue in order to unleash a campaign of mass agitation for its own ends. *Harian Rakjat* vigorously defended itself and a minor press war resulted, which did not terminate until the PKI daily was temporarily suspended by the military because of its criticism of the government.[117] In December 1961, the PKI was again in the forefront of those demanding an Indonesian military conquest of West New Guinea and the party consistently urged the government to liquidate the remainder of Dutch capital in Indonesia in retaliation for the Dutch occupation of West New Guinea. Then, when in the middle of 1962 the Dutch capitulated and Indonesia at last acquired control over the territory, the PKI was in the van of those opposing resumption of economic relations with the Netherlands, a position which ran counter to government policy. Even in radical nationalist circles the PKI's campaign against returning Dutch 'economic imperialism' has been looked upon with some suspicion.

NASAKOM calls for the unity of Moslems and Communists, but most Moslems cannot overcome the belief that the PKI is an organization of *kafir* (infidels) and is hostile to Islam. The very fact that the party aligned itself with Pantjasila resulted in criticism. First there were prominent Moslems who accused the party of opportunism and hypocrisy, since in their opinion the very theories of Marxism and Leninism made it impossible for Communists to accept the first principle of Pantjasila, namely belief in God. Repeated assurances by its leaders that the party fully accepted Pantjasila, indeed revised its Constitution so as to include specific acceptance of Pantjasila by formal action of its Seventh Special National Congress in April 1962, even the historical circumstance that throughout PKI history there have been a number of *kiajih* (Moslem clerics) who proclaimed the unity of Islam and Marxism,[118] did not alter this opinion in the slightest. This was partly because the adherents of Pantjasila as the state philosophy came to be more and more arrayed against those who demanded that Islam be made the basis of the state's constitution and not an essentially secular or 'man-made' doctrine like Pantjasila. The culmination of this conflict came, as was indicated earlier, with the crisis in the Constituent Assembly early in July 1959—a crisis which Sukarno resolved by the imposition of the 'secular' Constitution of 1945 on the country.

Whatever progress the party sometimes makes in removing the stigma of *kafir* is often nullified by other errors. For example, around the middle of June 1961, thousands of PKI members participated voluntarily in a much publicized effort to help the construction of the new Istiqlal mosque in Djakarta, all in the spirit of NASAKOM, but scarcely a month later *Harian Rakjat* was suspended again by the military authorities in Djakarta for having printed an article on Pantjasila in which mention of the first pillar of Pantjasila, the concept of 'belief in God', had been left out.[119]

Adhesion to the two-stage or multi-stage theory of revolutionary development has also brought the PKI in conflict with many of the currently prevailing plans about the Indonesian economy. Though economic planning theory in Indonesia has not been particularly realistic or specific, it does generally seek to balance extensive state control over major enterprises, distribution and foreign commerce, with a degree of private enterprise in fields designated by the government. Some of this balance has been accomplished so far, but sizable private foreign investment in the petroleum industry and in estate agriculture also remains, despite a politico-economic climate increasingly hostile to such investment and despite extensive government controls over the operations of foreign private capital. Viewing the lingering influence of this foreign capital and estate agriculture the PKI has asserted that it is absurd to talk about socialism prevailing in Indonesia today: 'All talking and shouting about a socialist society is a joke, a deception, is just showing off', Aidit has declared, 'a person cannot possibly talk seriously now about "building a socialist society in Indonesia" so long as imperialism and feudalism are still tolerated'.[120] Therefore, as the PKI daily noted sometime ago, 'there seems to be a paradox in Indonesia today. The Communists hold that Socialism is not a program for the present time, while the non-Communists are urging that Socialism be established'.[121] These non-Communists, however, who are seeking Socialism now are in fact encouraging capitalism in general, according to the same daily, because genuine socialism seeks to oppose capitalism: 'And how can you call it Socialism if all that is being expelled is the foreign retail shopkeepers while Indonesian capitalists are growing in strength'. And more than that, how can you call it Socialism if not only nothing is being done to interfere with the interests of imperialist capital invested in oil . . . but even worse, their profits are increased by allowing an increase in the price of oil?'[122]

The PKI opposes capitalism in general, certainly foreign imperialist capital; the only capital it seeks to protect at present is *national* capital, for protection of *national* capital which also suffers from the depredations of foreign enterprise is by definition anti-imperialistic. But to seek Socialism now, with imperialist capital still entrenched, with feudalism still prevailing, and with other nefarious capitalistic tendencies evident in the country is considered an absurdity. Thus it is not surprising that in the PKI view there should be no private capital injections from abroad to assist the current Eight-Year Development Plan. Available foreign loans (not foreign business investment) and the benefits that can be derived from land reform (i.e. the eradication of feudalism) and from compelling foreign capital and the rich to purchase development bonds are sufficient to achieve that plan, in Communist opinion.[123]

Those who advocate establishing Socialism in Indonesia now are in fact promoting the 'bourgeoisation' of the Indonesian revolution; this is an error, as PKI economic expert Sakirman has pointed out, which Marxists have made before, e.g. the leaders of the Second International and also the Mensheviks. That is why the proletariat must be in command during the first or bourgeois-democratic phase of the revolution, as well as in the second or Socialist phase, for only that way can the bourgeois-democratic phase deal thoroughly with imperialism and feudalism. To 'bourgeoisize' the first phase of the revolution is as dangerous as crying 'socialism now!', since in effect the conditions for the establishment of that socialism do not as yet (fully) exist. That is also why the two phases of the revolution, though linked, should be kept apart and not be mixed together, as 'revisionists' and deviationists are wont to do, thereby apparently thinking that they can have socialism while imperialist capital and feudalism still flourish in their midst. It is at this point that the bourgeoisie, with its vacillating characteristics is, and has been, such a danger to the party. Sakirman argues that the Russian and Chinese revolutions indicate how ambivalent the bourgeoisie during the first phase of the revolution can be, unless it is firmly guided by the proletariat, in which case it can be an ally of the workers and peasants. Hence, the demand for 'Indonesian Socialism', and the belief that this type of Socialism now exists, are both dangerous, for they may cause the bourgeoisie to think that Socialism can be reached within the bourgeois-democratic phase, whereas in fact that phase merely clears the obstacles to the establishment of a true Socialist society.[124]

Building on Sukarno's oft repeated phrase that the Indonesian revolution which began in August 1945, is 'not yet finished' and needs to be 'fulfilled', the PKI therefore, holds that this 'fulfillment' means the completion of a 'people's' and 'democratic' revolution, i.e. of its concept of the first stage of the two-stage revolutionary process. The fight for national independence of the Indonesian people is thus seen in the Leninist context of a kind of continuing 'national liberation' movement directed against imperialism and feudalism. The existing changes therefore, which the 'August revolution' has brought do not reflect 'socialist changes', for Indonesia 'is only at the stage of democratic change' and hence, 'it becomes clearer now that the achievement of socialism is not at all the problem today'. But this again does not mean that in this period of democratic change compradore bourgeois groups and 'feudalists' should be permitted to rule, but only that national capitalism is protected in this preliminary era, while the progressive forces are steadily pushing the first (bourgeois or national democratic) stage of the 'August revolution' to its completion.[125]

To keep momentum in this drive toward completion of the 'August revolution' and yet not move too far away from official Indonesian state ideology is perhaps the principal theoretical and tactical problem of the

PKI. During 1963, the Malaysia issue proved ideal for the party in this regard and allowed the PKI to recapture completely the ground it had lost in the aftermath of the July 8, 1960 'Evaluation' crisis (see chapter VII). Capitalizing on the temper of militant 'confrontation' and 'living dangerously', while at the same time the domestic economic chaos increases, the PKI is clearly aiming to push the government further and further to the left in the name of 'completing the August revolution', recapturing 'Indonesia's identity' or any other messianic verbalization. When on November 13, 1963, after the death of First Minister Djuanda, Sukarno announced a new cabinet, PKI leaders announced their dissatisfaction that a true NASAKOM or *gotong royong* cabinet (i.e. one which includes Communists) had not been formed 'at this propitious moment'. Demand for the inclusion of the PKI in the government is, of course, old with the party, expressing, as it does, the party's old policy demand for a national coalition government, and having been reaffirmed again at the Seventh Special National Congress of the Party in April 1962.[126] But to phrase it in terms of NASAKOM and *gotong royong* illustrates PKI tactics *ad oculos* and serves to emphasize again how useful the symbolism of the Indonesian state ideology is to the party.

Efforts to mesh party theory and tactics with the various concepts of Sukarno's mystagoguery and of the Indonesian state ideology are dictated not only by tactical considerations of the appeal to the masses of such a union of concepts, but also by the watchful eye cast by the military on all ideologies that might be interpreted as contrary to official policy. Acceptance of the 1945 Constitution and of *Manipol* is the price the party has had to pay for continued existence. In recent years censorship often made it difficult for the PKI to disseminate its Marxist-Leninist principles or to defend an ideological position that might be considered as deviating from the official state philosophy. The anti-Communist currents prevalent in the army (the agency principally concerned with the censorship of news media) places the PKI in an awkward position. A continued ideological 'bolshevization' of the party—a key principle of the *Sajap Leninis*—has sometimes been seriously jeopardized, and party leaders are called upon to exercise all their dialectical ingenuity to propagate party theory in the context of the official state ideology. Since the anti-Malaysia campaign, however, the party's position has improved in this regard.

To attain the party's aims in the first phase of the revolution depends, however, not only on an understanding of theory but also on a proper party organization and program. It is with these that the next chapter will be briefly concerned.

CHAPTER V

PARTY ORGANIZATION, PROGRAM, AND FRONT GROUPS

IN HIS EXPLANATION of the party's 1959 Constitution, the first vice-chairman of the PKI, M. H. Lukman, declared that the progress of the party in Indonesia had been the 'reward' for the proper execution of its constitution.[1] Since World War II the PKI has had five constitutions, but those of 1947 and 1951 were so brief and relatively unspecific that one learns little of the party's structure and operations from them. The Constitution of 1954, which was formally adopted at the Fifth Party Congress of that year, is the first in the PKI's history to spell out its aims and work in some detail. Five years later a much expanded and considerably revised version was adopted at the Sixth Party Congress. Then, in response to Presidential Decree no. 7/1959 and Presidential Decree no. 13/1960, which imposed uniform demands on Indonesian political parties, a special Seventh Party Congress, in April 1962, altered the 1959 Constitution. But the changes were minor and basically the 1959 Constitution continues in force. In the following analysis we shall be primarily concerned with the party's organization and program as laid down by this 1959–1962 Constitution, along with offering occasional comparisons with its predecessor of 1954.[2]

Party Organization. The Party, as the preamble of its 1959–1962 Constitution states 'is the organized vanguard and highest form of class organization of the Indonesian proletarian class', and its entire work is based upon the theory of Marxism-Leninism. Its immediate aim is the creation of a 'People's Democracy' in Indonesia, preparatory to realizing 'a Socialist society and a Communist society in Indonesia'. 'People's Democracy' in turn would be realized by first fulfilling the bourgeois or national democratic stage of the revolution (see *supra*, p. 86). The organizational structure of the party as outlined in Chapter III (articles 23–35) is based on the principles of 'democratic centralism':

1. For the whole of Indonesia there is the National Party Congress, the Central Committee (C.C.) and the National Party Conference;

2. For each so-called first-level area of local government[3] there is a Major District Party organization, a Major District Party Conference and a Major District Committee (MDC);

3. For the capital city of Djakarta, there is a special Djakarta Party organization and Conference and a Djakarta Party Committee whose status is the same as those of section 2 above;

4. For each island or for several islands, as determined by the Central Committee, there is an Island Party organization or Islands Party organization, an Island or Islands Party Conference, and an Island or Islands Committee (I.C.), which is under the direct leadership of either the Central Committee or the appropriate MDC;

5. For the special district of Jogjakarta (Central Java), and for the city of Jogjakarta, and for such other towns as will be selected by the Central Committee, there are distinct district and town party organizations, district and town party conferences, as well as separate district and town committees which are directly under the leadership of the MDC;

6. For second-level areas of local government, and for areas below this level as determined by the Central Committee, there are Party Section organizations, Section Party Conferences and Section Committees (Secom);

7. For third-level regions of local government, or for districts below this level as determined by the MDC or the IC, there are Party Subsection organizations, Subsection Party Conferences and Subsection Committees (Subsecom);

8. For factories, mines, villages, offices, business enterprises, schools and other institutions there is either the Major Party Branch organization, the Major Party Branch Conference and the Major Party Branch Committee (MBC), or if the unit involved is small, the Party Branch organization, Conference and Committee (BC);

9. Branches, finally, are divided into Groups which consist of a maximum of 10 persons each who live or work close to one another.

Article 26 of the 1959–1962 Constitution provides that during the period between two Branch meetings, two Party Conferences and two National Congresses, the Party Committees elected by these meetings, conferences or congresses act as the supreme leading bodies of the party organization at each respective level. Supreme leadership lies with the National Party Congress, which according to article 36 in ordinary circumstances will be held once in every five years. But if at least one-third of the major regional organizations, representing more than half of the entire membership of the party, request it through decision taken at their respective conferences, then a National Congress must be convened. The National Party Congress is legal only, however, if it is attended by at least one-third of the membership of the Major District Party organizations, representing, again, more than one-half of the entire membership of the entire party. However, the number of voting delegates attending a National Party Congress and the method of their election will be determined exclusively by the Central Committee. PKI members and candidate members may speak at congresses but not vote. In his commentary on the 1959 Constitution, Lukman comments that secret as well as open elections have both their good and their bad sides and suggests that a good deal of variety is possible in election methods according to the desires of the CC and the interests of local party organization.[4] The same flexibility in voting, it may be observed is expected to exist at party conferences at the local level. The functions and powers of the National Party Congress are very broad and include revision of the program and constitution of the party, discussion, revision and endorsement of reports submitted by the Central Committee and other central organization bodies, the power to elect the Central Committee, and so on. The number of members and candidate members of the Central Committee is decided upon also by the National Party Congress.

Just as the CC is elected by the National Party Congress so lower executive committees are elected by their respective regional or local party organizational conferences (e.g. an Island Committee is elected by the Island Party Conference) and the hierarchical principle is strictly observed. According to the constitution (article 23) lower party organizations must periodically report on their work to the organizational level above them and are expected to request instructions from the higher level whenever necessary. For each election of a party committee the National Congress or the appropriate regional party conference shall set up an election commission and, as indicated, the election procedure is quite flexible, i.e. it can be carried out by secret or written ballots, by voice vote, and so on. In order to be nominated as a candidate for membership of a party committee the individual must have been a party member for a specified length of time. If he seeks a CC post he must have been in the party at least 8 years; an MDC post 5 years; IP, TP or Secom post at least 3 years; Subsecom 2 years; and Branch Committee one year. The CC according to article 41 shall elect a Political Bureau and an executive of this Bureau, a CC Secretariat, a CC Chairman and deputies and CC secretaries. These elections will be held at plenary meetings of the CC which will be convened by the Politburo every six months, although postponements and the holding of earlier than scheduled plenary sessions lie within the Politburo's power. The Politburo and its Executive Committee carry out the functions of the CC between the latter's plenary meetings, and the Politburo's executive Committee is in fact the highest and most powerful day-to-day policy-making body of the entire PKI, since the CC secretariat is primarily occupied with routine matters.

Among the most important powers of the CC is the authority to convene one or more so-called National Party Conferences 'to discuss and decide upon pressing political and organizational questions' during the period between two National Party Congresses. The 1959–1962 Constitution makes no provision as to when such National Party Conferences are to be held; the CC may convene them or not as it chooses. A Party Conference is legal only if attended by delegates representing more than one-half of the Major District party organizations. The number of delegates to a National Party Conference and the method of their election is determined by the CC. The constitution provides for a kind of stand-off in power between the CC and a National Party Conference. For example, the latter may dismiss CC members and candidate members 'who have not carried out their responsibilities as they should have done' and may elect replacements for them up to one-fifth of the total CC membership. But all decisions taken by the National Party Conference, including action on dismissals and replacements of CC members are valid only if subsequently ratified by the CC. Elaborate provisions appear in the 1959–1962 and the 1954 party Constitutions on the operations of regional and local party organizations. For example, Major District party organizations are required to have a party conference one every three years; Island, Town and Section organizations every two years; and subsection organizations every year. All regional committees (i.e. committees above the level of the Branch organization), like the Major District Committees, Island Committees or Section and Subsection Committees are required to convene a conference of their particular organization if requested to do so by more than one-half of the total number of party organizations directly under them or on the proposal of the party organization directly above them, such a conference being legal only if attended by delegates from at least one-half of the party organizations directly under the organization in question, and representing more than one-half of the members in the particular region. The various local and regional committees hold regular plenary meetings (for example, Major District Committees, Island Committees and Town Committees must hold a plenum every four months, Secoms every three months, and Subsecoms every two months) and then elect executive committees, secretaries and deputies. The local committees call the local conferences at prescribed intervals, and such conferences may dismiss members of the appropriate local committees, so long as the number of committee members replaced is not more than one-quarter of the total number of persons on the committee and so long as the party committee involved as whole subsequently endorses the replacement. All decisions of the local or regional conference require approval of the cognizant committee in order to take effect.

Increasingly since the advent of Aidit direct party work among the masses has been stressed. At the lowest or basic level of the party (the Major Branch, Branch or Group) organizational discipline and indoctrination receive paramount attention. Anywhere, whether in factory or school, village or office, a group or basic party organization can be set up if there are at least three party members. The Branch has a membership of up to 100, the Major Branch beyond it. Major Branch, Branch and Group organizations are given detailed instructions: they must carry out propaganda and organizational work among the masses; they must implement party decisions from above; they must 'constantly pay heed to the sentiments and demands of the people' by reporting mass sentiment and by aiding the people 'to solve their problems themselves'; they must draw in new members, collect their dues, exercise discipline over them, organize their study and aid them in becoming literate; and they must disseminate the party publications. Branch meetings are held at least once a month, Major Branch conferences at least once every two months. Heads of Groups are required to attend the Branch meetings and delegates of the Branch committees are expected to attend the Major Branch Conferences. Branch meetings and Major Branch Conferences elect Committees, which in turn elect the Secretaries. A Branch unit, such as a Group, which has less than 10 members does not have a Committee, although it has its Group Head and Secretaries.

Purposely, no specific provision is made as to how frequently the Party Group is to meet. At this level members must form an intimacy and cohesion among themselves which makes both formal and informal meetings a natural and extremely frequent occurrence. Continuous proliferation of the party organizations is a principle of the PKI. For example, article 55 of the 1959–1962 Constitution provides that 'Party Branches with many members must divide their members up into Groups each of which consists of at the most 10 persons'. The same article provides that at the basic level women party members may set up their own Group. This provision was probably made as much in deference to prevailing Indonesian social and cultural traditions which, especially in a rural context and also because of the influence of Islam, looks askance at the commingling of the sexes in social and political organizations, as to party belief that a separate women's organization promotes women's leadership.

Chapter VII of the 1959–1962 Constitution takes special cognizance of the position of party members in a non-party institutional setting. Thus provision has been made for the so-called Party Fraction, denoting a group of at least three party members who hold positions of some importance in a non-party organization. Such Fractions are led by the appropriate party committee and the status of such Fractions in the National Party Congress or in lower level party conferences is determined by the party committee leading the Fraction. A Party Fraction may also be created in various representative bodies of central and local government, where they 'must staunchly defend the interests of the people'. Party Fractions shall be led by the appropriate party committee (e.g. the PKI 'Fraction' in the Indonesian parliament is led in the first instance by the Djakarta Committee which, it may be recalled, has the same standing in the party hierarchy as a Major District Committee). The Party Fraction has its secretary and if it has more than 10 members it will have its own Working Committee, but in all matters the Fraction is subordinate to the Party Committee leading it.

Centralized control over the party in the interests of greater discipline and of a more closely-knit organization has increased with the party's 1959–1962 Constitution. The 1954 Constitution had already provided for party Control Commissions but the 1959–1962 Constitution added 'Verification Commissions' to these. The Central Committee of the party, as well as the Major District, Island, Town, and Section Committees, are required at their respective plenary meetings to establish Control Commissions. The composition of the lower Control Commissions requires approval by the party committee directly above. The Control Commissions have what might be called a 'personnel' supervisory function; they examine violations by party members of the constitution, party discipline, and morals, they may impose or rescind disciplinary measures and handle complaints or appeals made by party members. Control Commissions at all levels are under the leadership of the Party Committees at the same level, and higher Control Commissions have the right to examine, to revise or to endorse the decisions of lower Control Commissions. While the work of the Control Commissions has been specified in some detail in the Constitution, this is not the case to the same degree with the Verification Commission. The 1959–1962 Constitution does provide that the National Congress and the various District Conferences shall elect Verification Commissions and that the task of the Verification Commissions is to control party administration, party funds and property and to supervise the 'productive undertakings' of the party (e.g. the mass campaigns which the PKI periodically stages to collect funds, or the assistance the party gives in public construction projects, or the sales campaigns of the party to strengthen its treasury), but no mention is made in the Constitution of the organizational level to which the Verification Commissions are responsible. According to Lukman's commentary on the 1959 Constitution the Verification Commissions report directly either to the National Party Congress or to Party Conferences (presumably either National Conference or Major District Conferences) and the Commissions' task is to 'thwart bureaucracy'.[5]

An entirely new provision in the 1959–1962 Constitution is the explicit recognition given in Chapter X to the youth front of the party—the *Pemuda Rakjat* ('People's Youth'), which according to the Constitution declared itself at the Fifth National Congress to be 'the loyal and trusted assistant' of the PKI. This is the only front group to be accorded specific recognition in the present PKI Constitution. The Constitution enjoins party organizations at all levels to pay close attention to the work of the *Pemuda Rakjat*, to provide it with ideological training and to see that close bonds are maintained between it and the rest of the youth of the country.

The 1954 and the 1959–1962 Constitutions make class origin an important criterion of membership eligibility. Thus article 8 of the 1959–1962 Constitution separates applicants for membership into divisions according to socio-economic background and this classification determines how long applicants must be candidate members and how involved their sponsorship has to be. Workers, agricultural laborers, poor peasants or 'the urban poor' can become party members after having served six months as candidate members, and if they are recommended by two party members. Approval of the Branch party meeting and endorsement by the Subsection Committee is also necessary. For so-called 'middle' peasants, office workers, intellectuals and independent professional persons the procedure is more difficult: a one-year period of candidate membership is required, and the two party members who must give the necessary recommendation must themselves have been members of the party for at least one year without interruption. Approval by the Branch meeting and by the Subsecom concerned is again required. Persons of 'social positions' other than those mentioned above (e.g. the wealthier peasants or members of the national bourgeoisie) who wish to join the party encounter still stricter requirements. For them a two-year period of candidate membership is necessary, and the two sponsoring party members must have been members of the party for at least three years continuously. Branch and Subsecom approval are again required for this category. These requirements also confront ordinary members of other political parties who have left their party and are now seeking PKI membership. Perhaps the most difficult requirements are for those who have held a regional or national executive position in other political parties and who wish to join the PKI. A two-year candidacy period, recommendation by two party members who have been in the party for at least five years without interruption, and endorsement by the Branch, Major District Committee and sometimes by the Central Committee are required. All members of the party have, moreover, to meet the uniform requirements of *(a)* Indonesian citizenship, and *(b)* the minimum entrance age of 18 years. At the time a person enters the party as a candidate member, and again when a candidate member is accepted as a full party member, the following oath is taken:

I, . . . declare my agreement with the program and the Constitution of the Communist party of Indonesia and hereby declare my readiness to become a candidate-member/member of the CPI. I pledge to fulfill all Party responsibilities; to guard the unity of the Party; to carry out Party decisions, to become an example in the struggle for my country and my people; to strive to become an example in everyday life; to strengthen the ties between the masses and the Party; to strive to deepen my consciousness and master the principles of Marxism-Leninism; to be frank and honest to the Party; to obey Party discipline; to guard the safety of the Party.

This is my declaration and vow to the Communist Party of Indonesia, the Party which I hold high and love.

In accordance with Leninist teaching, class background is, however, not the only criterion for entrance into PKI membership. Ideological training is equally important. In his commentary Lukman emphasizes that 'social basis' does not determine the nature of the PKI, but rather broad and intensive indoctrination in Marxism-Leninism.[6] The obligations of party members have been spelled out in considerably greater detail in the 1959–1962 Constitution than in the 1954 version. Along with the duty to study Marxist-Leninist theory diligently, to promote the unity of the party and 'continuously raise' his understanding 'of the party's political line', the party member must place the party's interest ('that is the interests of the masses') above personal interests, carry out 'criticism and self-criticism', overcome feelings of complacency and conceit, and always be loyal to the party. A member has the right to participate in free discussions in party meetings, or in party publications, about the theoretical or practical problems of party policy, to vote in party elections and hold office in the party, to propose, criticize and to defend his point of view 'if he does not agree with a decision, side by side with having to carry out this decision unconditionally'. Improper conduct of party members may lead to their being 'criticized and educated' and disciplinary measures may be taken against them. These disciplinary measures, in order of their severity, are: warning, strong warning, removal from work decided upon previously, the giving of trial work, or expulsion from the party. Every disciplinary action requires the approval of the Group meeting and must be approved either by the Control Commission or by the Party Committee at the organizational level directly above the one at which disciplinary action was taken. The more severe forms of disciplinary action (such as expulsion) taken against members of Party Committees can only be imposed by the Party Conference that elected the particular Committee member to office; in case of action against a member or candidate member of the Central Committee approval of at least two-thirds of the members of the Central Committee and of the National Party Congress is required. Appeals by the offending party member are possible to a higher Party Committee, to a Control Commission and also to the Central Committee. Party members who have been expelled may only be received back as members by decision of the Party Committee that expelled them or by a higher Party Committee.

Over the years, and particularly since the advent of the *Sajap Leninis* in the party, admission to party membership has become more difficult. The Constitutions of 1954 and of 1959–1962 go into considerable detail concerning the prerequisites and training of candidate party members. Before anyone is accepted as a candidate member the Party Committee concerned must appoint a party functionary in order 'to hold the broadest possible exchange of views with the person wishing to become a candidate member so as to get to know him and investigate him thoroughly'. Party education is necessary and the Branch meeting or Party Committee concerned may prolong (but also shorten) the required period of candidacy. If it becomes evident that the candidate does not possess the necessary requirements, his status of candidate member 'shall be withdrawn'. However, candidate-members as well as party members are free to leave the party upon their own request, although the Party Committee concerned, if it wishes, 'may try to suggest' that the resignation be reconsidered. Active party work is required of all and members or candidates who, in a six-month period after having been duly warned, continue to be inactive, or do not pay party dues for legitimate reasons, shall be automatically considered as having left the party, and the decision to delete their names from the membership list will be taken by the Branch meeting and reported to the Party Committee immediately above for endorsement.

Finally, a word may be said about party finances. The 1959–1962 Constitution provides that the party shall be financed by members' entrance fees, by dues, by 'productive undertakings of the Party' and by voluntary and 'non-binding' contributions (including those from non-members). The entrance fee is the same as one month's dues. Dues are comparatively small and range from a monthly contribution of half a Rupiah on gross monthly earnings of up to Rp. 250, to at least one percent of all gross earnings for those with monthly incomes of Rp. 1,000 and higher. Since 1954 the dues have been slightly reduced. In the 1954 Constitution, a half

Rupiah contribution was demanded of all of those with gross earnings of up to Rp. 150 a month, and those with monthly incomes between Rp. 251 and 350 paid Rp. 2 monthly, while the 1959–1962 Constitution asks only a contribution of Rp. 1 a month for those with monthly earnings ranging from Rp. 251 to 500. All party members who hold paid positions in the party must hand over all their other earnings to the party and they receive a stipend from the party in an amount not stipulated by the Constitution, but left to the regulations of the party organization involved. Ten percent of all entrance fees, monthly contributions and other monthly income received by all units and organizational levels of the party is sent to the Central Committee. The remaining 90 percent is destined for the Major District Committee, or where necessary, for the Island or Islands Committee. Thus the MDC or the IC is the hub of the party's financial wheel, receiving all money obtained by lower level organizations (i.e. Town Committees, Secoms, Subsecoms, Branch Committees and Groups). The financial needs of these lower level organizations are handled by the MDC or IC. Fiscal autonomy below the Major District organizational level is thus in theory absent in the PKI.

A comparison with the 1954 Constitution reveals increased concern with organizational discipline and ideological purity. Duties and obligations of members and the responsibilities of various levels of party organization are more detailed and explicitly fixed in the latter document. The 1954 Constitution demanded of members the reading of 'Marx, Engels, Lenin, Stalin, and the thought of Mao Tse-tung, along with the great revision of Muso'. The comparable passage in the 1959–1962 Constitution, however, demands of party members diligent study of 'Marxism-Leninism', and reference to the names of other Communist luminaries has been wholly omitted. This change is, of course, in keeping with the conviction of the *Sajap Leninis*, that 'Marxism-Leninism' is a single comprehensive ideology of universal scientific validity.[7] Lukman in his commentary remarks that the references to Stalin and Mao have been removed from the party constitution because their teachings are already included 'in the general principles of Marxism-Leninism', while Muso's 'great revision' is no longer mentioned, because this revision has already been 'effected completely'.[8]

How well does the formal party structure as described in the 1959–1962 Constitution function? A detailed answer falls outside the scope of these pages and would, in any case, demand an intimacy with the party's operational secrets unlikely to be found outside the circle of the party's top cadres. Even so some insight into PKI operational practices is possible for the implementation of the constitutional directives has in recent years been spelled out in a variety of party publications, particularly in the PKI journal *Kehidupan Partai* ('Party Life'). Daily participation in the class struggle is here emphasized as a major form of correct ideological training. The tendency of some party committees to think of training as primarily a matter of lectures given in party schools is severely criticized. 'Practical education' is also necessary and involves the participation of every party member in various party approved organized bodies, in order, for example, to assist in 'revolutionary actions of the workers'; it includes criticism, self-criticism and the active fostering of a feeling of responsibility on the part of members toward the party and toward the people; it encompasses in day-to-day party life the holding of discussions 'about practical or about theoretical problems', which must be carefully directed, based on proper preparation by each participating member, and in which the leadership, while maintaining a strong fundamental position in harmony with the party line, still is expected to encourage the cultivation of 'the creative ability' of every member of the group.[9] To combat subjectivist tendencies party members must know 'the method of knowing the situation', the 'method of study' and the 'importance of synthesizing experiences at the correct time'. The best way to achieve the first objective is 'to become part of daily revolutionary life' as well as to participate in 'guided' research activities. Research is not merely a matter of gathering figures, or of interviewing a few government officials, but of actively participating in the life of the masses. The 'method of study' is the judicious use of time, proper selection of books, and finding active application of what has been studied. Self-discipline, the 'persistency' in reading, and devising a proper study agenda are all considered essential. Finally, all experiences, successes as well as failures, 'must be synthesized at the proper time'. However small the experience, a proper conclusion should be drawn from it, but this is not to be regarded as an invitation to develop new theory or to add to Marxism-Leninism. Experience may constitute a theory 'if it has already become the experience of the working class in general', i.e. if it confirms existing revolutionary theoretical principles.[10] Constant training in these fundamentals is a duty of every member.

But while all this might be interpreted as a caveat against the dreaded practice of 'subjectivism', experience of PKI cadres in various parts of Indonesia shows the limits of the class theory now generally expounded by the party leaders. In this class theory, it will be recalled, the problems of 'feudalism' and landlordism are heavily underscored, particularly in the party's appeals to the peasantry. But what of a society consisting largely of migratory peasants, using the shifting or slash-and-burn method of cultivation in a thinly populated area where there are no landlords? This is the case in Central Borneo and the PKI leader in that area has recently pointed out that 'it is necessary for us to seriously consider the classification of our peasantry in Central Borneo so that we will not make a mistake in determining the line of policy of the party toward said peasantry'. The danger of theoretical rigidity is thus checked by practical cadre experiences and in Central Borneo the party apparently sees it as its task not the indoctrination of the peasantry in the intricacies of the class war and the evils of feudalism, but in aiding the populace to become sedentary, adopt better cultivation methods and mitigate unsatisfactory living conditions.[11]

Next to the evil of subjectivism the problem of bureaucracy (or of 'commandism' as party spokesmen sometimes call it) receives attention as a major impediment to effective party organization. Such bureaucracy is regarded as a danger to the party; it is seen as but the expression 'of the interests of a certain class' (as one Communist writer has put it) and it defeats the principle of democratic centralism in which stress must be placed equally on the elements of 'democracy' and of 'centralism'. For example, receipt of a general instruction by a higher Party Committee should not lead to its mechanical execution without any discussion about the manner of implementation, for in this way 'only centralism is functioning'. This also creates the danger of separating theory from practice, because the particular conditions in which a general directive must be executed are not given adequate attention and it also threatens to separate the leadership of the revolutionary movement from the masses.[12]

'Democratic centralism' in the context of a society like Indonesia's has often meant a high degree of authoritarianism in party leadership and party organs have frequently stressed the dangers of 'élitism'. Relations between the various organizational levels of the party nevertheless have generally a highly centralized character, and the power of local and regional committees within their respective spheres is virtually absolute. Rank-consciousness seems to be a pervading feature of organizational life and on occasion one finds writers in party journals and papers complaining of the 'militaristic' manner in which some zealous cadres are said to be organizing members and candidate members.

Party publications often stress the threats to the party coming from its own successful growth; the larger the organization the more difficult it is to maintain true unity and to maintain true rapport.[13] The necessity of developing and keeping a spirit of comradely intimacy is, therefore, regarded as primary to successful organization as is evident not only from the constitutional directive that Party Branches with many members must split up into Groups with at the most 10 persons each, but as is equally clear from the techniques which party cadres are told to use in winning contributors for the party. Such contributors should be carefully selected and cultivated; they need not be party members and are frequently persons who for various reasons hesitate to enter into the 'household' of the party; they are also often professional people with an above-average standard of living. Cultivating such contributors widens the cadre's horizons, helps to erase an 'inferiority complex' and provides an opportunity to exercise 'revolutionary patience'. Before actually contacting the potential contributor the party cadre should study his habits and hobbies and only then should he attempt to have 'a heart to heart' exchange on questions of home and family, national and international problems. Persistence is necessary and though contributions are volunary tthey should be or become regular. The cadre is told especially to ingratiate himself with his potential contributor's wife and family ('each time we are ready to leave we must bid his wife good-bye, carry and play with the infant children, bring sweets and picture books for the children'), for when the contributor's wife is won over it will mean 'that the root of the Party is deeply planted in the household of the contributor (this is important; always remember)'.[14]

As indicated, the 1959–1962 Constitution makes provision for units of Party organization in the representative bodies of government and Party work in such bodies is considered extremely important, because by it the Party can gain 'improvements, however small for the people'.[15] Party organizational journals devote considerable attention to the activities of the party in the parliamentary sphere. An example is a recent report on the work of the PKI in the legislative council of the Second Level Autonomous region of Kediri in East Java, where in view of the limited authority of local government the party has deemed it necessary to apply its power to 'its maximum'. In the Kediri local council the PKI 'Fraction' assisted in the legalization of the action of nearby peasants who had taken over the land from a Chinese landlord in the area, aided in obtaining flood relief from the central government, and generally attempted to articulate the 'people's demands' and to render the masses more politically conscious.[16]

Party functionaries who hold positions in local government have been instructed to be particularly active in aiding public works projects, such as the construction of schools and houses, and in the clearing of debris after a natural calamity. Party cadres are expected to bring pressure to bear on local government to initiate more *gotong royong* (mutual cooperation) in local economic development, and the techniques of mobilizing other political and social organizations and the populace generally for such purposes are discussed in great detail at party meetings and in publications. Indeed, no party in Indonesia surpasses the PKI in its attention to, and in providing the necessary training for its members in, what is generally called, 'group dynamics'. Experience in the mass movement is first of all defined as experience in applying manipulatory techniques. The rapid growth of the party precisely in those densely populated areas in Indonesia where mass phenomena are most conspicuous is due not in the least to the successful application of these organizational techniques. But the party leadership still sees itself as far from successful in this respect, for party organizational directives and publications continue to call attention to cadres who are not active enough, who are 'too theoretical', who decline to go among the masses (especially among the peasants), who do not display the proper initiative in starting *gotong royong* drives, public works projects, or public collection campaigns, and so on.

Flagging spirits are constantly incited by new organizational drives and ceaseless sloganizing; especially in the period 1960–1961, when the party confronted a serious crisis in its relations with the government as well as being wracked by dissension among top leaders, campaigns urged cadres to 'put in effect the "Five More"': more courageous, more clever, more shrewd, more unyielding and more persevering'.[17] The 1962 Party Congress adopted the 'Five More' slogan, along with Aidit's demand for the fulfillment of the final part of the party's Second Three Year Development Plan, i.e. 'the Movement of the Four Increases: to increase party schools and people's courses; to increase the membership of party and mass organizations; to increase the number of candidate members who become full-fledged members; and to increase the collection of dues'. In order to implement the 'Four Increases Movement' a separate 'corps of functionaries' was organized at each committee level to be sent down to each subordinate party level organization 'as far down as the groups', and this 'movement to go down to the ranks on a large scale' was designed to interlock with a new program of ideological training in party schools ('There are no stupid cadres and no bad cadres if they are well led and treated justly').[18] Commenting on the Seventh Party Congress Aidit admitted that 'there are comrades who maintain that the difficulties we encounter in our work to reach the targets of the Three Year Plan are due mainly to two factors: first, democratic rights are too limited, and second, life is too difficult'. However, declared the PKI chairman, an expansion of democracy and improvement of living conditions 'must be fought for', and this struggle can only be successful 'if the Party and the masses represent a mighty political force'.[19]

At the Plenum of the PKI Central Committee, in February, 1963, Aidit reiterated the scope of the 'Four Increase Movement', and announced that a new Four Year party development plan was being readied. On this occasion Aidit also delved deeply into questions of leadership practice, stressing the necessity to keep in touch with 'mass demands'. It has been the PKI's experience, Aidit declared, that the principal reason for an organizational breakdown is the lack of a single united leadership body which ceaselessly keeps itself informed of mass needs. Party leaders, at whatever level, should know the problems of subordinate party members intimately, for only in that way can they make an effective appeal. (From this exhortation it would seem that the PKI still has not been able to rid itself of the old problem of 'élitism' which had been the cause of so many criticisms in the past). The collection and systematisation of the 'opinions of the masses', scientifically summarized and then 'disseminated back' among the masses, is, argued Aidit, the best means of realizing the objectives of true party leadership: 'from the masses, back to the masses'.[20]

Within the framework of the 'Four Increases Movement' and the continuing emphasis on getting close to 'mass demands' the PKI in the second half of 1962 initiated a number of so-called 'short term' movements, originally in the pilot area of Central Java, and with the intent to broaden such movements subsequently to include the entire country. Thus there was the 'May movement', revolving around May Day as well as the anniversary of the party on May 23; there was the 'August movement' welcoming the anniversary of the August 1945 Revolution; this was followed by the 'November movement' centering around the November 1926 'national Indonesian uprising against imperialism'. Each of the movements stressed a particular feature of the 'Four Increases', e.g. the 'May movement' emphasized recruitment of new party members among workers and increasing membership in the mass organizations, while the 'November movement' focused in particular on 'more and better' political schools and 'people's courses'.[21] Similar 'short term' movements are now being readied for East Java and North Sumatra, particularly in conjunction with the establishment of new party schools, which in turn is a feature of the current Four Year Plan (to be discussed presently). These party schools are rapidly becoming a new organizational base of importance to the party; all party cadres at all levels, as well as the great majority of party members, are now expected to have had training at a party school, where, in addition to instruction in Marxist-Leninist fundamentals and in 'problems of the Indonesian revolution', close attention is paid to problems of party building and of 'the united national front'. By the beginning of 1964 some kind of party school had been established in 80% of the third level regions of local government or subsection party organization levels.

In April 1963, the PKI announced the formal completion of its second Three Year Plan, and the following August the Politburo announced a new 'Four Year Plan on Culture, Ideology and Organization'. This new plan was said to have been drafted both 'democratically' and 'realistically' and after consultations at all levels of party organization 'from top to bottom'. Noting the continuing need for the 'mastery of proper methods of leadership' the plan divides instruction into two parts, general education and ideological training. As for general education (particularly for, though not necessarily confined to, cadres) provision is made for the establishment of 'academies' and 'faculties' at the Central and Major District levels, for 'People's Universities' (which will presumably give instruction equivalent to senior middle schools) at each Section organizational level; for 'Houses of People's Knowledge' (equivalent to lower middle schools) at the Subsection organizational level; and for 'Leagues of People's Knowledge' (at the elementary school level) for each Branch or Major Branch. Teachers' training institutes as well as correspondence courses are envisaged by the Four Year Plan and it is intended that the party's anti-illiteracy program, especially in areas beyond Java, will be stepped up. To coordinate the activities under the Four Year Plan a special Cultural Department of the party, under the direct supervision of the Central Committee, is to be set up and the regular holding of Conferences on Art and Culture, also in conjunction with LEKRA, the PKI's cultural front organization (see below) is being planned. As for ideological training existing party training facilities are to be expanded and emphasis is to be placed henceforth or integrating the Marxist-Leninist philosophy with the problems of national Indonesian society, so that Communists will be capable 'of combining proletarian internationalism with working class patriotism, and . . . the general truth of Marxism-Leninism with the concrete practice of the Indonesian revolution'.[22]

Judging by the difficulties experienced in implementing the PKI's earlier two Three Year Plans, it is doubtful if the new Four Year Plan will achieve the great expansion of training facilities and the intensification of ideological indoctrination that is envisaged. The PKI's first Three Year Plan began on August 17, 1956, with the attempt to provide systematic ideological instruction to cadres, and according to an evaluation by Aidit of party training made in September 1963, no less than 301,884 cadres were trained during the first Three Year Plan—'over 30 times the number of full and candidate Party members in 1951'.[23] The Party has thus far not released details on the relative success of the second Three Year Plan, but only some 150,000 cadres are believed to have been trained during the period 1959–1962. For the period of the second Three Year Plan coincided with a relative trough in the party's political fortunes, increased military supervision over all party activities under emergency regulations, tight censorship over party publications, and so on. With the lifting of emergency conditions in most of the country early in May 1963, the time seemed ripe for a new organizational departure, and the PKI's Four Year Plan is designed to be just that. At the Central Party school difficulties arose earlier due to lack of qualified staff; this is the instructional center for the deeper mysteries of dialectical and historical materialism, but the relative absence of outstanding intellectuals and theoreticians (with the exception of a few figures like Aidit, Lukman and Adjitorop) in the PKI so far, has rendered the Central Party school into an institution of little or no significance. During the first Three Year Plan, moreover many of the party' educational aims could not be reached due to financial difficulties, and facilities even now are altogether lacking at many Subsection levels, despite the party's claim that instruction is in fact being given there. The new Four Year Plan, in short, will be obliged to cover old ground, while attempting to break new. But undaunted Aidit has promised that the party 'will launch a large scale movement to raise the cultural level of the working people', also through 'the establishment of all sorts of colleges and universities'.

Indispensable to the party, and closely linked to its organizational efforts, are its party publications and periodicals. The PKI has its own publishing firm (*Jajasan 'Pembaruan'* in Djakarta), half a dozen printing concerns and scores of booksellers and retail outlets for its publications throughout the country. No single political party in Indonesia is so intensively concerned with publishing its views as is the PKI. Particularly noteworthy are the party's inexpensive translations of Communist classics. The party's principal journal is *Bintang Merah*, devoted to the study of Marxism-Leninism, and for a wider audience the party also has published an English-language periodical, *Review of Indonesia*, which for some years was exported in considerable quantities to India, Malaya and Hong Kong. Of a more specialized nature are the quarterly *PKI dan Perwakilan*, which deals primarily with parliamentary and local legislative affairs, and *Ekonomi dan Masjarakat*, a quarterly devoted to economic and financial problems. Both the Central Committee and Major Branch Committees publish additional journals (those of the latter appearing only infrequently and often in poor form), but these, like *Kehidupan Partai*, are particularly intended for party members. Party fronts, such as the labor federation SOBSI and the peasants movement BTI, have their own publications.

Probably the most important single medium of communication for the PKI has been its daily newspaper *Harian Rakjat*, which claims a circulation of 60,000, in several editions, including a weekly summary edition which is also distributed beyond Java. *Harian Rakjat* began its career in January 1951, and its birth was the direct consequence of the rise of the *Sajap Leninis* in the PKI, which soon turned the existing small party newspaper into one of Indonesia's biggest dailies. Today party cadres, including Central Committee Chairman Aidit, assist in selling the paper 'in the streets, at railway and bus stations and in market places; they describe briefly the contents of the particular issue and hold talks'[24] and periodic circulation campaigns offer an ideal opportunity to party members and neophytes to participate in the prescribed form of 'mass action'. The editor-in-chief, Njoto, is a member of the Politburo, and a second vice-chairman of the PKI. In some factories and in villages one may see the daily issues of *Harian Rakjat* posted on special stands and when (because of frequent suspensions imposed by the military censors) the paper cannot appear, the workers' 'feeling is such as not having had breakfast, and this they state', as a recent eulogy puts it.[25] For some time the paper carried a special feature for those learning to read and generally it has sought to stress labor news and party policy pronouncements on important national and international issues.

Little is known of the financial affairs of the paper, but considering the distribution and collection problems of all Indonesian papers, it is obvious that income from subscriptions and the few advertisements alone have not been able to meet the paper's expenses. According to Njoto the printing establishment 'P.T. Rakjat', which publishes *Harian Rakjat*, has lost 'several hundred thousand rupiahs' because of the paper's suspensions (in 1960 alone the paper was suspended for a total of 57 days) and in order to make up the deficit a 'Harian Rakjat Assistance Fund' was created by the party. During 1960, according to Njoto, over Rp. 130,000 was donated to this fund, while 'P.T. Rakjat' also floated a bond issue which brought in Rp. 900,000.[26] In attempting to reach all layers of society and to bring some news from as many sections of the country as possible, other regional and local news, even from the Djakarta area, is frequently ignored. A recent evaluation of the paper states that a 'great deal of regional news from estates and shops does not yet get sufficient space in *Harian Rakjat*. This is proved by the many friendly letters regarding news not printed'. On the other hand it is claimed that:[27]

Certainly in addition to workers, peasants also love the *Harian Rakjat*. Peasants read the *Harian Rakjat* on the slopes of Mount Merapi. In the mountains bordering the Malang-Blitar area the peasants read *Harian Rakjat*.

And arriving on the boundaries of estates in Sumatra and in Sanggau, West Borneo peasants are seen reading the *Harian Rakjat*. They do not read it just to pass the time, but read it for study and to teach. They discuss its contents together.

In celebrating the paper's tenth anniversary the editors declared that 'the rise or fall, life or death of *Harian Rakjat* depended on the strength of its relations with the masses'.[28] By the end of 1961 the collapse of the paper seemed imminent, not, however, because its relations with the masses had necessarily weakened, but because of the military 'state of war' administration in Djakarta. On November 3, 1961, the Djakarta 'war administration' suspended *Harian Rakjat* for an 'indefinite period' because of a cartoon celebrating the Twenty-Second Soviet Communist Party Congress. The war administrator deemed the cartoon to be in violation of previous regulations governing the material published in papers and journals, declared that the editor-in-chief 'had violated the vow' he had made in applying for a publication license to defend the 1945 Constitution and support Indonesian Socialism and Indonesia's independent foreign policy. He noted that although *Harian Rakjat* had been repeatedly warned and suspended in the past (e.g. the paper had been suspended for a week in August 1961, and for more than two weeks in the previous February, while in 1959 and 1960 it had suffered the same penalty even more frequently), it was not showing sufficient willingness 'to abide by the provisions and directives given to it and had even given the impression of making a deviation from *Manipol/Usdek* . . . the State policy of the Republic of Indonesia'.[29] The latter phrase confirmed the suspicion of many observers that the mere propagation of Communist theory in party journals was rendering the PKI increasingly liable to attack on grounds that such propagation was contrary to official Indonesian ideology. The party thus could advocate only one type of Socialism, namely the Indonesian variety, as expounded in '*Manipol*' and *Usdek;* any other exposition (such as a defense or a eulogy of Leninism) might bring action by the censor. Even before the November 1961, suspension of *Harian Rakjat* the effect on party publications by the new climate of monolithic state ideology prevailing in Indonesia had begun to show itself and many such publications (e.g. *Bintang Merah*) had become less and less regular in their appearance, and some, indeed, ceased altogether. With the lifting of emergency conditions in May 1963, the news and publications climate improved somewhat, and in November 1963, after a three year absence *Bintang Merah* appeared again and other party and front group publications either reappeared or became more regular.

The Party Program. The Seventh Special National Congress of the PKI in April 1962, reaffirmed, with minor changes, the party program adopted at the Sixth National Congress in September 1959. This 1959–1962 party program, based on the general line of 'fulfillment' of the August revolution, embodies the following ten principal points:[30]

1. The Indonesian state system should be a 'people's state system . . . that is a People's Democratic State', based on the masses and on the national united front of peasants and workers led by the working class. A dictatorship of the proletariat is not possible in Indonesia in view of the undeveloped state of the economy and the task of the people's government is therefore not to carry out Socialist reforms but to carry out democratic reforms, i.e. the abolition of feudalism, the giving of land free of charge to the peasants, the defense of national industries, the improvement of living conditions of the workers, the abolition of illiteracy, and so on.

2. Indonesian democracy should not be the old type democracy, but 'People's Democracy,' led by the working class, and capable of attracting the broad support of all layers of society.

3. The abolition of imperialist and feudalist influences should not give rise to the accession to power of the domestic bourgeoisie, but to the joint power of all anti-imperialist and anti-feudal classes because only in this way it is possible to eliminate the 'injustice' that millions of peasants, workers petty and national bourgeoisie and intellectuals 'do not participate in determining the political orientation of the government'.

4. A democratic centralist principle should prevail in government, i.e. there must be 'a strong central government that manages general affairs', while regional power should develop a mutually reenforcing relationship with the central government.

5. The armed forces should not oppress the people but should be the servant of the people. It is natural, considering their revolutionary antecedents, that the members of the armed forces should seek to implement the August revolution. (It may be noted that this point recognizes in principle the right of the armed forces to participate in politics while expressing concern over the degree of this participation.)

6. The Indonesian economy should be developed in such a way that prime place is given to the State sector (i.e. the area of State-owned enterprises), and that industry and trade undertaken by the national capitalists is not hindered and in fact is encouraged. The economic influence of imperialism and feudalism should be resisted.

7.   All land owned by foreign and Indonesian landlords should be confiscated without compensation (in an apparent deviation from PKI theory the 1959–1962 party program does not at this point distinguish between 'patriotic' and 'imperialist' landlords, as described in Chapter IV above, although such a distinction is implicit in another demand of the program, to be noted presently). Land should be distributed free of charge to the peasantry, especially to the landless and poor peasants. But distribution is to take place on an individual basis and there must be private ownership by the peasant of the land. Estates which are modern in operation and forest land should not be distributed among the peasantry, but should be placed under the control of the state. This provision, it may be noted, runs counter to some radical peasant sentiment in Indonesia, which advocates a break-up of many or most estates for distribution among the land-hungry peasants, but the provision is essentially in accord with government policy. Moreover, the criterion of modernity with respect to estate operations gives the party some room for maneuvring, especially because of the demand that 'all' land of foreign landlords be confiscated. The land of the rich and the middle peasants, the program continues, should not be confiscated (land of the middle peasants should in fact be 'protected' by the state) although all 'feudal slavery systems' (such as mortgaging the harvest in advance) should be abolished and the debts of the peasantry and fishermen and the handicraftsmen to money-lenders should be cancelled. Migration of peasants to less densely populated areas of Indonesia and irrigation improvements should be encouraged.

8.   Working conditions should be national, not colonial in character, namely, minimum wages, two weeks annual vacation with pay, 'social guarantees' for all those that are injured or unemployed, prohibitions against child and women's labor, and introduction of the six hour working day for those engaged in 'underground mining and other industries detrimental to the health'. Development of trade unions and the right to collective bargaining should be guaranteed. To ameliorate the workers' standard of living strict price control should be established.

9.   Colonial culture is 'unscientific and anti-people', and Indonesian culture should be truly national. Free compulsory education for all children up to the age of 12 should be introduced, and the work of scholars and artists should be encouraged. All groups are entitled to use their own regional languages in the schools and in the courts, as well as to the use of the national Indonesian language as 'the language of unity'. A broad popular health system, capable of eliminating the sources of malaria, dysentery and other diseases, should be developed.

10. Indonesia's foreign policy should defend 'independence, territorial integrity and world peace'. A struggle must be waged for 'the liberation' of West New Guinea and for its incorporation into Indonesian territory. An anti-colonial, peace-loving policy must be implemented on the basis of the principles of the Asian-African Conference at Bandung in 1955. War propaganda should be prohibited and economic and cultural cooperation with all countries should be encouraged.

Two other sections of the program deserve brief mention. One describes in some detail the establishment of the 'United National Front', points to the difficulty of effecting a peaceful, parliamentary transition to 'a system of people's power' (although the possibility of such a peaceful transition is not excluded) and urges the working class to lead 'the struggle of the entire people' including of the peasantry, and to assume the leadership of the united front. The other section lists fifty specific demands based on 'a Marxist analysis of the concrete situation and the balance of forces', which are essentially a repetition and elaboration of the basic ten points described above. The fifty demands are divided into six categories. The first category, sub-headed 'For National Independence', urges the Indonesian people 'to organize all forms of their resistance against the Dutch occupation of West Irian' and demands nationalization of all the Dutch enterprises, including those enterprises with only some Dutch capital. All foreigners who have aided counter-revolutionary movements as well as Indonesians who led such movements (specific mention is made here of the PRRI and Darul Islam) should receive death sentences.

In the second category, entitled 'For Democratic Rights', repeal of all colonial laws is urged, a democratization of village government by creating defined levels of local government is demanded as is the 'serious' implementation of regional government, and the holding 'on time' of direct general elections for parliament and local councils is stressed. This category also states that 'the broadest possible democratic liberties' must be given to the people and to their organizations, and that all laws restricting 'the freedom of the patriotic movement' be repealed. All citizens, regardless of sex, origin, political conviction or belief should have equal rights. Implementation of the 1945 Constitution in conformity with the 'anti-imperialist and democratic' spirit of the August revolution of 1945 is also included. This second category concludes with a demand that good relations be established between the army and the people, and between the officers and men and that the 'democratic rights' of the members of the armed forces be respected.

The third category of demands, called 'For Better Living Conditions', asks for general improvements in the working conditions and living standards of workers and peasants, by the raising of wages, elimination of crop mortgages, by reducing interest rates on loans, requiring money lenders to register themselves, by the legalization of ownership of land taken by peasants from foreign estates, confiscation of land of those landlords who have sided with 'counter-revolutionary terrorists' (here the theoretical distinction between 'patriotic' and 'imperialist' landlords is apparently made), by giving the peasants the right to arm themselves (under the leadership of the army) to defend themselves against terrorists, and so on. This category also provides for special relief to fishermen and special protection in the form of credit and tax cuts to small enterprises. A special clause includes demands for improvements in the living conditions of and special treatment for members of the armed forces.

The fourth category, 'For Economic Improvements', is perhaps the most specific. It demands that owners of foreign estates be required to cultivate rice on estate lands in order to increase the output of this staple and that the owners must also help the peasants with seeds, fertilizer and implements. Protective tariffs for the benefit of national enterprises against foreign competition are demanded, along with price control. Changes in foreign investment legislation are also demanded so as to control the foreign exchange earned by the foreign oil companies and to guarantee adequate supplies of oil to the people and the armed forces. All mining concessions which have not been utilized should be withdrawn and be exploited by the government itself. Import and export trade and all important enterprises should be under complete government control and all forms of communications, especially in the regions outside Java, should be improved.

The fifth category ('For Cultural Progress') demands expansion of the physical plant of the school system, and a reduction of educational costs to parents and students, urges that 'imperialist subversive activities in cultural affairs' (as manifested by poor quality motion-pictures, reading material and music) be eliminated, and requests an increase in the number of public meeting-halls for cultural activities as well as in the number of medical clinics.

The sixth and last category ('For World Peace') opposes the rearmament of Japan, urges the U.S., Britain and the Soviet Union to stop testing nuclear weapons and to dissolve all military agreements, and demands implementation of an anti-colonialist policy, based on the African-Asian Conference of 1955, and of an independent policy which seeks improved economic and cultural relations with all countries but resists every effort to be drawn 'into the bloc of war and aggression'.

A comparison with the 1954 program of the PKI reveals many similarities and some, although comparatively minor, differences.[31] The threats of imperialism and feudalism, the united national front approach and the classes involved, the objective of the people's dictatorship (not the dictatorship of the proletariat) are key concepts that appear in both the 1954 and 1959–1962 party programs. Nevertheless the turbulent events between the constitutions have left their mark. The demand for a 'centralized' structure of democracy, the various clauses spelling out the role of the army and its place in national political life, increased concern for political liberties, the greater stress on the West New Guinea issue, and most of the entire section 'For Cultural Progress' were new with the 1959–1962 program. In contrast to the brevity and the generalities of previous party programs one is struck by the increasing attention to detail, the widening of the scope of party interest and activities, and the 'openness' with which such interest and activities are expressed.

Between 1960 and 1962, however, the propagation of the program—indeed its very publication—became extremely difficult for the party. The increasing watchfulness exercised by military over the propagation of any ideology held to be in conflict with the Constitution of 1945, Pantjasila, *Manipol—Usdek* and other concepts of the approved State political philosophy seemed to make program less and less useful to the PKI. The PKI, as the price of its continuing existence, formally accepted *Manipol—Usdek* into its program, and while, Aidit, Sakirman and other theoreticians employed all their dialectical ingenuity to reconcile Marxism-Leninism with the Indonesian state ideology, the advocacy of the party program had to be expressed, if at all, in ever more circumspect terminology and in ever broader generalizations, despite the moral support the PKI leadership from time to time got from a Sukarno lashing out against those in his country inflicted with 'Communist phobia'. Since the beginning of 1961 no important commentaries on the PKI program were published, and the danger seemed real that for practical purposes Marxism-Leninism would have to submerge itself completely in the vague vocabulary of the currently accepted version of revolutionary charisma, as interpreted largely by the PKI's enemies—the officers of the Army.

In Aidit's report to the Central Committee's plenum in December 1960 the party's policy in a democracy that has become more and more 'guided' in character was outlined.[32] 'With loyalty, grimness and cleverness' the party was now attempting to implement its program and other decisions of the Sixth National Congress, Aidit declared and although the political situation was shifting to the left, the 'objective conditions' making for the rise of 'new right-wing elements' remained unchanged. These new right-wingers, declared Aidit, carried on anti-Communist propaganda and thus threatened the unity of the nation under NASAKOM:[33]

We must make an all-out effort to unite all possible people for the implementation of *Manipol*. Also, if we do not want to fail, we must reveal and attack these enemies with all our strength who are anti-nation and anti-people. The victories won by the party and the people have dismayed both old and new imperialist and right-wingers. . . . Right-wingers are very active in the universities; among other things they interpret the Pantjasila in a way that is contrary to President Sukarno's speech 'The Birth of Pantjasila' of June 1, 1945, and they misinterpret and oppose *Manipol* and its planning. In their frenzy they slander us and purposely misinterpret our party's constructive critics, they strive to rob us of the victories which the people have won, and impede the people from winning still more victories.

In accordance with Presidential Decree no. 7/1959 concerning the 'simplification of parties' and Presidential Decree no. 13/1960 concerning the 'recognition, control and dissolution of the parties', Aidit in his report recommended, and the Central Committee Plenum on December 31, 1960, approved an addition to the party constitution (in the preamble), reading as follows:[34]

The PKI accepts and defends the 1945 Constitution, that is the Constitution of the Republic of Indonesia, which begins with an expression of the desires of the Indonesian people for a life of freedom, unity, sovereignty, justice and prosperity, and considers Pantjasila the law of the nation, which aims at constructing a just and progressive society in accordance with the individuality of the Indonesian people and based on the work program of the Political Manifesto together with the specifications designated by the First Session of the MPRS (People's Congress) on November 19, 1960, as the General Line of National Development for the Indonesian Republic.

Indicative of the difficult position in which the PKI found itself in the period 1960–1961 is the history of how this and other constitutional additions were ultimately incorporated. In August 1960, the Central Committee announced that shortly a Plenary Session of the Central Committee would be convened to discuss preparations for a special Seventh Party Congress which would ratify proposed changes in the party constitution, so as to bring them in line with the relevant presidential decrees. But on December 31, 1960, a Central Committee Plenum declared that it would not be necessary after all to convene a special party congress in order formally to change the party constitution. This decision apparently had been made largely by Sukarno who, according to the Central Committee, on November 23, 1960, after consultation with party leaders had 'specifically stated that in order to fulfill Presidential Decree no. 7, it is not necessary to hold a special congress, thereby cancelling the need for an extraordinary Seventh National PKI Congress'.[35] Sukarno's decision may well have been motivated by the consideration that granting permission to the party to stage yet another national congress (so soon after the last national congress in September

1959) and while public tempers were still aroused over the party's July 8, 1960 'Evaluation' (see below, chapter VI) might be somewhat impolitic. The Central Committee by itself agreed, therefore, to incorporate the required phrases rendering obeisance to Pantjasila and the 1945 Constitution (as demanded by Presidential Decree no. 7/1959) into the party's constitution and to add a clarification of its concept of 'People's Democratic Government' so as to make clear that this concept does not refer to 'the power of the proletariat, but the power of the people', i.e. the joint power 'of all anti-imperialist and anti-feudal revolutionary classes'. The latter concession was apparently made particularly in order to emphasize the 'national' character of the PKI. Concepts like 'People's Democracy' and even 'Socialism' and 'Communism' were given a specific Indonesian context, the first being made synonymous with *gotong royong*, the second and third being described as adapted to 'Indonesian conditions'. By equating 'People's Democracy' with *gotong royong* the PKI in effect sought to reconcile whatever differences might still be felt to exist between the party's announced 1955 election aim of national coalition government and 'Peope's Democracy'. For the entire PKI effort to enter into a national coalition also was described as based on *gotong royong*, it will be recalled (*supra*, p. 165), and the 'native' *gotong royong* symbol thus was made to serve as a useful instrument for equalizing party objectives. The Central Committee in line with Presidential demand also pledged the party to the path of peace. But within the PKI pressure to hold a special congress soon increased, however, reflecting the demands of a militant element, with leanings toward Peking, and for whom there had already been too much acquiescence to government pressures as a result of the July 1960 'Evaluation' crisis. Moreover, the 1959 Constitution clearly seemed to demand such congressional approval of constitutional changes. By the end of 1961, the Central Committee, noting that 'an official request' had been made for formal congressional ratification of the constitutional changes, agreed to convene the Seventh Congress.[36] As indicated, this Congress, meeting in the closing days of April 1962, approved the earlier cited addition to the party's constitutional preamble, an explication of the nature of 'People's Democratic Government' (also incorporated in the new preamble), and the 'clarification' that the youth front *Pemuda Rakjat* (People's Youth), specifically mentioned in the 1959 Constitution (articles 68–69), is in fact an organization 'sheltered' by the PKI within the meaning of Presidential Decree no. 7/1959 (see also *infra* pp. 241–242).

By the end of 1962, with the new anti-Malaysia campaign gaining momentum, the PKI's resurgence became particularly noticeable in party and front publications, which displayed a new aggressiveness and theoretical experimentation, unawed—as was the case barely two years before—by the army's supervision over the party's ideologizing of current events. New commentaries on party tactics and program now appeared again in growing numbers, especially after Aidit's February 1963 report to the Central Committee Plenum. The practice of publishing many of the lectures now being given to the higher party schools shows that leading cadres feel free once again to comment publicly and at length on the application of the party program to 'concrete conditions'. Recently the party has even noted the differences between its program and the Political Manifesto.[37]

The Peasant Front. Among the front groups the Indonesian Peasants Front (*Barisan Tani Indonesia*—BTI) merits particular attention because one of the most emphasized principles of the *Sajap Leninis* has been the need for effective mobilization and incorporation of the peasantry into the Communist movement. 'A national front without the active participation of the peasants is like a bale of jute without contents, empty and light, and hence easily blown by the wind', Aidit has declared, and one of the most popular slogans of the party has been '*Belanda angkat kaki, tuan tanah angkat tangan!*' ('Dutchmen take to your heels, landlords stick your hands up!').[38] Before describing the PKI's work among the peasantry and the role of the BTI it is necessary to say a word about the structure and problems of Indonesia's peasant economy as determinants of Communist policy.

The pivotal problem of the Indonesian peasant economy today, as in decades past, is the acute shortage of arable land. This shortage is by no means general throughout the Indonesian islands, since population densities vary markedly from region to region, but it is particularly evident in all of Java (where more than 60 percent of all Indonesians live) and in sections of Sumatra, and of the Nusa Tenggara (Lesser Sunda Islands). Land shortage in Java, and the problem of the rural proletariat are, as was noted in Chapter I, by no means recent phenomena, but they have begun to make themselves felt with redoubled force in the past decade. By 1957 some 66 percent of the Indonesian peasant landholders in Java held less than 0·5 hectares (1·23 acres), 32 percent held from 0·5 to 2 hectares (1·23 to 4·94 acres) and 2 percent had holdings larger than 2 hectares. For the country as a whole the situation had certainly not improved since 1940, when 70 percent of all peasants held less than 0·5 hectares, 25 percent held from 0·5 to 1 hectares and the rest 1 hectare and up.[39] The seemingly inexorable population pressure (from 1940 to 1962 Indonesia's total population rose from 70 to 96 million, Java's alone rising from about 48 to more than 65 million) has resulted in a steady sub-division and sub-tenancy of miniscule holdings, in an enormous labor intensivity and in the spread of wasteful labor-absorptive methods of production. Under-employment and disguised unemployment in agriculture have reached alarming proportions: according to one calculation more than 31 percent of the total agricultural labor force of 23·5 million people in the country is in excess of need and qualifies to be designated as 'disguised unemployment'; estimates for Java alone show roughly the same percentage.[40] The evils of progressive indebtedness and loss of control over the peasants' land to landlords or creditors have become more and more pronounced in a number of areas. One Indonesian student has well described the fate of the small farmer thus:[41] 'It frequently happens that within a month or so after harvesting this rice they are already contracting new debts. It is evident that the fruit of their harvest has been divided among their creditors. Such a state of affairs often persists until they are obliged to sell a portion of their land'.

Particularly noteworthy has been the spread of large and absentee landownership. Under prevailing conditions of rural indebtedness and sub-tenancy even a peasant with relatively small holdings may find it possible by judiciously leasing out his land or by advancing credit to other small-holders (who are often apt to default on their debts) to become a landlord, and 'an increasing concentration of landownership and land usage rights' has thus become evident.[42] In the village case-studies made by Adiwilaga concentrations of up to 50 percent of the arable land in the hands of absentee landlords, accompanied by fierce competition among the growing tenants' group for the scraps of land that can still be rented out, have been noted.[43] The very fragmentation of the land, precluding adequate production methods and resulting in inevitably low yields, seems to encourage concentration of land in the hands of a few, since with an inadequate crop the peasant is pushed into usurious indebtedness which ends with his losing whatever land he still has and with his sinking into the debt-ridden tenant and share-cropper group.[44]

Adiwilaga notes that conditions of personal servitude have begun to emerge, with tenants having to perform special services or making special payments to a landlord who 'is exercising his seigneurial rights', while 'The landlord in turn will give each of his tenants as little land as possible just in order to have more servants at his disposal'.[45] These feudalistic conditions are by no means confined to overcrowded Java. After a survey of land tenure conditions in the eastern part of Nusa Tenggara, the Agrarian Affairs Minister, Sadjarwo, declared in May 1961, that farmlands and pasture lands there are in the hands of tribal chiefs who are at the same time landlords as well as cattle 'kings' owning hundreds of cattle. By 'seigneurial' right the cattle graze freely over the land with the result that 'the peasantry which formed the majority of the population was pushed aside and has no chance at all to own farmland', and, according to Sadjarwo, the landless peasants live 'as serfs of the tribal chiefs and are unable to free themselves'.[46]

Sadjarwo's views generally closely parallel those of the PKI, and the actual conditions of the 'serfs' in Eastern Nusa Tenggara, reflecting rapidly eroding traditional class distinctions in the area, require further analysis, but it is indisputable that a polarization of classes, based on the widening distinctions between the landowning and the landless is—as Goeritno also has shown in his survey of a Central Javanese village[47]—a social dynamic of major importance in contemporary Indonesia. Any Indonesian statistics must be used with caution but according to Sadjarwo, citing data compiled by his Ministry of Agrarian Affairs, 60 percent of all peasants in the country are landless; on the island of Lombok (Nusa Tenggara) peasants had pawned 42 percent of the total area of (presumably arable) land to landlords, while in some villages in Java one-third of the land is in the hands of landlords.[48]

We have already noted the emphasis on the role of the peasant and on the need for land reform in PKI theory and tactics. In line with the party's policy of the 'Three Togethers' (i.e. party cadres must 'live together, eat together and work together' with the peasantry) an intense and broadly conceived campaign of ideological indoctrination and continuous party branch and group formation among the village masses began, tied to rendering practical assistance to the peasant and his work. It is to party functionaries that the peasantry is encouraged to turn for relief of the age-old practices of *rodi* or *idjon* (crop mortgaging in advance of the harvest) which the PKI has branded as 'feudal', and party functionaries bring pressure to bear on the landlord on behalf of a debt-ridden peasant or seek to legalize possession of land by land-hungry squatters who have moved on some landlord's or estate's property. Practical advice is also provided through the party's 'Five Principles' campaign, encouraging peasants to 'plough deeply, plant closely, use more fertilizer, improve seeds and irrigate better'.[49]

On occasion this campaign involves the party in considerable controversy, as was illustrated by the 'Martosuwondo affair'. All during 1959 a certain Martosuwondo, a villager in Central Java, claimed to have increased his rice production from the usual 25 or 30 quintals per hectare, to between 1,000 and 2,000 quintals. The PKI, and its peasant front the BTI, hailed and widely publicized Martosuwondo's efforts as a demonstration of the efficacy of the 'Five Principles', but criticism by government officials soon deflated Martosuwondo's and Communist claims. The Minister of Agriculture and several members of the Supreme Advisory Council declared that their investigation failed to substantiate the results claimed, but the party, through its chairman, D. N. Aidit, castigated the skeptics by declaring them to be still dominated by 'textbook thinking'.[50] Possibly also because of such headlong ventures into the problematic area of agricultural production the enthusiasm of party rank and file members for work among the peasants is somewhat less than the party leadership apparently likes to see and the Central Committee's general report to the Sixth National Congress noted that party cadres were still not sufficiently informed on 'the agrarian relation-ships' and that there were 'still many party functionaries who evade work in the countryside'.[51] A report by a PKI sponsored 'Peasants Conference' held in April 1959 echoed this complaint: 'It is not unlikely that some of the cadres leading the Party Committees or the revolutionary peasants organization have family ties with landlords and have not yet received sufficient ideological education'.[52]

In the context of the multi-stage revolutionary theory the basic policy of the PKI at present is to strengthen the peasant in his capacity as a private producer and landowner. The implementation of this policy is perhaps best illustrated by what the party has called its 'small yield' campaign, i.e. limited achievements in general peasant welfare. 'Small yield' action involves party agitation to cut interest rates on peasant indebtedness, wage increases for landless laborers, and defending the peasant's cause when he happens to find himself in legal difficulties. It also includes the so-called 6:4 campaign, i.e. agitation for a change from the traditional pattern of payments by tenants to their landlords, by which each gets half the harvest cultivated by the tenant, to an arrangement by which the tenant keeps 60 percent of his crop. The landlords to whom the 6:4 ratio is applicable, it should be noted, are 'patriotic' ones (i.e. they 'oppose imperialism' and the PRRI and Darul Islam rebels). The land of 'imperialist' or *Darul Islam* landlords should be confiscated. Also part of the small-yield action is a campaign to distribute uncultivated lands to landless laborers, especially uncultivated lands belonging to estates.

The party is also expected to raise the general cultural level of the peasantry. Strictly adhering to the principles of 'voluntariness' and 'democracy' cadres should assist the peasants to organize in all types of appropriate organizations such as 'pooling of money' clubs (a kind of small-scale lottery arrangement, generally popular in Indonesia, by which each member puts in a small amount of money in a common pool and the winner takes the entire pool, whereupon the collection begins again) mutual assistance associations, funeral groups (for the purpose of sharing funeral expenses), sports', educational and cultural organizations, and so on. 'Only by carrying out with perseverance the work among the peasants will the confidence of the peasants in the party grow and will the party's fighting abilities be increased', Aidit has said.[53]

The development of cooperatives has been of particular concern to the party. At its special 'Peasants' Conference' held in Djakarta in April 1959 the PKI emphasized that the type of cooperatives which it desired were what might be called 'national front' organizations of laborers, peasants, fishermen and handicraftsmen. The party is not, at this stage, seeking 'Socialist cooperatives', because 'the conditions for these do not yet exist'. However, the leadership of true 'working people's cooperatives' must be in the hands of Communists, because only in that way can the 'fundamental principles' of cooperative organization be observed: (1) 'voluntariness', (2) mutual interest; and (3) 'democratic methods' of work and leadership. The 'Peasants' Conference' excoriated the 'capitalist cooperatives of the Hatta style' (former Vice-President Hatta, who is detested by the PKI, is generally regarded as perhaps the principal advocate of the cooperative movement in Indonesia), because Hatta believes, it was alleged, that the economic crisis of the country can be solved by cooperatives and that 'it is possible to oppose capitalism and imperialism with cooperatives'. All this is misleading, according to the PKI, because Hatta's cooperatives (the term evidently used for all cooperatives not under Communist control) are really 'capitalist cooperatives' designed to lull the Indonesian people into believing that it is unnecessary to organize and mobilize against imperialism and landlords by revolutionary means. The principle of 'voluntariness' is to be advocated in opposition to the allegedly involuntary practices of the 'Hatta cooperatives'. The latter, though paying lip service to the voluntary principle, are said to coerce people to join by means of thinly concealed commands of government officials. Neither mutual interest nor democratic methods are allegedly observed in the 'Hatta cooperatives' for their leaders are said to be in league with 'landlords, capitalists and moneylenders'. True (i.e. Communist-led) cooperatives must in no way abridge the activities of revolutionary peasants' organizations; indeed, they must assist the latter, for the more damage is done to the landlords and the more land redistributed, the more favorable the conditions for cooperatives will be.

It is evident from all this that the PKI regards the cooperatives as adjuncts of the revolutionary peasants' struggle against imperialism and feudalism. The stress on 'voluntariness', on mutual interest and on democratic methods in the PKI program seems designed to exploit the problem arising from the rather elaborate bureaucratic structure which the spread of the cooperative movement (there are some 12,000 cooperatives of various types in Indonesia today, with a total membership of 2·5 million and with nearly 500 million Rupiah in capital) has engendered, and to underscore the difficulties which the small producer may experience in a cooperative organization of sometimes thousands of members.[54] In June 1961, a government controlled central cooperative body, the so-called KOKSI, was formed, in line with the state's general supervisory policy under 'guided democracy', but BTI cooperatives were to all intents and purposes able to retain their independence, and by early 1963 KOKSI had largely atrophied. Of late PKI directives on the cooperative movement have become increasingly practical and technical in character, affording detailed analyses of the consumption and production problems of the members of cooperative societies.

Next to the party the BTI is the principal agency concerned with the implementation of Communist policy directives. Founded on November 25, 1945, in Djokjakarta the BTI has gone through three principal stages of development.[55] From 1945 to 1949 it was primarily a para-military organization of the PKI, but besides participating in the revolutionary fighting it also undertook, at the revolutionary Indonesian government's request, to cultivate neglected foreign estates in an effort to increase food production and it promoted a 'democratization' of the villages (e.g. by aiding in the formation of local government institutions). In early 1948, according to one BTI spokesman, the organization was particularly active in opposing restoration of agricultural estates in Djokjakarta and Surakarta to their former owners. With the Madiun affair the BTI also went into eclipse, and like the PKI it experienced a period of reorganization and then of expansion between 1949 and 1953, the period now described as the second phase in the BTI's development.

On February 6, 1949, BTI elements formed a new organization, the Indonesian Peasants Association (*Rukun Tani Indonesia*—RTI) which originally had as its declared principal objective the mobilization of the peasantry in areas occupied by the Dutch. The RTI in effect took over operations from the temporarily 'underground' BTI, but with the formal transfer of sovereignty to the new independent Indonesian government the BTI revived. The RTI continued on its own way, however, especially attracting a following on the islands beyond Java, and both BTI and RTI were subsequently active in propagating labor unrest on Western estates and arousing the peasantry generally on behalf of lower prices and land reform. In part because of this unrest the Sukiman government, it will be recalled, arrested scores of Communists in 1951, including a number of BTI and RTI activists. Though agrarian unrest in Indonesia was becoming increasingly ready for exploitation, other parties (including some bitterly opposed to the PKI) were organizing their own peasant groups, and in order to present a stronger front toward their competitors the RTI and BTI formally merged in September 1953.

With this merger a new phase set in, marked by increased organizational activity, ideological indoctrination of members and by fusion with still other peasant splinter groups. The BTI now urged immediate 'appropriation of the land controlled by foreigners in Indonesia, without compensation', and 'the free distribution of said land among the peasants, particularly among the poor peasants and the landless peasants', the plots of distributed land to 'be owned individually'. Ever more closely the BTI echoed the Communist program and at the organization's Fifth Congress, held in Surakarta in September 1957, 'expanding mass peasants' actions in order to foster the growth of progressive forces' were stressed as the BTI's major aim. In the general program adopted by the BTI at this Congress the struggle against 'feudalism' and the realization of a true 'national independence' are seen as taking place within the context of a united national front, and the entire document has a pure Marxist-Leninist flavor.[56]

With its more than 5 million members the BTI by early 1964 was the largest peasant organization in Indonesia, harboring within its ranks not only avowed PKI members and candidate members, but also remnants of Trotskyite and left-nationalist peasants organizations (some of them dating from the revolution) as well as fellow-travellers and sympathizers. In élite-conscious Indonesia the BTI has served a considerable number of ambitious radicals, often unwilling for opportunistic reasons to identify formally with the Communist Party, but sharing its radical agrarian program and desirous of climbing to prominence via the party's peasant front program. The relative respectability of the BTI derives not merely from the increasing legitimacy and power of the PKI after 1951, but also, and perhaps primarily from its announced 'practical' approach to agrarian problems, its interest in promoting better cultivation methods, in providing credit to the farmer and in having special regard for the educational hunger of the younger generation in the rural areas.

Both BTI and PKI are forever 'discovering' villagers (like Martosu-wondo) who as a result of allegedly Communist-propagated cultivation methods have been increasing their production by fantastic percentages. Although the BTI has been widely accused of being only interested in

such spectaculars for propaganda purposes and of having no real interest
in production, there can be little doubt if one looks at the volume of
BTI instructional literature, the trainnig courses given by BTI 'specialists', and the organization's assistance program to needy peasants that,
whether for propaganda purposes or not, much of the BTI's attention
is in fact devoted to the practical problems of increasing peasant output.
The relative effectiveness of the BTI in this respect probably stemmed
in part from its tight organizational structure which closely parallels
that of the PKI.

On November 25, 1959, the BTI embarked upon a Three-Year Development Plan which was expected to double the organization's total membership by the end of 1962. Membership quotas were set for BTI provincial and district organizational levels and detailed instructions were
issued for the mobilization of mass support through the 'small yield'
campaign. 'The majority of the peasant mass is made up of those who
can only understand things by what they experience', as one directive
put it, and the expansion of membership can only take place if BTI
activists concern themselves with solving the 'practical problems' of the
masses. Close control was to be exercised over the BTI membership
drive: 'organizationally a clear cut division of labor among the activists
must be introduced; vertical control over the execution of the plan
must be exerted; reports must be submitted; and periodic gatherings
to compare experience must be held'.[57] Communist jargon frequently
appears in the BTI campaigns. Just as Communist theoreticians may
speak of 'left' and 'right wing' deviations, so the BTI cadres have been
made familiar with the errors of 'leaning on the right' and of 'leaning
on the left'. 'Leaning on the right' means that the activist or BTI section
is placing too much emphasis on propagandizing for food production
increases and expansion of crop cultivation, and is not being sufficiently
concerned with 'small yield' actions, such as seeking wage increases
for landless workers, implementation of the 6:4 principle, or a cut in
interest rates on peasant loans. 'Leaning on the left', indicates too great
a pre-occupation with 'small yield' action and not showing enough
interest in food production, strengthening cooperatives among the
'middle' peasantry and in bringing about organizational unity in peasant
ranks.[58]

The earlier mentioned 'small yield' campaign is but a dimension of a
wider and continuously activating organizational dynamic that seeks to
mobilize the peasantry through a succession of 'maximum effort' or
'full production' drives under BTI or direct PKI auspices. Since 1960
much 'small yield' activity has been formalized in a *Gerakan 1001*
('The Thousand and One Movement') under which, in a 'thousand and

one' different ways, the social and economic position of the peasantry is fortified through production increases while its political consciousness is being mobilized.[59] In January 1963, a *Gerakan 1001* seminar was held in Djakarta offering detailed directions by BTI chairman Asmu in current production problems.[60] An earlier part of the *Gerakan 1001* has been the 'Six Good Movement' which has as its aim: decreasing land rents, decreasing interest rates, increasing wages of peasant laborers, increasing agricultural production, raising the peasants' cultural level, and raising their political consciousness. Peasant militancy ('*Satu tangan pegang bedil dan satu tangan pegang patjul*'—One hand on the rifle and one hand on the hoe) has been fostered—always with a weather eye on the reaction of local army commanders—in connection with popular resistance against *Darul Islam* marauders, the campaign to acquire West New Guinea, and more recently, with recruitment of 'volunteers' for the anti-Malaysia campaign. The BTI has, in fact been in the forefront of organizations denouncing Malaysian premier Tunku Rahman and the concept of the Malaysian federation.[61]

Both PKI and BTI seek to integrate themselves with pattern of peasant demand. In areas under estate cultivation emphasis is placed not only on getting higher rents and wages for those who lease land to the estates, or who work there as laborers, but also on squatters' rights, even if in clear contravention of government land guarantees to estate owners or managers. In villages with sizable numbers of semi-employed or unemployed youths various community 'beautifying' campaigns are initiated, involving repair of roads, bridges and other civic projects. Here the PKI youth front *Pemuda Rakyat* lends a hand, just as special courses for peasant women bring the collaboration of activists of *Gerwani*, the PKI's women's front organization. Physical training and recreation is not lost sight of, and neither are anti-illiteracy campaigns or 'current events' courses that can be integrated with other BTI work. Everywhere the BTI, sustained by local PKI organization, seeks to overcome resistance to the implementation of land reform legislation and to the execution of the minimum 50–50 crop division law passed in 1959, largely as a result of Communist insistence. Always stressing the economic basis of social activity the BTI has in the past three years also encouraged the formation of small separate organizations for landless peasant laborers, small holders who own and work their own soil, tenant farmers, women laborers, and so on, and these so-called *klompok* serve as functional subsidiaries, especially in certain 'small yield' activities most meaningful to them.[62]

As part of its 'Go down to the masses' campaign the PKI, supported by the BTI, has primarily since 1956 carried on research in land tenure and rural social relationships, with a view to buttressing its demand for 'land reform' and its charges of incipient 'feudalism', aggravated land-lordism' and general empoverishment of the Indonesian peasantry. This research has been carried on by cadres in Java, Sumatra and portions of the Nusa Tenggara and some results have been published in party literature.[63] For example, in the village of Tjaruj (Sidaredja district, Central Java Province) according to PKI findings 44 percent of the village population holds 4·3 percent of the total land area, having an average holding of 32·1 hectares. In contrast some 43 percent of the total population, designated as 'poor peasants' by the PKI survey, holds on the average only 0·5 hectare per household. In the village of Gelung (Paron district, in East Java province) 2·2 percent of the population, designated as 'landlords', possesses 27 percent of the village land area, while 62 percent of the total population are described as 'peasant laborers' and hold no land. In Semboro village (Djember district, East Java Province) 8 percent of the population, again designated as 'landlords', holds 54 percent of the village land, while 54 percent of the population, classified as 'laborers' and 'poor peasants', holds only 13 percent of the land. Peasant indebtedness has also come in for analysis and according to party surveys interest rates set by landlords-usurers may be as high as 200 to 300 percent per half year, while the rendering of 'feudal' duties (i.e. various kinds of unpaid labor performed for the benefit of the landlord) is becoming common. According to Sidartojo, PKI leader in North Sumatra, the amount owned by peasants to moneylenders in the Karo area of North Sumatra alone totals Rp. 1·5 million and while the agreed interest rate is 24 percent, in practice it is much higher because all sorts of 'fees' drive the interest rate up to 150 percent. In the Karo region the moneylender element is closely tied to the landlord group and, according to this account, there can be no doubt of the 'feudalistic exploitation practices which so far operate under the guise of traditional customs'.[64]

In line with these findings, and as a part of its general policy, the PKI and BTI have been in the forefront of the supporters of so-called land reform legislation in Indonesia. The party paper has asserted, 'Socialism cannot be achieved without land reform'.[65] But although both PKI and BTI have closely supported such measures as the minimum 50–50 crop division law, this kind of legislation, according to the Communists 'will not put feudalistic exploitation to an end', for the very principle of tenancy itself is a perpetuation of 'feudalistic' practice.[66] Also, the 50–50 division falls short of the party's recommended 6:4 ratio. More-over, the party has complained that government officials 'seem to be in no hurry to implement the crop sharing agreements law' and that, therefore, success of the measure lies not least in 'the strength of the peasants' unity', i.e. pressure by the peasants themselves.[67] Still, the PKI and BTI have urged faithful implementation of the law by all concerned.

The same qualified approval has been extended to the government's 'basic agrarian law' of September 1960, and subsequent agrarian legislation, which set definite minima and maxima for size of landholdings, abolished remnants of colonial agrarian legislation, provide for distribution of the land, for compensation to owners whose holdings are taken, and and so on. Perhaps the most important provision of the law was that which set maximum limits on the size of holdings (for Java the maximum, exclusive of estates, was set at 5 hectares of irrigated or 6 hectares of unirrigated land for each family) in each regional administrative unit.[68] Establishment of definite maxima has always been stressed in party publications,[69] but the implementation of these and other provisions of the new agrarian legislation seems to be occurring only slowly, due to a variety of objections and barriers, and a note of impatience has been repeatedly struck by the party and the BTI. It seems clear, however, that land reform legislation is still in a condition of development. In November 1961, Agriculture Minister Azis Saleh declared that although 'there is already a land reform act and a crop share act in Indonesia . . . it is still deemed necessary to bring about a revolution in the field of agriculture'.[70] But whether the present state of land registry and the pattern of rural socio-economic relations does in fact allow for a speedy implementation, and whether, the enacted measures can materially contribute to increased food production as is officially expected, remains to be seen. The PKI and the BTI, however, have not been reluctant to stress their own long standing demands for what the new agrarian legislation now seeks to accomplish, and to continue their own 'small yield' campaign in conjunction with it. *Harian Rakjat* has reported that in Semarang regency the BTI has been organizing lectures and information services about the government's agrarian and crop sharing legislation for the benefit of local villagers. Meanwhile the BTI assists in various campaigns to increase wages for rural laborers and in destroying rodents that are plaguing the peasants' crops. When some landlords decided to feed their tenants with cassave instead of rice, the BTI brought pressure to bear and rice was again distributed to the tenants.[71] It is through work of this type that the Communist party continues to endear itself to the swelling ranks of the rural poor.

The Labor Front. Unlike its organizational interest in the peasantry, the PKI's concern for, and attempts to dominate, the Indonesian labor movement go back to the very first years of the party (see Chapter I above), and all during the colonial era this interest persisted. In the period of the Indonesian revolution the tempo of organization and action in the labor movement notably quickened, and a large number of unions and union federations came into being.[72] The need for a single overall organization was increasingly felt during these years and late in 1946 a single federated body, the All Indonesian Central Labor Organization (*Sentral Organisasi Buruh Seluruh Indonesia*—SOBSI), came into being, led by Harjono (who later participated in the Madiun Affair, and was executed in January 1949, for his part in the affair), Njono, a dedicated PKI activist (now a member of the party's Politburo) and the present SOBSI chairman, and by prominent figures in the *Buruh* (Labor) and Socialist parties. From the start SOBSI was a Communist-directed organization; many of its leaders participated in the Madiun affair and like those of the PKI subsequently suffered incarceration or death as a result or went underground. The Madiun rebellion cost the SOBSI dearly: some 50 percent of its membership withdrew, rival federations were established and uncertainty about the desirability of further militant labor action brought continuing crises in leadership. Like the PKI, SOBSI also experienced a gradual revival in the period after 1951. In 1952 its membership was 1,561,750. By 1963 it claimed 3,865,000 members (out of a total of about 7 million organized workers in Indonesia), making it the largest single labor federation in Indonesia.

In 1957 some 39 national unions and more than 800 local unions were affiliated with SOBSI. Among the more important of these were the Union of Plantation Workers of the Indonesian Republic (*Serikat Buruh Perkebunan Republik Indonesia*—SARBUPRI) with about 600,000 members, the Union of Sugar Workers (*Serikat Buruh Gula*—SBG), with 305,000 members, the Union of Stevedores and Seamen (*Serikat Buruh Pelabuhan dan Pelajaran*—SBPP) with 50,000 members, the Union of Railway Workers (*Serikat Buruh Kereta Api*—SBKA) with 68,000 members, the Union of Motor Transport workers (*Serikat Buruh Kendaraan Bermotor*—SBKB) with 50,000 members, the Union of Postal, Telegraph and Telephone Workers (*Serikat Buruh Pos, Telegraf dan Telefon*—SB POSTEL) with about 20,000 members, the Union of Petroleum Workers (*Persatuan Buruh Minjak*—PERBUM) with 35,000 members, the Union of Textile and Clothing Workers (*Serikat Buruh Tekstil dan Pakaian*) with 60,000 members, the Union of Defense Ministry Employees (*Serikat Buruh Kementerian Pertahanan*—SBKP) with 60,000 members, the Union of Employees in the Ministry of Public Works (*Serikat Buruh Pekerdjaan Umum*—SBPU), with 48,000 members, and the Union of Employees of Autonomous Regions (*Serikat Buruh Daerah Autonoom*—SEBDA) with

73,000 members. SOBSI encompasses affiliates in all major phases of the country's production and services processes and it is in this respect better balanced, and potentially more dangerous, than other non-Communist or anti-Communist labor federations. According to SOBSI the organization covers all first-level autonomous areas in Indonesia and branches have been established in virtually all second-level autonomous areas including in the chief cities of these areas. SOBSI is affiliated with the Communist-led World Federation of Trade Unions, of which SOBSI chairman Njono is a vice-president.[73]

At SOBSI's Third National Congress in August 1960 (the two previous national congresses were in 1947 and 1955), a new constitution was approved, which affirms participation in the 'united national front' of workers and peasants to wage the fight for complete freedom (the Dutch hold on West New Guinea and continuing Dutch 'economic domination' were regarded as evidence that Indonesia 'has not achieved complete freedom'), and against imperialism and feudalism, for better living conditions and for 'rights of freedom of labor unions and other democratic rights', and expresses adhesion to the Pantjasila, and *Manipol—Usdek*. Article 1 of SOBSI's Constitution declares that the federation is 'non-partisan', and its official song (next to the national anthem) is the 'Internationale, the song of the workers of the world'. Article 3 provides that members of individual unions affiliated with SOBSI are also members of SOBSI.

The organizational structure parallels that of the PKI and the BTI. A National Congress, held every four years, is the highest authority not only in SOBSI but also of the individual affiliated union (article 14). A National Council is the supreme authority between National Congresses and a plenary meeting of the Council is held once a year. A Presidium of the Council is the supreme body of the organization during intervals between Council meetings. There are also a Central Bureau for the handling of routine, day-to-day matters, and various special bureaus (e.g. for Education-Information, Foreign Relations, Economic Affairs and Development). Article 8 provides that the structure of the federation is based 'on field of work and on geographic division', with workers in a given enterprise forming a labor union or 'basic organization', reaching up to 'area organizations' with their appropriate conferences and executive bodies. 'Base organizations' also have their executive boards, elected by the membership. The rather elaborate pattern of interlocking control by the higher over the lower levels of the organizational pyramid shows fidelity to the principle of 'democratic centralism' and the constitution provides for the appointment of Verification Commissions at all levels to 'supervise the task of the organization in the field of administration, finances, inventory and productive efforts'. Members may be expelled and reinstated according to a definite procedure. Article 28 also provides that SOBSI may only be dissolved by a National Congress specifically called to consider the question of dissolution. The significance of this clause loomed larger in 1962 because of the Indonesian government's efforts to merge all labor federations and unions into a single, government-controlled labor organization.[74]

In its relations with the rest of organized labor SOBSI has followed the Communist party line of unity with the 'progressive' forces, cooperation, where possible, with 'middle of the road' forces, and hostility to 'die-hards'. In practice this has often meant SOBSI action in cooperation with such labor federations as the Central Labor Organization of the Indonesian Republic (*Sentral Organsasi Buruh Republik Indonesia*— SOBRI) which has about 90,000 members and is controlled by the small, independent Communist Murbah Party, the late Tan Malaka's organization. SOBRI, founded in February 1951, is also affiliated with the World Federation of Trade Unions, and despite the ideological differences between the Murbah and Communist party leaderships frequently acts in close concert with SOBSI. The 'middle of the road' labor forces have been primarily those non-Communist labor organizations or federations which maintain close ties with the more radical nationalist parties. An example is the Democratic Workers Union of Indonesia (*Kesatuan Buruh Kerakjatan Indonesia*—KBKI) which since its founding in 1952 has been generally identified with the *Partai Nasional Indonesia* (PNI). KBKI claims over 500,000 members, a figure which like the membership figures of other labor federations (including SOBSI's) is probably exaggerated. There has been a strain between the KBKI and SOBSI over the government-sponsored single labor federation, an idea which KBKI supported and SOBSI generally opposed. The 'die-hards' in the labor movement, according to the PKI and SOBSI, are those unions allied with the Masjumi and Socialist (PSI) parties, many of which have been dissolved with the enforced demise of the Masjumi and PSI (a few of which, have reconstituted themselves, and later won new government approval). Comparatively, SOBSI despite its size is better organized than most of its smaller competitors. There is an 'élite mindedness' about the Indonesian labor movement which amply confirms Michels' iron law of oligarchy; the rank and file is fluid and frequently poorly integrated with the leadership. It has been pointed out, for example, that 'It is hard to determine exactly how many trade union members there are in Indonesia since the collection of dues often is not over ten per cent of the so-called membership'.[75] The autocratic tendencies of union leadership and the frequent formation of new unions and dissolution of old ones tend, however, to strengthen SOBSI in seeking to place its sympathizers in key positions in other labor organizations, and thus effecting advantageous tactical alliances.

In the last analysis the factor which has aided SOBSI's policies most is the continuing stagnation of the Indonesian economy and the deterioration of workers' living conditions. Recurrent shortages of basic necessities like rice, clothing and kerosene for fuel have—despite increasing restrictions on all popular demonstrations—permitted SOBSI and other Communist fronts, such as *Gerwani* to agitate for better living conditions. The import, production and distribution of food and clothing in Indonesia today verges on the chaotic. With inflation still unchecked, the index of retail prices of 19 basic foodstuffs on the Djakarta free market rose from 100 in 1953 to 397 in January 1961, and another analysis of indices shows that 'the prices of cloth and footwear have registered the biggest increase in the last three years from 116 in March 1958 . . . to a peak of 694 in August 1960'.[76] In May 1963, in a lecture on Sukarno's economic policy statement *(Dekon)* of March 28, 1963, Aidit cited another index of twelve basic foodstuffs, which he claimed showed a rise of from 100 in 1953 to 1910 in 1962.[77] Government food imports have over the years brought only very brief and slight relief, and while conditions are not uniformly bad throughout the country, the fundamental unbalance in the economic relationships between most Indonesian cities and the surrounding rural areas is spreading. In Java certainly the food supplies to the cities from the countryside have been diminishing since the Second World War, while the cities themselves have markedly grown, and hunger oedema and malignant malnutrition have by now threatened to become endemic in a number of rural areas.[78] The furore occasioned by the Indonesian government's stepped up campaign to acquire West New Guinea in the closing months of 1961 could not obscure the increasingly grave problem of scarcity of staples and other necessities. As one Djakarta paper editorially put it late in October 1961:[79]

A hard fact is the steadily increasing living standard (cost) in the country. Rice which only a month ago sold for Rp. 7 a litre has now reached the peak of more than Rp. 20 in the open market. Together with rice, prices of other crops or commodities keep increasing as rice is more or less regarded as the price-regulator in the market. Coconut oil usually selling at Rp. 25 a bottle is now out of stock and is superseded by the so-called vegetable oil selling at Rp. 30 the bottle. The same is true with sweet potato and cassave as the foremost rice substitutes. Kerosene for cooking is also very hard to get and if there is any can only be had clandestinely at the cut-throat price of Rp. 3 a bottle, three times the official price.

The various reasons for what the Governor of West Java by the end of November 1961, chose to call 'the fantastic increases of prices of essential commodities'[80] fall outside the scope of this study. Suffice it to note that these problems continued in the following years so that toward the close of 1963 the PKI daily could report that in areas of West Java the pirce of rice had risen so high that people were compelled to eat mango seeds and that they could afford to eat only once every three days.[81] By February 1964, thousands were being treated for hunger oedema and malnutrition in Central Java, and the general economic stagnation, compounded by the effects of the 'confrontation' against Malaysia, provided the setting of a general *verelendung* and popular misery which already the year before, in February 1963, had caused one Djakarta daily to editorialize that 'this year's Lebaran will be the most difficult for the people during the 17 years of our independence'.[82] The problems of seriously deteriorating living standards, spiraling prices and recurrent shortages of popular necessities have increasingly become a conspicuous and alarming feature of the Indonesian economy, especially since the middle of the previous decade.[83] At the same time the question of providing adequate employment to the country's burgeoning population has become more and more acute. In this way there has emerged an ideal climate for continuing radical labor agitation, a climate which SOBSI has fully sought to exploit.

An analysis of SOBSI's most publicized demands over the years reveals them to be primarily concerned with furthering the Communist Party's political and economic objectives, as well as with improving living and working conditions. Instances of the former include SOBSI demonstrations on behalf of Indonesia's claim on West New Guinea, protest actions against the restoration of estate lands to the foreign estate companies, support for *Manipol—Usdek* and for the '*gotong royong*' parliament that excluded the Masjumi and the PSI, demands for stronger action against *Darul Islam* and PRRI rebels, further nationalization of the remnants of Dutch capital in mixed enterprises in Indonesia, and so on. During the government crisis in March 1957, occasioned by the fall of the second Ali Sastroamidjojo cabinet, SOBSI threatened to call a general strike throughout Indonesia if the new cabinet would include Masjumi but exclude PKI members, while SOBSI affiliated unions in South Sumatra (including oil, estate, mine, railroad and harbor workers) called a 24-hour sit-down strike in that province presumably 'in support' of President Sukarno's call to defend the Republic and the unity of the Indonesian people.[84]

SOBSI's militancy in struggling for better working and living conditions is also noteworthy however. SOBSI has repeatedly made studies of the cost of daily necessities of workers and in 1953 excused the various labor difficulties that had arisen that year (and for many of which it was itself largely responsible) by pointing to the 'daily rising costs of living' or workers, and suggesting minimum wages.[85] Any military intervention in the rights of the laborer SOBSI has strongly resisted. Perhaps the first noteworthy case of such intervention came early in 1954 when the military arrested a number of workers at a Surabaya industrial establishment on charges that the workers had 'not been adequately performing' their duties.[86] SOBSI led the movement of protest against this military action, and subsequent military control over much of the Indonesian production process exercised through various 'cooperative' organizations SOBSI leaders have given every indication of resenting. Even before the Indonesian economy reached its present plight SOBSI made known its opposition to all government interference in free action on the labor front. A case in point was the big strike in support of higher wage demands involving several hundred thousands of laborers called by SARBUPRI (one of SOBSI's strongest affiliates) on foreign-owned estates on Java and Sumatra in September 1953, which involved production losses of 10 million Rupiah a day.[87] The strike was in clear violation of a government arbitration decision, but government threats of legal action against the workers were sharply attacked and were of little avail. In the late nineteen-fifties it was especially PERBUM (SOBSI's petroleum workers' affiliate) and SOBSI-connected civil servants associations which were active, with the support of the entire federation, in higher wage and pension benefit campaigns, while PERBUM in particular agitated against the progressive lay-off of workers necessitated by the automation introduced by the foreign oil companies in Indonesia.

Protests against rising living costs reached a high point in 1959 and 1960, when SOBSI-affiliated unions and other Communist-front groups, especially women's groups, repeatedly marched on government offices in various cities to present their demands. Early in 1959, Mohammad Munir, SOBSI's first deputy chairman, urged a nation-wide campaign for reduction in prices while another SOBSI leader and parliamentary deputy, F. Runturambi, accused the government's price control agency of 'becoming nothing but an office legalizing price rises'.[88] In its May Day 1960 statement, entitled 'Under the Banner of Unity Continue the Mass Actions for Food and Clothing and for Democracy', the Central Bureau of SOBSI declared that 'economic conditions have worsened', excoriated the state enterprises 'which are full of corruption' and which 'still resemble ordinary private commercial business hunting for maximum profits', and demanded a 25 percent across the board increase in wages which SOBSI considered 'realistic, even low' in view of the fact that the cost of living in Djakarta alone over the past year and a half had jumped by 73 percent.[89] On June 14, 1960, SOBSI returned to the attack, publishing an evaluation of the 'working' *(karya)* cabinet, which foreshadowed the much discussed July 8, 1960 evaluation of the PKI Politburo. Its evaluation noted 'the race between increasing prices and the needs of the working people' and declared that the cost of living index in Djakarta had risen from 294 in July 1959 to 382 in April 1960, while at the same time an attempt was being made to reduce workers' wages in the nationalized, former Dutch enterprises, thereby intensifying 'the sufferings of the workers'. The evaluation charged interference in trade union activity by the government ('Trade unions which are the expression of the workers' organized consciousness are prohibited from holding strikes and demonstrations and their meetings are interfered with'), also through the intended creation of a government controlled central labor federation, the United Organization of Laborers in Indonesia (*Organisasi Persatuan Pekerdja Indonesia*—OPPI) membership in which 'is based upon coercion, something which has never before existed in Indonesia. Only under the rule of the Hitler Reich could such a thing happen'.[90]

Though, as indicated in the following chapter, the military acted quickly to counter these Communist criticisms, the Third National Congress of SOBSI in August 1960 heard Njono repeat them; he declared, for example, that workers' living conditions were worsening, that production in the state and nationalized enterprises was declining due to 'certain cliques which have become bureaucratic capitalists', and that economic conditions in Indonesia were still 'colonial' in nature. He also repeated his opposition to OPPI.[91] Despite the difficulties faced by the PKI, SOBSI and other fronts in their relations with the government and the army through the remainder of 1960, these criticisms continued to be voiced by the party fronts.

Moreover, SOBSI's point about government intervention in trade union activity was well taken. Since 1953 when Indonesian business leaders expressed their concern over an intended modification of the 1951 arbitration regulation and over the government's alleged intention to recognize an 'unlimited freedom to strike',[92] compulsory arbitration, virtual prohibition of strikes and lockouts in essential enterprises, and supervision over all trade union activity, has become ever more conspicuous. Compared to the early 1950's, when strikes annually numbered in the hundreds and man-days of work lost numbered in the hundreds of thousands,[93] strikes in the past five years have become progressively rarer and indeed have by now virtually disappeared in most major areas of production and service. This, notwithstanding the fact, that (as yet another government regulation banning strikes in vital enterprises in areas under a state of emergency put it) the right to strike is 'a fundamental right' which should be upheld.[94]

As a result of the military emergency occasioned by the PRRI rebellion and of the increasing recognition given to the military in all aspects of public life, labor-military 'cooperative' bodies (*Badan Kerdja Sama Buruh dan Militer*—BUMIL) were set up, centralized in Djakarta and with regional and local levels of operation, by means of which military commanders increasingly came to direct labor policy and trade union activity. The culmination of this process of government control came with the announcement in the middle of 1960 that the government intended to establish a central federative labor organization, the 'Fascist' OPPI, as SOBSI put it, and Labor Minister Ahem Erningpradja (formerly a leading figure in SARBUPRI and SOBSI, and more recently in KBKI), once in the relative good graces of the PKI and SOBSI, became OPPI's principal proponent, a role which was soon to bring him a great deal of Communist hostility.[95] OPPI was meant to be quite all inclusive; as article 5 of its draft statutes put it: 'Every working citizen who receives regular payment in whatever form from an employer shall belong to this (i.e. OPPI) organization. This membership cannot be withdrawn so long as a working relationship exists between him and the employer'.

SOBSI's objections to the forming of OPPI not only stemmed from the involuntary character of OPPI's membership but also from the 'compulsory reduction' in workers' wages which OPPI membership dues would impose and from the fact that the Labor Minister would have the right to appoint and dismiss OPPI's executive and committees. The latter provision SOBSI interpreted—in line with the general opposition of the Communists to any allegedly interference with 'democratic liberties'—as an abridgement of the workers' political rights. The same thought underlay SOBSI's objection to the clause in OPPI's draft statutes providing that OPPI committee members and executive officers be prohibited from joining any political party. In September 1960, Njono called attention to the 'persisting idea expressed in the press' that a 'simplification' of the trade union movement, via the establishment of OPPI, 'would mean the dissolution of SOBSI'.[96] The old issue of freedom of political action for Communists and their sympathizers which the PKI had kept in the foreground of its demands over the years thus was raised once again. While Ahem Erningpradja was not without support, these objections of SOBSI, along with demands for intensive modification of OPPI's draft statutes from the side of other non-Communist trade unions and federations, were sufficient for the government not to insist too strongly on further adhesion by the trade union movement to the single labor federation.

Since the beginning of 1961, little was heard of OPPI. Officially the Labor Minister was proceeding with 'consultations' to implement the decision to create OPPI. In fact a kind of stalemate had been reached, somewhat similar to the stalemate in the development of the single National Front incorporating all parties, an idea which the PKI has also vigorously opposed. Organizationally SOBSI and other labor organizations remained intact, ostensibly with the blessing of the Labor Minister, and while SOBSI's operational freedom was somewhat curtailed in the next year, some of its affiliates continued to be restless. On November 17, 1961, a mass demonstration of several thousands took place in Kediri, East Java, which was organized by SARBUPRI, one of SOBSI's principal mainstays which is under effective Communist control. The demonstration was presumably directed against intentions to mechanize agricultural production in the area although squatter agitation was probably also involved and in the fighting between the demonstrators and the military which subsequently ensued six were killed and a score wounded. Though an immediate news blackout was imposed on the incident it was evident that SARBUPRI's hold on agricultural workers had not notably weakened. In Surabaya, the city which has replaced Semarang as a principal Communist stronghold, SOBSI activists and local PKI leaders have been in repeated conflict with the military authority of the city since 1961 and a score of Communists and their sympathizers have been detained.

It has become quite evident that the SOBSI leadership, like that of the PKI, will not abandon freedom of action without a struggle. The SOBSI National Council has reiterated that 'contradictions in the field of national cooperation' can be solved by peaceful negotiation, but that when 'it is deemed necessary mass action may be used'. These mass actions, moreover, must be enduring and 'must be able to stand the test'. In strict accord with Communist theory SOBSI regards the 'contradictions' between workers and the military as traceable to 'contradictions within the people themselves'. While SOBSI in principle favors cooperation with the military in various common bodies, it looks with regret on the alleged fact that through these common bodies workers' rights have been curbed.[97] The monolithic organizational structure of the Indonesian state characterizing the development of 'guided democracy' in Indonesia appears to have found a by no means negligible opponent in SOBSI.

Officially SOBSI has never shown discouragement. The 'domestic and the foreign political situation are consistently moving to the left', as the general report of SOBSI's National Council to the organization's Third National Congress in 1960 put it. SOBSI continued to proceed with its membership drive, with its anti-illiteracy campaign, with the distribution of its periodical *Bendera Buruh* (Flag of Labor) and with the campaign to improve registration of its base organization even in the 1960–1961 period of crisis. SOBSI's National Council also called for combatting 'pessimism and cynicism' in the implementation of the National Eight-Year Development plan, but it has equally continued to emphasize that 'democratic freedoms' must be guaranteed, and that a 'truly national cooperation' must prevail in national political and economic life.[98] Implementation of the Eight-Year Plan gave SOBSI new reason for action and detailed plans were in fact been drafted by the organization's economic experts. This interest in the Eight-Year Plan is again illustrative of Indonesian Communism's technique of exploiting every aspect of official national policy by means of which Communism can be both rendered officially respectable and be organizationally strengthened.

By the end of 1963, OPPI, though still nominally being in process of formation, had in fact been aborted. The nearest thing to a rival which SOBSI by that time had left to fear was SOKSI, another army inspired labor-management cooperative body in the state enterprises, which also includes a number of small peasant and estate workers groups. Because of its access to government subsidized supplies of food and clothing SOKSI units have occasionally had an organizational advantage in the present hand-to-mouth Indonesian economy. But by the beginning of 1964 there reportedly was beginning to arise a desire on the part of some SOKSI branches to affiliate with SOBSI, indicative that the latter's dominance in the labor field is not easily challenged, and that it, like the PKI, had successfully weathered the 1960–1961 crisis. SOBSI along with the Party youth front, *Pemuda Rakjat*, took the lead in the attack on the Malayan and British embassies on September 16, 1963 and the take-over of British enterprises and estates at that time, as well as in January 1964, when Deputy Prime Minister for Foreign Affairs Subandrio termed the SOBSI take-over action 'heroic'.[99]

Other Party Fronts—Front Relations with the Party. Communist influence operates at at many social and economic levels. We have already noted the *Pemuda Rakjat* (People's Youth) the Communist Youth Front, and the special importance assigned to it in the present PKI constitution. The close involvement of Indonesian youth groups in the development of nationalism and in the Indonesian military resistance during the revolution against the Dutch made the youth movement a political force of major importance with which the PKI, also after the fight for independence had been won, sought to ally itself as a matter of course. Much of the basis of the Communist Youth Front today was originally made available by the Indonesian Socialist Youth group (*Pemuda Sosialis Indonesia—Pesindo*), which had provided the PKI with a good deal of its strength during the Indonesian Revolution and which at its third congress in Djakarta in November 1950 changed its name to *Pemuda Rakjat*.[100] By 1962 *Pemuda Rakjat* claimed about 1·5 million members (as compared to about 30,000 in 1950), but in keeping with the policy of other front groups it has consistently attempted to stress its non-partisan character. *Pemuda Rakjat* has been by no means the only Communist Youth front. The Generation of Reconstruction Youth of Indonesia (*Angkatan Pembangunan Pemuda Indonesia*—APPI), also under Communist control, was primarily active in Sumatra. 'National Communist influence (i.e. that exercised by the *Partai Murbah*) determined the policies of the Generation of Communist Youth (*Angkatan Comunis Muda*—ACOMA), an organization which ran as a party in the 1955 national parliamentary elections and won one seat. Though independent of the PKI and supposedly hostile to it, ACOMA frequently pursued policies that in fact dovetailed with those of the PKI and *Pemuda Rakjat*. *Pemuda Rakjat* is a principal organizational ally of the PKI; as one of its leaders has described its role:[101]

The People's Youth of Indonesia is a reliable assistant of the Communist Party, the vehicle for its policy among the masses of youth. Distinguished from the other youth organizations by its class consciousness, it is the reserve of the Party. At the same time it is an independent mass organization of young people which includes not only workers and peasants, but also other sections, particularly middle strata. . . . People's Youth helps in forming progressive and democratic youth organizations, associations and unions . . . (and) considers it to be its principal task to secure unity of action with all other democratic organizations of the youth, and it must be said we have had quite considerable success in this respect, particularly in sports societies and cultural organizations which at one time we wrongly dismissed as being 'non-political'. . . .

The aims of the youth movement are reflected in the slogans, common programmes and joint resolutions of the youth organizations which stress that socialism can be achieved only after victory in the struggle for a completely independent and democratic Indonesia. This, naturally, does not mean renouncing propaganda of the ideas of socialism. On the contrary, we widely popularize scientific socialism and the advantages of the socialist system, and use concrete examples for this end. But at the same time we concentrate on more immediate democratic tasks, those associated with the struggle against imperialism and feudalism.

Primarily through the *Pemuda Rakjat* the PKI has attempted to infiltrate the *Partindo*, a small political party which in 1958 was formed, with the blessing of Sukarno, by younger and more radical elements in the PNI. The new *Partindo* was expected to emulate the radicalism of its pre-World War II predecessor but in practice this turned out as an imitation of PKI aims without reference to Marxist-Leninist terminology. By 1963 *Partindo* had become, in effect, a kind of tactical satellite of the PKI, useful to the party in influencing the PNI with which *Partindo* retained informal relations.

The principal vehicle of Communist control over and influence in the Indonesian women's movement has been the *Gerwani* (*Gerakan Wanita Indonesia*—Indonesian Women's Association), which in 1962 claimed to have about 750,000 members. *Gerwani's* leaders, like Mrs. Mudikdio Marah Umar, Mrs. Umi Sardjono and Mrs. Suharti Suwarto, are all party members, and represent or have represented the PKI in the Indonesian parliament. Like other Communist fronts, *Gerwani* has advocated both general Communist policy objectives as well as a program expressive of its own particular character. The return of West New Guinea, action against PRRI and *Darul Islam* rebels, and stricter measures against 'imperialist' capital have thus appeared in the organization's program, along with frequent agitation on behalf of lower prices and better living conditions. In March 1954 the second *Gerwani* Congress drafted a five-point program which included the following demands:[102]

1. The need for a new marriage law for Indonesia, with guarantees of the legal equality between men and women.

2. Greater allocations in the government's budget for public health and welfare programs for the benefit of women and children.

3. Increase in the number of schools and intensification of the fight against illiteracy.

4. Broadening of social welfare regulations for the benefit of women factory workers.

5. Sincere pursuit of a policy of international peace and friendship by the government.

In defending women's rights *Gerwani* has especially stressed the evils of what it calls lingering 'feudal' survivals in Indonesian society, e.g. traditions and customary laws in a number of areas which may force a girl into a marriage which she does not want. The majority of Indonesian women, declared *Gerwani's* executive in a press statement issued just before the elections for the Constituent Assembly in 1955, do not enjoy the same rights as men, partly because successive Indonesian governments have not been able to implement the guarantee of equal rights as provided by the provisional Constitution, and because a 'democratic marriage law' does not exist.[103] Appealing to the U.N. Declaration of

Human Rights, the *Gerwani* statement urged women to participate actively in the Constituent Assembly elections. *Gerwani's* (and the PKI's) opposition to 'feudalism' has particularly involved a Communist conflict with the Islamic principal of polygamy and the generally subordinate position of women in traditional Islamic marriage and divorce law. Due to the influence of Islamic *kiajih* in Indonesian society, women may on occasion be pressed into an unwanted union with such a *kiajih* and *Gerwani* has been in the van of organizations publicizing and protesting such practices. More restrained has been *Gerwani's* demand for a government regulation establishing the rights and duties of the nation's 'first lady', a question which became particularly delicate after President Sukarno's second (polygamous) marriage.

The organization has also served as a Communist means of mobilizing peasant opinion. In January 1961, for example, *Gerwani* sponsored a 'Peasant Women's Seminar' in Djakarta, which drew primarily on the support of its branches in the smaller cities and villages of Java. Among the proposals adopted by the seminar were the following: (1) landownership rights of women peasants should be guaranteed by law; (2) unpaid labor duties, traditional in many villages, should be abolished; (3) traditional laws which provide for a greater share of an inheritance for sons than for daughters should be abolished; (4) women peasants should have the right to participate in community projects such as the construction and repair of irrigation dikes; and (5) traditions which look askance on the woman who is childless should be combatted.[104] All these proposals it should be stressed, have the backing of the PKI (the current program of the PKI adopted at the party's Seventh National Congress, it will be recalled, emphasizes the equal rights of men and women in politics, employment opportunities, marriage and divorce, etc.), but the party also sees the women's movement as a partner in the struggle to realize its more overtly political and international objectives. As the PKI daily has put it:[105]

Women, together with other patriotic forces, must actively follow the struggle to return West Irian to the territorial jurisdiction of the Republic of Indonesia. They must actively take part in the liquidation of the consequences of foreign capital domination which still regulate the life of the Indonesian people. . . . Women are actively participating in the implementation of the regulations for guaranteeing production and in the redistribution of land, meaning they are actively participating in cutting off the hand of imperialism. Victory in the attainment of these national and democratic tasks can only be assured if women develop their own firm and strong policy of unity.

Like the BTI *Gerwani* too has been concerned with organizing for 'small yield' actions, involving women with a particular vocational or social interest, e.g. teachers, midwives, peasant laborers, and so on.

In the period 1960–1961 these subsidiary organizations or clubs proved particularly useful in venting popular grievances over food shortages and rising prices, again at a time when the PKI was virtually enjoined from doing so. Of late *Gerwani* has particularly proliferated its own front publications, and has adopted Kartini (the Central Javanese regent's daughter who died in 1904 and who has been a symbol of the emancipation of Indonesian women) virtually as its patron saint.[106]

Communist front activity in Indonesia has exhibited a good deal of flexibility and adaptability and relies by no means on nationwide, mass movements alone. The Neighborhood Association of the city of Surabaya (*Rukun Kampung Kota Surabaya*—RKKS) is an example of a local front suited to the needs of a particular area. During the period of the Japanese occupation of Surabaya in World War II people living in the same street or alley, or in a closely knit cluster of houses near a bridge or a crossroads were organized in a neighborhood association under an approved leader. It will be recalled that the Japanese had used this system of control and security in their own homeland and in other areas they occupied. After the Japanese surrender, all during the revolutionary period and thereafter the Surabaya neighborhood associations continued to function and early in 1952 began to come under effective Communist control.[107] PKI cadres became association leaders and promoted party influence in their own neighborhoods. What could be described as political wards in the American manner began to emerge, and people continued to turn to their *rukun kampung* for help in getting jobs, free rice, small loans, information about political happenings, and so on. In time the PKI added 'security guards', often from among the ranks of young toughs in the *Pemuda Rakjat*, levied dues and brought effective pressure to bear on municipal government. A central coordinating body of all *rukun kampung* was established which in the middle and late nineteen-fifties was able to mobilize quickly thousands for demonstrations, supportive actions in strikes, and so on. To the impoverished new immigrant, or to a squatter in a wretched hovel in an overcrowded *kampung*, the RKKS not only offered a means of keeping body and soul together, but also provided the heady wine of a revolution not yet completed. In the populous living quarters of what is now, with considerable accuracy, called 'Red' Surabaya, where frustration easily and frequently explodes in incidents of violence, the RKKS always stood ready to take up the cudgels against 'the imperialists and their followers'.[108] Around 1959 the RKKS began to decline, however, primarily because of the increasing intervention of the military in civil affairs and because of the imposition by the government of ever more monolithic forms of organizational control under 'guided democracy'. But the *rukun kampung* are by no means gone, even though local and provincial governments have looked askance at them and have attempted to minimize their influence and today the neighborhood associations continue to provide the Surabaya PKI with much of its stength.

Flexibility, in keeping with the presumed hyper-individualistic character of its supporters, is characteristic of another Communist front, the League of People's Culture (*Lembaga Kebudajaan Rakjat*—LEKRA). Founded in 1951, it is the Communist front of 'cultural workers', and includes primarily artists, writers, many professional journalists, teachers and scholars. Membership figures have not been published recently but estimates hover around 6,000. Essentially élite-minded, despite frequent exhortations by LEKRA members that art must reflect the aspirations of 'the people', the organization has been particular active at national Indonesian cultural and scientific congresses where it displays considerable power in pushing the Communist line[109] (e.g. 'artistic coexistence', need for emphasizing 'national values', opposition to imperialist 'excesses' such as American films, meeting the 'people's cultural interest', and so on). At the time of the sixth national congress of the PKI in September 1959, an exhibit of the works of 'progressive painters' was held in Djakarta, which according to Aidit, 'showed a "leap forward" in the efforts to attain "two highs", i.e. a "high level of ideology" and high artistic level' and 'the unity of the painters with the life of the masses and the revolutionary struggle of the Indonesian people was reflected by many paintings'.[110] There have not (as yet) been any *causes célèbres* of artistic denunciation in the annals of the Indonesian Communist movement, as one finds them, for example, in the USSR or People's China, possibly because such doctrinaire rigidity in cultural matters might be inappropriate for a country still in the 'first' phase of revolution.

Something of the character of LEKRA can be learned from the proceedings of its first national congress held in Surakarta, on January 29, 1959.[111] Preceded by a painting exhibition in Djakarta and a 'cultural week' in Surakarta the LEKRA congress was attended by dignitaries from China, Korea, Germany, by foreign cultural attachés in Indonesia and received congratulatory messages from American singer Paul Robeson, Dutch Communist author Theun de Vries and People's China's leading author Mao Tun, as well as from the CC of the PKI, and from SOBSI, BTI, and other Communist front groups. SOBSI's message stressed the common interests between SOBSI and LEKRA's 'cultural workers'; for example, 'extremely difficult living conditions' confronted both groups, while government support was still miniscule ('annual expenditures for cultural activities amount to less than Rp 0·25 per person'). In his general report LEKRA Secretary General Joebar

Ajoeb traced the 'development of Indonesian Culture' since the outbreak of the 1945 revolution, stressing that the national revolution had broken the fetters of Dutch and Japanese control over art and science and that 'a great number of artists, scientists and other cultural workers' had participated in the revolution, thereby demonstrating their unity with the people. Ajoeb noted a continuing conflict between two principles, 'Art for the People', and 'Art for Art's sake'. Though the principle of 'Art for the People' has the upper hand in this conflict, the struggle continues, because two other tendencies have emerged in it, against both of which a resolute fight must be waged. These two nefarious tendencies are the belief that 'Art for the People' will never be able to achieve high artistic standards, and the belief that 'Art for the People' *need* not achieve high artistic quality.

Ajoeb noted various other dangers to the development of people's culture, among them the attempt to split culture and politics. LEKRA rejects 'chauvinism, fascism and cosmopolitanism' and considers as one of its principal achievements the 'unearthing' of 'the wealth of the regional people's art . . . which has beautiful and progressive prospects'. This achievement has been made possible also by LEKRA's policy of providing for 'cultural pages' in 'progressive' papers and magazines, encouraging painters, writers and other to work on 'people's themes' and by promoting the proper kind of 'cultural exchange among nations'. Ajoeb's report noted that more encouragement still needed to be given to specific kinds of local and regional art forms like the *lenong* (Djakarta theatrical art) and the Central Javanese *wayang* and *ketoprak* (shadow-play theatre), as well as to the campaigns to increase more literacy and scientific development (in view of 'the progress made by Soviet technicians especially in launching Sputnik and the man-made planet'). LEKRA's first national congress concluded with the adoption of the following resolutions: (1) a ban on nuclear weapons and immediate disarmament; (2) free cultural exchange among nations 'in accordance with the Bandung, Cairo and Tashkent Conferences'; (3) the inclusion of artists and their functional representation in the new Indonesian parliament; (4) implementation of regulations establishing third-level autonomous government; (5) abrogation of foreign investment legislation; (6) recognition of the value of regional languages and opposition to the use of regional language 'for imperialist, reactionary and separatist agitation'; (7) intensification of 'culture' education in the schools; and (8) endorsement of various measures to improve culture, science, folklore, music and dancing, and so on. A new central executive board was approved by the Congress which included, among others, Pramudya Ananta Tur, one of the leading younger Indonesian writers, Rukijah Kertapati, a woman author, and Njoto, chief editor of *Harian Rakjat* and PKI Politburo member. Ajoeb was re-elected secretary general, one of his deputies being Henk Ngantung, a noted painter and presently a vice-mayor of Djakarta. President Sukarno concluded the Congress with a speech in which he expressed hope that LEKRA's principles of art and science for the people would include within them an understanding of 'Art and Science from and for the People', and he took this occasion to criticize the LEKRA-sponsored painting exhibition in Djakarta just before the Congress, declaring that it had included elements of 'liberalism and impressionism, surrealism, cubism and the like' which were far from being understood by the people. Sukarno hoped that painters would mend their ways so as to achieve high artistic standards 'understandable to the people in order to heighten the spirit of reconstruction'.[112]

Through LEKRA the PKI has attempted to augment its top cadres with leading figures among the national intelligentsia, and the comparative shortage of intellectuals in the PKI has long been grievously felt by the Central Committee. In 1961 Politburo member Jusuf Adjitorop sketched the outline of a campaign to draw more intellectuals into the party, in which he noted the need to identify party tactics with intellectual demands for better living conditions, more intellectual freedom and assistance to scholarship. He emphasized that the nucleus of Indonesia's academicians still consisted of those who had been trained in the colonial period and that it was therefore vitally necessary to increase the number of intellectuals from the ranks of the proletariat and the peasantry. A segment of the existing intellectual group, argued Adjitorop, had 'democratic' leanings, but there were also those with 'right wing' Socialist views and the party's task was clearly to appeal to the former while confronting the latter.[113] In 1962 the party formed a scholars' front, the Organization of Indonesian Scholars (*Himpunan Sardjana Indonesia*—HSI) which has proved quite influential and has about 2,000 members. The PKI in its cultural policies has also been aided by the emphasis on 'national identity' and Sukarno's not always successful opposition to Western forms of popular dancing and music.[114] Artistic and 'cultural' purity, have also received particular stress, of late, in *Zaman Baru*, LEKRA'S fortnightly.

The continuing exploration of the revolutionary Marxist dimensions of the Indonesian 'national identity' in party publications is but one feature of the PKI's planned cultural transformation of the country.[115]

The Communist Party in Indonesia has had considerably less success in establishing veterans and para-military fronts. Undoubtedly this has been due to the policies of certain prominent figures of the Republic's armed forces leadership over the years, who, mindful of the danger repeatedly posed to the Indonesian Republic by ill-controlled units of irregular forces allied with political parties during the revolution, have attempted to minimize the power of such para-military forces by dissolving them or by bringing them under the effective control of regular army commands. Tactically, moreover, the PKI's attempt to maintain military bands like the forces of 'the Merapi Merbabu Complex' and the *Bambu Runtjing* (see Chapter II above) proved to be a blunder, for it provided anti-Communists in Indonesia with ammunition for their charges that the PKI was trying to overthrow the government at the very time when PKI policy was to make the party look as respectable as possible by insisting that it was not a party of 'coup-ists', as Aidit put it. And so, while the PKI has insisted on the villagers' right to form their own local defense organizations against *Darul Islam* marauders, it did not oppose strict army control over these security guards; nor has the party resisted the progressive absorption of its veterans organization (PERBEPSI, founded in 1952, which had a membership of about 265,000 in 1957) into the National Veterans' Legion.

In light of the ever widening power of the army in all areas of security and in view of the party's own national united front policy, more or less independent para-military fronts are not possible. Unquestionably, Communist cadres are active in a number of groups affiliated with the People's Defense Organization (*Organisasi Pembala Rakjat*—OPR), the army-controlled civil 'guards' now operating in the rural areas, whose principal task was to combat the Darul Islam, and who subsequently joined anti-Malaysia volunteer groups, but the rural front activity would be extremely difficult to carry on in the OPR, and it is not likely to develop in the future unless the PKI leadership decides on a major tactical change and actively would begin to promote creation of a Communist national liberation army, a move which would almost certainly lead to civil war.

The strength of the Communist fronts today is attenuated in part by the influence of non-Communist and anti-Communist competitive organizations in the same field (e.g. all the major parties now permitted to exist, such as the PNI and NU, have their own *aliran* or ideological and organizational conduits in the labor, youth, women's and other movements, and many of the smaller parties have one or two such auxiliaries), but of course, also by the monolithic tendencies of Indonesia's 'guided democracy', implemented by the army leadership and directed toward the 'simplification', i.e. unification and amalgamation of all partisan groups, whether in politics or labor, or among youth, veterans or women, into single state directed organizations required to subscribe to one government supervised ideology. Given the strong tendencies toward *aliran* formation and action in Indonesian public life, however, this has meant the imposition of a degree of uniformity that runs counter to much of Indonesian national experience. For authoritarian constructions of this kind (which have, for example, resulted in the banning of Rotary Clubs, and Masonic Lodges, and even in the dissolution of the Boy Scout organizations) have generally not found much support 'among a people whose "native movement" under the colonial regime already gave evidence of a whole color spectrum of opinions'.[116]

The PKI and its fronts have therefore not been alone in expressing their apprehension over such monolithic developments, and as a result monolithic constructs like the National Front have largely remained ineffective. The army created National Front for the Liberation of West Irian was, in January 1960, replaced by Sukarno's own National Front, on the grounds, ostensibly, that the army organization was not sufficiently active in mobilizing the West New Guinea campaign. Actually the reorganization was probably due to Sukarno's fear that control over the mass movement was coming too much in army hands, for the Front was designed to fuse and supervise all existing partisan political organizations and their functional satellites. But while Sukarno succeeded in substituting his own National Front for that of the army, the fact that the PKI and other parties resisted any move of being absorbed by the Front, while at the same time Indonesia's President needed the support of the parties to balance the army's power, meant that Sukarno's National Front remained but a loose and ineffectual federative body with little or no real influence. Late in February 1963, the National Front's secretary general, Sudibjo, was still complaining that the front was ineffectual, 'that people at present are still unaware of the great importance of the National Front', that many National Front leaders were 'deliberately' neglecting their duties in the hope that the Front would meet with destruction, and so on. The PKI has paid but the barest lip-service to the role of the Front, and its organizational activity has continued successfully to bypass it.

More than ever the party's fronts have insisted that they are 'mass organizations' free from any partisan control and that, despite their particular political position, they are not to be considered as 'Communist'. The party's front groups persist in this line, even though their organizational structure—whether one looks at *Gerwani* or at SOBSI—is closely modeled after the PKI's and after the latter's principle of organizational 'democratic centralism', and even though the top leadership of the fronts consists of PKI members or known fellow-travellers, and even though known cadres are in command in the critical lower echelon positions. As one student of SOBSI has put it:[117]

In their statements, insisting on the independent character of the SOBSI, spokesmen both of the federation and of the Communist Party, while admitting the presence of so many Communists in the SOBSI, always try to minimize the significance of this situation. They contend that their presence is only a fortuitous concidence, caused by the correctness of their principles and policies and their devotion to the national well-being of the Indonesian people. Typical of this kind of communist mentality is the content of a letter written and sent on December 4, 1954, by Mr. Njono, Secretary-General of SOBSI, to Mr. D. N. Aidit, Secretary General of the Partai Kommunis Indonesia, on the occasion when Mr. Njono applied for the PKI membership after having been the top leader of the SOBSI and a strong sympathizer of the Communist Party for many years. Mr. Njono concluded his letter with the expression of the expectation that his application for Communist Party membership would certainly be seized upon [by] the capitalists and reactionaries to renew their accusation that the SOBSI was dominated by the Communist Party.

In their constitutions, SOBSI, BTI, and other front organizations continue to declare themselves to be non-partisan. When in the aftermath of the PKI's sensational July 8, 1960 'Evaluation' of the government the party and its front groups were banned by military authorities in a number of areas in Indonesia, SOBSI protested the ban, denying that 'it is connected organizationally with, or is patronized by, the Indonesian Communist Party', while about the same time the BTI followed suit, affirming its 'sovereignty and independence' and rejecting the contention 'that it "shelters" under or is "tributary" to any political party'.[118] There is no evidence, however, that these avowals of organizational independence made much of an impression on government and military leaders. They may, however, provide front-group leaders with a sense of justification for political action which the PKI itself feels no longer free to engage in. After its July 8, 1960 'Evaluation' had run into heavy government opposition, the PKI slackened somewhat in issuing critical comments on the domestic economic and political situation for a while, but SOBSI and BTI continued to do so, apparently quite prepared to court further repressive measures by the military. In the closing weeks of 1960, at a time when it was still banned, along with the PKI and other fronts in a number of regions, SOBSI for example began a campaign against Belgian investments and interprises in Indonesia, in retaliation for 'Belgian imperialism' which 'is the power behind the chaotic situation in the Congo', as SOBSI's first deputy chairman, Mohammad Munir put it.[119] The campaign bore fruit in March 1961, when estate workers affiliated with SARBUPRI (one of SOBSI's mainstays, it will be recalled) occupied eight Belgian estates in the Labuhan Batu area of North Sumatra, although in other areas workers were prevented from taking over Belgian plantations in pursuance of a government decision to place such Belgian possessions temporarily under government control, in view of the tensions aroused by the Congo situation.[120] In April and May SOBSI activists began a campaign for a worker's take-over among the personnel of the Belgian owned 'Faroka' cigarette factory in East Java, a campaign facilitated by the fact that 'Faroka' personnel is affiliated with the Indonesian Tobacco Workers Union (*Serikat Buruh Rokok Indonesia*—SBRI), a member of SOBSI. Though at one point the take-over was nearly successful, the army quickly quelled it, an army spokes-man criticizing 'certain groups' that were using the workers 'in a political controversy aimed at achieving their own ends'.[121] Earlier in the year the army had already had occasion to denounce a series of brief, wildcat strikes in state-owned enterprises in North Sumatra, instigated by SOBSI-affiliated unions. Accusations that SOBSI was aggravating the seriousness of the national economic condition became a favorite line of army commanders dealing with SOBSI inspired labor unrest. During 1962 SOBSI was particularly vociferous in criticizing economic conditions, from rising prices to mismanagement in the state enterprises (the latter a slap at the army, since many state enterprises are directly supervised by army officers), and in December demanded that the government 'take immediate steps to smooth the distribution of rice and other daily necessities'.[122] In January 1963, it reiterated this demand, and during the remainder of that year called for more drastic measures against speculators, foreign capital and 'corruption' in the bureaucracy. SOBSI, along with *Pemuda Rakjat* showed its strength toward the close of 1963, and again early in 1964, when it mobilized mass agitation against British and Malayan holdings, and SOBSI's theoretical independence of the PKI, while at the same time faithfully articulating the party line, has continued to prove to be one of Communism's major assets in Indonesia.

PART III

THE CHANGING BALANCE OF POWER

CHAPTER VI

THE 1960 CRISIS AND ITS AFTERMATH

TOWARD THE CLOSE of 1959 it seemed that the PKI was beginning to become more and more critical of the Sukarno-Djuanda
government and of the state of affairs after Sukarno, on July 5, 1959,
had unilaterally imposed the 1945 Constitution and had begun to issue
a great many executive decrees, thereby seemingly reducing parliament
to a mere appendage of the process of government. This apparent
aggressiveness in Communist circles was probably encouraged by the
additional prestige won for the party by its Sixth National Congress in
September 1959, and by a certain solidarity manifest among virtually
all parties represented in parliament in the face of what seemed to be
increasing executive encroachment on customary parliamentary operations. With considerable frequency the organs of the PKI and its fronts
began to take the government to task. No doubt this Communist
criticism also reflected increasing concern among party leaders that the
freedom of operations of the PKI and its fronts was being jeopardized
by the autocratic position of President Sukarno and of various army
commanders. Possibly, too, the PKI believed that the circumstances
surrounding the return to the 1945 Constitution and the formation of
the Sukarno-Djuanda *karya* (work) cabinet on July 10, 1959, augured
a possible 'opening to the left', giving the PKI a right to demand a seat
in the cabinet in view of its strength and its support (however guarded)
for the 1945 Constitution. The criticism may well have been calculated
to press the government to bring the Communists into the cabinet.

Whatever the motivation, the Communist campaign soon moved into
high gear. A statement issued by the Economic Affairs section of the
PKI Central Committee on November 19, 1959, noted 'the growing
unrest' among the masses as a result of economic hardships and asserted
that the standard of living was declining and that prices of daily
necessities were steadily going up and seemed to be uncontrollable.
Dismissals of workers and arbitrary eviction of peasants were said to
cause 'an ever greater number of unemployed and narrowing employment opportunities'. All these ills the statement attributed mostly to
government distribution and price policies, which had the tendency to
encourage speculative and parasitic business ventures and to drive the
cost of living ever higher. The national income, the statement concluded
was mostly in the hands of 'foreign monopolists, landlords, commercial,
capitalists and speculators', and therefore the government should orient

itself more toward the working people and their pressing needs.[1] On January 12, 1960, M. H. Lukman again severely criticized the government for its inability to bring prices down, indirectly also criticizing the military because they were getting 37·8 percent of the 1960 state budget, while only 13·1 percent was being allocated for the program of supplying the population with its basic necessities of food and clothing. Lukman also attacked allegedly undemocratic procedures in the appointment of heads of local governments ('the persons being appointed as Heads of Regions are precisely those local government officials who do not have the support of the people'), and concluded by saying that while the new Sukarno-Djuanda *karya* cabinet had already been in office for six months 'during all this time there has been no sign that the Ministers in this cabinet are capable of implementing its program'; he hoped, therefore, that the cabinet's composition would be changed.[2] If this was yet another PKI bid to join the cabinet, it had no effect, and on February 10, 1960, the Politburo issued a sharply critical evaluation of the government emphasizing the 'deteriorating economic situation', condemning the profit-oriented policies of the state-owned trading corporations taken over from the Dutch, and pointing to scarcity, higher prices and an increasingly heavy tax burden.[3] In March 1960, conflicts arose between the supervisory office of the nationalized Dutch enterprises and their SOBSI-affiliated workers over the Lebaran (day ending the Muslim fasting period) gratuities to be paid to the workers, but Army Chief-of-Staff Nasution nipped an intended strike action in the bud—a move which brought new, if veiled, criticisms of the military. On March 21, 1960, *Harian Rakjat* was suspended again by the military administration of Djakarta, among other reasons for having criticized the military-enforced state of emergency laws in the country, which in the paper's opinion were stifling the development of democratic and 'national' forces.[4] On May 1, 1960, SOBSI issued a lengthy critique of government policies, declaring that economic conditions were continually worsening, criticizing the state enterprises for their 'hunting' after maximum profits, as well as the government's price policy which placed essential commodities out of the people's reach. Again the military were attacked; Nasution was criticized for his intervention in the dispute over the payment of Lebaran gratuities, while the military as well as the government in general were condemned for inhibiting the 'democratic rights' of the workers:[5]

The Political Manifesto has underlined the concept that guided democracy is still a democracy, yet there are still many military regulations and actions which restrict democratic rights. The workers are not only encountering various prohibitions, but more than that in some districts because of their activities to solve labor problems or to lead natural, reasonable and just mass actions, dozens of cadres and activists of the SOBSI and the trade unions affiliated to it have been detained or put into prison.

Next day (May 2) SOBSI gave a general reception in Djakarta attended by Aidit and Lukman. Njono gave a speech at that time in which he noted again that workers at present were experiencing the 'contradictions caused by military regulations and measures which restrict the right to assemble, to hold meetings, and to express opinions either orally or in written form, the freedom of the press and other democratic liberties'. The 'contradiction' between the workers and the army was, however, still a contradiction 'among the people', as Njono put it in Leninist-Maoist fashion, and the contradiction would not sharpen so long as workers' actions remained natural, 'with just, reasonable and know-the-limit demands'.[6] Njono noted that SOBSI early in the year had forwarded several demands to cabinet ministers to stop the further deterioration in the living standards of the people. Late in June the Central Committee of the PKI again took the government to task for its attempt to reform the regional councils, declaring that the freezing or dissolution of the councils by executive order would do great harm. 'It is very untactful' the CC declared, 'that the Government at the present time does not try to smoothen and stabilize the regional governments but acts to the contrary'.[7]

The July 8 'Evaluation'. After this barrage of criticisms the statement issued by the Politburo on July 8, 1960, did not seem especially newsworthy. Entitled 'Evaluation of One Year of the Karya Cabinet', and published both in *Harian Rakjat* and other party organs as well as in brochure form, it criticized the cabinet in terms of the cabinet's announced three-point program (bringing food and clothing to the people, establishing security, and combatting imperialism, especially through the struggle to regain West New Guinea) and pointed out the shortcomings in each of these three fields. Again the government's economic and financial policies were attacked, the rising costs and the shortages of basic commodities were noted, and the ascendancy of 'bureaucratic capitalists' making use of the state-of-war regulations to hunt for profits in the state enterprises taken over from the Dutch, was excoriated once more. Government policies in the national development field were also criticized, the 'Evaluation' alleging that the government was intending to make economic development dependent on foreign monopoly capital and to continue to be hospitable to 'imperialistic' foreign capital investments in the country. The Minister of Trade was accused of orienting Indonesia's trade in favor of the capitalist West, while the

Minister of Labor was charged with failing to look after the economic interest of the workers and of ignoring the democratic rights of trade unions. There was criticism of the security policy, the implication being that military action against the rebels was lagging inasmuch as the Political Manifesto of 1959 had stated that security would be restored within two to three years, whereas General Nasution in the middle of 1960 declared that this would still take three years. Security policy was criticized indirectly also by the charge that the process of democratizing village governments—the responsibility of the Interior Minister—was being ignored.

The cabinet's foreign policy was also unfavorably reviewed. The struggle to regain West New Guinea, it was alleged, was making little if any headway. Indonesia's support of Tito and of Tito's idea of holding a conference of nations pursuing an independent foreign policy was severely criticized because it implicated Indonesia in an attempt to create 'a new world' based on the Yugoslav revisionist ideology. Foreign Minister Subandrio was criticized for allegedly having said that there were no problems between the U.S. and Indonesia that needed settling. Relations with the Chinese People's Republic had worsened, declared the 'Evaluation', a development that went contrary to the principles adopted at the Bandung Conference of Asian-African nations.

In publishing this new critique the PKI made it plain that it had apparently still not lost hope of gaining a seat in the cabinet, for in an editorial comment on the Politburo 'Evaluation' the party newspaper pointed out that the time had come for the cabinet to consider carefully its basic line *and its membership*, and to heed the 'voice of the people'. By attacking the policies of individual ministers the 'Evaluation' strengthened the impression that the party was looking for cabinet seats, although such individidual attacks are part of established party policy, as we have seen, since in that way the party hopes to avoid criticism that it is attacking the government as such, or the figure of Sukarno. After the furore over the 'Evaluation' had broken out the paper declared that the 'resounding and prolonged echo' left by the statement was indicative that it reflected 'the innermost thoughts' of the majority of Indonesians of all walks of life.[8]

The first wave of criticism of the PKI's 'Evaluation' came from the press. Anti-Communist papers like *Abadi*, *Pedoman* and *Nusantara* took note of allegedly 'new aggressive tactics' of the Communists, professing to see an attempt to split the army from the president in the evaluation and hurling terms like 'anti-national' and 'deceitful' at the PKI. The 'Democratic League', which had been formed to protest Sukarno's new *gotong royong* parliament and by implication opposed the whole drift toward executive autocracy, issued a call for 'the greatest possible national vigilance' in view of the strength being exhibited by the PKI. Even left-wing papers like *Bintang Timur* appeared somewhat embarrassed over what another paper called 'the hard punch blows' delivered by the PKI to the government in its evaluation.[9]

With public opinion seemingly aroused the army now moved against the party. On July 16, Politburo member Sakirman, a vice-chairman of the National Planning Council, was (according to a statement issued by the PKI Secretariat on July 17) 'taken from his house by uniformed men in Bandung early in the morning' and 'has since then not returned home'. The announcement caused a spate of rumors, 'and for some days', according to a PKI publication, 'the CC Secretariat was unable to find out where Sakirman was'. It appears that Aidit took up directly with Sukarno the matter of Sakirman's whereabouts and after he had done so a spokesman of the West Java Military Command in Bandung at last disclosed, on July 20, that Sakirman had been arrested in Bandung by 'state law-enforcing agencies' on behalf of the Djakarta Military Command. Thereupon he had been sent to the capital, where he was in the custody of the Djakarta Military Command. The spokesman of the West Java Military Command in Bandung declared that 'the reason for Sakirman's detention was the concern of the Djakarta Military Garrison Command'. It soon became apparent why Sakirman had been arrested, for also on July 16 the 'War Administrator' of Djakarta, Colonel Umar Wirahadikusuma, ordered suspension of *Harian Rakjat* for an 'indefinite period' (it was allowed to appear again on August 2), because it had published the July 8 'Evaluation' of the Politburo; this, in the Military Command's opinion, seemed designed to play off President Sukarno 'against a number of Ministers', suggested that the army was unduly favoring the rebel groups in the country, and sabotaged the security policy of the government. (For good measure the anti-Communist daily *Nusantara* was also suspended on the same day for having carried articles allegedly implying that the government was violating the 1945 Constitution). In its announcement banning *Harian Rakjat* the Djakarta military command went, however, into much greater detail than in its statement on *Nusantara;* it pointed out, for example, that by publishing the July 8 'Evaluation' *Harian Rakjat* was breaking an agreement reached between its editors and the Djakarta War Administrator the previous April, in which *Harian Rakjat* had agreed not to publish articles 'having the nature of playing the President off against the Armed Forces' or of 'playing off one armed service against another' and had agreed not to make itself 'available' as 'a tool of another foreign power' but place national interests paramount.[10] In the agreement, according to the War Administrator, *Harian Rakjat* also accepted the necessity of the condition of 'emergency' (i.e. martial law) and thereby the need of military censorship. By publishing the July 8 'Evaluation' *Harian Rakjat* allegedly had violated all these April agreements. Following the banning of *Harian Rakjat* the Djakarta military command also declared the pamphlet version of the 'Evaluation' to be illegal. A deadline of July 29 was set, by which date all persons holding the pamphlet were required to turn them into the authorities. But the order had apparently only limited effect, since subsequently an undisclosed number of persons were arrested for still having the outlawed pamphlets in their possession.[11]

Also on July 16 Nasution publicly arrayed himself against the PKI. Speaking in Kutaradja during a military inspection tour of Acheh, Nasution put the PKI in the same category as the PRRI and the Darul Islam as comprising those who 'disapproved' of the government's policies. It was as near as Nasution had ever come in classifying the Communists as being among the country's outlaws. The Army Information Chief, Lt.-Col. Sunarjo, reiterated in a statement issued on July 24 what was to become the army's favorite line toward the 'Evaluation', saying that 'a certain group' (obviously referring to the PKI) was again attempting to play the army off against the President. The 'group' in question, said Sunarjo, opposed stability in the country, because stability 'means the wiping out of its breeding ground'. In addition to Nasution, other cabinet ministers, notably Foreign Minister Subandrio and National Planning Council Chairman Mohammad Yamin criticized the 'Evaluation'. Yamin characterized as 'ridiculous and untrue' the Communist charge that he was advocating the use of foreign capital investments as a means to defray the costs of Indonesia's new overall development plan.[12] Meanwhile the controversy was waxing hotter over press reports, quoting the Djakarta War Authority, that PKI leaders, having been summoned to appear before the authority, were trying to 'evade State officials in the performance of their duty'. For on July 19 the Djakarta Military Command summoned Politburo members for questioning in connection with the 'Evaluation'. According to Aidit Politburo members did not receive a summons from the Djakarta War Administrator on that date, although he declared he had on July 19 received an instruction from the President, who, as 'Supreme' War Authority, had directed him and three other Politburo members to appear before the Djakarta War Administrator on July 21. Whatever the significance of this distinction, it soon became the basis of further arguments between the army and PKI leaders. For when Aidit on July 19 publicly stated that Politburo members had not received summonses from the Djakarta War Administrator, his statement was flatly contradicted three days later by the Administrator. The PKI countered this denial with a complaint and with a demand for an investigation of the Djakarta War Administrator's statements, urging that if necessary legal action be taken, because the honor of the Politburo members in question had been besmirched. On July 21 Aidit and Njoto, in compliance with the Presidential instruction, presented themselves to the Djakarta War Administration and were ordered to return the next day for interrogation, which they did, along with M. H. Lukman and Sudisman. By July 30 the interrogation was completed and while Aidit, Njoto, et. al. had not been formally detained during the interrogation, as had happened to Sakirman, they were, according to a statement of Aidit's, 'during the week or so of investigation placed in a position in which it was not possible for us to leave Djakarta'. All in all, according to Aidit, the Politburo members that were interrogated answered a total of 679 questions, and their interrogation covered '190 pages of closely-typed folio'.[13]

During and well after the period of interrogation rumors filled the capital about the possibility of a Communist *putsch* and an army counter-*putsch*, about special protection being provided for high-placed officials, about allegedly illegal measures being taken by the army in detaining Communist cadres, about dissension and conflict in the ranks of the armed forces, and so on. Matters reached such a pass that a spokesman for the Djakarta War Administration felt constrained to issue a warning on July 28 against the rumors, which, he said, were aimed at 'playing off the Army against the President' and at 'splitting the Army'. The spokesman also announced that immediately after the July 8 'Evaluation' by the PKI, 'a certain group' had been launching false reports of 'non-actual happenings'.[14]

The frequent reports by the War Administrator's office on the controversy themselves contributed to keeping the rumors and the speculation alive. On July 30, for example, the War Administration issued yet another statement announcing the arrest of 12 persons (not all belonging exclusively to 'one or other group') for having organized a meeting without a license and for having the brochure version of the PKI's 'Evaluation' illegally in their possession, while he also announced that 'the second stage' of the investigation of the Politburo members interrogated earlier would commence soon. By August 25 the War Administration announced that there were 'strong legal grounds' for a court suit against the PKI and that such a suit was being contemplated by the judiciary.

All the while the July 8 'Evaluation' affair was having repercussions throughout the country. On July 28 some 3,500 persons, mostly youths affiliated with Masjumi and Socialist organizations, demonstrated in Palembang, South Sumatra, marching on the Territorial Military Headquarters, and carrying banners demanding the banning of the PKI, the dissoluton of the new *gotong royong* parliament appointed by Sukarno, and a firmer stand in the struggle to regain West New Guinea. Following the demonstration the PKI Major District Committee headquarters in Palembang was attacked, sustaining considerable damage.

On August 18 a similar demonstration of 4,000 youths, also demanding that the PKI be banned, was staged in Malang, East Java, followed by an anti-Communist demonstration in Surabaya on August 20, in which about 1,000 persons, including youths, students and 'betja' (pedicab) drivers, reportedly participated. Earlier, on August 2, in Bandjermassin, South Kalimantan, a public meeting had been held also urging the PKI's dissolution, and on August 5, a Friday morning prayer meeting attended by a large throng of Muslims in Bandung, West Java, heard prayers offered up against 'kafirs (unbelievers) and atheists'. On August 11 PKI cadres were arrested in the rural districts of East Priangan, West Java and accused by military authorities of having 'repeatedly held prohibited meetings'.[15] The Indonesian press continued to keep the issue alive and was almost unanimous in criticizing the PKI for its 'opportunism', its 'incorrectness', its policy of 'discord', and so on. Ironically, some papers, like the leftist *Bintang Timur*, which had extensively reported or commented on the July 8 'Evaluation', were subsequently themselves ordered suspended by the military authorities because of the nature of their comments.

It was left to President Sukarno to make the next move in the affair. It will be recalled that on March 27, 1960, he had announced a new *gotong royong* parliament, which excluded the Masjumi and the Socialist Party (PSI), on the grounds that these parties had not purged themselves from that section of their membership actively leading or supporting the PRRI rebellion against the government. On August 17, 1960, in his Independence Day address, Sukarno announced that he had ordered Masjumi and PSI to dissolve themselves within one month; failure to do so would cause them to be marked as outlawed. This decision was made, he declared, because these parties were 'endangering the State'. In light of the PKI's July 8 'Evaluation' the dissolution order of the Masjumi and PSI provoked bitter reactions in anti-Communist circles, nowhere more perhaps than in certain military territorial commands in various part of the country. A feeling that Sukarno seemed to be more concerned with the alleged danger coming from anti-Communists than with that from the Communists found further confirmation in various statements which he was making at this time (to be discussed presently) which seemed calculated to give the PKI strength and comfort in its dispute with the military over the July 8 'Evaluation'. Shortly after Sukarno suspended parliament it will be recalled and before he announced his new *gotong royong* parliament, leading army officers, Masjumi leaders, Socialists and members of confessional parties, as well as a few followers of Nahdatul Ulama, had formed the 'Democratic League'. The League was anti-Communist and was ostensibly formed to preserve parliamentary democracy but even before the July 8 'Evaluation' some of its members were urging the army to seize the government.[16] Nasution, while not actively opposing the League, declined to heed its wishes, however, but regional army commanders, as in the past, seemed more disposed to take drastic action. On August 24, 1960, the Commander of the Military District of South Kalimantan 'temporarily suspended' the activities of the PKI and its subsidiary organizations, including SOBSI, BTI, *Pemuda Rakjat*, *Gerwani* and LEKRA. The reason given was that 'the ideology, objectives, principles, short as well as long term programs, of the Indonesian Communist Party (PKI) are clearly in contravention to the Government's program, and aim at the violent change of the principles and objectives of the Indonesian Republic based on Pantjasila'. The suspension announcement accused the PKI of trying to play off the state's agencies against one another, and noted that inasmuch as a recently announced Presidential order had liquidated the Masjumi and Socialist parties, 'public opinion in South Kalimantan believes that the PKI should also undergo the same fate'.[17] All PKI publications as well as those of the Chinese People's Republic's embassy, were also banned. Soon afterwards followed the announcement by the War Administrator of South and Southeast Sulawesi suspending all activities of the PKI in the area by August 27, in view of the fact that 'progress now being made in the security field in South and Southeast Sulawesi has reached the final stage at this moment' and also 'in the interest of the continued implementation of the Political Manifesto'. The South Sulawesi decree also noted that following the presidential decision dissolving Masjumi and the PSI 'attempts have been made by certain groups to create new problems which might disturb law and order' in the context of implementing the Presidential decision.[18] Almost simultaneously an announcement by the Military Commander of South Sumatra and Djambi suspended all activities of the PKI and of organizations which were said to support the PKI, such as the SOBSI, BTI, the oil workers union PERBUM, the estate workers union SARBUPRI, and also *Gerwani*, *Pemuda Rakjat* and 'other social, economic and cultural institutions which are affiliated with the PKI'. Violators of the suspension orders were threatened with a maximum one-year jail term or a maximum fine of Rp. 50,000. An explanatory note, issued by the South Sumatra Military Command, declared that after the Presidential decision dissolving the Masjumi and

PSI had been announced, 'the following symptons' were noted in Djambi and South Sumatra, which presumably justified the military command's decision to ban the PKI:[19]

1. An instruction of the PKI Central Committee ordering all its branches throughout Indonesia to impede the implementation of the government regulation on the ban of alien traders in rural areas, and to 'obstruct' workers on all estates, in oil industry establishments, and in coal and tin mines, who were not affiliated with PKI-sponsored labor organizations;

2. Evidence of preparations being made by PKI members to hold a 'showdown' with Masjumi and PSI members;

3. Actions by PKI sponsored organizations aimed at instigating workers to occupy estate lands as much as possible 'so as to block the government's endeavors to boost production';

4. Preparation by the SOBSI-affiliated PERBUM oil workers union to stage strikes 'following a radiogram of the Supreme War Administrator of August 16, 1960 on the intention of certain workers to take over foreign enterprises such as Unilever, Shell, etc.';

5. Failure by PKI leaders to turn in the banned brochure version of the July 8 'Evaluation'; and

6. An 'absence of concrete support' in the PKI for the War Administrator of South Sumatra and Djambi.

The Djakarta military command must have felt heartened by these suspensions and on September 1, 1960, it took the initiative in staging a parade in Djakarta, which included elements of the Indonesian Army, Navy, Air Force and State Police, with armored cars, tanks and other motorized units. The parade, described as a 'mass patrol', was generally interpreted as a show of strength for the benefit of the Communists and their sympathizers and designed to demonstrate the unity of the armed forces in view of the alleged Communist attempt to create discord in the ranks of the military and the government agencies. The spokesman for the Djakarta War Administration said the parade constituted 'a positive proof and answer to certain elements wishing to see the emergence of a rift among the Armed Forces of the Republic of Indonesia' and asserted that the armed forces 'have remained an integrated unity'.

But as the anti-PKI drive seemed to be accelerating among territorial military commanders, and in the midst of speculation that a party suspension might soon also be imposed in East Java province, Sukarno, ever adroit in preserving a balance of power, summoned the war administrators of South Kalimantan, South Sumatra and Djambi, and

South and Southeast Sulawesi to the capital for reports and consultation, and by September 13, 1960, had all but disavowed the military action against the Communist organizations. He declared that it would have been better if the regional war administrators had first consulted him in his capacity as Supreme War Administrator before issuing their suspensions of the PKI and that there should be closer coordination between regional military administrators and himself.[20] Sukarno reportedly told the regional war administrator also that the PKI 'is known to agree with the Pantjasila' and advocated freedom of religion without being opposed to religion. He insisted that all revolutionary forces, including the Communists, should find a place under the shelter of Pantjasila. This Presidential pronouncement was only one of a number apparently designed to bolster the sagging prestige of the Communists. As early as July 25, 1960, during the annual congress of the National Indonesian Party (*Partai Nasional Indonesia*—PNI), the organization with which he is frequently identified, Sukarno criticized those PNI leaders who had a 'Communist-phobia', and who continuously pointed out their differences with the PKI, as a result of which they were becoming 'rightists'. Speaking of himself Sukarno declared: 'I do not fear Communism. I have no leftist phobia. I continue to sleep nicely even if people say that I am a Communist'.[21] The President noted that he and the PKI had some 'differing views', but that on such matters as anti-colonialism, anti-imperialism, the struggle to regain West New Guinea, the position of the peasants and workers he and the PKI shared an identical outlook. While addressing a large group of students in Surakarta on July 27, Sukarno urged his audience not to fear being called 'leftists', declared that his own philosophy was 'Marxism adapted to the Indonesian situation', and finished by saying 'I am a Marxist myself, besides being a believer in God'. On almost the same day in August that a spokesman for the Djakarta military command was saying that a substantial basis for an anti-PKI court suit existed because of the publication of the July 8 'Evaluation' by the party, a message of Sukarno's was read to the Third National SOBSI Congress in which he declared that the Congress was being held at 'an opportune moment' since the nation was busy clarifying the course of the Indonesian revolution along the lines laid down by the Political Manifesto and that the Indonesian workers were the 'functional group which best understands the Call of the Age'.

There is little question that Sukarno's influence acted as a brake on the anti-Communist drive following the July 8 'Evaluation'—a fact which many PNI members did not appreciate. The PNI South Kalimantan branch had issued a statement supporting the military decision to suspend PKI activity in the area, a pronouncement which had caused considerable dissension in the PNI's national leadership, particularly after the PNI national executive ordered PNI regional branches to abstain from organizing demonstrations and making 'public statements of a political nature'.[22] *Suluh Indonesia*, the PNI's mouth-piece, found it necessary to comment at length on the differences between the PKI and the PNI while paying lip service to Sukarno's warning against 'Communist phobia'.[23]

The PKI, meanwhile, made strenuous efforts to rescue itself from its predicament. It stressed its ideological conformity with Sukarno's national philosophy, particularly as laid down in such recent formulations as the Political Manifesto, *Djarek* (the abbreviated designation for the President's address on August 17, 1960) and in Sukarno's speech before the United Nations' General Assembly on September 30, 1960. During August the party's Central Committee announced that the PKI was also readying various changes in its constitution in order to bring it in line with recent Presidential decrees on the function of political parties. Party pronouncements during this period seemed at pains to stress the PKI's 'national' orientation. The party also established special liaison with the President and government officials in order to have the suspensions revoked. On August 26, 1960, a PKI delegation led by M. H. Lukman called on the deputy attorney-general and the staff of the Supreme War Administrator, specifically in connection with the party's suspension in South Kalimantan; subsequently a party spokes-man indicated that the PKI might bring the issue before the Supreme Court so that the suspension question could be settled 'in line with the course of the Indonesian State and according to existing laws'. Another delegation, again led by Lukman, called on First Minister Djuanda on August 31 to ask that the ban on the party in South Sumatra and South Kalimantan be lifted, and the PKI announced that the party had for-mulated a statement of policy toward the bans placed on local branches which had been submitted to Sukarno, Djuanda, Nasution, the Supreme Court, and the Regional War Administrators involved. On September 1, Aidit and Jusuf Adjitoropo met with Sukarno and Nasution on the same question, and in subsequent days the Supreme War Administrator's Office appears to have been concerned with little else but the suspensions of the PKI.

All these protests were slow in producing significant effect. To be sure, the ban on the PKI was lifted in South Sumatra-Djambi and in South Sulawesi on December 1, 1960, but the ban on *Harian Rakjat* in the former region remained in effect for a year longer, and all PKI leaders entering or leaving the area were required to report to military authorities, while the holding of all party gatherings, even closed ones, necessitated prior approval of the regional war administrator. As for the South Sulawesi area, by the middle of December 1960, the PKI Central Committee was still protesting to Home Affairs Minister Ipik Gandama that Communists were obstructed in holding public meetings and also were being excluded from second level regional legislative councils in such towns as Makassar and Pare-Pare, but the protest was to no avail. On July 8, 1961, military authorities in South Kalimantan made a point of reminding the community that the suspension on all activities of the PKI and its 'supporting and/or affiliated groups' continued to remain in force, and in a circular all State and private enterprises were prohibited from negotiating with any of the banned organizations—a measure particularly affecting such Communist dominated groups as the SOBSI. There was little doubt that the continuation of the PKI suspension in South Kalimantan had the approval of Sukarno in his capacity as Supreme War Administrator, for Presidential Decree no. 7/1960 expressly stipulated the right of regional war administrators, as of December 1, 1960, to forbid political activities in their region if circumstances warranted it. However, under this decree regional war administrators must also first obtain the approval of the Supreme War Administrator before they can impose such bans.[24] On August 28, 1961 the ban in South Kalimantan was finally removed.

Despite the suspensions Sukarno demonstrated his official endorsement of the general legitimacy of the PKI. On August 16, 1960, Sukarno appointed Aidit, Njoto and Henk Ngantung to the executive board of the New National Front, the organization designed to unify all political currents in the country behind the completion of the Indonesian revolution. On September 16, 1960, Aidit was named as a member of the special Indonesian delegation, headed by Sukarno himself, to the fifteenth General Assembly meeting of the United Nations. On December 27 Sukarno established another council, also headed by himself, to revise the Eight-Year National Development Plan and in this council Aidit and Lukman were given seats. On December 28, Lukman was designated one of three vice-chairmen of the Sukarno appointed *gotong royong* parliament. To be sure, in all these posts Communists found themselves in the company of representatives of other approved political organizations and of the military. But even so it is clear that whatever damage the July 8 'Evaluation' had done to the party, it had certainly not eliminated it from official participation along with other centers of powers in the highest councils of government and policy, though such participation (in the context of Sukarno's and the military's autocratic powers) was and is somewhat nominal. Again and again Sukarno in the course of 1961–1962 reiterated the importance of

NASAKOM, the unity of nationalist, religious and Communist political movements in the nation. For good measure—and doubtless mindful of the army's frequent charge that the PKI was trying to drive a wedge between himself and the army—he excoriated the 'imperialists' who, 'even want to play Bung Karno off against the Armed Forces'. These 'imperialists', said Sukarno 'want Bung Karno to quarrel with General Nasution. But Bung Karno is no child, neither is General Nasution. And hereby the imperialist strategy has collapsed'.[25] On January 29, 1962, in an address before delegates of *Partindo* (the radical offshoot of the PNI) which by this time was steadily being infiltrated by the PKI and which had turned the vague collectivist ideology of the PNI called *marhaenism* into a Communist front doctrine, Sukarno emphasized again the importance of NASAKOM and stated that the true follower of *marhaenism* 'may not suffer from Communist phobia'.

For its part the PKI endeavored to remove the impression that it might be suffering from an 'army phobia'. For example, as early as October 5, 1960 (the fifteenth anniversary of Armed Forces Day) which came in a period when the dispute over the party's July 8, 'Evaluation' was still having its repercussions, the PKI sent the army a congratulatory message expressing the hope that 'democratic mutual assistance be preserved among the Armed Forces, parties and people' in line with the Political Manifesto and the directions given by the President and Supreme Commander.

The PKI and Sukarno. Party activity since the middle of 1960 has unquestionably been inhibited but the limits on its operations were the result of gradual changes in the pattern of public power in Indonesia, occurring over several years; comparatively sudden and isolated events, like the furore over the July 8 'Evaluation' were not primarily responsible for the recent restrictions. True, the PKI and its fronts were suspended in a number of areas, its newspaper suffered frequent suspensions, and the antagonism between the party and the army with its regulatory powers sharply increased because of the 'Evaluation'. Yet, in a significant sense, the July 8 affair was not the cause but a symptom of tensions between the party and the government, of a conflict which perhaps was unavoidable since each fresh political crisis in the previous two years allowed Sukarno to move forward with the support of the army in imposing a near dictatorial monolithic government in which party activity became steadily more difficult. The emasculation of parliament and of the last vestiges of ministerial responsibility, the widening scope of public power exercised by army commanders, the increasingly stricter controls over press, education, and even religious life—all betokened a state of affairs in which the wonder was not that the July 8 'Evaluation' furore occurred, but that when it did it had relatively moderate repercussions and that the inherent legitimacy of the party within the national philosophy of NASAKOM and within the structure of government was not affected by it. Presidential Decrees no. 7/1959 and no. 13/1960 which regulated the structure, membership and to a large extent the aims of political parties also confirmed the party's position in national public life, and when Sukarno, on September 13, 1960, temporarily suspended all political activity until November 30 in the interests of presenting Indonesia's case at the United Nations (and possibly also to forestall any untoward happenings while he was away from home), an additional damper was put on the few flickering embers in the public discussion of the July 8 'Evaluation'. Aidit instructed all PKI branches to carry out the President's decree temporarily banning all political activity 'with high Communist vigilance and spirit'.

By the early part of 1961 some PKI leaders felt that the party could begin to adopt with caution a more critical tone once more. A meeting in April 1961, between Sukarno and principal party leaders on the implementation of the decrees 'simplifying' the existing political organizations aroused a good deal of PKI concern not because the PKI was directly in danger— as was indicated the Communist Party's position as such was confirmed by the simplification decrees—or because the party had any real qualms over the elimination of certain lesser parties as a consequence of the decrees, but rather because the remaining parties would be expected to adhere more fully to the new National Front, the organizational expression of NASAKOM. Though Aidit, early in 1961, was appointed chairman of a National Front 'team' which went to North Sumatra to assist in the formation of a provincial branch of the Front there, he made it a point to stress at a mass rally in Medan that the formation of the Front did not mean the end of the political parties. Rather, as he put it, the National Front was designed to 'consummate' the national revolution by liquidating imperialism, forcing landlords to surrender their privileges, drive the Dutch from West New Guinea and carry out development for the achievement of a just and prosperous society.[26] In other words, the Front was to be an instrument in the completion of the first stage of the multi-stage Communist revolution. That this particular emphasis was in all probability not shared by other supporters of the Front goes without saying, but Aidit's statement indicates that the PKI would resist submersion in the National Front, and would express adhesion to the Front only in the terms of established Communist strategy.

Officially, however, the PKI remained in accord with the state-approved catechism of political ideology. On April 26, 1961, the PKI gave extensive publicity to its constitutional revisions adopted by the Central Committee the previous December. While maintaining Marxism-Leninism as the foundation of its work and the establishment of 'People's Democracy' as the party's objective, the party announcement also included acceptance of the 1945 Constitution and of the Political Manifesto (see *supra*, pp. 190–191). 'People's Democracy', moreover, was interpreted to mean 'a system of *gotong royong* (mutual help)', while the terms 'Socialist' and 'Communist' societies were said to refer to societies 'without exploitation of man by man', and as being 'adjusted to Indonesian conditions'. The explanation pledged the party not to aim at a revision of the foundations of the state and to pursue only 'peaceful and democratic ways'. All party members were called upon to uphold the 'Banner of the National Front, the Banner of Party Development and the Banner of the 1945 Revolution', along with the party program.[27]

These interpretations of and changes in the party constitution had been approved with minor alterations by the Office of the Supreme War Administrator, and ultimately were officially approved by the Seventh National Party Congress, in April 1962. The constitutional changes showed once again the party's readiness to de-emphasize its revolutionary Marxist-Leninist identity and take on the protective coloration of its ideological environment. But the party's seeming flexibility, which had appeared to make the constitutional revisions but a simple matter, continued to mask, of course, the real dynamics of the power-conflict and the national power-balance involving President, army and PKI. Only a few days before it had published its new constitutional provisions, the party had been reminded of these dynamics. For on April 13, 1961, Sukarno, in his function as Supreme War Administrator had summoned the principal PKI leaders, Aidit, Lukman, Njoto, Sudisman and Sakirman and had declared that after having received the advice of First Minister Djuanda, Defense Minister Nasution, Attorney-General Gunawan, National Police Chief Sukarno Djojonegoro, and others, it had been decided to bring no formal legal indictment against the PKI at this time because of its July 8 'Evaluation' and instead to 'temporarily freeze' the case against the PKI on a certain condition. The condition was that should the party leaders or party members again violate the Penal Code (as according to Sukarno's statement they were deemed to have done by publishing their July 8 'Evaluation') then a lawsuit would be instituted.[28] In a sense the party was put on probation, but taken in context with Sukarno's other utterances about the party PKI leaders might well feel that they had won something of a victory.

Renewed Conflict. In any event, some party organs soon showed that they were still prepared to carry on the now covert, now overt conflict with army commanders. On February 3, 1961, *Harian Rakjat* was again suspended for 18 days and early in May 1961 it was reprimanded and given a 'stern warning' by the Djakarta War Administrator's office. Next month it received another 'sharp warning' for having carried an article in its June 4 issue, which had discussed the Pantjasila and had—either by accident or design—omitted the concept of 'belief in God' (one of the pillars of Pantjasila). On August 2 the paper was banned again 'indefinitely' (though publication resumed on August 9) for having printed an article criticizing the American weeklies *Time* and *Life* which the paper declared opposed 'continuation of Indonesia's revolution'. This article was declared 'tendentious' by the War Administrator and considered to be an attempt to influence Indonesia's 'independent active foreign policy'. On November 3, 1961, the daily was again suspended for an 'indefinite period' for having carried a cartoon in its November 1, 1961, issue, which had the caption 'From capitalism—imperialism towards Socialism-Communism'. The cartoon referred to the Twenty-Second Congress of the Communist Party of the Soviet Union then in progress, and in the opinion of the War Administrator it violated the editor's promise to defend 'Indonesian Socialism', the 1945 Constitution, the 'active and independent foreign policy of the Republic of Indonesia' and not to become 'an instrument' of the 'current cold war between foreign blocs'. The cartoon had depicted the Congress of the Soviet Party as the harbinger of a bright future for the world; any such suggestion was apparently considered a deviation from approved Indonesian state ideology and foreign policy, as interpreted by the Djakarta military.

Meanwhile SOBSI displayed a new aggressiveness in the period 1961–1962. Developments in the Congo provided the impetus for the earlier cited SOBSI campaign against Belgian capital and enterprises in Indonesia, and around the middle of December 1960, it demanded strong action against 'Belgian imperialism'. The demand was repeated in March 1961, when SOBSI leader Mohammad Munir declared that in confronting Dutch imperialism in Indonesia and Belgian imperialism in the Congo the Indonesian government should confiscate remaining Dutch enterprises as well as Belgian estates and enterprises in the country. Munir's technique of linking Belgian to Dutch imperialism and thereby to the explosive West New Guinea problem proved an effective tactic, in line with the Indonesian government's official sympathies for Patrice Lumumba and with general opposition to colonialism as part of the country's 'active independent foreign policy'.

But while SOBSI spokesmen were permitted to propagandize for a take-over of Belgian enterprises, the military as has already been indicated did not allow an actual expropriation by workers of the Belgian estates in North Sumatra or of the 'Faroka' cigarette factory in East Java. Still, SOBSI, sensing a relatively permissive atmosphere, and in any event committed to support of high Lebaran gratuities for all workers, began early in 1961 a new campaign among laborers on government (formerly Dutch-owned) estates and in government enterprises— a repetition of the campaign a year before—thus again provoking a conflict with military commanders. The North Sumatra branch of SARBUPRI (the estate workers union) as well as the North Sumatran branch of the SBKA (the union of railway employees), both affiliated with SOBSI, instigated a series of brief 'unofficial' strikes in July and early August 1961, against the management of state-owned plantations and against the nationalized Deli Railway Company in North Sumatra. Wage increases and protests against deteriorating conditions of living were the ostensible reason for the strike. Union activists remained in the background, however, and the wildcat strike was said to be an outburst of 'spontaneous' dissatisfaction among some workers. Taken in the context of SOBSI's earlier difficulties with the military, the strike action in the government enterprises seems primarily to have been another Communist show of strength, perhaps primarily to demonstrate the PKI's continuing vitality. But this time SOBSI thought it wise not to be officially involved.[29] The War Administrator of North Sumatra declared in Medan on August 9, 1961, that 'the strikes of the last few few days are known to have been staged by . . . individual instigators who have a certain interest', that is, they 'had the intention of obliterating the state's economy; this is especially so because the actions have been directed against state owned plantations and companies'. With evident chagrin another North Sumatra War Administration statement declared that 'those who have instigated the strikes have saved their own necks and denied all responsibility to avoid further investigation and official prosecution'.[30] This was as much admission of defeat by the military as the Communists could have hoped for, since neither SARBUPRI, SBKA or SOBSI were ever officially implicated. The August strike did show the potential value of such 'unofficial' and 'spontaneous' workers' resistance under Communist auspices, a kind of 'hit and run' tactic on the labor front.

Perhaps encouraged by this, Communist leaders returned to the attack, this time even publicly restating some of the criticisms the PKI had made in its 1960 'evaluation'. SOBSI chairman Njono declared at the SARBUPRI Congress in Surakarta on September 10, 1961, that the fall in production in the government enterprises had not been caused by strikes but by the 'inefficiency and mismanagement' of the enterprises concerned. He reiterated the problem of high prices of food and clothing and the unfavorable living conditions of workers, recalling Sukarno's speech shortly before that the people could be patient but that 'a hungry stomach could not wait too long'. What is stirring the workers, he concluded, is that 'the Political Manifesto be implemented consistently and that the national development plan be carried out in a democratic way'.[31] A month later it was Aidit's turn. Addressing the opening sessions of a People's Youth congress in Djakarta, he stated that he saw no improvement in the living conditions of the people in spite of various efforts to strengthen the economic position of the country. Although there were 'signs of rapid improvement in the political level', this was not what was important to the people, he declared, and 'bureaucratic capitalists are gaining a stronger position, foreign capital still dominates over the private national entrepreneurs and the call for the mobilization of all the progressive "funds and forces" has become vague'.[32] This was as strong a critique of the government as the party leadership had permitted itself since the 1960 'Evaluation', and it repeated two essential points of that 'Evaluation', namely, the difficult living conditions of the masses, and the allegedly nefarious activities of the 'bureaucratic capitalists' in the various military-supervised state enterprises. The second point, in effect, constituted an indirect attack on the military, but there were no repercussions this time, which was even more remarkable when one considers the conclusion of Aidit's same address in which he again intimated the need for a cabinet change, thus by implication criticizing the cabinet much as had been done more directly the year before. Aidit stressed the 'imperativeness to muster the available people's potentials' and to place the people in their 'appropriate' position where they might contribute to the solution of national problems. Referring directly to the capacity of a cabinet, Aidit said it was wrong to assume that political improvements could be made without a change in the composition of a cabinet so as to bring it 'in line with the wish of the people'.[33]

Meanwhile other party fronts were attempting to keep up the pressure in the fields of the government's economic and security policies. *Harian Rakjat* in September, spoke darkly of extensive 'sabotage' of the government's land reform laws, a fact allegedly known to the Agriculture Minister, and demanded stronger action on this and also against 'armed counter-revolutionary gangs' which were said to be supporting the prevailing system of landownership. SARBUPRI's congress in September 1961 concluded with a demand for the 'democratization' of the management of estates, both state owned and private by inviting workers' representatives to sit with management in executive deliberations. SARBUPRI also demanded that the government repeal existing foreign investment legislation and reject all foreign capital investment in whatever form. Another SOBSI affiliate, the Indonesian Sugar Workers Union (*Serikat Buruh Gula*—SBG), also concluded a congress in September 1961 by demanding that the government, in line with the Political Manifesto, recognize and guarantee the rights of workers to express their opinion 'in the spoken as well as the written form' and that state of emergency laws (by which the military regulate political life) be revoked in some areas so that 'when the general elections are held the state of normalcy will have been restored completely'.[34] On February 26, 1962, SBKA demanded that the government halt the rise in prices and appealed directly to Sukarno to bring about price stability. It also urged the government to confiscate all foreign enterprises in which the Dutch still had capital 'as an answer to Dutch obstinacy' in the West New Guinea dispute. These demands, it will be clear, meant another indirect criticism of the position and powers of the army. Equally evident, by the end of 1961, was the fact that the PKI was relying heavily on its fronts to safeguard its freedom of operations.

Communist instigation of labor unrest in this period turned at least one major port city, i.e. Surabaya, into a scene of almost continuous conflict with military and civil authorities. Communist strength lies in the city's SOBSI-affiliated trade union organizations (especially stevedores, sailors and civil servants), and in students' and youth groups aligned with *Pemuda Rakjat*. Revolutionary agitation, a carry-over from the days of the Indonesian Revolution against the Dutch, when Surabaya and its environs were an important battlefield for Indonesian irregulars against the English and Dutch, has been perpetuated through earlier mentioned Communist-dominated *rukun kampung* (neighborhood associations) and has been amplified by the human flotsam that has entered the city from the East Java countryside in the aftermath of the revolution, and by the tensions among the volatile inhabitants of the neighboring island of Madura who have long regarded the city as an area of opportunity. All during 1959–61 there were minor skirmishes between street-gangs, laborers and youth groups and the military authorities. The fact that the city's civil government is heavily infiltrated, if not dominated by Communists, caused lines of conflict to emerge ever more sharply. Arrests of leaders of wildcat strikes and of illegal demonstrations by the military led to local press campaigns and agitation by PKI cadres and SOBSI executives, who alleged maltreatment of prisoners by the military. In this campaign some city officials tacitly concurred. This, in turn, brought further arrests and still further demonstrations demanding release of those arrested in September and October 1960. Matters reached such a pass that on March 23, 1961, the Military Garrison Commander of Surabaya issued a communique warning the city population not to be misled by provocations and rumors designed to heighten the unrest. The communiqué charged that 'certain groups' were trying to stage illegal demonstrations and to spread leaflets and pamphlets in contravention of military regulations.[35]

Despite the subsequent imposition of jail terms on PKI and SOBSI agitators, the conflict persisted and local Communists in Surabaya in the closing months of 1961 were quick to seize on the quickening West New Guinea campaign as a further means of demonstrating their strength; *Pemuda Rakjat* sections, fortified by SOBSI affiliates, took the lead in staging 'spontaneous' demonstrations in November and December 1961, and later in attacking U.S. consular and information service buildings on February 16, 1962.[36] These actions were of a type which embarrassed military commanders and the police found difficult to prevent because of the government's accelerating West New Guinea campaign and its explicit policy of mobilizing public opinion behind this campaign. The Communist policy of being *plus nationaliste que les nationalistes* is an old one, and in the framework of the Indonesian government's stepped up efforts to take over West New Guinea it provided the PKI with a valuable tactic to counter the influence of its enemies in the Army and to keep its image before the public.

But, as in the case of the Djakarta War Administrator's policy toward *Harian Rakjat*, army commanders did not let many opportunities pass to bear down on the Communists. Since 1958 no other flag than the national Indonesian one could be displayed on May Days by order of the military. This measure, originally announced on March 31, 1958, was not always rigorously applied in outlying regions, although in Djakarta even May Day speeches had to be cleared in advance. May Day, 1960, was under effective army supervision throughout the country, however, and not even 'The Internationale' could be sung. The same supervision has been applied to May Day celebrations in following years. Army commanders were quick to interpret regulations in such a way as to minimize the area in which the PKI could still speak its mind about national policy. A case in point was the party's vain attempt to express its views on recent government tactics with respect to PRRI rebels and on other security questions. On July 18, 1961, the West Java War Administrator's Office in Bandung warned the West Java Provincial Committee of the PKI that all reports or statements connected with the settlement of the question of the rebels and with security matters generally required prior approval of the information department of the West Java War Administration. This warning came after the Provincial Committee had issued a statement criticizing and raising questions regarding the army's policy toward the *Darul Islam* rebels; implied was the suggestion that the army was not as forceful in wiping out the rebels as it might be.

The War Administrator's warning in effect nipped in the bud an intended PKI campaign directed at one of the more controversial aspects of recent domestic policy, namely the amnesty for, and rehabilitation of, rebel forces throughout the country. Individually, various local military commanders, especially in South Sulawesi and in Sumatra, had been encouraging the surrender of various rebel groups, including followers of the PRRI, and of the Muslim extremist Kahar Muzakkar, since the end of 1959. Such surrenders, although not carrying a blanket amnesty with them, were taking place at least informally on the understanding that there would be no prosecution if the returning rebels involved showed their readiness to demonstrate loyalty to the central government—an arrangement backed by the army commander's authority in his own theatre of operations, though not necessarily finding favor in other, especially political, quarters. Here lay the origins of a major conflict between army leaders, and especially between Chief-of-Staff Nasution, and the PKI. For by the end of 1959 Nasution appeared to have become fairly well convinced that a successful military action against the scattered PRRI units and *Darul Islam* guerillas would take several years and would overtax Indonesia's already strained economy. While Nasution's subsequent appeals to the Darul Islam leaders in West Java had little or no effect, a conciliatory policy toward the PRRI remnants in Sumatra and their allies in Sulawesi seemed to be more promising and informal discussions about a 'return' of these rebel groups 'to the lap of the Republic' began taking place between local military commanders and rebel representatives as early as the middle of 1960.[37] First by tens and sometimes hundreds, and by the beginning of 1961 by thousands, supporters of the PRRI or of a 'Unitary Indonesian Republic' (*Persatuan Republik Indonesia*—PRI) as the PRRI rebel movement had been officially calling itself since 1960, now began to return. In a statement released on February 24, 1961, the PRRI-PRI issued an appeal to its followers everywhere, calling on them to return 'to the fold of the Republic' in order 'to end the sufferings of the people and unnecessary sacrifices for the sake of attaining stabilization and normalization in all fields'.[38] Leading rebel figures and military commanders such as Maludin Simbolon, Achmad Husein and Zulkifli Lubis, and their units commenced to surrender in ever larger numbers, and by the end of August 1961, the PRI President, Sjafruddin Prawiranegara, and his Defense Minister, Burhanuddin Harahap, had given themselves up and the PRRI-PRI movement had for all practical purposes ceased to exist.

The PKI viewed all these developments with covert hostility, but was powerless to express its opposition openly. The PRRI-PRI rebellion had after all resulted from the dissatisfaction of leading Masjumi and Socialist politicians and of military commanders with the entire course of events in the country since 1956, and in this dissatisfaction grave apprehension over rising Communist influence had been a major factor. The PRRI-PRI had been led by major enemies of the PKI in the Masjumi and Socialist Party leadership, and by fanatical anti-Communist army officers like Zulkifli Lubis. An amnesty, indeed a promised rehabilitation of the rebels by the government (strongly encouraged by Nasution), would provide sudden legitimacy to numerous opponents of the Communists, and rob the PKI of a major source of justification for its 'anti-imperialist' policies. Indeed, on October 9, 1961, Nasution even declared that the returning rebels had not lost their voting rights, and that a new electoral law, now in the making, would be more explicit about the matter.[39] Apart from army control over security affairs, PKI opposition to the amnesty and rehabilitation procedure was complicated by the fact that by Presidential Decree no. 449/1961, effective August 17, 1961, a formal amnesty and abolition of punishment was granted by the government to all involved in the PRRI rebellion and its corollary (the socalled *Permesta*) in Sulawesi, to the Muslim extremists of the Darul Islam, and its allies in the Islamic State movement in Acheh and South Kalimantan, as well as to the followers of the 'Republic of the South Moluccas' (*Republik Maluku Selatan*—RMS) in East Indonesia, provided they reported to the central government authorities by October 5, 1961. Moreover it was known that Sukarno, although originally reluctant to the idea, had in fact endorsed the amnesty procedure around the close of 1960.[40] An open and too vociferous criticism of the amnesty policy now would be tantamount to a criticism of basic security policy, and would re-align the party against Sukarno as well as Nasution. On May 14, 1961, Nasution after an inspection trip through recently 'liberated' areas of North Sulawesi, had already warned against 'certain elements' who opposed the government's amnesty policy toward the rebels,[41] an indirect allusion to the PKI. The earlier mentioned warning by West Java War Administrator's warning to the PKI that any statement about the settlement of the question of the rebels required prior army approval made public discussion of the issue by the PKI impossible, and in light of the army's action against the party following the July 8,

1960 'Evaluation', there seemed little that the PKI could hope to accomplish, unless it was prepared for a complete rupture with the government.

Meanwhile army pronouncements on the subject only infuriated the PKI. Thus on July 22, 1961, Army Commander Suryosumpeno in West Sumatra declared that the army did not feel itself 'the winner' now that the rebels had returned; rather 'we should thank God' for 'the return of our brothers'. On August 30, 1961, Nasution appointed Brigadier-General Suprapto to head a special Defense Department committee, charged with the rehabilitation and resettlement of the rebels in coordination with educational programming, provisioning for health, relocation in villages, and so on, and since then Nasution has repeatedly and publicly demanded that rebel rehabilitation procedures be quickly implemented. On October 22, 1961, he declared in Palembang that the security situation in the country would not be fully restored until 1962, but added that current security policy, including the granting of amnesty to the rebels had 'yielded enormous success', and that some 130,000 former rebels had thus far returned to the authority of the central government, turning in 35,000 pieces of arms. By the beginning of January 1962, the PKI was reduced to issuing a general and vaguely worded 'encouragement' for strong action against those rebels who had not yet returned by the government's deadline of October 5, 1961, especially against the West Java *Darul Islam* insurgents, who continued, and later even intensified, their depradations and spurned all offers of compromise and amnesty.

Another issue, equally important to the party's future, but also seemingly moving rapidly out of its control and out of the arena of public discussion was the freedom of the press. By March 1960, at the ninth annual convention of the International Press Institute meeting in Tokyo, Indonesia was described as the Asian country with the severest suppression of news. The history of the Indonesian Republic has been marked almost from the beginning by increasingly frequent government attempts to clamp down a degree of official censorship that imitates the worst practices of the colonial era. As early as October 1953, the attorney-general's office requested the press not to publicize parliamentary proceedings which could create tension and dissension and it opened the possibility of a 'repressive supervision' of the national press[42]—remarks which produced sharp, adverse reactions in the Indonesian journalistic world in which *Harian Rakjat* fully concurred. An ordinance issued by the Army Chief-of-Staff to the press in October 1956, prohibiting the publication of 'destructive and provocative' news items,[43] brought a new storm of criticism, and in the face of almost universal parliamentary indignation over the ordinance (in which PKI deputies went along with the majority) the application of the ordinance was to considerable degree mitigated. The rapid political changes in the context of 'guided democracy' since then, however, brought ever more severe application of military censorship powers, while subsequent government regulations promulgated by the President required all newspapers to support *Manipol-Usdek*, and to refrain from commenting on such matters as security policy, the rice situation and economic conditions generally, except with the knowledge of the military commanders concerned. By February 1959, the Minister of Information declared that the idea of a free press was long past, and was as obsolete as other 'liberal democratic ideas'.[44] Increasingly heavy censorship began to extend to all media of communication (thus, on August 1, 1961 the Djakarta Army War Administrator's Office even placed the more than 200 private printing presses in the capital under its direct supervision), and despite the occasional efforts on the part of many editors to circumvent press controls (just prior to the 'indefinite' suspension of his paper in November, 1961, the editor of *Harian Rakjat* was accused by the Djakarta War Administrator of trying to evade army objections to certain stories by issuing different editions of the paper), the next year and a half saw the destruction of the few remaining remnants of freedom of expression in the country. The government's proposed press control bill introduced into parliament in June 1961, treated the press as 'an inanimate object which is so hemmed in by "conditions" and "permits" that we could speak of a "licensed press"' as one non-Communist paper, in one of the few fairly sharp public criticisms of the bill to be published, put it editorially.[45] *Harian Rakjat* with a long list of suspensions behind it by the time the bill was introduced, contented itself, as did a few other papers, with asking 'questions of clarification' about the bill, thus hoping to evade censorship. By the beginning of 1962, however, the entire question of press freedom seemed to be becoming increasingly academic because a drastic shortage of newsprint necessitated the appearance of newspapers only half their normal size, while the Information Ministry declared that no consideration would be given by the government to new applications for newsprint as of January 1962.[46]

The Party and Indonesian Foreign Relations. In one fairly broad area the PKI retained a measure of freedom of expression and operations in this period of conflict namely in those selected fields of foreign policy (e.g. anti-colonialism, Western variety) where a kind of general concensus prevails in official circles and where under 'guided democracy' the nation is expected to be of one mind. As has been indicated earlier, PKI organs repeatedly risked action by military censors when they ventured too open an endorsement of Communist bloc countries or even a moderate criticism of or opposition to the U.S. and its close allies. But the party was left, from time to time, with some room to issue statements on foreign affairs that were not likely to bring suspensions of publication. A case in point was the question of world peace. In January 1960, the party staged a National Indonesian 'Peace Congress', in Bandung, during which Sukarno, in a message which must have been gratifying to the PKI, lashed out against those who branded the peace movement as a Communist movement only. Sukarno agreed to bend every effort to get the entire nation to support the peace movement. The Congress approved 'general and absolute disarmament' (carefully omitting any details on how this was to be achieved); urged 'complete elimination of racialism' (here citing South Africa's *apartheid* policies, the 'racial outrages' against Negroes in the U.S., and the outbreak of 'fascism and anti-Semitism in several countries of the West'); declared that the love of peace should be fostered as part of the nation's educational program; favored 'peaceful co-existence for cultural cooperation' with the proviso that 'culture of an Asian-African character should be the basis for cultural cooperation' (presumably among all the countries of the world); issued a 'vigorous protest' against the 'arrest and persecution of peace fighters' in such countries as Kenya, Nyasaland, Portugal, Algeria, Greece, West Germany and others; sent a message to 'the Australian people' expressing 'high tribute to the solidarity of the people of Australia who supported the struggle of the Indonesian people against imperialism, the source of exploitation, poverty and world war', and noting that 'the Indonesian people too are striving for justice, construction and for West Irian'; and expressed full support for Sukarno's 'command that the entire Indonesian people should be peaceminded and fight for lasting world peace'.[47] In endorsing Castro the PKI has also found no obstacle in its way, although officially the dispute between the U.S. and Castro's Cuba has elicited little more in the way of Indonesian reaction than hopes for 'peaceful settlement' and condemnation of armed aggression against Cuba. Aidit fulsomely praised and supported this official Indonesian position, declaring in a statement released on April 21, 1961, that 'I am of the opinion that the stand of the Indonesian government on the latest developments in the Cuban question which clearly upholds the Cuban government is in harmony with the feeling and thought of the people. . . . I feel that the government needs to continue strenuous efforts with the fullest initiative from within as well as from outside the U.S. to speedily stop U.S. imperialist aggression against Cuba, which makes the world situation very tense and which threatens world peace'. Under the protective cover, so to speak, of the

Indonesian governments' own official criticism of the Cuban invasion, Aidit in the same statement, felt free to attack the American government further, this time suffering no reprisal from the army censor for doing so. Thus Aidit recalled on this occasion one of his earlier comments on the inauguration speech of U.S. President Kennedy early in January 1961, that the 'Kennedy cabinet would keep reflecting the representation of capitalistic monopoly groups' and that in view of its attitude toward Laos and the Congo it was 'just as imperialist as Eisenhower's'.[48]

Aidit's support for Cuba, it might be noted, was already manifest at a time when many observers were still unconvinced of the Communist character of Castro's revolution. The PKI never appears to have had any doubts on the point. At the Sixth National Congress of the PKI in September 1959, a 'fraternal delegate' from Cuba (Ursinio Rojas, a member of the executive of the People's Socialist Party of Cuba) was present at the invitation of the Central Committee of the PKI. During his visit there was 'an exchange of views' from which the following conclusion was derived, according to the PKI:[49]

The victorious revolution in Cuba under the leadership of Fidel Castro . . . provides important lessons and experiences for the Indonesian People. Cuba's experiences show that in the present international situation it is not impossible for a small island nation, even though it is geographically isolated and close to the centre of world imperialism, to win a revolution, to overthrow a reactionary tyrannical military power that bows down in servitude to U.S. imperialism, and that is helped by the imperialists and to establish a national, democratic and independent government. Cuba's experiences show that imperialism is no longer able to prevent countries, however small, from taking the path of independence and progress. . . .

These experiences are extremely important for Indonesia because Indonesia is continually being subjected to attacks and threats from the imperialists. The policy being pursued by the Fidel Castro Government in Cuba— reorganizing the entire State apparatus on an extensive scale with the help of the whole people by means of completely stamping out militaristic elements and eradicating the government apparatus which has been utilized by the imperialists, and replacing all this with a democratic apparatus that serves the people and the entire nation—is a policy which sets a good example for Indonesia. The policy of returning to the 1945 Constitution so as to continue with and win victory for the August 1945 Revolution indeed cannot be successfully implemented without getting rid of moribund and reactionary norms and completely overhauling the State apparatus to bring it into line with and serve the aims and interests of the Indonesian Revolution. . . .

The fraternal delegate of the brother Party in Cuba declared during the discussions that the Cuban people fully support the struggle of the Indonesian people for the liberation of West Irian . . . both sides joyfully saluted and gratefully congratulated the Soviet Government on the great victory of Soviet science with its success in launching the first rocket to land safely on the moon. This event is of paramount and decisive international significance in international relations.

The above quotation is of interest not only because of a recognition of the nature of the Castro revolution by the PKI as early as September 1959 (and probably even earlier), but also because a parallel is drawn between the reform of the 'State apparatus' under Castro in Cuba and the return to the 1945 Constitution in Indonesia. PKI support for the latter and recognition of the worth of the former would seem to suggest that developments in Cuba and Indonesia might both be considered from the point of view of Communist theory as steps on the road of the 'bourgeois democratic' revolution, although presumably Cuba has made comparatively more rapid strides of late toward completing the 'bourgeois democratic' phase and entering upon the 'Socialist' phase than has Indonesia. PKI support for Cuba continued without qualification in coming months and the Seventh National Party Congress in April 1962, in a special resolution entitled 'Don't Touch Cuba!', warned 'American imperialism' of the folly of attempting to counter the revolutionary Cuban struggle.[50]

Another foreign policy area where the PKI was able to speak out because its views were close to those of the government was the Congo. Official Indonesian recognition and support of the regime of Patrice Lumumba won the party's hearty approval and when Lumumba was assassinated the party spearheaded a brief mass campaign of protest carried on by various 'Action Committees Against the Murder of Lumumba' which appear to have had the tacit approval of local military commanders. Refusal to let the 'Action Committees' operate would in fact have been difficult, partly because of the Indonesian government's own official condemnation of the Lumumba murder, but also because the 'Action Committees' managed to win support from local civil and regional government officials. For example, the rally sponsored by the North Sumatra 'Action Committee' on March 22, 1961, in Medan was attended by the mayor of Medan and the head of the North Sumatra provincial legislative council. The resolutions adopted by this rally were reflected in those of many similar rallies held throughout Indonesia: condemnation of Lumumba's murder, demands that Belgian-owned enterprises be confiscated and that diplomatic relations with Belgium be broken off, and demands for the punishment by the United Nations of Congolese leaders Moishe Tshombe, Joseph Kasavubu and General Mobutu.[51] In line with this campaign the Communist-dominated municipal council of the city of Surabaya decided to change the name of the Darmo Boulevard, one of the largest streets in the city, to Lumumba Boulevard, and LEKRA (the PKI's cultural front organization) published a book under the title 'We all are Lumumba', featuring poems by Indonesian writers, including Njoto, and honoring the slain Congolese premier. With the approval of the authorities the book was distributed among delegates attending the Asian-African People's Solidarity Council conference in Bandung in April 1961. For sometime after Lumumba's murder the Indonesian government recognized Antoine Gizenga as Lumumba's rightful successor and as the premier of the central Congolese government, and the PKI was permitted to voice its support of Gizenga and its condemnation of Gizenga's enemies, like Katanga President Moise Tshombe, without hindrance. In line with the earlier mentioned tactic of letting front groups carry a major portion of the burden in pushing the party line forward, SOBSI early in February 1962 protested to U.N. Secretary-General U Thant against the arrest and isolation of Gizenga after the latter's fall from power. In its protest SOBSI urged the U.N. to save Gizenga's life 'from the anti-Lumumba gang' and demanded that he be restored to his post in the Congolese government in Leopoldville.[52]

With Sukarno as a protective cover the PKI was also able to voice its support for various Communist demands to reorganize the U.N. When in his address to the Fifteenth Assembly of the U.N. on September 30, 1960, Sukarno urged that U.N. headquarters be moved from New York as well as a reorganization of the United Nations and a revision of its charter, the party was given another opportunity to delve into international affairs with little danger of repression by the military. The existing structure of the U.N., declared Sukarno, 'is a product of Western state system'. Though he 'greatly' respected it, he, Sukarno, could not regard it with 'reverence' or with 'very much affection'. Pointing to the rise of 'the socialist countries' since the day when the U.N. was established in 1945, and to 'the great wave of national liberation and economic emancipation' and to the 'great scientific advance' relating to the exploration of space, Sukarno urged a revision of the U.N. Charter. He remained altogether vague about the nature of this revision but seemed to intimate that the underdeveloped countries living 'in the midst of a Revolution of Rising Demands' should be given a larger role. Sukarno did not mention the Soviet *troika* plan, but did indicate that the U.N. Secretariat should 'reflect the true position of our present world'.[53] As if on cue the PKI reacted. On October 25, 1960, Aidit speaking on the national Indonesian radio network in connection with observances of the Sixteenth U.N. Day called for a 'retooling and revision' of the U.N., declaring that 'the world developments in the last fifteen years were not reflected in the leadership and other bodies of the U.N.'[54] Supporting Sukarno's suggestion that U.N. headquarters be moved to another part of the world 'free from the cold war climate', Aidit alleged that African-Asian states, which together with the Latin American nations were in a majority in the U.N., 'were not included in the bodies which determined the policies and course of the U.N.' Aidit's inclusion in the Indonesian delegation headed by Sukarno to the U.N. Assembly meeting in New York in September 1960 apparently justified all these remarks, but in the same radio address and on other occasions he also seized the opportunity to castigate the 'several imperialist states' which were trying to use the U.N. to enforce their national policies and stated that in the Korean War and in the Congo United Nations intervention benefitted 'imperialist countries'. Aidit's role as a delegate to the U.N. was brief, however, and he content-ed himself by declaring that during the Fifteenth General Assembly of the U.N. a 'deeper understanding had been reached among non-bloc nations, Indonesia and the Socialist countries' in such matters as the seating of People's China, the urgency of disarmament, the need to reorganize the U.N. Secretariat and on the need to remove the U.N. from New York, 'the very center of the cold war', as he put it.[55]

In no area of Indonesian policy, foreign or domestic, did the PKI feel as free to agitate openly as in the West New Guinea crisis. It will be recalled that the very rise of Aidit and the *Sajap Leninis* in the PKI was accompanied by an alteration of party policy on the West New Guinea problem, away from the approach of Alimin favoring a more or less independent West New Guinea loosely united with Indonesia, and toward a radical nationalist policy of proclaiming West New Guinea to be rightfully part of Indonesian national soil and of agitating for its 'return'. The radical nationalist orientation in the West New Guinea dispute was and is an integral part of the party's particular anti-im-perialist policy and for this reason the PKI always opposed any apparent slackening in the West New Guinea campaign. When in July 1959, Foreign Minister Subandrio announced that Indonesia would not introduce its dispute with the Netherlands over West New Guinea into the United Nations that year, but would instead concentrate on a 'contest of power' with the Dutch, the PKI immediately interpreted this as an abandonment of traditional firmness and criticized the government so severely that other papers began to accuse the party of seeking to exploit the West New Guinea issue for its own purposes. As it turned out, the new 'contest of power' strategy involved an accelerating diplomatic pressure,[56] punctuated by psychological warfare, press campaigns, an arms build-up and an increasingly threatening tone, with all of which the PKI closely identified itself. The fact that in this campaign of 'confrontation' Indonesia relied heavily on the support of Communist bloc countries (e.g. the $400 million arms agreement of January 1961 with the Soviet Union) gave added strength to the PKI's own position, and the party newspaper generally found itself in the vanguard of opinion denouncing recent Dutch development efforts in West New Guinea—especially in connection with the establishment of a representative body for the area during 1960-1961.[57] As this Dutch development program began to strike a responsive chord in articulate Papuan opinion and the threat of war became increasingly serious,[58] the PKI joined in the government's campaign to arouse Indonesian opinion, declaring in a statement issued on September 30, 1961, that the entire Indonesian people stood ready to 'liberate West Irian by whatever means', charging the Dutch government with a lack of goodwill and asserting that any form of trusteeship or 'internationalization' of the area was unacceptable because 'we do not want a repetition of the Congo's bitter experience with the United Nations'.[59]

During the Twenty-second Congress of the Communist Party of the Soviet Union in Moscow in October 1961, Aidit reportedly 'consulted Communist and workers parties' leaders of five continents' in attendance at the congress to explain to them the 'resoluteness of the Indonesian people and government to liberate West Irian with all available means from the Dutch colonial yoke'.[60] During the Congress also, the Dutch and Indonesian Communist party delegations adopted a joint statement, rejecting the 'shameful' policy of self determination for West New Guinea (the cornerstone of Dutch policy in this area, it will be recalled) as a 'barely disguised attempt' to use the United Nations as a cover for 'the U.S.-Dutch colonization of West Irian', affirming that the only way to settle the problem lay in an immediate and unconditional transfer of West New Guinea to Indonesia, and warning that if 'Dutch reactionaries' persisted in their refusal of an immediate transfer 'they will deliberately provoke a war with Indonesia over West Irian'.[61] The freedom of operation which the party felt in its policy toward the West New Guinea crisis was further given justification by the official Indonesian attitude toward the attack on the U.S. embassy in Djakarta on February 5, 1962, and on U.S. and Japanese consular buildings in Surabaya on February 16, 1962. Both attacks, which were inspired and led by Communist youth agitators, were officially regretted by the Indonesian government and promises of payment of compensation were given, but at the same time the government all but exonerated the attackers by pointing to the 'state of tension' of the Indonesian people in connection with 'the present stage of struggle for the liberation of West Irian from the Dutch colonialists'.[62] Before the arrival of U.S. Attorney—General Robert Kennedy in Indonesia, *Pemuda Rakjat* handed, amidst considerable publicity, a list of questions to the Foreign Affairs Department for transmittal to Kennedy. One question inquired what the real attitude of the U.S. government was towards Indonesia's 'legal right' to West New Guinea, and another asked if the U.S. would not side with the Dutch in the event that 'Indonesians settle the West Irian issue by means of confrontation in all fields, now or in the future'.

The party's encouragement of, and involvement in, the government-directed mass campaign to acquire West New Guinea later aggravated the conflict between the PKI and the army leadership. Despite the fact that Nasution seemed agreed to the eventual use of force, particularly after the PRRI-PRI rebel movement had collapsed, he was also interested in reaching a peaceful solution of the problem and appeared determined not to launch a sizable attack until Indonesians could fully utilize the vast quantity of military hardware received from the Soviet Union, Yugoslavia, Poland and other countries.[63] The debacle of the attempt at a small-scale Indonesian invasion of West New Guinea on January 15, 1962, during which one Indonesian torpedo boat was sunk and two others fled, and which cost the life of Commodore Sudarso, acting-chief of the Indonesian Navy, underscored for Indonesian military leaders the serious logistic problems involved in an effective armed attack on and occupation of West New Guinea. But the ignominious defeat of the January 15 invasion force, coupled to the attempted assassination of Sukarno on January 8, 1962, in Makassar, led Communist and radical nationalist leaders to ever more forceful demands for an immediate settlement of the West New Guinea question. The January 15 debacle also brought an unfavorable development for the Communists, for on January 19, 1962 Air-Marshal Suryadarma, Air Force Chief-of-Staff, was relieved of his command and Air Vice-Marshal Omar Dhani, named as his successor. Suryadarma was given a new, ill-defined post as Minister-Military Adviser. Though Sukarno, in a special order of the day on January 22, ordered the armed forces to 'keep away from other interpretations' about this change of command (than the official one that it was made in line with plans for the 'rejuvenation of the Air Force'),[64] speculation that Suryadarma had been relieved of his post because of some error in the January 15, 1962 invasion strategy persisted. Of all the Armed Forces Staff Chiefs Suryadarma might be described as the only avowed leftist, and his change of post was probably not welcomed by the PKI, particularly when, shortly thereafter on February 6, 1962, Sukarno promoted Nasution to be Deputy Supreme Commander of the Armed Forces, a post which not only strengthened such operational control over all the nations' armed forces as Nasution already possessed as Defense Minister, but also seemed to strengthen his position as a possible heir-apparent to Sukarno. In the absence of a vice-president (during Sukarno's frequent sojourns abroad supreme

executive powers have been temporarily vested in a variety of functionaries) Nasution's new position could hardly give encouragement to
the PKI.

The Narrow Range of PKI Freedom. Quite apart from the July 8
'Evaluation' affair there were other disquieting developments for the
PKI. The process of establishing monolithic, state-controlled organizations continued, posing an ever increasing danger to the freedom of
operations of the party and its fronts. For example, considering the
attempt the PKI made to control the cooperative movement, especially
among peasants, and in view of its attack on the 'Hatta cooperatives',
the formation of the earlier cited 'All Indonesian United Cooperative
Organization' (*Kesatuan Organisasi Kooperasi Seluruh Indonesia*—
KOKSI) by presidential decision in June 1961, was not encouraging
for the further spread of party influence among peasant groups. The
earlier mentioned outburst of peasant unrest in Kediri, East Java, in
November 1961, in which SARBUPRI had played the leading role, led
to the suspension of major Communist mass organizations in the entire
Kediri residency (the ban was not lifted until September 1962) and the
arrest of prominent PKI cadres. During 1960–1961 the government gave
unmistakable indications that it would not tolerate any kind of organizational or ideological independence, however seemingly harmless. The
national Indonesian Boy Scouts' organizations are no more; they too,
as of the middle of 1961, were brought under a single national youth
organization called *Pramuka* (derived from the Sanskrit terms *pradja*,
muda and *karana*, meaning 'people', 'young' and 'work', according to
a military spokesman of the organizations' founding committee).[65] Since
March 1961 such organizations as the Rotary Club, the Freemasons,
the Moral Rearmament movement and the Rosicrucians have all been
banned, on the grounds that the 'principles and goals' of these organizations were 'founded in and originated from territories outside Indonesia',
which made them 'inconsistent with the principles of the Political
Manifesto which have been adopted as the main course of the State'.[66]
PKI leaders, aware that their party has frequently been branded as
based on an 'alien' ideology, might well reflect that the justification
given for the banning of Rotarians and Masons strikes dangerously
close to home and sets a precedent that can also threaten its own position
in the future. And while PKI theory has generally sought to emphasize
the congruency between Communist principles and the official state
ideology, government spokesmen stressed that the reform and planning
theories carried out by the state were specifically not Marxist in character.
Even such PKI sympathizers as Agrarian Affairs Minister Sadjarwo
declared that the government's land reform program was 'not Communist-

inspired' and was not modeled after the Soviet Union's agrarian policies, while Foreign Minister Subandrio emphasized that 'Indonesian socialism' is 'different from Marxism under which all details are imposed upon the community' and that under Indonesian socialism instead the people are provided with 'general outlines' but are left free to implement them.[67] Such pronouncements do not merely reflect a strong nationalist desire to give substance to what is believed to be a unique national identity; they are also reflective of a hostility to 'alien' influences, that is part of a strong undercurrent of xenophobia, largely anti-Western, but also directed against Marxism in an international political sense. When in August 1961, a Soviet Embassy secretary was ordered to leave Palembang by the local military for reasons unexplained, Indonesian press speculation about the affair clearly showed the extent of this anti-Marxist and anti-Communist undercurrent, though this is by no means as prominent as the anti-Western bias.

It was again Sukarno who has acted as a principal buffer for the PKI against charges that Communism is an 'alien' element in Indonesian life. It was and is he who, with such concepts as NASAKOM, aided the party in its attempt to acquire an indigenous and national character. And the restraints on the party particularly in 1960–1961 were and are in an important sense also restraints on Sukarno. An example again was the West New Guinea issue. Using the Sukarno-dominated popular campaign for the take-over of West New Guinea as a means of demonstrating its continuing strength, the PKI, like Sukarno, ran against the more conciliatory approach of army leaders, notably of Nasution. By its display of aggressiveness the PKI unquestionably hoped to maneuver the anti-Communist army leadership into a position where it could be charged with being 'soft' on the West New Guinea issue, but in order to do so the PKI, as usual, needed Sukarno as a front. However, Sukarno, despite his inflammatory exhortations and 'commands' could not ignore military advice and the army leaders indicated that an invasion of West New Guinea would require more extensive preparations and that there could be no thought of a massive attack until the armed forces had become thoroughly familiar with their newly arrived equipment. Thus the president (and his Communist supporters) were in the position where they could neither afford to lose the momentum of the mass campaign they had unleashed, while at the same time they could not let the momentum continue without some braking, given the military exigencies. But the army too was aware that a military failure in the West New Guinea campaign would strengthen the Communist's hand with Sukarno. On February 21, 1962, Sukarno declared that he hoped that during the Muslim fasting month of Ramadan the Dutch would be prepared to hold negotiations, and that the nation favored a solution of the dispute without bloodshed. These words were widely interpreted as indicating a readiness to ease the tension and as demonstrating the availability of yet another period for negotiations. They may also have been prompted by the President's awareness that the country was in serious economic difficulties and was far from ready for extensive hostilities with the Dutch. But at about the same time Sukarno also ordered the general mobilization of all Indonesians between 18 and 40 in order to channel the 'people's spontaneity' and to make them ready 'voluntarily and actively to take part in the struggle to liberate West Irian'. While Indonesian diplomatic officials and government spokesmen continued to insist on a transfer of West New Guinea as the only basis of negotiations, informally other Indonesians (among them Nasution's representative in Europe, the Bandung publisher Oejeng Suwargana) were seeking a compromise in which immediate transfer of the disputed area to Indonesia would be abandoned for some interim period of joint administration, possibly under U.N. auspices, only at the end of which a transfer would take place, ostensibly with some regard for the wishes of the native Papuans of West New Guinea. Sukarno, was thus by no means the only dynamic factor in the West New Guinea question. In the PKI's contest of power with the army leadership in the West New Guinea issue Sukarno thus, sometimes, proved to be a comparatively weak support. At the same time he had also become relatively more dependent on the PKI and on the radical nationalist temper generally with which the Communists have identified themselves, and this for two reasons: (1) Sukarno, given the nation's deteriorating economy needed a flaming issue of which he would be the principal spokesman in order to retain prestige and power; and (2) he needed support from quarters independent of, or hostile to, the army leadership, lest he become himself a mere front for the army and ultimately be pushed aside by it.

The cabinet reshuffle of March 6, 1962 again revealed how Sukarno was steering between the conflicting demands of Communists and anti-Communists in the country. The replacement of Attorney-General Gunawan and Public Works Minister Dipokusumo, both of whom had been targets of PKI criticisms, might be described as a concession to the Communists, but the replacement of Sudjono, a radical, as minister for parliamentary relations, and of Ruslan Abdulgani, a principal purveyor of Sukarno's ideological mystiques, as vice-chairman of the Supreme Advisory Council, could only please anti-Communist elements. The cabinet reshuffle also provided for ministerial status for PKI vice-chairman, M. H. Lukman, a vice-speaker of parliament, and for D. N.

Aidit, a vice-chairman of the Provisional People's Congress, whenever they were to attend socalled 'State Leadership' meetings, which are also attended by the President and other top cabinet officers. Though it might appear as if the PKI had thus come significantly closer to formal parti- cipation in the top executive level of government, in fact the ministerial appointment had little or no practical meaning, since army officers and the leaders of PNI and NU also held comparable executive positions in parliament and in the People's Congress and were similarly appointed to ministerial rank when attending 'State Leadership' sessions. Rather than as a promotion, the ministerial appointments of Aidit and Lukman should be considered as but another indication of how the PKI seemed to be enveloped and 'neutralized' by the monolithic structure of govern- ment under 'guided democracy'. With NASAKOMIL (an acrostic, it will be recalled indicating the unity of the military along with the principal political currents in the country, including nationalism, Communism and religion) the PKI could feel relatively assured of its official position, but with this concept it was also in serious danger of becoming a spent force and of being progressively 'hollowed out' through the army's restric- tions on its operations.

The PKI's dependence on Sukarno thus seemed to aggravate the complexities of united front strategy. As was indicated earlier (see chapter IV) this strategy under Aidit has tried to combine an approach both 'from above' and 'from below', but given the structure of the army's power and the general monolithic character of the state further reliance upon a united front approach 'from above' seemed more and more ineffective because the party's maneuverability and independence in such an approach (e.g. under NASAKOM or in the context of the government's new National Front) could not be assured. At the same time it became clear that NASAKOM and similar ideological constructs were indispensable to the survival of the PKI, and for that matter, also to Sukarno in his own power struggle with the army. With the demise of parliamentary democracy, the increasing restrictions on party opera- tions, and the virtual impossibility of driving an effective wedge into the National Front, the PKI could only keep its strength by continuous mass action through the front approach 'from below', e.g. through an advocacy of increasing militancy and 'volunteer action' in the West New Guinea campaign, or through continuous agitation via SOBSI, *Gerwani* and other fronts over the country's economic problems. Such militancy 'from below', however, might well bring the party eventually to a new and total rupture with the army, from which even the President might not be able to save it. Thus it was not only the army which prevented an effective front 'from below' policy, but also the PKI's dependence on Sukarno, and his on it. In this precarious mutual balancing act all sudden or forceful moves might well be fatal to both participants. But with neither an effective approach 'from above', nor with one 'from below' the PKI, by the end of 1961, seemed to have become something of a bird in a gilded cage, with only a process of slow atrophy lying ahead.

The Basis of a New Departure. Yet the dynamics of the Indonesian political and economic system were even at the close of 1961 already forming the foundation for a new development for the party. The ever mounting mass agitation in connection with the West New Guinea campaign, an agitation subsequently captured by Sukarno's exhortation to his nation to *vivere pericoloso!* ('live dangerously!'), gave the PKI, as rarely before, the opportunity to hitch its fortunes to a new momentum of nationalistic fervor and so acquire respectability as a party truly identified with national aims. In the early months of 1962 no party outdid the PKI in articulating a quality of reckless daring that would somehow manage to bring West New Guinea into the Indonesian fold. And it was precisely within this context that the party felt strong enough to hold its Seventh National Party Congress. Compared to the Sixth Congress of September 1959, the Seventh Congress which was held from April 25 to April 30, 1962, was much less of a spectacle. Its principal accomplishments involved endorsement of constitutional revisions already described, and adoption of various resolutions calling for speedy general elections, 'democratization' of regional government, support for the Eight Year Development Plan, opposition to 'neo-colonialism' (e.g. in Malaya where the idea of a Malaysian federation was gaining ground, as well as in the Congo and Latin America), support for Cuba, for the 'democratic people' of Portugal struggling against Salazar, and so on. The Congress also affirmed that only a *gotong royong* cabinet, i.e. a government that included the PKI, would be able 'to rally the national forces' to cope with present difficulties. This affirmation was essentially *pro forma:* it was not until later in the year that the PKI would redouble its efforts on behalf of a *gotong royong* régime. As was the case at the Sixth Congress, Sukarno also addressed the closing session of this Congress and in his speech he emphasized that there was no need for the Indonesian people 'to indulge in Communist phobia' and that 'There is nothing which can shake the fact that the Indonesian Republic can only exist with Nasakom as its axis'.[68] But the real significance of the Seventh Congress was that it was held at all, particularly considering Sukarno's earlier directive that no special congress would be necessary to ratify the changes in the party constitution.

The PKI seemed to have accommodated itself, by the time of the Seventh Congress, to living in a condition of continuous tension with the army and to a policy of equally continuous 'reality testing', i.e. pressing its demands and agitating through its fronts against the quarantine network thrown over Communist activity by the army. There were obvious 'safe zones' in all this, that is areas of activity, such as the West New Guinea campaign, and certain other fields of foreign relations, where the army would be unable to touch the party. 'Danger zones', by the same token, involved party demands for greater 'democracy' in areas under direct martial law, or criticisms of living conditions, or of the management of state run enterprises, or strike actions against foreign establishments. Well aware of the tactical problems posed by these conditions some PKI leaders in the course of 1961 reportedly favored a 'break through', i.e. a stepped up aggressiveness, bringing, if necessary, the conflict with the army to a head in a short period of time, and counting on the balancing influence of Sukarno and on mass support in the context of the West New Guinea campaign and as a result of deteriorating living conditions. PKI economic expert Sakirman and SOBSI leader Njono were said to sponsor such a course. Apparently this approach did not envisage a *coup d'état* by the PKI, but rather a creation of a state of tension well short of a coup but soluble through a new *modus vivendi* in which Sukarno, as so often before, would be the architect of the new accommodation. The majority of the party leadership, particularly vice-chairman Lukman, is said to have opposed the Sakirman-Njono policy, because of the undue risk involved, and advocated instead a continuous upbuilding of the party and a slow but steady ascent toward more and more actual Communist participation in the government. Aidit seems to have been primarily concerned with preventing an explosion among his top lieutenants, although he was described as favoring the militants. The extent and duration of this dissension in the party's leadership, its relationship to the developing Sino-Soviet conflict, and the manner in which it was ultimately resolved, are still shrouded in mystery, but there is little doubt that the Malaysia issue and the opportunity it afforded for a new expansion of the party, and indeed for a shift in the domestic Indonesian balance of power provided the principal avenue of reconciliation (see below chapter VII). But precisely in order to accommodate the militants the staging of the Seventh Congress became necessary, and this in turn may well have influenced Sukarno in going back on his earlier decision on the need of such a congress. For Sukarno's position, it need hardly be stressed, depends on a strong and viable PKI as much as it depends on a strong and viable army. Serious dissension in either one of these balancing power centers, would soon render him the prisoner of the other. Paradoxically, therefore, the reported rift in the PKI leadership, was something of an asset to the party, in that its militancy could not be safely ignored or repressed.

Meanwhile Communist aggressiveness could continue to feed on economic stagnation and popular misery. Rapidly dwindling gold reserves, recurrent scarcities and soaring costs of basic commodities seemed to edge the economy ever closer to complete chaos. By the beginning of 1962 the rice crisis, always latent in the country, was as serious as it had ever been, not just because of adverse weather conditions, but also because of fundamental distribution problems arising from the overcontrolled economy[69] One informed Indonesian estimate put the price of rice in the free market in December 1961 at 1,000 percent higher than in 1953.[70] In Djakarta alone, according to another analysis, the cost of a litre of rice increased from about 10 rupiahs in the middle of 1961 to an average of 35 rupiahs by December of that year.[71] Early in March 1962 some 2,000 people staged demonstrations in front of the residences of the mayor of Surabaya and of the Governor of East Java Province demanding lower prices. Meanwhile the government frantically endeavored to purchase more rice abroad, and to establish 'cheap rice shops' *(warung nasi murah)* and 'rice purchasing commands' throughout the country.[72] Rice was rapidly assuming a political significance intertwined with the West New Guinea issue and with domestic political freedom:[73]

'For Rice and Democracy to Help Us in the Struggle for West Irian'—so ran the wording on an unusual banner one noticed among the thousands which President Soekarno saw before him on December 19 (1961). He was speaking in Jogjakarta, giving his 'final command' for the wresting of West Irian from the Dutch. The slogan was a bold example of the sort of brinkmanship in which opponents of the Indonesian government engage these days, when they venture into the field of public politics. 'Democracy' is on the way to becoming an opposition world. 'Rice' is that already.

As always the PKI was quick to capitalize on the situation. From March 26 to March 31, 1962 the Central Java Major District Party Conference of the PKI met in Semarang and urged rapid extension of branches of the province's *Komando Anti Lapar* ('Anti-hunger Command') by including representatives of 'mass organizations' (i.e. PKI fronts) in the divisions of the 'Command', improvements in the distribution of food and clothing, and an across the board wage increase of 50% for the workers of state enterprises.[74] Throughout 1962 party branches led demonstrations in a number of cities in Java demanding improvement in living conditions.

The long-range prospects of the economy, even when considered in the light of the relative relief brought by the end of the PRRI rebellion, were discouraging. Between the end of 1960 and the end of the third quarter of 1961, Indonesian foreign exchange holdings dropped by about 50 percent and an overall trade deficit threatened for the first time in 9 years; export earnings in the first half of 1961 were one-fourth lower than in the first half of 1960.[75] By the end of 1961 the government had decided to ban further textile imports. The position of Indonesia's principal foreign exchange earners, oil and rubber, became increasingly precarious and especially the drop in exports of the higher quality estate rubber since 1953 has been ominous. 'One by one Indonesia's export products are being ousted from the world market', a prominent spokesman for one of the country's national exporters associations was quoted as saying. 'Indonesia's raw materials have been ousted by the trade of its neighbor countries and the newly independent countries in Africa which produce similar products. Indonesian products are insufficiently competitive at world markets, mainly owing to low quality, shipping difficulties, shortage of cargo space, and lack of guarantees concerning regular supply'.[76] Domestic industrial growth remained sluggish as import restrictions and shortages of raw materials continued to impede development.

Added to these factors, finally, was the rather abrupt end of the West New Guinea crisis. By March 1962, thanks to U.S. pressure on the Dutch, Indonesian and Dutch representatives under American aegis were commencing a series of discussions which despite occasional obstacles ultimately led to a settlement on August 15, 1962, providing for the transfer of West New Guinea to Indonesia by May 1, 1963, after an interim United Nations' administration. The circumstances surrounding the reaching of this agreement are not of particular significance here,[77] suffice it to note that the settlement immediately raised problems for Indonesia's balance of power and future development. With the acquisition of West New Guinea, and earlier with the end of the PRRI-PRI-*Permesta* rebellion, the whole issue of the future position of the army, of its oversize 'volunteer' groups and of its role as administrator in the prevailing state of emergency became a pressing one. Could continuing restrictions on partisan political activity be justified further? What would be the effect of army demobilization? What was to be the course of future economic development, especially in the context of the American sponsored long range stabilization plan by an international consortium? In all these questions the PKI saw immediate tactical opportunities. Very shortly the Malaysia issue was to provide the party (and indeed the country) with a framework for a solution to the problems raised by the end of the West New Guinea campaign and with new avenues for the expansion of Communist power.

CHAPTER VII

THE MALAYSIA ISSUE: THE NEW DYNAMIC

ON May 27, 1961, at a meeting of the Singapore press, Malayan premier Tunku Abdul Rahman voiced an idea that ultimately was to have far-reaching consequences for Southeast Asia's political future. Speaking of his nation's destiny, the Tunku said:[1]

Malaya today as a nation realises that she cannot stand alone and in isolation. Outside of international politics, the national one must be broadly based. Sooner or later she should have an understanding with Britain and the peoples of the territories of Singapore, North Borneo, Brunei and Sarawak. It is premature for me to say now how this closer understanding can be brought about, but it is inevitable that we should look ahead to this objective and think of a plan whereby these territories can be brought closer together in political and economic cooperation. . . .

With Whitehall's cautious support the plan for a 'political and economic cooperation' among the territories named went forward in the following months, and by and large the concept of a Malaysian Federation met with substantial majority approval in Singapore, Sarawak and Sabah (North Borneo), although in Brunei the position of the Sultanate and the question of the oil revenues proved ultimately to be insurmountable obstacles. Soon it became apparent what had been among the Tunku's principal considerations in advancing the concept of Malaysia, particularly when Communists throughout Asia denounced the scheme. As the Malayan premier put it, late in 1962:[2]

I think the only objection by the Communists is that they thought that all these areas (i.e. the component parts of Malaysia) would fall to them one day and as soon as possible, but with Malaysia it would not be so easy. And as a result they introduce in all their charges this bogey of imperialism . . . but I can tell you, and you can take it from me, that there is no imperialism as bad as the Communist imperialism.

A federation conceived as a bulwark against Communist advances in Southeast Asia; conceived, moreover, with the active support—also militarily—of its colonial suzerain; economically viable and on the best of terms with private Western capital—such a federation was a challenge which Communism, and in particular the PKI, would not be likely to ignore.

The Politics of the Malaysia Issue. Already at its plenary session at the end of December 1961, the PKI Central Committee had passed a resolution condemning the Malaysian Federation as 'a form of neo-colonialism', and asserting that Britain would see to it 'that the Federation of Malaysia will be smuggled into SEATO'. British interest in such a Federation, the resolution went on, stemmed from the fact that Britain was no longer able to contain 'the growth of the democratic movement and the influence of patriotic political parties' throughout the Malaysian area, and hence through the Federation, Britain would be able to safeguard her position in the region. Malaysia would, therefore, only serve to 'strengthen the position of the imperialists in Southeast Asia', and the Indonesian people should therefore 'heighten national vigilance' against them. The resolution ended with the prophesy that 'The Indonesian people will certainly support the righteous, patriotic and just resistance of the people of Malaya, Singapore, Sarawak, Brunei and North Borneo against the efforts for the establishment of Malaysia'.[3] In the months following this resolution, *Harian Rakjat* and other party and front organs kept up their attacks on the idea of Malaysia, being virtually the only publications in all of Indonesia to do so. Indeed, Lord Selkirk, former British Commissioner General in Southeast Asia, has remarked that when around September 1961, he informed Indonesian Foreign Minister Subandrio of the formation of Malaysia, Subandrio declared that this was 'entirely a matter for the people concerned and did not concern Indonesia'.[4] The Indonesian government has in fact admitted that it originally had 'no objections' to the idea of the Federation and that it wished Sarawak, Brunei, and North Borneo 'success with this merger' with Malaya and Singapore.[5] Pre-occupied with the final stages of the West New Guinea campaign this official Indonesian indifference seems understandable. The PKI's continuing denunciations, particularly in the resolutions of the Seventh National Party Congress in April 1962, seemed to have but little effect at the time.[6]

Yet there were compelling reasons why the PKI had to keep hammering on the Malaysia issue, quite apart from the obvious necessity to express opposition to an avowedly anti-Communist political concept. One stemmed from the earlier mentioned dissension in the PKI top leadership and from the related problem of the party's narrowing range of operational freedom. The need for militancy to prevent slow atrophy became by the end of 1961 a major tactical necessity for the party and whenever and wherever it could engage in its 'reality testing' with the army, particularly in the relatively 'safe zones' of foreign relations, it did not fail to do so, as we have seen. The militants in the Central Committee (and these apparently included Chairman Aidit) seemed intent on adopting a Peking style 'hard' line, not only at home but in Southeast Asia as a whole, in keeping with Chinese Communism's views of the aggressive role of the international Marxist-Leninist movement. The Malaysia issue was ready made for such a tactic. The other reason for the PKI's persistent opposition resulted from the fact that apparently anti-Malaysia left wing groups in Malaya itself were beginning to approach the PKI for help. Malaya's Minister for Internal Security, Dato Ismail, revealed in the Malayan parliament in March 1963, that members of the left wing, anti-Malaysia *Party Rakyat* in Malaya had gone to Indonesia during the previous two years for PKI cadre training, and that Aidit had instructed the 1962 Malayan Socialist Conference to pass resolutions denouncing Malaysia.[7] Earlier, in February 1962, premier Rahman stated that the declaration of the Malayan Socialist Front (which embraces the *Party Rakyat*) opposing Malaysia was 'word for word' in agreement with the PKI's own expressed opposition to Malaysia, and that Socialist Front members had recently gone to Indonesia to attend a conference of *Partindo* (which, by this time had in effect become an informal PKI front). *Partindo*, declared the Tunku further, had among its leaders the Malayan nationalist Ibrahim Yaacob, described as a 'well known Communist' by the Tunku, and as having been banned from entering Malaya.[8] While the details of these charges have not as yet been published there is little doubt that Rahman, from the beginning, regarded the PKI as the principal activator of the campaign against Malaysia. He so stated publicly in December 1962, for example, adding that so long as the PKI had freedom of operation Malaya and Indonesia would continue to drift apart.[9] The following January he accused the PKI of trying to subvert the Malayan people 'by making use of certain Malayan politicians to carry out its objectives', and warned that unless the PKI was 'crushed' Malayan-Indonesian relations would continue to be strained.[10] And again early in December 1963, at a United Malays National Organization rally in Kuala Kedah, North Malaya, Rahman stated that Malaysia could never become friendly with Indonesia as long as there were Communists in Indonesia.

By June 1962, a notable strain was beginning to develop in relations between Kuala Lumpur and Djakarta. According to the Indonesian government its own relative friendliness to the contemplated federation changed as a result of 'a growing hostile attitude toward Indonesia' in Malayan Government circles, accompanied by 'provocative public statements in certain branches of the ruling party in Malaya for the Indonesian island of Sumatra'.[11] Remembrance of alleged Malayan shelter and assistance given to PRRI rebels also are said to have compounded this growing Indonesian enmity. Be that as it may, the more important reason, undoubtedly, why the PKI rather suddenly found that its anti-Malaysia position was finding favor in official Indonesian circles, stemmed from the West New Guinea settlement and its aftermath. Fundamental to an understanding of this settlement was the U.S. policy consideration that no significant economic stabilization could be accomplished in Indonesia until the furor over West New Guinea had died down, i.e. until the disputed area had been acquired by Indonesia. This consideration was basic to the great pressure exerted on the Dutch by the U.S. in the early months of 1962, and related to it also was the planned inauguration of a new U.S. assistance program for Indonesia, in conjunction with an international consortium. This program would be based on the recommendations of the so-called Humphrey report, drafted by a team of six American experts and transmitted formally to the Indonesian government in August 1962.[12] The spectre of a disciplined and realistic development effort largely under the aegis of major Western industrial powers, and involving (sooner or later) a whole range of controversial and unpopular decisions, including retrenchment of the swollen bureaucracy, rationalization and technical improvement of production, imposition of labor discipline and wage control, fiscal reform and drastic reassessment of budgetary priorities, began to loom ever more ominously on the Indonesian political horizon, as the day which would formally mark the settlement of the West New Guinea question also neared.

U.S. expectations that Indonesia, by the middle of 1962, could take such a development effort in hand were, of course, quite unrealistic, for neither U.S. policy makers nor indeed the writers of the euphemism laden Humphrey report seem to have sufficiently understood the vicious circles of the Indonesian economy and their political implications,[13] nor indeed the long standing Indonesian reluctance, commented on by other students of the Indonesian economy, to take definite decisions 'regarding the form of the economy and the society, relations of Indonesia to the West and the like'.[14] The torrent of symbols and ideological concepts which has been poured out over the country in the past decade, particularly by Sukarno far from articulating such decisions, has served to postpone making them. The fact is that the planned development envisaged by American policy makers would not now be possible because of the inevitable and probably calamitous consequences they would bring in the balance of power. Pressure on Sukarno from the trade unions, but also from the ranks of the bureaucracy, from the national business group long propped up in the export and distributing trade by a host of protective measures, from groups like the PKI for whom the idea of development under a Western consortium was *ipso facto* anathema—all rendered an overhaul of the tax system, creation of a more favorable climate for investment, rationalization of the external trade machinery, a more realistic development policy than that contained in the mystagoguery of the official Eight Year Development Plan and many other measures, politically simply impossible. To Sukarno, and to those segments of the socio-economy which particularly look to him for protection and leadership the Malaysia issue offered itself as the most immediately available means to perpetuate the *status quo* i.e. the condition created by the West New Guinea campaign, by the precarious balance between army and PKI, and by the incessant ideologizing and manipulation of the masses under 'guided democracy' and *vivere pericoloso*. For dangerous as the anti-Malaysia campaign might turn out to be for the country's already chaotic economy, Sukarno, with some justice, could feel that the U.S., ever fearful of Indonesia drifting yet further toward Communism, would not allow the complete collapse of her economy, whatever restrictions on direct assistance might be imposed.[15]

Finally the position of the army should be considered briefly.[16] The quick settlement of the West New Guinea question necessitated an incisive evaluation of the army's position and future role, and even before the formal announcement of the Dutch-Indonesian accord on August 15, 1962, the army had begun to consider the problems surrounding demobilization. With approximately 280,000 officers and men, including various 'volunteer' groups formed during the West New Guinea campaign, the army had for years wrestled with its swollen size and with projects for streamlining its operations. In 1952 an attempt at retrenchment and modernization of the army, it will be recalled, had led to a major political crisis and the fall of Nasution, then Army Chief of Staff, and since then solutions have continued to be postponed. Even the naval high command, early in 1962, declared that it needed but 40% of its total complement of about 40,000 men, and the navy's proposal seemed but a reflection of repeatedly formulated but always stillborn. Army reorganization schemes based on rapid mechanization and training of highly skilled younger personnel and envisaging a compact force of at the most 125,000 men. But the political consequences of a sizable demobilization have, since 1952, always been unthinkable, and with the outbreak of the PRRI rebellion in 1958 the desirability of a large infantry army, with its volunteer satellites and appropriate to manpower absorbing anti-guerilla combat, became evident, justifying again postponement of reorganization. Subsequently the Indonesian paratroop landings in West New Guinea and the prospect there of a new field for extensive guerilla warfare further strengthened the opponents of reform.

With the end of the West New Guinea campaign however and with the Sumatra rebellion wiped out, the modernization question became pressing once more. It now assumed, in a sense, the appearance of a conflict between generations: older officers, many of them building primarily on their reputation in the revolution and unwilling to accept a squalid retirement or adjust to a new role of the technocratic military specialist, confronted growing numbers of younger subalterns, many of them trained in Western war colleges and staff schools and ambitious for advancement in their service specialty. But neither of these two groups of officers were particularly enamoured of the new 'civic mission' program *('Operasi Bhakti')*. For years previously army territorial commanders had employed their units in various public works and economic development projects, and with the end of the West New Guinea campaign such 'civic' activity seemed to become the army's new, major function.[17] An example was the *Operasi Bhakti* conducted in the southern part of Tasikmalaja regency in West Java during October and November, 1962, during which various army units assisted in construction and repair of schools, roads and bridges, cleared rice fields and even took 'the initiative in agricultural and fishery activities', as the army's press release put it.[18] Almost from the start there was considerable resentment in the army over its new 'civic' responsibilities, notwithstanding eloquent directives and exhortations by Nasution. Especially younger officers and staff specialists resented their new 'civic' responsibilities, having a different conception of the martial life. But as a measure forestalling both demobilization (with all its consequences in the currently stagnating Indonesian economy) and army modernization *Operasi Bhakti* could only be improved upon if the condition of the West New Guinea campaign, with its manpower absorbing guerilla warfare requirements, were to return. Again, the Malaysia issue provided just that: as for so many other groups in Indonesia it afforded a chance to retain the *status quo* as it existed before the August 15, 1962 Dutch-Indonesian agreement.

After Sukarno had thrown his power behind the anti-Malaysia campaign, moreover, it would have been difficult for the army to follow a contrary course unless it was prepared to risk a new breach between its commanders and Sukarno and the PKI. Such a breach, so soon after the quelling of the various outbursts of disaffection by army colonels ever since 1956—outbursts which so gravely undermined the army's prestige and which provided the PKI with so much ammunition against the army leadership—could hardly be a welcome prospect for Nasution and his associates. Also, in the ranks of the army's satellite 'volunteer' groups, mobilized during the West New Guinea campaign, the PKI's influence was and is by no means negligible. For these 'volunteer' groups, as well as the younger ranks of the regular army, were accurately described as 'armed farmers' by the PKI, 'and therein lay the military's dilemma. It commanded the guns to defend the revolution but the guns were in the hands of 250,000 young men who were as susceptible as their brothers in the villages to Communist promises of a better life'.[19] While the top commanders and even most of the officer corps might see the PKI as their principal enemy and might well have some doubts about participation in PKI instigated anti-Malaysia campaign, the ranks were not necessarily immune to PKI blandishments and to the party's steadily growing influence in all walks of life. The anti-Malaysia campaign could thus not easily be discredited. Finally, the army had a legitimate strategic interest in the anti-Malaysia campaign. For although some observers have been inclined to ridicule official Indonesian pronouncements—including ones by army leaders—that Malaysia is a threat to Indonesia, such a threat is nonetheless felt to exist. Army commanders who fought the prolonged campaign against the PRRI-PRI-*Permesta* cannot easily forget that Malaya and Singapore provided important sources of supply as well as sanctuary to the rebel leaders, and that from this protected base new insurrectionary movements might well be launched in the future. A completely friendly and pliable Malaya as a strategic necessity alone could readily justify the anti-Malaysia campaign.

It has been necessary to describe these motivating factors in the army and in the pattern of Presidential power at some length, in order to emphasize the PKI's new importance as the country's vanguard in the anti-Malaysia campaign. In the Malaysia issue the PKI found that it did not have to conform to a new ideological venture or policy already set by others, but that this time it had set the trend and that others were following. Moreover, while for Sukarno, for the power groups dependent upon him, and for the army, the Malaysia issue afforded an opportunity to retain the pre-August 1962 *status quo*, for the PKI it was not just the *status quo* (which it despised in any case) but a new avenue to increased power that was being opened up, a chance to break through the 'quarantine' network imposed upon it. Not only did this seem likely as a result of an anticipated new wave of popular fervor, a continuation of the *vivere pericoloso* that had marked the closing stages of the West New Guinea campaign and with which the PKI had fully identified itself (not least in hopes of being able to enter the government in the spirit of *gotong royong* and NASAKOM), but also in consequence of the fact that through the anti-Malaysia campaign Indonesia, officially and unofficially, would find itself the ally—indeed the main support—of the anti-Malaysia Communist elements in Malaysia itself, and beyond these of People's China, which was also becoming involved in the campaign. In short, the Malaysia issue seemed to promise not just a new party organizational momentum, but a significant shift in the balance of power with far-reaching consequences for the Southeast Asian area.

The Brunei Revolt and its Aftermath. By September 1962, Indonesia's Foreign Minister Subandrio was saying that Indonesia 'could not remain indifferent to Malaysia' and that if a military base were to be established in Sarawak, Brunei or Sabah, after these areas had entered the new federation, Indonesia would have to take 'counteraction'; specifically, said Subandrio, if an American base were to be established, 'we shall then arrange for a Soviet base in our part of Borneo'.[20] The PKI sometime earlier had already raised the spectre of 'imperialist encirclement' posed by the formation of Malaysia, and as British-Malayan defense talks emphasized retention of British and Commonwealth military facilities in Singapore and Malaya after formation of the Federation, the PKI's organs found further substance for this charge. Meanwhile opposition to Malaysia was solidfying within the Malayan area itself, and also in Sarawak, where the Sarawak United People's Party (SUPP), largely Chinese, a forum for the Communist underground in the area, and with ties to the China mainland, spearheaded the anti-Malaysia campaign. The Malayan *Party Rakyat*, and the Singapore *Barisan Sosialis* (also Communist influenced and like the SUPP a vehicle for Chinese cultural chauvinism and communal political aspirations) worked in close liaison with Brunei's *Partai Rakjat*, led by A. M. Azahari, a member of Brunei's Legislative Council and a veteran of the Indonesian Army in the revolutionary war.[21] Azahari also skillfully capitalized on the Philippine claim on North Borneo, which since early 1962 was being pressed with greater intensity. Late in November 1962, Azahari's emissaries reportedly also had informal contacts with government officials and party leaders, including of the PKI and *Partindo*, in Djakarta.

The sympathies of both Indonesia and the Philippines appear to have been decisive with Azahari. At dawn on December 8, 1962 about one thousand of his followers, several scores of whom appear to have been Indonesian migrants in the Brunei area, launched a revolt in Brunei, attacking oil installations, while in the immediately adjacent areas of Sarawak and Sabah there were also minor eruptions. From Manila Azahari proclaimed Brunei's Sultan head of a new 'Kalimantan Utara' state and named himself premier. But within 48 hours the Sultan had repudiated him, and the revolt had been crushed by several companies of Gurkhas flown in from Singapore. Azahari announced a 'struggle to the finish' but most of his followers were either rounded up or fled over the border into Indonesian Borneo. For the PKI and the Indonesian government the revolt offered definitive justification for their anti-Malaysia campaign, and in the weeks following the rebellion, the PKI and its fronts took the lead in staging demonstrations (with the obvious approval of army authorities) and protest rallies. On December 13, 1962, Aidit called on the Indonesian people to render all assistance to the 'revolutionary struggle of the people of North Borneo' and to oppose any effort at breaking the North Borneo people's struggle, and simultaneously similar expressions of support were voiced by SOBSI, BTI, *Gerwani*, and *Pemuda Rakjat*, as well as by other political parties, including by the PNI ('on behalf of the entire "Marhaenist Front"').[22] The next day it was announced by the West Borneo *Partindo* branch chairman that all *Partindo* members in Kalimantan would be expected 'to take care of and house any revolutionary fighters who may cross the border'. The 'Indonesian Peace Committee', recently formed front, issued a statement on December 24, 1962, urging 'more positive and concrete assistance' to North Kalimantan, by granting 'de facto or de jure recognition of the North Kalimantan Revolutionary Government headed by Sheik Azahari'. This demand was to be heard frequently in the next year in various party organs. On December 23, 1962, several thousands participated in a PKI inspired rally in Djakarta, during which effigies marked 'British colonialists' were taken from a bamboo coffin and burned. SOBSI meanwhile urged the government to stop using or chartering ships flying the British flag 'or flags of its allies', and various SOBSI affiliates joined in a protest against Britain's 'cruel suppression of the people's movement in North Kalimantan'. The Communist campaign reached such a pass that by December 28, 1962, Sukarno felt constrained to announce that 'the sympathy of the Indonesian people for the struggle of the North Kalimantan people was definitely not the result of Communist influence', but was based solely on 'the Indonesian people's love of freedom' and this sympathy was not restricted to the North Kalimantan rebels but included also 'the Congolese, the Angolans and Algerians'. Lest he be misunderstood Sukarno quickly added that those who accused Indonesia of being Communist influenced in her North Kalimantan policy were 'in fact paying great tribute to Communism'. On the other hand, he said they also suffered from Communist-phobia.[23]

While an official representative of Azahari opened his office in Djakarta, and as Subandrio formally announced on January 20, 1963, that Indonesia was compelled to adopt a policy of 'confrontation' against Malaya, the Indonesian Army in West Borneo began to act as a training and supply center for not just the remnants of Azahari's band, now operating as the *Tentara Nasional Kalimantan Utara* (National Army of North Borneo-TNKU), but also for young, Communist influenced Chinese, many of them cohorts of SUPP, who, as the day of the formal formation of Malaysia steadily approached, were prepared to begin a fullscale guerilla war in Sarawak.[24] Before the middle of 1963 Indonesian 'volunteers' and other military were leading bands of these Chinese and Indonesian guerillas, along with TNKU elements, and by the end of November 1963, the Sarawak government announced that armed Indonesian terrorists had landed along the coast of Sarawak and that Sarawak 'Communists are giving the Indonesians their full and willing cooperation'.[25] By this time also the Malaysian government had revealed the creation of special bases in Indonesia for infiltration into Malaysia, and the actual and growing influx of Indonesian terrorists and underground organizers into Sabah, Malaya, and Singapore.[26] Government sloganizing, and symbol and mass organizational manipulation in Indonesia meanwhile once more reached the level of the last stages of the West New Guinea campaign when steady infiltration by guerillas had also been the Indonesian military tactic. The 'status quo' was being restored.

Typically, the PKI sought to utilize the accelerating anti-Malaysia campaign to gain political advantages. At a mass rally in Bandung, on December 16, 1962, Aidit declared that a *gotong royong* cabinet, 'with NASAKOM as its core' (i.e. a cabinet with full PKI participation), should be set up immediately to overcome 'present difficulties'. Considering that the nation was confronted by 'a very strong enemy, namely American, British, Japanese and West German imperialism, the landlords and their pawns, the capitalist bureaucrats, who have brought our economy into a mess', the formation of a 'National Unity Front' which would bundle the strength of 'all legal parties' was absolutely necessary. (*Inter alia* one might note that America, Britain, Japan and West Germany would have been the principal participants of the international consortium designed to finance the long range Indonesian development plan at the conclusion of the West New Guinea campaign, and that the term 'capitalist bureaucrats' has become PKI-ese for army officers, since many of them are supervisors of state enterprises). The 'National Unity Front' did not mean a fusion of parties but rather the framework of a common political effort. 'Let life in Indonesia flourish like the many colored flowers of a beautiful garden', Aidit went on, 'and let the people choose for themselves which flower they like the most'. This Maoist exhortation was followed by the assertion that Sukarno had long wanted the establishment of a *gotong royong* cabinet, but that 'the dark forces manipulated by the imperialists who still play a role in political life' had thus far prevented it. Yet a *gotong royong* cabinet could alone break down the 'mismanagement in all fields of activity'.[27]

Clearly this speech revealed the PKI's desire for greater operational freedom as well as its renewed campaign to enter the government. The groundwork for the latter approach, long since laid with the PKI's demand for a national coalition government, was strengthened again in

September 1962, when PNI chairman Ali Sastroamijojo made a strong plea for 'the right of political parties to exist in Indonesia', endorsing a *gotong royong* cabinet.[28] Ali's plea was as significant as an indication of the restiveness in political circles over the continuing army imposed state of emergency, as of the PNI's willingness to collaborate with the Communists in the cabinet. On January 3, 1963, Ali repeated his party's readiness to form a cabinet with PKI representation and, five days later, a *Partindo* spokesman also expressed the hope that a 'gotong royong cabinet with NASAKOM as its core' be formed.[29] By this time, it might be noted, premier Rahman was under no illusion as to what direction the wind was blowing from in *Partindo;* in his New Year's message on January 1, 1963, Rahman, for example, had linked both the PKI and *Partindo* to the Brunei rebellion, an association for which *Partindo's* secretary general formally 'thanked' the Malayan premier.[30] In February 1963, PKI and front branches took to holding 'commemorative gatherings' to celebrate the forthcoming 'sixth anniversary' of Sukarno's 'conception of a gotong royong cabinet' and after one such commemorative service, early in March, SOBSI leader Njono, on behalf of his organization cabled Sukarno urging him again 'to set up a gotong royong cabinet, with NASAKOM as its core' declaring there was no further reason to delay the creation of such a cabinet.[31] Again utilizing the momentum it had helped to create the PKI Central Committee's Plenum in February 1963, called on the government to speed up the drafting and passage 'of a bill on a democratic general election' and exhorted the government to hold such elections as soon as possible, since 'there are at present no reasons whatsoever to delay', and since 'the present situation requires expansion of democratic rights for the whole of the Indonesian people'.[32]

The PKI campaign, however, puzzled some observers, who were quick to point out that if the PKI actually would enter the cabinet it might soon find itself in a position similar to that of the Armed Forces which also, since the late 1950's increasingly entered into high level government work but which, in consequence, were also 'increasingly discredited by association with unpopular and unsuccessful policies, particularly in economic affairs'.[33] Why then would the PKI really wish to enter the government? The strength of the PKI and the effectiveness of its demands precisely lay, it was pointed out, in the party *not* being represented in the cabinet. Furthermore it seemed that the PKI, paradoxically, was warning not to expect too much from a *gotong royong* cabinet—at least not in the early stages of its operation—even as party and front spokesmen were urging that such a cabinet be formed. Thus

Aidit, in June 1963, declared that while the formation of a NASAKOM cabinet was 'the first political step which must be taken', it was true 'at the same time' that 'a NASAKOM cabinet does not yet mean that the situation will immediately improve; a NASAKOM cabinet is not an Aladdin's lamp'.[34] The seeming ambiguity of the PKI's position probably stemmed from the conviction of its leaders that in its campaign for a *gotong royong* cabinet the party, as in the past when it re-emphasized this demand, could not lose. Given the opposition of the army leadership to inclusion of Communists in the government it was most unlikely that a *gotong royong* cabinet would come into existence; at the same time the demand for such a cabinet had significant agitational value, particularly when it was related to the country's economic miseries. Thus by not heeding the PKI's call for a 'National Unity' cabinet, army and government only helped to strengthen the party and its 'agitprop' work. And should, in fact, the party be invited to enter the government, then this circumstance alone (considering what Communist entry into coalition cabinets has meant in other countries since World War II) would be of such immediate tactical value that the party's position might well become wholly unassailable, even if there were no immediate economic improvements. As it turned out the party calculated rightly: army opposition to a *gotong royong* cabinet continued overwhelmingly strong, and here again the Malaysia crisis may well have come to the army's aid since it might reasonably be argued that so long as the national security was not firmly established neither a general election nor a decisive alteration in the composition of the government was a responsible step. Indeed, by November 8, 1963, Aidit warned that 'certain people' in Indonesia were using the government's anti-Malaysia 'confrontation' policy as a pretext to justify reimposition of martial law. The unity of the people, the government and the armed forces, he said, should not be weakened by resumption of martial law.[35] But if the army was unwilling to accept a *gotong royong* cabinet or general elections it then would have to compromise on the growing demand—not just from the PKI but also from other parties—for a lifting of emergency and martial law conditions. On May 1, 1963, the day also that administration over West New Guinea was formally transferred from the United Nations Temporary Executive Authority to the Indonesian government, Indonesia formally returned to a state of 'civil order', the offices of the Supreme War Administrator *(Peperti)* and of the Area War Administrators *(Peperda-Peperda)* terminating their functions. However 'to safeguard the cause of the Revolution' a secretariat of 'The Council to Assist the Revolutionary Leadership' (largely an army body) with vague supervisory powers over political life was set up, and earlier both Nasution and Sukarno had repeatedly pointed out that the lifting of the emergency did not mean a return to 'liberal democracy'. The sphere of party operations for the PKI notably widened, but a network of executive powers and regulatory supervision continued to remain in the hands of the President and regional army commanders.

Aidit's earlier cited warning in November, that resumption of martial law would be harmful to the country, reflected the party's continuous sensitiveness to army pressures. Already in his report to the Central Committee Plenum in February 1963, Aidit had warned that 'capitalist bureaucrats' (the increasingly common PKI term for army commanders and 'reactionaries' were busily trying to create a new emergency situation just as the government was attempting to end the existing emergency. In many areas declared Aidit 'they are continuing to exercise dictatorial powers', replacing local officials by appointees of their own.[36] Local party branches were instructed to be vigilant in supervising the 'democratization' of regional administration, in line with the decisions of the Seventh National Congress, and party organs subsequently 'interpreted' at length the 'practical' effects of the lifting of the emergency on May 1. But the party in the next few months, moved with considerable caution in pressing its 'democratization' views, and the principal beneficiary in this early period of the restoration of civil controls, as far as the party was concerned, were its own and its fronts' publications, which in the latter half of 1963 began to appear again in great profusion. It was primarily after the founding of Malaysia on September 16, 1963, that the party again stepped up its agitation for domestic reforms, although prior to this, it continued intermittently to call for a *gotong royong* cabinet.

PKI Intransigeance. In the early months of 1963 Indonesia's next step in the anti-Malaysia 'confrontation' appeared at first to be uncertain. A semi-official 'Committee for Solidarity with the North Borneo People's Revolution', which includes cabinet ministers, army officers and party leaders, including PKI members, was formed to channel popular interest and mass organizational activity, while reports circulated that the Indonesian Army was now taking a hand in training Chinese from Sarawak and TNKU remnants for extended guerilla warfare in the future. But significant and expected Afro-Asian support for Indonesian 'confrontation' remained lacking. And in Manila, as well as in Washington and London, efforts were being made to prevent a complete rupture in Malayan-Indonesian relations, even though the Tunku and Sukarno embroiled each other in unedifying name calling. As Whitehall gave every indication that Indonesian opposition would not deter it from proceeding with the creation of a Malaysian Federation Sukarno declared that 'we must remain faithful to our principle' and 'must keep opposing the neo-colonialist effort and the movement for Malaysia'.[37] This sentiment was repeatedly cited by PKI spokesmen, as in the meantime Army Chief Ahmad Jani declared that 'the Indonesian Army fully backs the Indonesian government policy of opposing the formation of the Malaysian Federation'.[38] A meeting of Rahman and Sukarno in Tokyo (May 31–June 1, 1963) at which the two leaders agreed to 'refrain from making acrimonious attacks' on each other in the future, and in which they recognized the 'desirability' of restoring friendly relations, was greeted with an ominous silence in PKI media. The silence was quickly broken, however, when on July 8, 1963, the United Kingdom and Malaya, Singapore, Sarawak and Sabah (Brunei decided to stay out of the federation) agreed to the formation of Malaysia on the following August 31, and PKI hostility now also turned more and more against Britain. Soon SOBSI, predictably, would be calling for the expropriation of British holdings in Indonesia. The details of the subsequent Manila tripartite conference between Rahman, Sukarno, and President Diosdado Macapagal of the Philippines (July 30–August 5, 1963), and the 'Declaration', 'Joint Statement' and 'Accord' which it produced with their provisions for a United Nations' 'ascertainment', complete with 'observers' from Indonesia and the Philippines, of the political wishes of the people of the Borneo territories prior to the formation of Malaysia, with its affirmation by the signatories to 'maintain fraternal relations', and its contemplated creation of a 'Mapilindo' (Malaysia-Pilipinas [Philippines]-Indonesia) Federation, are of little relevance here.[39] No matter what would have been agreed upon in Manila, short of the Tunku's readiness to abandon the Malaysia project completely and turn the British out altogether, the PKI would have opposed it. As *Harian Rakjat* put it in its comments on the Manila Conference: 'Malaysia remains a neo-colonialist project. The spirit of national independence, of African-Asian solidarity, and the spirit of confrontation must be used to face the Manila Agreement'.[40]

The Tunku's determination to proceed with the creation of Malaysia even before the United Nations 'ascertainment' in the Borneo territories had fully taken place, the tangled question of the Indonesian observers at the 'ascertainment', and the unequivocal British assurances of military support for the new Federation, all allowed the PKI to drive its agitation to a new crescendo. All suggestion of compromise or moderation became treasonous in Communist eyes, and when on September 16, 1963, the Malaysian Federation formally came into existence, just after the U.N. 'ascertainment' showed substantial majority support for Malaysia, thousands of screaming anti-Malaysia demonstrators with SOBSI and

Pemuda Rakjat cadres in the lead stormed the Malaysian and British embassies in Djakarta, hurling stones, smashing windows, and breaking furnishings, while police and security forces ineffectually attempted to restrain the mob. In the wreckage of the British Embassy *Pemuda Rakjat* leader Unwar Nasution informed the British Ambassador, Andrew Gilchrist, that Indonesian students would 'always fight for the people of Northern Borneo to help them gain freedom from imperialism'.[41] Meanwhile SOBSI entered British commercial establishments, attempting to run up a red flag, and harassing proprietors and personnel, while elsewhere in West Java attempts were being made to seize British owned rubber and tea estates.

The seizures, though at first seemingly countermanded by the government as British-Indonesian relations neared the breaking point, were in fact the beginning of a steady expropriation process. Unquestionably unrelenting Communist pressure played its role in this. Despite Indonesian government assurances that British holdings would be returned eventually, there occurred instead, in subsequent weeks, a process of steadily advancing supervision and control by the government, including by Army officers, which reached its culmination in January 1964. At that time two Indonesian pilgrim ships were being detained in Hong Kong, presumably by creditors, and Britain reportedly also had refused shipment of Indonesian aircraft engines and military equipment bought by the Indonesians in Hong Kong. But this appears only to have been a pretext for what followed. For on January 17, 1964, President Sukarno met with U.S. Attorney General Robert Kennedy in Tokyo. The latter had been sent by President Johnson on a peace and mediation mission to Manila, Djakarta and Kuala Lumpur, and with the immediate aim to arrange for a cease-fire in the accelerating guerilla conflict in Sarawak. On the day that Sukarno and Robert Kennedy met, *Harian Rakjat* carried a statement by Aidit, who insisted that 'it is our obligation to avoid efforts which have the nature of compromise', and that efforts to 'crush Malaysia' be continued. The Aidit announcement appears to have been something of a signal, for the next day SARBUPRI activists entered the British P & T Company rubber and tea estates in West Java, while other SOBSI members ran up the red flag at Shell Oil Company properties in Djakarta. Unilever workers in Djakarta seized the switchboard, and bolted the main doors of the plant, while warning British staff away from the building. The walls of the Shell office building were plastered with signs reading 'Indonesian property', which proved to be a prophetic announcement, for ten days later the Indonesian government in fact decided to assume formal control over British enterprises seized by the workers. On February 2, 1964 the government's

Badan Penguasa Perurusahaan2 Inggris (Supervisory Office of British Enterprises) began functioning in order to 'safeguard' and 'exercise control' over the British concerns.

In its way this government take-over marked something of a turning point in the operations of the present Indonesian power structure, because there is little question that the government was coerced or let itself be coerced into taking this step and that as a result of Communist pressure it went back, in effect on its own decisions.[42] For after the take-over by SARBUPRI of the P & T Company rubber and tea estates, where workers hoisted the red flag side by side with the Indonesian national flag, acting President Johannes Leimena (Sukarno was in Tokyo conferring with Robert Kennedy) appealed to workers to 'faithfully observe' Sukarno's previous decree forbidding workers from taking over enterprises without authority.[43] In London British officials reminded the Indonesian chargé d'affaires of the assurances given after the seizure of British property the previous September that British holdings would not be nationalized. But in Djakarta Leimena's appeal was in fact ignored, as workers proceeded to take over Unilever and Shell Oil offices. And even as Sukarno, who had speedily returned to Djakarta on January 20, 1964, confirmed and endorsed all measures taken by Leimena, SOBSI had already seized the offices of the British-American Tobacco Company. A hurried meeting of the Supreme Operations Command, attended by the armed forces' chiefs and principal cabinet officers, concluded with a new warning 'to the people' to obey presidential orders. But whatever assurances SOBSI may then have given the government, or the government may have given the British Foreign Office, the fact was that neither Sukarno nor the army now felt free any longer to ignore anti-Malaysia sentiment and the pressure of Communist mass organizations and formally restore British property. The decision to place the British enterprises under state control may have been clothed in the garb of extending 'protection' and 'safety' to them so as to create the impression that the government was actually protecting the enterprises from the workers, but in fact in this indirect way Indonesian officials have now managed to assume managerial functions: 'While the British officers of the firm still have authority to write checks, they must now be countersigned by the government representative'.[44] Given the deepening tensions of the Malaysia issue a return of the taken-over enterprises seems unlikely. Although SARBUPRI and SOBSI have subsequently protested the appointment of army officers as supervisors over the taken-over estates, and have demanded more 'democratic' control (i.e. control by SARBUPRI representatives), the Communist unions and the PKI generally might well feel that they had scored a victory by the government take-over. Aidit's warning on January 17, 1964 had apparently not been without effect; the Communists would no longer tolerate a course of compromise or moderation in the Malayan crisis.

PKI intransigeance now in effect became Indonesia's intransigeance, dooming all efforts at a peaceful settlement of the dispute, amidst rumors that Sukarno was willing to compromise but was no longer able to do so. Only a few hours after U.S. Attorney General Robert Kennedy had won the agreement of the Philippines, Malaysia and Indonesia to participate in a foreign ministers' conference of the three nations in Bangkok and the assurances of Indonesia and Malaysia that they would agree to a ceasefire in the Borneo guerilla war, Sukarno, on January 23, 1964, in addressing a youth rally, announced a continuing drive to crush Malaysia. 'Indonesia may change its tactics but our goal will remain the same', he stated, and *Harian Rakjat* duly praised him for it. Despite elaborate standfast and ceasefire announcements the guerilla war went on; in fact it went on all during the fruitless Foreign Ministers discussions in February and March, 1964. Meanwhile the decision to send the U.S. Seventh Fleet to the Indian Ocean provided Aidit with another opportunity to denounce the 'imperialist encirclement' of Indonesia, of which Britain's 'neo-colonialist Malaysia' and the 'puppet state of South Viet Nam' were deemed to be striking examples. The PKI therefore called on the entire Indonesian people to oppose the 'posting of the U.S. Seventh Fleet at the country's threshold'.[45]

On March 16, 1964, Sukarno endeared himself further to the PKI with a call-up to the nation for volunteers to increase the nation's defenses and 'preserve the National Revolution'. The appeal seems to have particularly been intended for youth and Sukarno urged them to enlist in what he called a new struggle to save the country 'from the people of the North'. *Pemuda Rakjat*, the Indonesian Students Association and other youth groups 'ethusiastically responded', some youth units indicating their immediate readiness to be sent to 'the North' and help 'the North Kalimantan people' in their 'liberation struggle'. The Indonesian Red Cross began a drive for 'needed volunteers', as if the nation was readying itself for war. But although Sukarno's March 16, 1964, appeal presumably had been made in response to Malaya's newly announced conscription drive, Nasution, on March 17, declared that general mobilization in Indonesia 'at present is not necessary', and that what should now proceed would be Indonesia's 'total' confrontation against Malaysia.[46] What this 'total' confrontation might entail however was indicated by Sukarno's March 16 speech, in which he called on the entire nation to proceed with 'voluntary action' and recalled that during the final stages of the West Irian campaign some 'seven million boys and girls' had registered as volunteers. The new volunteers, Sukarno declared, not only would receive military training 'in how to handle weapons', but would also receive instruction in how to further the revolution, and would engage in 'efforts to increase national production'. Sukarno's subsequent defiant indifference to the U.S. decision to cut aid to Indonesia unless the Malaysia dispute was settled, his unequivocal endorsement of the North Viet Nam régime, at this time and his constant reiteration of *'ganjang Malaysia!'* ('crush Malaysia!') all seemed to suggest that he had now fully identified himself with the PKI momentum.

Early in March 1964, in an interview with visiting Filipino journalists, Aidit gave an indication of his idea of the price of peace. The people of North Kalimantan should be given an opportunity to express 'their preference', he declared. This necessitated withdrawal of all British troops from North Kalimantan, release of 'political prisoners' and then the holding of a new plebescite or referendum, with the North Kalimantan choosing between independence or affiliation with Malaysia. (*Inter alia* it might be noted that Aidit was echoing Sukarno's call, at this time, for another, 'truly democratic' ascertainment of the wishes of North Kalimantan inhabitants). If, Aidit went on, the people of North Kalimantan agreed to Malaysia, 'then we accept this status, but we must maintain our vigilance in Kalimantan'. As an Indonesian, Aidit also declared at this time, he would reject any move to establish foreign military bases in his country, but he felt bound to point out that the Philippines had U.S. bases on its territory. Finally Aidit took the occasion to deny that there was any power struggle between himself and Nasution, declaring: 'Both Nasution and I and the other leaders of Indonesia are influenced by the common political concept of *musjawarah* or mutual consultation. Besides Nasution and I are personal friends. We fought the Japanese together'.[47] Clearly the PKI chairman saw continuing virtue in his concept of the 'national unity front' in the Malaysian 'confrontation', and *musjawarah* and NASAKOMIL served the party well as the symbolic formulations of its own relentless organizational dynamics.

By the end of 1963 a spirit of reckless intractability seemed to have become the official Indonesian policy norm, notwithstanding the gravity of the economic situation. In an address to a delegation of visiting Filipino veterans in Djakarta, on December 5, 1963, Foreign Minister Subandrio declared that Indonesia was deliberately neglecting her economy so that she could concentrate on regaining her national identity and on reviving the 'iron spirit' of her people. This was a kind of

approach in line with the PKI's own zealous advocacy of Sukarno's
vivere pericoloso! Other utterances around this time by Subandrio, who
had been given prime responsibility in the direction of Indonesia's
economic confrontation policies against Malaya seemed to suggest the
curious air of unreality and volitional omnipotence prevailing in the
higher regions of government.[48] 'To hell with your aid!', said Indonesia's
President, in a remark directed at the United States on March 25, 1964,
'we'll never collapse'.[49] Yet chaos has become a pervading feature of
the Indonesian economy. The food shortage continued critical, with the
price index of 19 main foodstuffs in Djakarta rising to 4,620 by the
beginning of December 1963 (1953 is 100).[50] Declining exports and
lower world market prices sharply reduced Indonesia's reserves and
necessitated further cutdowns in imports. Already late in November
1963, 75 per cent of the small industrial concerns in Central Java had
stopped operating due to lack of raw materials.[51] By the beginning of
1964, one authoritative analysis pointed out that 'Indonesia owes her
foreign creditors something in the order of US $3,500 million, and she
appears to have no foreign exchange left in her treasury. In a reasonable
year she earns $800 million from export, but almost half of this is eaten
up by debt repayments and rice imports'.[52] Money in circulation at the
end of 1960 was estimated at 46,200 million Rupiah, while by May
1963, according to a statement by First Minister Djuanda it was 150,000
million Rupiah.[53] Relentless inflationary pressures, chaotic fiscal policies,
and recurrent shortages of all kinds of essentials have long since made
a shambles of any serious development effort. The PKI furiously
attacked Indonesian negotiations for an U.S. $82 million loan from the
International Monetary Fund. The PKI in fact demanded that Indonesia withdraw from the IMF which it termed 'an agency in the international imperialist conspiracy', and *Harian Rakjat* charged that the
government's decision to let prices of a number of commodities rise in
line with the May 26, 1963 economic reforms was 'a condition for
getting credits from the imperialists, whether from the IMF or directly
from the U.S. itself'.

This assertion was not very far from wrong, because the May 26
regulations, the latest in a seemingly endless series of tinkerings, were
reportedly introduced at U.S. insistence as a prerequisite for further
U.S. aid and assistance under the one time projected international
consortium for Indonesia. The May 26 regulations, which opened the
door to a measure of free competition, dropping price controls and
allowing for sizable increases in fares, remained virtually without
significantly beneficial effect, however (they were revised by December
1963) because of the gathering momentum of the Malaysia confrontation

and the resulting cancellation of foreign dollar support. *Harian Rakjat* and SOBSI organs sharply attacked the May 26 reforms, also because of the initial rise in prices and because of the increase in transportation fares. By February 1964, there were widespread crop failures and famine stalked parts of Java again. All through 1963 the government announced new campaigns to uproot corruption and economic malversations. In June 1963, 'major economic crimes' were said to be under investigation among state trading company officials and by March 1964, Nasution was still announcing the uncovering of 'massive monetary manipulations' by state enterprises' managers.[54]

Such revelations were especially grist to the PKI's mill, which has for some years now and with almost ritualistic fervor attributed much of the sorry state of the nation's economy to corruption and inefficiency in the management of state enterprises.[55] The fact that many former Army officers have managerial posts in the state enterprises, and that the Army continues to have responsibility for certain aspects of labor-management relations, has given PKI denunciations of the malversations of 'bureaucratic capitalists' in the state enterprises a special edge. But PKI statements on the nation's economic problems generally echoed the same attitude of insouciance that characterized those made by its leaders. On February 25, 1964, for example, Aidit criticized 'certain groups of people' who were suggesting that Indonesia should stop her confrontation against Malaysia, because they feared that the Indonesian economy would otherwise collapse. 'Indonesia shall not founder because of economic difficulties', Aidit emphasized, adding, however, that Indonesia would certainly triumph if she would but launch her confrontation 'as a revolutionary war'.[56] As will be indicated presently the latter phrase was suggestive of the PKI's adhesion to the line of militant expansion of revolutionary movements in Southeast Asia, which in turn reflected the party's (and Indonesia's) currently close relationship with Peking.

On November 7, 1963 First Minister Djuanda died, adding new impetus to a cabinet reorganization which was formally announced on November 24, 1963. Aidit and Lukman retained their ministerial ranks, along with other principal party leaders, in their respective positions as Provisional People's Congress' Vice-Chairman and as House of Representatives' Vice-Speaker. But the cabinet, despite the party's earlier mentioned campaign for PKI inclusion in the government, was still no closer to actual *gotong royong* status. Significantly, front organizations like *Pemuda Rakyat* and SOBSI expressed their disappointment over the cabinet reshuffle primarily in economic terms. No significant improvements in the economy were likely to be forthcoming, various front organs intimated, unless a government 'with NASAKOM as its core' was established. Clearly between the poles of continuing economic misery and anti-Malaysia popular fervor the PKI hoped to be able to generate the spark that would lift it to power.

The Drift toward Peking. In the wake of its anti-Malaysia campaign and the related drive to expand its domestic power, the PKI, especially in the latter half of 1963, began to project a role of leadership in the revolutionary development of Southeast Asia. In so doing it not only continued to associate itself closely with Peking's insistence on the need for militancy in the international Communist movement, in particular in the underdeveloped part of the world, but in fact seemed to assist in pushing official Indonesian policies as a whole closer toward those of Communist China. This process, in turn fed back upon the party's own domestic intransigeance and thrust to power. For Malaysia at any rate it seemed that Indonesia was closely aligning itself with Peking's ambitions in Southeast Asia, and on October 13, 1963, for example, Tun Abdul Razak, Malaysia's Vice-Premier, asserted that President Sukarno's confrontation policy was due to pressure from Communist China and that Sukarno was following the directions of the PKI.[57]

In an address on September 29, 1963, at party headquarters in Djakarta, on the occasion of the return of a PKI delegation (led by Aidit) from a tour through the Soviet Union, Cuba, the German People's Republic, People's China and North Korea, during the preceding ten weeks, Aidit noted that[58]

Not only has the international Communist movement made progress in the process of choice, crystallization and consolidation, but world revolution too is developing everywhere. Everywhere, and primarily in Asia, Africa and Latin America, the struggles of the peoples are being intensified. . . . People may argue about where the focus of the world revolution is today. But the fact is that at present the most acute anti-imperialist struggle is in Asia, especially in Southeast Asia, where the sound of gunfire has not stopped since the end of World War II. The people of South Viet Nam, Laos and other places in Southeast Asia have been waging an armed struggle. This is also the case with the Philippines and Malaya where the people's armed struggles are still continuing even though on a small scale.

In Southeast Asia there are already a socialist country and largescale revolutionary movements of the masses. There are also Communist parties which exert a very broad influence on the revolutionary movement, like the Communist parties of Indonesia, Burma and other countries. It may be said that all the Communist Parties in Southeast Asia are holding high the banner of Marxism-Leninism. There is no market for revisionism in Southeast Asia. Conditions both objective and subjective are very favorable in Southeast Asia. The Communists and other revolutionaries of Indonesia should feel fortunate and happy that we are in such an area. We are in the forefront of the struggle against world imperialism.

In subsequent pronouncements by party leaders this line was further elaborated, indeed Aidit felt justified to openly side with Peking's interpretation of the internal political situation in India, launching a sharp attack on Nehru and the 'Dange clique' (S. A. Dange is chairman of the Indian Communist party which has been critical of Peking), and called on 'true Communists' in India to form a real Marxist party, offering the support of foreign parties, including the PKI for such a move.[59] Did Aidit begin to envisage Indonesia as a kind of Cuba, ready to export revolution to other parts of Southeast Asia? Between December 23 and 26, 1963 the party's Central Committee met for its usual plenary session and described Southeast Asia as one of the world's focal points of 'major contradictions'. In the Southeast Asian area, the Plenum said, the people have attained a high level of political vigilance and are 'rich in experience in revolutionary struggle, including armed struggle', while there is already a large section in the area which has overthrown capitalism and has established socialism. The Plenum declared itself to be aware of 'the tremendous responsibility' of Indonesian Communists in the national independence struggle in Southeast Asia, particularly in light of the great importance of the Indonesian revolution. The Plenum emphasized that the Marxist-Leninist parties of Southeast Asia, which are still struggling for national independence, have the same basic tasks: (1) to attract the masses as widely as possible and to organize them into a national front; (2) to enter the villages as deeply as possible in order to strengthen the worker-peasant alliance; (3) to strengthen party leadership in the mass movement and 'to be skilful in utilizing all forms of struggle'; and (4) to strengthen cooperation between the peoples and the Marxist-Leninist parties of Southeast Asia.[60]

The notion that Indonesia had a revolutionary role to play in her foreign relations appeared also to be echoed in non-Communist quarters. On March 23, 1964, Foreign Minister Subandrio declared that if at a certain point Indonesia is made to choose 'between the conventional and revolutionary aspects in the implementation of her foreign policy she will choose the one which will benefit the Revolution'. Indonesians have consistently proclaimed, Subandrio went on, that their revolution had yet to be consummated, and so they have been concentrating their efforts 'at building a new world'. Subandrio stressed that 'Indonesian politics is the decisive factor which can mark the downfall of the imperialists and colonialists' and that this struggle could not be won by way of a strong economy or a strong army alone, but by way also of 'the solidarity of the peoples desiring a new world'. The Indonesian Revolution, the Foreign Minister concluded, is not only a great revolution compared to other revolutions, but 'it might even be the last revolution'. For the Indonesian revolution is adapted 'to the growth and demands of the present era stage by stage, sometimes defying rationalization'. Indonesia's revolution can 'meet the demands put forward by the present revolution of mankind'. These views, as well as the PKI's, tended to underscore a particular image of the 'confrontation' (one of considerable popularity in Indonesia) as a contest between an essentially 'feudal' Malaysia, an anachronism in twentieth century Asia, and a 'modern' Indonesia, whose revolutionary aspirations are in harmony with those of 'the new emerging forces', to the leadership of which Indonesia has been none too subtly aspiring.[61] Thus 'confrontation' could be interpreted in terms of a uniquely revolutionizing mission, specifically that of bringing Malaysia into the 'new world'. In effect such an approach also sanctified Indonesia's alliance with the left radical and Marxist elements in the Malaysian territories which also oppose Malaysia, and the support given to the 'volunteer' scheme by the earlier mentioned Malayan nationalist Ibrahim Yaacob, who in March 1964 promised Nasution that 'thousands of members of the Free Malaya Association' (which Ibrahim heads) were ready to become 'volunteer fighters' in the struggle to 'crush Malaysia' is, along with Indonesian involvement in guerilla and underground terrorist activity in Malaysia, indicative of the manner in which Indonesia is planning on implementing her policy of 'revolution'.

This, precisely, is what has endeared Indonesian 'confrontation' tactics to Peking. 'Indonesia's just stand of opposing the neo-colonialist scheme of Malaysia and supporting the revolutionary struggle of the people of North Kalimantan', Liu Shao-chi declared during his visit to Djakarta in April 1963, 'constitutes a serious blow to the colonialists, old and new', and with this Indonesia 'has become an important force opposing imperialism and colonialism' in Southeast Asia. Already early in January 1963, only a few weeks after Azahari's unsuccessful coup in Brunei, Communist Chinese premier Chou En-lai had expressed 'resolute support' for the 'just struggle of the people of Brunei'. And in September 1963, during a visit of an Indonesian parliamentary delegation to Peking, Chu Teh, chairman of People's China's National People's Congress, reiterated that the Chinese people 'firmly supported' Indonesia's struggle against 'neo-colonialism propagated by the imperialists in the name of Malaysia'. On the first anniversary of the Brunei revolt Peking proclaimed that only 'the first round' of the North Kalimantan struggle had ended, but that since this struggle was part of the 'liberation fight in Southeast Asia', the cause of the North Kalimantan rebels would triumph, 'with Indonesia's backing and the growing support of the peoples of Asia and the whole world'.[62] Peking's own conflict with

Moscow feeds upon the Malaysia conflict, for this conflict is of course a test case of Peking's continuing emphasis on the need for revolutionary militancy in the Communist movement of the world, particularly in the underdeveloped countries. But by the same token the PKI has seen its position strengthened because of Peking's 'hard line' in Southeast Asia, and along with it the party has the satisfaction of being the principal activator of an undoubtedly rapidly developing Sino-Indonesian partnership in foreign affairs.

Indications of this partnership are not just found in the Malaysia issue. At the Asian-African People's Solidarity Organization meeting in Nicosia, Cyprus, in September 1963, no less than at the earlier Asian-African Conference in Moshi, Tanganyika, in February 1963, the Sino-Indonesian entente showed itself clearly. In Nicosia, for example, the Indonesians were second only to the Chinese in attacking the Soviet supported nuclear test ban treaty, while at Moshi it was primarily Sino-Indonesian insistence which led to the passage of a resolution extending official recognition to Azahari's 'Unitary Government of North Kalimantan'. At the Afro-Asian journalists' conference in April 1963, the discomfort of the Soviet delegation was as conspicuous as it had been at Moshi, and the predominantly political resolutions passed by this conference largely reflected the 'hard line' of Peking, while Peking generally was considered to be the manipulator of the gathering.[63] Even more blatant was Peking's financing of Indonesia's 'Games of the New Emerging Forces' (GANEFO) in November 1963, in which apparently the PKI acted as middleman between Djakarta and Peking in providing the needed financial assistance to the Indonesian government.[64] Peking subsequently reached new heights in the use of superlatives in its eulogy of the games.[65] Matters apparently reached such a pass that early in March 1964, the newly appointed Indonesian ambassador to People's China, Djawoto, felt constrained to note that Indonesia had not become 'the tail' of Peking. The Indonesian Republic, declared Djawoto, is fighting for the 'emancipation of all nations and moves equally with all countries in the world'.[66]

It is, perhaps, particularly remarkable that this new warmth between Djakarta and Peking was able to grow despite the anti-Chinese riots in Java in March and May, 1963. Especially as a result of riots in the latter month (the socalled 'May 10 affair' as it has come to be called in Indonesia), notably in Bandung, a new breach in Sino-Indonesian relations might have seemed likely (the riots left 13 Chinese dead, hundreds wounded, and Chinese and other property losses estimated at 4 billion Rupiah).[67] The causes of the disturbances are obscure and may have involved long standing Chinese-Indonesian communal tensions as much as the harrowing plight of many Indonesians in the stagnating economy of their country. There is little doubt that in some areas the riots had a distinctly anti-government, rather than an anti-Chinese character. On May 19, 1963 Sukarno gave the official explanation of the riots: they had been caused, he declared, by 'counter-revolutionaries as well as by foreign subversives' identified with the banned Masjumi and Socialist parties, which had exploited the Chinese minority problem 'because we have lately been in close contact with People's China'.[68] Peking immediately took up this explanation: the riots were instigated by 'imperialists' and 'counter-revolutionary groups', it said, for the purpose of sabotaging 'Sino-Indonesian friendly relations'.[69] Considering how vociferously Peking reacted to earlier anti-Chinese measures and demonstrations, the mildness of its reaction this time demonstrated *ad oculos* that Indonesia had come to occupy a special place in Communist Chinese foreign policy.

PKI reaction to the riots was in line with official views. Aidit declared on May 27, 1963, during an address in Djakarta commemorating the party's forty-third birthday, that recent 'racialist acts of terror' were anti-Sukarno, anti-Chinese and anti-Communist. The President was quite correct in blaming Masjumi and other counter-revolutionaries for the incidents, Aidit said, for the 'counter-revolutionaries do not like to see what they call the Sukarno régime succeed in carrying out its food and clothing program'. Hence the destruction of property during the riots, for this destruction increases 'the people's suffering', and in such a state of popular misery counter-revolutionaries believe the people can be more readily goaded against Sukarno. Those behind the riots, Aidit went on, 'want to practice an Alabama style American way of life, in which racialism is being fanned and Verwoerdism too', and they also wanted to damage relations between Indonesia and People's China. Finally, he argued, the instigators of the riots had an 'anti-communist policy' which 'is clearly perceptible from the fact that they are acting against Indonesian Communists with the main purpose of frustrating the formation of a Nasakom cabinet'.[70]

In seeking to project its own image in the underdeveloped world Peking appears to have found Djakarta a useful ally, indeed, occasionally, a useful frontman. Indonesia's own search for 'grandeur', particularly among the new nations, may well eventually conflict with Communist China's ambitions, but for the time being Indonesia appears to find it essential to stage one dazzling Afro-Asian conference after another, if only, it may be supposed, to divert attention from its economic miseries. Hardly had the 'Games of the New Emerging Forces' ended or Sukarno was urging a 'Conference of the New Emerging Forces', and on cue

Peking also called for 'a second Bandung conference' of Afro-Asian states, which would 'provide a suitable meeting place for the new emerging forces to compare notes' on the progress made since the 'spirit of Bandung' first activated the Asian and African peoples 'in their struggle against imperialism and colonialism'.[71] Just as the first Bandung conference of 1955 was noteworthy for Peking's attempts to ingratiate itself with its suspicious Asian neighbors, so a 'second Bandung' would mark Peking's steady advance in the expansion of her influence in the Afro-Asian community today, an advance in which Indonesia can and has been useful to her. The PKI, meanwhile, by emphasizing Indonesia's own revolutionary destiny in Southeast Asia, feeds the official pursuit of Indonesian 'grandeur', and in so doing not only further stabilizes and strengthens the party's position, but also drives Indonesia as a whole toward closer cooperation with a Communist world power.

Under the circumstances a new coolness in Soviet-Indonesian relations is not surprising at present, not least because Indonesia has found it increasingly difficult to meet the repayment schedule of the millions of dollars in credit and assistance granted Djakarta by Moscow (e.g. in February 1961 Sukarno boasted that Khrushchev had provided Indonesia with a grant of from $700 to $800 million, of which military credits amounted to at least $400 million; but how and to what extent the funds have been allocated thus far remains a mystery). In June 1963 'a debt repayment alleviation' was agreed to by the USSR, but it is doubtful if, given the economic effects of the 'confrontation' of Malaysia, even this modified schedule can be met.[72] Moscow is known to be far less enthusiastic than Peking over Djakarta's new anti-Malaysia campaign. Yet, undoubtedly alarmed over Djakarta's recent drift toward Peking, Moscow appears recently to have been willing to overlook the repayment problem. The visit to Indonesia, late in June 1964, of Anastas Mikoyan, then Soviet Deputy Premier, resulted in a promise of a fresh supply of Russian transport planes, helicopters and other military hardware for Indonesia, along with Mikoyan's unequivocal pledge of Soviet support for the Indonesian campaign to 'crush Malaysia'. It has been reported that Mikoyan's mission was facilitated by intimations of Indonesian spokesmen in Moscow that Sukarno was becoming 'alarmed' over his nation's apparent dependence on Peking and would welcome an official Soviet visit.

Meanwhile it is clear that the PKI is retaining its ideological affinity with the Chinese Communists. At the Central Committee's plenary session, from December 23 to 26, 1963 in Djakarta the party reaffirmed its opposition to 'revisionism' and its adhesion to the 1960 Moscow Statement.[73] Maintaining an 'independent and equal stand' in the international Communist dispute is essential, however, for thanks to such a position 'the differences within the international Communist movement have not had an unfavorable influence on the Indonesian Communist Party. The Plenum noted that today in the international Communist movement there are four types of Communist and Workers parties: (1) Marxist-Leninist parties; (2) parties whose leadership is controlled by revisionists but in which there is Marxist-Leninist opposition; (3) parties which are completely controlled by revisionists, while Marxists-Leninists within them have established Marxist-Leninist organizations, and (4) parties whose leadership is under complete control of revisionists but alongside of which new Communist parties have been set up. The PKI, the Plenum declared tersely, is a party of the first type.

The abovementioned classification, it needs no elaboration, is modeled upon the Peking line, and as if to underscore the PKI's continuing adhesion to the Chinese Communist strategy, the December 1963 Plenum, asserted that the 'correctness' of the 1960 Moscow Statement 'has been proved by revolutionary practice in every corner of Asia, Africa and Latin America, as well as in the world as a whole'. Indeed, 'the experiences of the struggle of the Indonesian people and other peoples of Asia, Africa and Latin America show that the anti-imperialist struggle is linked with the anti-revisionist struggle. Therefore a more determined struggle against imperialism means a more determined struggle against revisionism and vice versa'. The Plenum urged 'all Marxist Leninist Parties and all Communists' to hold aloft six banners to 'strengthen' international Communism: (1) the banner of Marxism-Leninism against revisionism; (2) the banner of revolution against capitulation; (3) the banner of concrete peace against abstract peace; (4) the banner of proletarian internationalism against great-nation egoism; (5) the banner of unity against splitting; and (6) the banner of revolutionary optimism against pessimism. One may justifiably conclude from the above phraseology—particularly from the manner in which Chinese Communists have hurled terms like 'revisionism', or 'great nation egoism', or 'splitting' against their Soviet opponents—that for the time being, at least, the PKI's position as an 'independent and equal' party means extensive use of Peking's vocabulary.

The PKI 'Breakthrough'. As a result of the end of the West New Guinea dispute and the state of emergency, and the accelerating intensification of the anti-Malaysia campaign the PKI, by March 1964, had managed to provide itself with more operational elbow room. The regulatory powers of the army and indeed of the Presidency had by no means wholly disappeared, to the contrary; but the political climate following the end of martial law and the constantly induced fervor of the 'confrontation' made a policy of keeping the PKI under quarantine as much as possible hardly feasible. For the central fact of Indonesian political life by the beginning of 1964 was that the nation and all its major and minor power centers were following or were made to follow the major foreign policy objective of the PKI, and that a revolutionary illuminism now no longer would serve as the domestic catechism of official ideology but was to be exported throughout Southeast Asia in line with the country's self conceived destiny. Thus the centre of political gravity had, for the time being, notably shifted in the PKI's direction, and no forces or factors were in sight that might be able to reverse the process.

CHAPTER VIII

CONCLUSION—A LOOK AHEAD

IN ITS MORE THAN 40 years of history the Communist Party of Indonesia exhibits a kind of recurring undulating pattern: a period of growth following the birth of the party in 1920 is abruptly terminated by a poorly coordinated and ineffectual rebellion, whereupon the party goes into decline. Another period of growth, this time during the Indonesian Revolution, is again suddenly ended by a disastrously haphazard insurrection, and once more the PKI seems all but to have destroyed itself. Again there is a steady advance, terminated by the near disaster of July 1960. At present the party has risen once more from the hollow of the wave and might be considered ready to take the plunge into open resistance and possible defeat once again. But the party which confronted, and successfully overcame the July 1960 crisis was and is no longer the party which led itself into the 'provocation' of Madiun in 1948. Present day tactical insights and organizational finesse are not likely to bring the party again to the disasters of 1926–27 and 1948. The earlier noted dissension in party leadership in the wake of the July 1960 'Evaluation' crisis did not involve the question of a violent seizure of power, but rather the relative degree of aggressiveness to be displayed by the party and its fronts in a period of particularly close supervision. Even if the arena in which the party now operates were to become smaller once more, or the dynamics of the Malaysia campaign in an as yet unforeseen circumstance were to redound back upon the party, the path of the *coup d'état* is not likely to be followed, certainly not so long as Sukarno is alive and in power and can provide the party with a modicum of protection and leverage. For much of the period since 1948 has been a time when the strategy and strictures of Lenin's 'Left Wing Communism, an Infantile Disorder' are particularly applicable to the PKI, and those now in command of the party, who style themselves the *Sajap Leninis*, know it. This is a time for patience, for husbanding one's strength, for maneuvring within a governmental framework partially favorable, partially dangerous to the Communist cause, a time for 'carefully, attentively, and skillfully using every, even the smallest "rift" among the enemies, of every antagonism of interest among the bourgeoisie of the various countries and among the various groups or types of bourgeoisie within the various countries, and also by taking advantage of every, even the smallest, opportunity of gaining a mass ally, even though this ally be temporary, vacillating, unstable, unreliable and conditional'.[1]

But such a period of cautious maneuvering, of resisting the efforts at quarantining by the army, of utilizing every tactical opportunity to expand its power, does not mean an end to militancy or aggressive 'reality testing' of the boundaries set on party operations. Not even in the dark days following 1948, or the equally dangerous months following the July 1960 'Evaluation', did the party crawl into a shell; the measure of its continuous aggressiveness and that of its fronts is its great and growing power on the Indonesian scene today. The assertion or implication that there has been a 'domestication' of the party at any time is quite misleading.[2] Such a view confuses party acquiescence to official state ideology or party conformity to prescribed limits of political activity, in the best traditions of united front strategy with an abandonment of distinct, revolutionary Communist ideology and tactical militancy; it overlooks the process of steadily 'radicalizing' official state ideology and policy by staying within them but while pressing against their limits all the time. It suggests that all or most of the 'adjusting' has to be done by the party, whereas in fact a case could be made for the view, particularly since the Malaysia crisis, that official Indonesian ideology and policy is 'domesticating' itself to the PKI. The 'crush Malaysia' campaign will be effective only, Sukarno declared on March 9, 1964, 'if all efforts are based on offensive revolutionary thinking'.[3] This seems but an echo of Aidit and Radio Peking.

What practical policy alternatives present themselves to the PKI at the moment? An astute Chinese student of the Indonesian Communists, Cheng Hsueh-chia, has suggested the following:[4]

1. Maintain the present line, beating a retreat and allowing for a relative weakening of the party, while aiding Sukarno in attaining full dictatorial power, as 'Lasalle helped Bismarch unify Germany'. In this manner the PKI would play a role similar to that of the German Social Democratic Party.

2. Prepare for an armed struggle while seeming to be in retreat. If at the same time Communist penetration of the armed forces could succeed, Nasution would become the Kornilov and Aidit the Lenin of Java. Only in this way could Aidit hope to use the island of Java in a further expansion of Communist influences.

3. Accelerate infiltration, presumably in all fields of governments, including in the armed forces, while preparing for the overthrow of Sukarno; give the appearance of beating a tactical retreat, while waiting for an expansion of Communist power throughout Southeast Asia (Laos, Viet Nam).

Cheng suggests that Aidit has determined upon the third course, partly because of the deterioration of the economy and because a renewed Communist offensive in countries contiguous to Indonesia would also strengthen the position of the PKI. But at least two of Cheng's suggested alternatives, including the one he favors, depend on Sukarno remaining in the picture. Indonesia's President has been ailing for some time, however, and is already old for an Indonesian of his generation; moreover there have been seven attempts at his life in recent years. Yet, for the time being, and given the balance which the President has provided for the PKI, especially in the last two years, it is most unlikely that the party would now challenge both Sukarno and Nasution in an open armed struggle. This does not necessarily mean that the party is not anticipating an eventual armed conflict; on the contrary. For such a clash may well occur after Sukarno's death if Nasution and the army should assume a dominant position in the state and decide to embark on an intensified anti-Communist campaign. It is by no means certain, however, that if Nasution succeeds Sukarno such an intensified anti-Communist campaign would necessarily follow. For an army directed anti-Communist campaign would probably antagonize left nationalist and other non-Communist quarters also. To crush all opposition to an anti-Communist campaign the army might well have to seek to establish military dictatorship which would solidify all center and left opposition groups into a popular front that could in the end play into Communist hands. Were Nasution to succeed Sukarno, a degree of additional restriction on party operations, if not too severe, might well continue to be borne by the PKI for some time, until dissatisfaction in the ranks of non-Communist parties, along with the effects of the continuing economic crisis, forced changes that would give all political groups, including the PKI, greater freedom of operation once again.

Cheng is undoubtedly right in ascribing major significance to an expansion of Communism in Southeast Asian countries contiguous to Indonesia. Here the steady pressures of Peking, also in conjunction with the anti-Malaysia campaign, and the likelihood of continuing radical Marxist opposition to Malaysia within Malaysia itself, all provide the PKI with a momentum that makes an outright *coup d'état* unnecessary except in a dire extremity. It might therefore well be concluded that (1) so long as Sukarno remains alive a Communist coup is very unlikely; and (2) if Sukarno dies, and if Nasution (or a régime wholly committed to Nasution) succeeds him, an outburst of Communist violence is only likely if the party sees no way of mobilizing sufficient popular front support to neutralize or undo the power of the anti-Communist military, and if it is therefore threatened with extinction.

As Sukarno (or, in future, some broadly acceptable substitute, like Vice-premiers Subandrio or Leimena) remains in power, the PKI faces several tasks. It must retain, as best as it can, its influence in its front groups by ceaseless exploitation of the economic crisis or external disputes. It must struggle to widen the area of its freedom of operations by drawing on the discontent in non-Communist (and even in anti-Communist) groups in Indonesia over the curtailment of political and civil liberties. The party must also try to accelerate its infiltration of the armed forces—a kind of 'hollowing out' of the opposition—especially in the enlisted ranks, in order to offset the anti-Communist orientation of leading officers. Finally, and from a theoretical point of view perhaps most important, the party must analyze anew the factors governing the present position of the national bourgeoisie in Indonesia, since in a significant sense the PKI's ultimate success or failure depends on such an analysis and the tactics based on it. The party's vigorous criticism of 'bureaucratic capitalists', of 'profit-hunting' managers of state enterprises taken over from the Dutch have all been part of an attack on the army leadership, but an attack that also had implications for the national bourgeoisie. At the same time the party has also leaned 'on the right' in recent years when it proved somewhat unenthusiastic about, or hostile to, such schemes of Sukarno's as the 'burial' of the parties, the formation of a monolithic National Front and the dissolution of the elected parliament. In this policy of leaning 'on the right' the party was admittedly most concerned with preserving its own freedom of operations as a party, but it also managed to convey its general support for the free formation of all partisan political opinion and party activity and for a parliament that reflected these in its membership, to other political groups equally concerned with their freedom of movement.

The July 8, 1960 'Evaluation', of course, by no means marked the end of the party's endeavors to continue to find supporters on the right. But it is true that the 'Evaluation' and similar criticisms which the PKI had made previously of segments of the national bourgeoisie has been in accord with a general dissatisfaction in world Communist circles—certainly in recent Soviet Russian theory—with the performance of the national bourgeoisie in recently 'liberated' lands like Indonesia. During 1961 Soviet periodicals published various attacks on national bourgeois governments in India, Burma, Indonesia, Pakistan, Egypt, the Sudan and other countries, in which these governments were either accused of 'inconsistency' and of being unable democratically to solve the land problem by eliminating feudalism (Near and Middle East), or of guiding national revolutions deliberately in such a way as to drive a wedge between 'the anti-imperialist movement of the masses' and the 'anti-feudal movement' (South and Southeast Asia).[5] In the latter countries the attitude of the national bourgeoisie toward foreign capital was held to be ambivalent and indecisive, resulting in a slowness and inconsistency in implementing the national bourgeois revolution to the point where a genuine people's democracy could emerge. From this point of view the PKI's July 8, 1960 'Evaluation', as well as its criticisms of government policies before it, and—in more covert form—after it, illustrate the alleged wavering and slowness with which Indonesia's revolution is being implemented. The Communist demand that measures be taken against those foreign enterprises operating in part with Dutch capital, the insistence that Indonesia's foreign trade pattern be turned away from the West, the cry for better living conditions and for a 'democratization' of village government, as well as the constant criticism of 'bureaucratic capitalists' all have far-reaching significance for the national entrepreneurial element. Only recently, again, the party has sought to define its relationship to that element, stressing at one and the same time the need for a 'patriotic' economy, in which there will be 'greater freedom of action' for the national capitalists 'in medium sized and small industry and in internal trade', and a control over the activity of 'national industrialists' so as 'not to enable them to run the state and to command the life of the people'.[6]

The difficulty is, that the PKI has not as yet been able to delineate clearly what segments of the Indonesian middle class it views as its allies at the present time, as it did, for example, in the mid-nineteen-fifties with respect to left nationalist and entrepreneurial elements in the PNI and other secular nationalist parties. The steady imposition of state capitalist forms of economic organization, as well as the decline of partisan parliamentary politics in the new Indonesian monolithic political order, have increasingly rendered the traditional process of forming factional alliances between party groupings, based on the free play of politico-economic interests, meaningless and impossible. Under the circumstances, then, the PKI's policy of simultaneously attacking and seeking support from the national bourgeoisie will require a sharper focus in the future. For example the party may well find it profitable to continue to attack 'bureaucratic capitalists' and managers in the state enterprises in a somewhat different way, i.e. with the aim of winning sympathy from private Indonesian business entrepreneurs who have found their sphere of operations increasingly circumscribed by state controls and by the dominant position of government corporations. Such an approach could be joined with an appeal for greater partisan political freedom and the restoration of political liberties (e.g. demands for a national election). This tactic would also have the advantage of delineating the military opposition in the bourgeois ranks more clearly, in view of the managerial power exercised by army officers in many state business and other enterprises and the army's influence in political life.

There will probably always be important segments of the national bourgeoisie which the PKI will be unable to win over. For example, in the more consciously Islamic community of traders and professionals allied with such parties as Masjumi (now dissolved) and Nahdatul Ulama the PKI continues to be detested on religious and ideological grounds,[7] and political developments in Indonesia since independence indicate that this Islamic self-awareness has increasingly become a basis of cultural and political identification for important groups in Indonesian society.

From this point of view, and also considering its anti-Communist implications, it might be said that the Islamization of Indonesian society is still in process, as Drewes has emphasized.[8] But this process, with its extraordinary mixture of modern-secular and orthodox dogmatic aspects, is by no means a uniform affair, and it embodies elements which are even potentially useful to the furtherance of a climate of opinion in which Communism can grow in the future. For along with a deepening of Islamic awareness, especially in the countryside in recent decades, has gone a steadily advancing secularization, and certainly in Javanese rural society new influences along non-Islamic channels are evident.[9] Islamic modernism itself, with its internationalism, its stress on education, on modern science and individual emancipation, and its adhesion to a program of moderate socialistic reforms, contributes to this advancing secularization in no small measure.

In this frame of reference the PKI's program fits very well. It is precisely the party's broad identification with national and collectivist principles and aspirations which has allowed it to become such a formidable force on the Indonesian scene and will probably allow it to remain so in future.[10] For the 'common ground' between the PKI and other groups is wide: it includes opposition to 'colonialism', support of national private entrepreneurial interests along with state control over major branches of the production process, approval of a broad spectrum of social reform (in land tenure, public services, and living conditions of workers) and cultivation of the national, if not nativistic, cultural traditions in language and the arts. Sukarno's mystique of 'socio-democracy',[11] with its anti-capitalistic orientation, could not be improved upon as a symbol of identification for the PKI at this stage of its strategy; so long as this mystique remains, and it is likely that it will for some time and even outlive its formulator, the PKI can always simultaneously find a niche in the official national ideology and in Communist theory. The rest is a matter of tactics.

For this reason too, the party has been able to find a vocabulary that can arouse mass sympathy if not open support. A student of recent socio-economic changes in the Jogjakarta area (long one of the more tradition-bound regions in the nation and the heartland of ancient Javanese cultural life) has noted the susceptibility of the common man to the vocabulary of 'socio-democracy' which the PKI employs so well: 'As an old man . . . put it to me: "In my days there were only *kulis* in the village, but now we have the *rakjat!*" The word *kulis* refers to the landholders burdened with many duties without definite rights, while the word *rakjat* denotes the people with the connotation of the sovereignty of the state being in their hands'.[12] The same student also indicates how well the PKI has been able to blend the symbolism of old and new. During the 1955 national elections in the Jogjakarta area the PKI organized village festivals centering around traditional *ketoprak* theatrical performances, in which popular stories were enacted but were interspersed with Communist slogans; the slogans were long remembered because of the attractive plays and performances.[13] By its 'common ground' ideological approach, of which the 'united front' is but the tactic, the party—in the midst of social frustration and economic retrogression and notwithstanding the recent limits on its operations—has a good chance of becoming an organizational crystallization of the popular, unfulfilled dreams aroused by the national revolution.

This chance is considerably improved because of certain other sociological aspects of the current political and ideological scene in Indonesia. Of these the party's tactical identity with what has been called elsewhere Indonesia's 'vertical' social development, is perhaps the most important.[14] With the ossification and long-term stagnation of the Indonesian economy only too evident in the past few years—factors which bear importantly on new forms of social stratification in the country—the dynamics of status change and class development are presently operating through and within new 'functional' groupings in Indonesian society, the product of the effects of a steady politicalization of national Indonesian life, especially evident since the Japanese occupation and the revolution. These 'functional' groups (peasant cooperatives, trade unions, veterans' organizations, youth groups, women's clubs, artists and writers' guilds, and so on) generally have their own channels of advancement, their own economic resources and their own considerable sphere of political influence. To some extent all these groups could be characterized as labor-absorbing devices, facilitating a functional and 'vertical' expansion of society, now that its 'horizontal' and traditional limits have been reached. It is advantageous today, to a degree undreamed of ten or twenty years ago, to be a kind of semi-professional 'veteran' or 'youth' or 'modern woman' or artist-intellectual in Indonesia and thus achieve comparative affluence and influence through the bureaucratization of politics and society.

No party in Indonesia has surpassed the PKI in expertly utilizing the dynamics of this vertical and functional status-revolution to win followers. The party offers a kind of career not just through its own organization, but perhaps even more through its fronts, and there is an economic necessity in front expansion that should not be overlooked. More than other parties (like the PNI) the PKI has taken special pains to win adherents among the young (witness the special position accorded the *Pemuda Rakjat* in the party constitution), and this has its *quid pro quo* aspect, especially in a land where the problem of the educated unemployed is becoming acute. It is not just a question of obtaining a salary or other emoluments from the party once one has attained a position of some significance in its bureaucracy; for such renumeration, though heavily shrouded in secrecy, is generally said to be rather small and generally reserved for higher echelon positions. Rather it is the status and power in an organization such as the PKI which can be translated into obtaining a well-paying position outside the organization, offered by supervisors or employers interested in labor peace, in obtaining favors at government bureaus, or in taking out insurance against unforeseen future events when having a well-treated PKI activist on the payroll might have great advantages.[15] The 'vertical' revolution and the bureaucratization of society, abetted by the monolithic functions of 'guided democracy', thus create their own new reciprocity patterns in which any center of power can learn to bargain effectively.

It will be seen that these developments, like the 'common ground' ideological approach mentioned above, fit in well with the Marxist-Leninist theory of united front tactics. The front idea is, so to speak, ready-made for Indonesia, in view of the structure of that country's power relationships. Another illustration of this is the *aliran* pattern. By an *aliran* ('current') is meant a political party surrounded by its satellite functional organizations, e.g. trade union federations, youth and women's groups, and so on. Frequently the term *aliran* designates the satellite organizations alone. Using the term in the latter sense for the moment, it has already been noted earlier (pp. 220–221) that all major parties and some smaller ones too have their *aliran*. To the extent that competitive *aliran* exist in major functional fields the PKI's political and tactical task may be rendered more difficult. But from a sociological point of view this basic *aliran* tendency in Indonesian life, already discernible at the end of the colonial era, and augmented by the Japanese occupation and the Indonesian revolution, is a continuing asset to the party since it conforms so closely to the structure of action as prescribed in Communist theory.

The course of national Indonesian politics has always been difficult to predict and it would be hazardous indeed to assume that the party's current ascendancy in the context of the anti-Malaysia campaign is likely to persist. But the PKI, by now, has become seasoned in 'reality testing', the ceaseless process of delineating what is and what is not currently possible in partisan political expression and activity. There are rarely sharp and dramatic reversals in such a process, and few sudden and spectacular victories. Rather the strategic emphasis is upon slow and steady advances and the progressive undermining of the opposition. In Indonesia the party's strategy in this regard is aided by yet another cultural tradition that will stand it in good stead, namely the disinclination of those participating in the indigenous pattern of status and power-seeking to push conflicts to a head, to pit extreme against extreme, and to abandon ever an appeal to a common ground of mutual interests, however fictional such a common ground may eventually turn out to be. This tradition of compromise is deeply embedded in ancient indigenous dynamics of power, especially in Java, and it has been demonstrated also in the Indonesian bureaucracy.[16] There is, under such circumstances, a kind of assumption of authority which is accepted on a reciprocal basis by others, so long, however, as this assumption of authority is not too greatly pressed in practice. A variety of an operational stand-off, or even a deadlock, in the structure of political power relationships thus ensues, in which charismatic symbols of unity (e.g. *Manipol* or NASAKOM) mask, and are frequently used effectively, to soften any total factional struggle for power. The PKI has used such symbols of unity with considerable skill in countering the criticism of its enemies and in insisting that since it accepts these symbols (thereby indicating in principle that it is willing to play the game according to the rules of total conflict avoidance), it cannot be banished or ignored in the making of the major decisions of national life. But this is not a one-way adaptation process, for the party also seeks to transform these symbols, sometimes quite subtly, in terms of its own ideological and tactical objectives; it 'radicalizes' the approved state ideology, pressing it, with its interpretations, into the directions which it wishes the nation to travel.

The significance of this 'radicalization' process seems sometimes to be obscured by paradoxical policy decisions about the party or by what seem to be efforts to contain its growth. In the cabinet reshuffle of August 27, 1964, for example, PKI second deputy chairman Njoto was appointed a minister seconded to the cabinet presidium. This was interpreted as a major victory for the party. Yet the appointment came in the midst of a barrage of criticism of the PKI, particularly in connection with the unrest and the 'arbitrary action' campaign instigated by its peasants' front, the BTI, in preceding months (cf. again p. 323, note 69), and also within the context of a minor press war by various papers and journals which questioned the PKI's adhesion to Pantjasila and *Manipol*. The party's campaign against American films being shown in Indonesian motion picture theatres also was arousing growing popular resentment. On September 15, 1964, moreover, Sukarno appointed a number of new 'territorial executive administrators' under the Supreme Operational Command (KOTI) which reports directly to Sukarno himself, and this move also was widely interpreted as a measure to curb widening Communist influence in the provinces. Nevertheless at that very time too the party's influence in facilitating or blocking appointments to key civil service and territorial military posts had become increasingly obvious, while Sukarno's militant, Peking-line, address sharply criticizing the values of 'peaceful co-existence' in Cairo, at the conference of non-aligned nations, on October 6, 1964, can hardly be interpreted as other than as an endorsement of the party's own world view. It is the long, but generally steadily ascending curve that gives the more accurate picture of the party's development since the advent of the *Sajap Leninis* in it.

The PKI, despite its difficulties, has moreover always retained an élan which is sustained by the general advance of Communism in our time, whatever the internal dissensions within the Communist world at present. It is this élan to which the equally ancient charismatic longings in Indonesian society (now intensified by the doctrines of revolutionary nationalism) continue to respond. It is the PKI which by virtue of its programmatic formulations perhaps most completely articulates the popular Indonesian mystique that the present era is one of tribulation, but that a glorious future lies ahead. The condition of charismatic and volitional omnipotence—a product alike of the pre-revolutionary era and of the revolution, and expressed by the whole tenor of national life in these first years of independence—may well lift the party into a dominant place in Indonesia in the near future.

NOTES

CHAPTER I

[1] On the pattern of these social changes see W. F. Wertheim, *Indonesian Society in Transition* (The Hague, Bandung, 1959, second edition), and J. M. van der Kroef, *Indonesia in the Modern World* (Bandung, 1954–1956), 2 vols.

[2] Cf. Harold R. Isaacs, *The Tragedy of the Chinese Revolution* (London, 1938), p. 61.

[3] Shortly after its founding party leaders substituted 'Indonesia' for 'India' (which had been a Malaicized version of the Dutch *Indië*, the common designation of the East Indies), while primarily since 1945 the word *Partai* (party) was substituted for the original *Perserikatan* (association). 'Kommunist' made way for the Indonesian *Komunis*.

[4] Virginia Thompson and Richard Adloff, *The Left Wing in Southeast Asia* (New York, 1950), pp. 269, 274, and 283; Robert van Niel, *The Emergence of the Modern Indonesian Elite* (The Hague, Bandung, 1960), p. 124; and Ruth Thomas McVey, *The Comintern and the Rise of Indonesian Communism* (Ph.D. Thesis, Cornell University, Ithaca, N.Y., 1961; University Microfilms, Ann Arbor, Mich.), pp. 380–381, notes 715 and 716. Alimin was adopted as foster son by Dr. G. A. J. Hazeu, the Dutch colonial government's Native Affairs Adviser, while Muso, a friend of Alimin's also was a protégé of Hazeu. Both Muso and Alimin attended secondary schools and were fluent in Dutch and English.

[5] D. M. G. Koch, *Batig Slot. Figuren Uit Het Oude Indië* (Amsterdam, 1960), p. 113. Literally Koch described Baars as '*een schrijftafelmarxist*' (a desk Marxist).

[6] *Ibid.*, p. 114.

[7] D. N. Aidit, 'Lahirnja PKI dan Perkembangannja', p. 409, in *D. N. Aidit. Pilihan Tulisan* (Djakarta, 1959), vol. 1.

[8] For the effect which education had and still has on the Indonesians in terms of heightening status consciousness, aversion to manual labor and aristocratic aspirations, see by J. M. van der Kroef, 'The Cult of the Doctor: An Indonesian Variant', *Journal of Educational Sociology*, vol. 32 (1959), pp. 381–391; and 'The Educated Unemployed in Southeast Asia', *The Journal of Higher Education*, vol. 4 (1960), pp. 177–184.

[9] W. M. F. Mansvelt, 'Onderwijs en Communisme', *Koloniale Studiën*, vol. 12 (1928), pp. 203–225.

[10] Nearly 40 years later the aversion apparently still exists; as the report of the PKI Central Committtee put it in 1959: 'Party cadres in general do not yet properly understand the agrarian relationships. There are still many Party functionaries who evade work in the countryside.' *Material for the Sixth National Congress of the Communist Party of Indonesia* (Djakarta, 1959), p. 82.

[11] J. Th. Petrus Blumberger, *De Communistische Beweging in Nederlandsch-Indië* (Haarlem, 1935, second edition), p. 18.

[12] *De Volkswelvaart op Java en Madoera. Eindverhandeling van't Onderzoek naar de Mindere Welvaart der Inlandsche Bevolking*, no. Xa, vol. 1 (Batavia, 1914), pp. 467, 476, 480, 495, 513, 528–530, 538, 548.

[13] J. M. van der Kroef, 'Indonesia: Centrifugal Economies', pp. 197–220 in James Wiggins and Helmut Schoeck, eds., *Foreign Aid Re-examined. A Critical Appraisal* (Washington D.C., 1958).

[14] *De Volkswelvaart op Java en Madoera, op. cit.*, p. 314.

[15] Cited from S. J. Rutgers, *Indonesië. Het Koloniale Systeem in de Periode tussen de Eerste en de Tweede Wereldoorlog* (Amsterdam, 1947), p. 112.

[16] J. Gerritzen, *De Welvaart van Indië. Voordrachten over Indische Economie gehouden te Leiden* (Haarlem, 1926), p. 147.

[17] Address of R. A. A. Djajadiningrat in the *Volksraad*, June 18, 1924, cited in Mohammad Hatta, *Verspreide Geschriften* (Djakarta, Amsterdam, 1952), p. 229.

[18] J. W. Meijer Ranneft en W. Huender, *Onderzoek naar den Belastingdruk op de Inlandsche Bevolking* (Weltevreden, 1926); and E. P. Wellenstein, 'Het Rapport Meijer Ranneft-Huender nopens den Belastingdruk op de Inheemsche Bevolking van Java en Madoera', *De Economist*, vol. 75 (1926), p. 261.

[19] Wellenstein, *op. cit.*, pp. 252, 275.

[20] *Verslag van den Economischen Toestand der Inlandsche Bevolking 1924* (Weltevreden, 1926), vol. 1. pp. 106–109.

[21] *Ibid.*, vol. 1, pp. 229, 259–266, 364.

[22] A good survey of the extent and character of Pan-Islamic action in Indonesia around the turn of the century is to be found in E. Gobée and C. Adriaanse, eds., *Ambtelijke Adviezen van C. Snouck Hurgronje* (The Hague, 1959), vol. 2, pp. 1615–1716.

[23] *Mededelingen Omtrent Enkele Onderwerpen van Algemeen Belang* (Batavia, 1919), p. 2; *ibid*, 1920, p. 5. Throughout the early nineteen-twenties PKI leaders seemed uncertain about the party's position toward the nationalist movement and the bourgeois-capitalist elements in it. Around 1919 and 1920 PKI leaders seemed generally agreed that nationalism could only have a limited appeal, because so much of the 'middle class' in Indonesia was composed of Dutch, Eurasians, Chinese, and so on. This meant, it was argued in some PKI circles, that the Indonesian revolutionary movement could combine the 'national liberation' and 'proletarian' stages of its struggle and proceed at once with the creation of a Socialist state (See Ruth Thomas McVey, *The Comintern and the Rise of Indonesian Communism*, *op. cit.*, pp. 106–107). This position, which expressed itself in an ambivalent attitude toward cooperation with the nationalist movement, was sharply criticized by those with a firmer foundation in Leninism and who saw 'adventurism' and 'Left Wing deviationism' in it. Tan Malaka also warned against a course that bypassed support of non-proletarian elements, urging the need for broadly based mass action in a 'united front' style movement that would include a phased accommodation of nationalist and other, non-Communist revolutionary interests.

[24] *Het Vrije Woord*, February 5, 1921, cited by Petrus Blumberger, *De Communistische Beweging*, *op. cit.*, p. 18.

[25] Petrus Blumberger, *De Communistische Beweging*, *op. cit.*, p. 23.

[26] *Ibid.*, pp. 28–32.

[27] *Ibid.*, pp. 24–37; J. Th. Petrus Blumberger, *De Nationalistische Beweging in Nederlandsch-Indië* (Haarlem, 1931), pp. 19–37; 55–89, 184–196. The 1924 PKI action program (see Ruth Thomas McVey, *The Comintern and the Rise of Indonesian Communism*, *op. cit.*, pp. 388–389, note 737), included demands for the establishment of soviets (from village and factory soviets to province, island and central soviets), freedom of speech, political action, and labor strike activity, the institution of the 8-hour working day and the abolition of the contract coolie labor system, the establishment of the graduated income tax and of universal free education until the age of 17, prohibition of receipt of interest and abolition of 'private estates', replacement of the armed forces by a people's militia, improvement of public health, housing and distribution of food, and so on.

[28] Cf. Iskandar Tedjasukmana, *The Political Character of the Indonesian Trade Union Movement* (Ithaca, N.Y., Modern Indonesia Project Monograph Series, Cornell University, 1959).

[29] J. Th. Petrus Blumberger, 'Vakbeweging (Inlandsche)', *Encyclopaedie van Nederlandsch-Indië* (The Hague, 1917–1935), vol. 7; p. 430.

[30] *Mededeelingen Omtrent Enkele Onderwerpen van Algemeen Belang*, 1921, pp. 12–15; see also Ph. Levert, *Inheemsche Arbeid in de Java-Suikerindustrie* (Diss. Wageningen, 1934), pp. 212–215, 226–259, who minimizes Communist influence and is on the whole more sympathetic to the wage policy of the sugar companies.

[31] Erich H. Jacoby, *Agrarian Unrest in Southeast Asia* (New York, 1949), pp. 65–61 and G. H. van der Kolff, 'An Economic Case Study: Sugar and Welfare in Java', pp. 188–206 in Ph. Ruopp, ed., *Approaches to Community Development* (The Hague, Bandung, 1953).

[32] *Indonesian Sociological Studies. Selected Writings of B. Schrieke. Part I* (The Hague, Bandung, 1955), p. 88, ('The Causes and Effects of Communism on the West Coast of Sumatra').

³³ Rutgers, *op. cit.* p. 159.

³⁴ *De Gang der Communistische Beweging ter Sumatra's Westkust. Deel 1 (Politiek Gedeelte). Rapport van de Commissie van Onderzoek ingesteld bij het Gouvernements Besluit van 13 Februari 1927*, no. 1a (Weltevreden, 1928), translated in, and here cited from, H. J. Benda and R. T. McVey, eds., *The Communist Uprisings of 1926–1927 in Indonesia: Key Documents* (Southeast Asia Program, Cornell University, Ithaca, N.Y., 1960), pp. 138–139. In a significant sense the Indonesian Communist experience paralleled that of the early Chinese Communists. Despite Comintern emphasis on the role of the peasantry, 'the prevailing interpretation of Marxism-Leninism in the young Chinese Communist Party tended to emphasize the role of urban workers and to de-emphasize the role of rural peasants'. (Shinkichi Eto, 'Hailu-feng—The First Chinese Soviet Government', *The China Quarterly*, October–December, 1961, p. 175). The same lack of appreciation of the peasants' role is a conspicuous feature of the early Indonesian Communists.

³⁵ Petrus Blumberger, *De Communistische Beweging, op. cit.*, pp. 60, 61, 68–69.

³⁶ On the revolt see *Inprecorr.*, November 25, 1926, p. 1391, and December 16, 1926, p. 1498.

³⁷ Cf. Lembaga Sedjarah PKI, *Pemberontakan Nasional Pertama di Indonesia (1926)*, (Djakarta, 1961), esp. pp. 102–127. This is an analysis of the 1926 uprising by the PKI's 'Historical Institute'. See also D. N. Aidit, 'Peladjaran dari Sedjarah PKI', *Bintang Merah*, vol. 16 (1960), p. 171. In its analysis of the rebellion (see Petrus Blumberger, *De Communistische Beweging in Nederlandsch-Indie, op. cit.*, pp. 145–148), the Comintern's executive essentially stressed the same points as does the PKI today.

³⁸ *Rapport van de Commissie voor het Onderzoek naar de zich in the maand November 1926 in verscheidene gedeelten van de Residentie Bantam voorgedaan hebbende Ongeregeldheden, ingesteld bij Gouvernementsbesluit van 26 Januari, no. X* (Weltevreden, 1926), cited from Benda and McVey, eds., *op. cit.*, esp. pp. 40–42.

³⁹ See J. M. van der Kroef, 'Javanese Messianic Expectations: Their Origin and Cultural Context', *Comparative Studies in Society and History*, vol. 1 (1959), pp. 299–323.

⁴⁰ Sjahrazad, *Indonesische Overpeinzingen* (Amsterdam, 1945), p. 67.

⁴¹ Bernard H. M. Vlekke, *Nusantara. A History of Indonesia* (2nd ed., Chicago, The Hague, Bandung, 1960), p. 377, describes prevailing Dutch sentiment in Indonesia after the rebellion of 1926–1927 as follows: 'The large majority of the Indonesians was loyal, it was believed, and if the "subversive elements" were weeded out, peace and order would be secure'.

⁴² Even critics of Multatuli's conduct in Lebak, Bantam, agree on the poverty and undeveloped condition of the area. See e.g. the essay 'De Zaak van Lebak' in R. Nieuwenhuys, *Tussen Twee Vaderlanden* (Amsterdam, 1959), pp. 184–185. Multatuli himself refers to Lebak's poverty in his celebrated 'Speech to the Chiefs of Lebak' and noted that 'the population of Bantam was anciently rebellious and restless' (E. Du Perron, *De Man van Lebak. Anekdoten en Dokumenten Betreffende Multatuli;* Verzameld werk van E. Du Perron, Amsterdam, Antwerp, n.d., p. 317). There is a parallel in this respect between the 1926 Bantam revolt and the Tjilegon rebellion in Bantam in July 1888. The Tjilegon affair was undoubtedly caused by the millenarian propaganda of a few Muslim clerics and agitators, but at the same time, as a government official reported after the insurrection, the population had legitimate reasons to complain, especially over labor and money taxes. J. E. B. Kielstra, 'De Wording en het Verloop van de Tjilegonsche Troebelen in Juli, 1888', *Indische Gids*, 1891, pp. 1137–1206, esp. 1200. And as in the case of the 1888 rebellion, the 1926 Communist insurrection was aided by the inflammatory teachings of Muslim clerics. Cf. M. W. F. Treub, *Het Gist in Indië* (Haarlem, 1927), pp. 11, 13.

⁴³ See e.g. R. A. van Sandick, *Leed en Lief in Bantam* (1892).

⁴⁴ W. F. Wertheim, 'Kijkje in Lebak na Honderd Jaar', *De Nieuwe Stem*, vol. 15 (June–July, 1960), no. 6–7, p. 472.

⁴⁵ The government's Bantam report is not exactly a model of precision and is replete with such generalities as: 'In Bantam the number of well-to-do people is in relation to the size of the population greater than elsewhere', and considers that the rebellion also broke out 'in what were economically the most prosperous areas and many of

the rebels could by no means be called poor'. Yet where the report is more specific, e.g., in the section on the tax burden, the report tends to confirm the suspicion that economic problems were certainly basic to popular grievances. Under the circumstances one becomes skeptical of the flat assertion that in Lebak district 'where there is least prosperity and in some districts even poverty', the PKI 'failed to gain a hold on the population'. (Benda and McVey, *op. cit.*, pp. 21, 26, 42.)

[46] For an analysis of the West Sumatran insurrection, see *De Gang der Communistische Beweging ter Sumatra's Westkust. Rapport van de Commissie van Onderzoek ingesteld bij het Gouvernments besluit van 13 Februari 1927 no. 1a* (Weltevreden, 1928) 4 vols; H. Bouman, *Enige Beschouwingen over de Ontwikkeling van het Indonesisch, Nationalisme op Sumatra's Westkust* (Groningen, Batavia, 1949); Benda and McVey, *op. cit.*, pp. 97–177; *Indonesian Sociological Studies, Selected Writings of B. Schrieke*, *op. cit.*, pp. 85–166.

[47] Daan van der Zee, *De S.D.A.P. en Indonesië* (Amsterdam, 1929), pp. 95–96.

[48] Roestam Effendi, 'Op 1 Mei marcheert Digoel mee in de proletarische gelederen' *Links Front*, May, 1934, no. 4, pp. 5–7.

[49] Mohammad Hatta, *Verspreide Geschriften, op. cit.*, p. 522.

[50] Petrus Blumberger, *De Nationalistische Beweging in Nederlandsch-Indië, op. cit.*, pp. 190–191, 205.

[51] Petrus Blumberger, *De Communistische Beweging in Nederlandsch-Indië, op. cit.*, pp. 151–162.

[52] Rutgers, *op. cit.*, pp. 177–178.

[53] G. Gonggrijp, *Schets Ener Economische Geschiedenis van Nederlands-Indië* (3rd. ed., Haarlem, 1949), pp. 227 and 211–243.

[54] B. C. van Suchtelen, 'Parallellen (Hongi-Tochten-Cultuurstelsel-Bijzonder Uitvoerrecht op Rubber)', *Koloniaal Tijdschrift*, September 1938, pp. 575–584. See also L. Götzen, 'Volksinkomen en Belasting', *Koloniale Studiën*, vol. 17 (1933), p. 479, whose calculations show a more than 44 per cent increase in the native Indonesian's tax burden between 1926–1932.

[55] C. B. van der Leeden, *Het Aspect van Landbouwkolonisatie in het Bevolkingsprobleem van Java* (Diss., Leyden; The Hague, 1952), p. 91. According to the government publication *Statistical Abstract of the Netherlands Indies 1940* (Pocket Edition, Batavia, 1940, p. 36) the amount of land available per head of native population in Java between 1930 and 1939 remained stationary at less than 0.2 hectares.

[56] J. van Gelderen, *Voorlezingen over Tropisch-Koloniale Staathuishoudkunde* (Haarlem, 1927), p. 116.

[57] See the brochure of the Communist Party of the Netherlands, *Redt de Muiters der 'Zeven Provincien'* (Amsterdam, 1933). See also Jeanne S. Mintz, 'Marxism in Indonesia', pp. 334–335, note 74, in Frank N. Trager, ed., *Marxism in Southeast Asia* (Stanford, 1959).

[58] On Pari see J. M. Pluvier, *Overzicht van de Ontwikkeling der Nationalistische Beweging in Indonesië in de jaren 1930 tot 1942* (The Hague, Bandung, 1953), p. 162.

[59] D. N. Aidit, 'Lahirnja PKI dan Perkembangannja', *op. cit.*, p. 415.

[60] D. N. Aidit, 'Peladjaran dari Sedjarah PKI', *op. cit.*, p. 172.

[61] D. N. Aidit, 'Lahirnja PKI dan Perkembangannja', *op. cit.*, 416–417.

[62] *Ibid.*, p. 417. For a description of the Indonesian 'resistance' and 'underground' groups during the Japanese occupation, see Benedict R. O'G. Anderson, *Some Aspects of Indonesian Politics under the Japanese Occupation: 1944–1945* (Cornell University, Modern Indonesia Project, Ithaca, N.Y., 1961), pp. 48–51.

[63] In the early thirties Tan Malaka spent some time in Japan and participated in the Communist movement there. According to his own autobiography, he returned to Indonesia in June, 1942, and went to work as an administrator in a Japanese-operated mine in West Java. He kept out of sight during most of the occupation but the extent to which he collaborated with the Japanese is uncertain. For these and other valuable insights into the life and times of one of Indonesia's most important revolutionaries, see Tan Malaka, *Dari Pendjara ke Pendjara* (Djakarta, Djokjakarta,] n.d.) 2 vols. In 1944 the Japanese naval chief, Maeda, established in Djakarta an *Asrama Indonesia Merdeka* (Dormitory for Free Indonesia), headed by Wikana, an old PKI

NOTES

309

activist, which was to prepare students for the task of national leadership, in line with the Japanese promise of Indonesian independence in the future. A similar school was established in Surabaya. Leading nationalist figures like Mohammad Hatta and Sutan Sjahrir lectured at the schools. The reason why the Japanese established these schools, where international Communism was a major course of study, is not clear, although one likely explanation is that the Japanese wished in some way to infiltrate and influence the PKI underground. Muhammad Yusuf, the founder of the PKI after the end of the Japanese occupation, was a disciple of Maeda. For various interpretations of the *Asrama* see George McT. Kahin, *Nationalism and Revolution in Indonesia* (N.Y., 1952), pp. 115–118; and Benedict R. O'G. Anderson, *op. cit.*, pp. 50–51.

[64] *40 Tahun PKI* (Djakarta, 1960), translated as and here cited from *40 Years of the Communist Party of Indonesia* (U.S. Joint Publications Research Series, no. 8209, May, 1961,Washington, D.C.), pp. 22–23. The extent of these alleged Communist outbursts of resistance against the Japanese has not been determined, and the nature of Communist led anti-Japanese organizations should be examined with caution. It is clear that the Japanese were concerned to control various youths with suspected 'illegal' leanings and to that end, for example, formed the *Angkatan Muda* (Young Generation) organization, where they could keep an eye on them. See, e.g. Benedict R. O'G. Anderson, *op. cit.*, pp. 51–52.

[65] *40 Tahun PKI, op. cit.*, p. 23.

[66] D. N. Aidit, 'Lahirnja PKI dan Perkembangannja', *op. cit.*, p. 418.

[67] Henri J. Alers, *Om een Rode of Groene Merdeka. 10 Jaren Binnenlandse Politiek Indonesië 1943–1953* (s.l., 1956), pp. 103–126, 175–176. There is still no satisfactory account of Tan Malaka's scheme to seize power in the new Indonesian state that was to follow on the heels of the Japanese surrender. Some Indonesian leaders of the Japanese sponsored Marxist training schools (see note 63 *supra*), among them Subardjo, Wikana, Iwa Kusumasumantri, together with Tan Malaka, appear to have planned their own revolutionary Indonesian government, and the kidnapping of Sukarno and Hatta by Sukarni, Nalik, Wikana and others on August 16, 1954, has been seen as an attempt to clear the way for a seizure of power by Subardjo and Tan Malaka. But at the critical time Malaka failed to form a strong armed unit with which to march into Djakarta, whereupon Subardjo, Wikana, Iwa Kusumasumantri and other covert backers of Tan Malaka changed sides and supported Sukarno and Hatta.

[68] Alers, p. 178.

[69] G. W. Overdijkink, *Het Indonesische Probleem. Nieuwe Feiten* (Amsterdam, 1948) p. 137.

[70] Alers, *op. cit.*, pp. 177–183; Kahin, *op. cit.*, pp. 210–212, 231–232, 259–277.

[71] Alers, *op. cit.*, pp. 187–194.

[72] Cf. Frank N. Trager, 'The Impact of Marxism', pp. 263–267, in Trager, ed., *Marxism in Southeast Asia, op. cit.* Whether Indonesian Communists at the Calcutta Conference were told to initiate an insurrection against the Indonesian government is not known for certain. Ruth T. McVey, *The Calcutta Conference and the Southeast Asian Uprisings* (Interim Report Series, Modern Indonesia Project, Cornell University, Ithaca, N.Y., 1958), p. 23, asserts that what the Caclutta Conference emphasized was all-out war against the Dutch. The subsequent stiffening of PKI policy did create growing antagonisms and thus made an outbreak of violence more likely.

[73] Alers, *op. cit.*, pp. 194–197. One aspect of the Madiun revolt, namely the alleged eruption in it of *abangan-santri* tensions in the Javanese countryside, may perhaps be dealt with here. Since pre-colonial days there has been a conflict between those Indonesians who take their Islamic beliefs as seriously as possible and who seek to live as orthodox Muslims (the *santri* element), and those who are laxer and who mix Islamic practice with ancient, animistic, and pre-Islamic tenets and practices (the *abangan* group). The tension between these two groups in Indonesian, and particularly Javanese, society and culture is not inconsiderable and was noted as early as the nineteenth century by various Dutch observers, while historically the conflict between them and the occasional violence to which it has given rise goes back even further. However, there seems to be a tendency among some American students of the Indonesian scene today to exaggerate the pattern of *abangan-santri* tensions in Indonesian life, and to ignore or unduly underemphasize syncretic elements and other antagonistic cleavages which either mitigate or obscure the rather simplistically drawn antithesis. During the

Madiun uprising PKI supporters and armed gangs unleashed a campaign of extraordinary violence and destruction against the *santri* element in the countryside around Madiun, killing Moslem teachers, pillaging schools and prayer houses, and this campaign has been interpreted as an aspect of *abang-santri* conflict. While the *abangan-santri* antithesis may have added its influence to this eruption, and while it is true that the PKI and its ideological position is closer to the *abangan* than to the *santri* sphere, the violent campaign of the Communist marauders in the Madiun affair has other factors behind it. There is, for one thing, the effect of the political conflict between Muslim groups and the radical left for hegemony in the Revolutionary Republic, a conflict probably deepened by *abangan-santri* religio-cultural tension but also reflecting a power struggle between élites and personalities and with ramifications in the armed forces, the auxiliaries and the various indisciplined gangs that constituted the revolutionary defense forces. Leadership clashes and personality conflict during the revolution were undoubtedly rationalized by *abangan* and *santri* appeals. For another, and perhaps most important, there is the psychological upheaval, i.e. the traumatic effects of the overthrow of the colonial system, the brutalizing consequences of the Japanese occupation and the turmoil of the revolution, creating grave disturbances in the personality organization of Indonesians (Cf. P. M. van Wulfften Palthe, *Psychological Aspects of the Indonesian Problem*, Leyden, 1949, and J. M. van der Kroef, *Indonesian Social Evolution. Some Psychological Considerations*, Amsterdam, 1958). The effect of this psychological disturbance was expressed in the *bersiap* (violent action) mentality evident all during the revolution, because encouraged by revolutionary tactics themselves, and it was especially evident after the Japanese occupation, when nameless horrors were perpetrated against whites, Chinese, Eurasians, and whomever seemed a likely target. The *santri* element, to the extent that it was the victim of the *bersiap* of Communist auxiliaries in the Madiun upheaval, was merely the convenient target of a violence engendered by serious trauma, experienced on a massive scale, in preceding years. Other targets could and were found in previous and in subsequent *bersiap* outbursts. The choice of the victim in such conditions of personality disorganization is often almost accidental, and lends itself to a high degree of rationalization in which the factor of availability usually predominates. To see the attack on the *santri* element in the Madiun uprising as an expression primarily of the *abangan-santri* antithesis is in any case a misleading over-simplification.

[74] This and the next paragraphs are based on *40 Tahun PKI*, *op. cit.*, pp. 25–32; Aidit, 'Lahirnja PKI dan Perkembangannja', *op. cit.*, pp. 418–429; and Aidit, 'Peladjaran dari Sedjarah PKI', *op. cit.*, pp. 172–173.

[75] Aidit, 'Lahirnja PKI dan Perkembangannja', *op. cit.*, p. 427.

[76] *Aidit Accuses Madiun Affair. D. N. Aidit's Defense Plea at the Trial in the Jakarta State Court* on February 24, 1955 (Djakarta, 1955?) pp. 16–28.

[77] See e.g. D. N. Aidit, 'The Success of the Sixth National Congress of the C.P.I. is a Mighty Victory for Democracy', pp. 10–11, in *C.P.I. Sixth National Congress*, Supplement to *Review of Indonesia*, September–October 1960.

[78] *Aidit Accuses Madiun Affair*, *op. cit.*, p. 26.

[79] *40 Tahun PKI*, *op. cit.*, p. 33.

[80] Aidit, 'Lahirnja PKI dan Perkembangannja', *op. cit.*, p. 429.

[81] Ruth T. McVey, *The Soviet View of the Indonesian Revolution* (Modern Indonesia Project, Southeast Asia Program, Cornell University, Ithaca, N.Y., 1957), pp. 71–83.

[82] Aidit, 'Lahirnja PKI dan Perkembangannja', *op. cit.*, p. 429.

CHAPTER II

[1] George McT. Kahin, *Some Aspects of Indonesian Politics and Nationalism* (Institute of Pacific Relations, Secretariat Paper no. 6, New York, 1950), p. 21.

[2] Aidit's views on the party's role in this period are developed in his essays 'Tentang Tan Ling Djie-isme' and 'Kembangkan Periode 1951', pp. 258–272 and pp. 274–277, respectively, in *D. N. Aidit. Pilihan Tulisan*, *op. cit.*, vol. 1. See also D. N. Aidit, 'Membolsjewikkan PKI', *Bintang Merah*, vol. 7 (1951), pp. 129–134, and M. H. Lukman, 'Timbulnja Faksi', *Bintang Merah*, vol. 7 (1951), pp. 18–19.

[3] *40 Tahun PKI (40 Years of the Communist Party of Indonesia)*, *op. cit.*, p. 35.

[4] Herbert Feith, *The Wilopo Cabinet, 1952–1953; A Turning Point in Post Revolutionary Indonesia* (Modern Indonesia Project, Cornell University, Ithaca, N.Y., 1958), pp. 37–38 note 33. According to Cheng Hsueh-chia, *Whither Indonesia? PKI and CCP* (Taipei, 1960), the PKI publication *Harian Rakjat* was restarted with the aid of funds collected by a left-wing Chinese member of the Indonesian parliament, Siauw Giok Tian, 'from the overseas Chinese who were sympathizers of the Peiping regime'.

[5] D. N. Aidit, 'Pembangunan Organisasi Penting, Tapi Lebih Penting Lagi Pembangunan Ideologi!', *Bintang Merah*, vol. 15 (1959), p. 234.

[6] Cf. *Program PKI Untuk Pemerintah Koalisi Nasional* (Djakarta, n.d.).

[7] *Bintang Merah*, May 1, 1951.

[8] D. N. Aidit, 'Lahirnja PKI dan Perkembangannja', *op. cit.*, p. 430.

[9] D. N. Aidit, 'Mengatasi Kelemahan Kita', pp. 6–40 in *D. N. Aidit. Pilihan Tulisan*, *op. cit.*, vol. 1.

[10] D. N. Aidit, *The Road to People's Democracy for Indonesia (General Report on the Political and Organizational Situation, delivered at the Fifth National Congress of the Communist Party of Indonesia, March, 1954)*, (Djakarta, 1955), p. 41.

[11] *Ibid.*, pp. 41–42.

[12] Some of Aidit's ideas in this period are reflected in his essays 'Menumpuh Djalan Rakjat' (originally delivered in May, 1952 commemorating the PKI's 32nd anniversary), 'Menudju Indonesia Baru' (originally delivered in May, 1953 on the occasion of the party's 33rd anniversary) and 'Djalan ke Demokrasi Rakjat Bagi Indonesia' (Aidit's report to the party's Fifth National Congress in March, 1954), respectively pp. 41–64, 92–124, and 207–257 in *D. N. Aidit. Pilihan Tulisan*, *op. cit.*, vol. 1. The last essay differs in some respects from the English version, *The Road To People's Democracy for Indonesia*, *op. cit.*, which has been used in these pages. See also M. H. Lukman, 'Menudju Front Persatuan', *Bintang Merah*, vol. 7 (1951), pp. 57–59.

[13] On *marhaenism* see S. Mangunsarkoro, *Sosialisme, Marhaenisme dan Komunisme* (Djokjakarta, 1955), and *Politik Marhaenis* (Djokjakarta 1952). See also 'Marhaenisme', p. 27 in *Kepartaian dan Parlementaria Indonesia* (Djakarta, 1954).

[14] Harry Goldberg, *Gerakan Buruh di Indonesia* (Djakarta, 1952), pp. 15, 19. Goldberg was in Indonesia at the time as representative of the Free Trade Union Committee of the American Federation of Labor. It should be noted that SARBUPRI though affiliated with SOBSI is virtually autonomous in its operations.

[15] Iskandar Tedjasukmana, *The Political Character of the Indonesian Trade Union Movement*, *op. cit.*, p. 59.

[16] On the fall of the Sukiman cabinet see J. M. van der Kroef, *Indonesia in the Modern World*, *op. cit.*, vol. 2, pp. 359–360.

[17] Feith, *The Wilopo Cabinet, 1952–1953; A Turning Point in Post Revolutionary Indonesia*, *op. cit.*, p. 89.

[18] See Hans O. Schmitt, *Some Monetary and Fiscal Consequences of Social Conflict in Indonesia 1950–1958* (Unpublished Ph.D. dissertation, University of California, 1959), esp. p. 17 and passim. On the politics of economic development during this period see also John C. Sutter, *Indonesianisasi: Politics in a Changing Economy 1940–1955* (Data Paper no. 36, Southeast Asia Program, Cornell University, Ithaca, N.Y., 1959), vol. 4, pp. 1106–1230. On the role of the importers' group, see especially Nan Grindle Amstutz, *Development of Indigenous Importers in Indonesia 1950–1955* (Unpublished Ph.D. Thesis, Fletcher School of Law and Diplomacy, 1958).

[19] Bruce Glassburner, 'Problems of Economic Policy in Indonesia 1950–1957', *Ekonomi dan Keuangan Indonesia*, vol. 13 (1960), p. 308.

[20] Sutter, *Indonesianisasi*, *op. cit.*, vol. 4, pp. 1200–1202.

[21] *Kewadjiban Front Persatuan Buruh* (CC, PKI, Djakarta, 1952), esp. pp. 15–16 and passim.

[22] D. N. Aidit, 'Menudju Indonesia Baru', pp. 92–124 in *D. N. Aidit Pilihan Tulisan*, *op. cit.*, vol. 1, and Aidit's *The Road to People's Democracy for Indonesia*, *op. cit.*, pp. 48–49.

[23] Feith, *The Wilopo Cabinet*, *op. cit.*, pp. 50–52, pp. 94–96.

[24] Sukarno, *Capitalism Creates Poverty* (Djakarta, Ministry of Information, 1958).

[25] Mao Tse-tung, *The Question of Independence within the United Front* (Peking, Foreign Languages Press, 1960), p. 4.

[26] Aidit, *The Road to People's Democracy for Indonesia, op. cit.*, p. 49.

[27] D. N. Aidit, 'Benarkah Front Persatuan Nasional "taktik Moskow"?', *Pembela*, August, 17, 1952.

[28] Aidit, 'Menumpuh Djalan Rakjat', esp. pp. 53–64, in *D. N. Aidit. Pilihan Tulisan*, vol. 1.

[29] In his address on October 19, 1951, in parliament, the acting head of the PKI delegation in the provisional Indonesian parliament, S. Utarjo, alluded to the dangers of this tactic of 'anti-Communism' by drawing on the history of the application of the Smith Act in the U.S. See 'Tentang Razzia jang bertentangan dengan Hukum dan Keadilan', *Bintang Merah*, vol. 7 (1951), no. 14–15 (October-November), pp. 1–8.

[30] On Aidit's views of the fall of the Wilopo cabinet and its aftermath see *D. N. Aidit, Pilihan Tulisan, op. cit.*, vol. 1, pp. 141–156. On June 26, 1953, in the middle of the cabinet crisis, some 3,000 railroad workers staged a demonstration in Djakarta. The demonstration was ostensibly designed to protest the depradations of the Darul Islam but was really directed against the Masjumi, some of whose members were suspected of being in league with the *Darul Islam*. The PNI and the PKI were generally regarded as having been the organizers of the demonstration which was supposed to embarrass the Masjumi and inflame public opinion so that Masjumi would be kept out of the next cabinet.

[31] *Nieuwsgier* (Djakarta), November 2, 1953.

[32] D. N. Aidit, 'Persatuan Nasional dan Kewaspadaan Nasional', *Bintang Merah*, vol. 9 (1953), pp. 366–370.

[33] *Nieuwsgier*, September 29, 1953.

[34] *Ibid.*, January 19, 1955.

[35] *Java Bode*, (Djakarta), April 29, 1955.

[36] *Ibid.*, January 17, 1955.

[37] *Nieuwsgier*, December 31, 1954.

[38] *Java Bode*, April 17, 1954.

[39] *Nieuwsgier*, June 9, 1954.

[40] See J. M. van der Kroef, 'Indonesia's Economic Difficulties', *Far Eastern Survey*, February, 1955, pp. 17–24.

[41] *Java Bode*, April 29, 1954.

[42] *Nieuwsgier*, October 23, 1954. A few NU leaders disagreed with this new 'soft' policy toward the PKI, and continued to call for the outlawing of the Communists.

[43] Cf. the address of the PKI deputy (and Muslim cleric) K. H. Achmad Dasuki Siradj in the now defunct Constituent Assembly in *Tentang Dasar Negara Republik Indonesia dalam Konstituante* (s.a.e.l., 1959?), vol. 2, pp. 326–336.

[44] *Nieuwsgier*, January 4, and 19, 1955. Repeal of emergency law No. 16/1951 had been a standard demand of Communist and other radical labor organizations since promulgation of the law and was particularly voiced as a matter of course during cabinet crises or changes of government.

[45] *40 Tahun PKI, op. cit.*, p. 41. Although he was removed from the Central Committee and subsequently saw his policies officially condemned by the Fifth Party Congress in March, 1954, Tan Ling Djie remained in sufficiently good standing to be one of the PKI's candidates in the national elections for the Constituent Assembly in December, 1955. In contrast Alimin's conflict with the party leadership was to deepen. All during 1955 Alimin did not hide his criticism of Aidit's policies and on March 24, 1956, Alimin denounced Aidit and the entire PKI policy since 1950 in a letter to the Central Committee. In this and other statements he called Aidit 'dishonest' and 'bombastic', branded the PKI as 'an ordinary bourgeois party' and as having followed a rightist 'class collaboration' policy especially in its alliance with the PNI, and declared that only his 'great age' had prevented him from making himself available for executive leadership at the time of the Fifth Party Congress. Alimin's criticism came at a particularly vulnerable time for the party since the PKI, despite considerable pressure, had failed in its attempt to be

included in the just formed second cabinet of Ali Sastroamidjojo. By implication Alimin attacked the whole 'national coalition' policy on which the party had decided to run in the elections of 1955. The PKI's Central Committee formally censured Alimin, and Aidit stated that age had never been a criterion for the selection of PKI leaders. Alimin's dissent from the party, according to Aidit, was moreover, a 'highly subjective' matter. Aidit also took occasion to point out that Alimin had rejected the Pantjasila (Indonesia's official national philosophy devised by Sukarno and comprising acceptance of 5 principles, viz., belief in God, nationalism, democracy, social justice and humanism) whereas, according to Aidit, the PKI could in fact accept Pantjasila (in line with the party's policy of identifying itself as closely as possible with national symbols), be it with some modifications, such as inclusion of constitutional guarantees of freedom of belief. (See *Harian Rakjat*, July 4, 1956 and *Java Bode*, July 7, 1956). Shortly thereafter Alimin left the PKI declaring that he remained 'a Communist at heart'.

[46] On the work of the Fifth National Congress see D. N. Aidit, 'Kongres Nasional Ke-V Partai Komunis Indonesia', pp. 279–292 in *D. N. Aidit, Pilihan Tulisan, op. cit.*, vol. 1.

[47] For these and other provisions of the program cited below see *Draft Programme of the Communist Party of Indonesia*. Adopted at the Fifth National Congress and prepared by the Plenum of the Central Committee of the Communist Party of Indonesia, October, 1953 (Agitprop Department of the Communist Party of Indonesia, Djakarta, s.a., 1954?)

[48] Aidit, *The Road to People's Democracy for Indonesia, op. cit.*, p. 48. Italics in original.

[49] *Nieuwsgier*, September 28, 1954.

[50] Njoto, 'Beladjar dari buku Lenin tentang Komunisme "sajap-kiri",' *Bintang Merah*, vol. 10 (1954), and 'Teori Leninis tentang masaalah kolonial', *Bintang Merah*, vol. 10 (1954), pp. 360–366.

[51] Cf. *Bintang Merah*, vol. 11 (April 1955), no. 4, which is entirely devoted to the Asian-African Conference.

[52] *Java Bode*, January 25, 1955.

[53] On this army crisis see J. M. van der Kroef, 'The Place of the Army in Indonesian Politics', *Eastern World*, January 1957, pp. 13–18.

[54] *Java Bode*, July 27, 1955.

[55] *40 Tahun PKI, op. cit.*, pp. 45–46.

[56] D. N. Aidit, 'Untuk Kemenangan Front Nasional Dalam Pemilihan Umum', esp. pp. 448–453 in *D. N. Aidit. Pilihan Tulisan, op. cit.*, vol. 1.

[57] *Java Bode*, November 2, 1955. Campaign donations to the party in East Java alone amounted to nearly half a million Rupiah according to a Communist spokesman in the Indonesian parliament.

[58] Herbert Feith, *The Indonesian Elections of 1955* (Modern Indonesia Project, Cornell University, Ithaca, N.Y., 1957), pp. 22–23.

[59] A. van Marle, 'The First Indonesian Parliamentary Elections', *Indonesië*, vol. 9 (1956), pp. 257–263.

[60] For Aidit's views on PKI strength see his 'Pertahankan Republik Proklamasi 1945', esp. pp. 472–473 in *D. N. Aidit. Pilihan Tulisan, op. cit.*, vol. 1.

[61] See in this connection J. M. van der Kroef, 'Indonesia's First National Election: A Sociological Analysis', *The American Journal of Economics and Sociology*, vol. 16 (1957), pp. 237–249, 407–420.

[62] The reason why the NU, PNI, and PKI all drew their principal strength from the same areas Central and East Java provinces) in the 1955 elections has thus far not been satisfactorily explained. That the PNI and the PKI would be strong in these areas is understandable if it is remembered that both appealed to the *abangan* orientation and the nativistic temper of traditional Javanese culture in these regions. NU is generally seen as *santri* in orientation and is presumed to have appealed particularly to the self aware *santri* element in East and Central Java. But this explanation overlooks the fact that Masjumi is equally *santri*, and yet Masjumi ran poorly in East and Central Java. Why did East and Central Java *santris* look toward NU more than toward Masjumi? The answer seems to lie in the direction of not drawing the *santri-abangan* antithesis

too sharply. NU, despite its appeals to Muslim orthodoxy, is and was much closer to traditional Javanism and to the *abangan* outlook than Masjumi with its modernism and cosmopolitanism. PNI, PKI, and NU thus all shared in some degree in the anti-modernistic nativism in the core areas of traditional Javanese life. See in this connection the editorial election analysis in *Nieuwsgier*, October 4, 1955.

CHAPTER III

[1] The PKI received 6,232,512 votes in the election for the Constituent Assembly and obtained 80 of the 514 elected seats. In the Constituent Assembly elections the PKI finished fourth after the PNI, Masjumi and NU.

[2] *Java Bode*, November 12, 1955.

[3] On November 9, 1954, Sukarno charged that he had received reports that there were Indonesians who were prepared 'to sell their country for the price of tens of thousands of rupiahs which they have received from foreigners'. He never specified the charges, although Masjumi leader Jusuf Wibisono subsequently revealed that the President might have had him and Tadjuddin Noor of the PIR in mind. Both strongly intimated that the basis of the charge was false and the work of an agent provocateur. A year later, the Indonesian press revealed that the President's charge was based on a false document, purporting to prove that the Chinese People's Republic was plotting with a subversive organization in West Java with which leading army officers were affiliated and which supplied the Communist *Bambu Runtjing* organization with weapons. Details of the action taken by the government, if any, on the basis of Sukarno's charges, were not revealed. See *Java Bode*, November 10, 1954; *Nieuwsgier*, November 15, 1954, November 14, 1955.

[4] In April, 1955, at the Bandung Conference of Asian-African nations a Sino-Indonesian Citizenship treaty was agreed upon by the Foreign Ministers of Indonesia and China. The treaty provided that anyone eighteen or over, or under eighteen and married, and holding the dual nationality of the two countries, would be given two years from the date of formal ratification to choose between them. Failure to chose would give the individual the citizenship of his father. There was a long delay in formal ratification of the treaty and in Indonesia there were varying degrees of opposition from the left as well as the right. The PKI, while declaring the treaty to be imperfect in some respects, generally approved of it (see *Harian Rakjat*, May 17, 1955). In June, 1955, a further exchange of notes between Peking and Djakarta took place designed to meet some of the criticisms made of the treaty, but not until December, 1957, did the Indonesian parliament approve it, after Masjumi and Socialist party deputies had left the chamber in protest. The standing Committee of the People's Congress of the Chinese People's Republic also ratified it in December, 1957. Disagreement about the implementation continued however, punctuated by various outbursts of Sino-Indonesian tension over the economic positions of the Chinese in Indonesia. Not until December 15, 1960 was the implementation of the treaty formally agreed upon between the two governments. See *Suluh Indonesia* (Djakarta), February 7, 1961; David Mozingo, 'The Sino-Indonesian Dual Nationality Treaty', *Asian Survey*, December, 1961, p. 25–31; and Donald E. Willmott, *The National Status of the Chinese in Indonesia 1900–1958* (Cornell University, Modern Indonesia Project, Ithaca, N.Y., 1961, revised edition), pp. 44–66.

[5] *Nieuwsgier*, March 6, 1956.

[6] *Java Bode*, January 7, 1956.

[7] *Ibid.*, March 19, 1956.

[8] *Ibid.*, March 17, 1956.

[9] D. N. Aidit's 'Bersatulah untuk Menjelesaikan tuntunan-tuntunan Revolusi Augustus 1945', pp. 33–98, in *D. N. Aidit. Pilihan Tulisan, op. cit.*, vol. 2.

[10] See B. Glassburner, 'Problems of Economic Policy in Indonesia, 1950–1957', *op. cit.*, pp. 314–315.

[11] *Java Bode*, July 7, 1956.

[12] For these developments see J. M. van der Kroef, 'Instability in Indonesia', *Far Eastern Survey*, April, 1957, pp. 49–62; and also 'The Place of the Army in Indonesian Politics', *op. cit.*, pp. 16–18.

[13] *Java Bode*, December 28, 29, 1956; January 21, 22, 1957.

[14] *Ibid.*, January 11, 1957.

[15] The idea of 'guided democracy' had been in Sukarno's mind for some time prior to his February, 1957 'concept'. On November 26, 1956, for example, he declared that Indonesia had its own 'original form of democracy which is not imported from abroad'. Therefore, he continued, 'there must be a guided democracy in this country, a democracy with leadership'. *Java Bode*, November 27, 1956. This pronouncement came shortly after Sukarno had made an extensive tour through major Communist countries, including the Soviet Union, Yugoslavia, Outer Mongolia and People's China. It has been suggested that the idea of 'guided democracy' and the solidification of all parties came to Sukarno during this tour and that it reflected Communist political organization. However the concept of strong executive guidance in political life and of a unified mass movement go to the very origins of Sukarno's political thinking and were evident in his writings and speeches as early as the late nineteen-twenties.

[16] See J. M. van der Kroef, 'Guided Democracy in Indonesia', *Far Eastern Survey*, August, 1957, pp. 113–124.

[17] *40 Tahun PKI, op. cit.*, p. 47.

[18] van der Kroef, 'Guided Democracy in Indonesia', *op. cit.*, p. 117.

[19] Among the critics of the idea of a National Council, and indeed of Sukarno's entire *konsepsi*, was former Vice-President Hatta. During the early days of April, 1957, the PKI and its fellow-travellers appear to have been genuinely concerned that in response to pressures from rebellious provinces Hatta might return to the government in a leading role. To forestall this the PKI supported a determined campaign, which included the dissemination of pamphlets and leaflets, accusing Hatta of theft of funds entrusted to him during the Revolution and of various other acts of corruption. The accusations proved baseless, however, and Hatta was able to clear himself without effort. See *Java Bode*, April 9, 10, 1957.

[20] *40 Tahun PKI, op. cit.*, p. 47.

[21] D. N. Aidit, 'Ubah Imbangan Kekuatan untuk Melaksanakan Konsepsi Presiden Sukarno 100%', pp. 193–246 in *D. N. Aidit. Pilihan Tulisan, op. cit.*, vol. 2.

[22] Cf. *Java Bode*, July 19, 22, August 3, 12 and 14, 1957.

[23] *Ibid.*, August 12, 24; September 3, 1957. The reasons for the 'anti-anti-Communist' policy of some PNI leaders are difficult to gauge. They may well have stemmed from Sukarno's obvious play to win the favors of the Soviet Union (as *vide* his reception of Kliment Voroshilov, the Soviet head of state in early May, 1957) suggesting that 'Sukarno was transferring his party "allegiance" from the PNI to the PKI', as Arnold C. Brackman, *Indonesian Communism. A History* (New York, 1963), p. 238, has put it. To stabilize their own position some PNI stalwarts evidently believed that security lay in hitching their wagon to the rising red star.

[24] *Review of Indonesia* (Djakarta), December, 1957, p. 10. This is the English-language monthly issued by the Secretariat of the Central Committee of the PKI.

[25] On these developments see generally van der Kroef, 'Disunited Indonesia', *Far Eastern Survey*, April, 1958, pp. 49–63; May, 1958, pp. 73–80.

[26] *Indonesian Observer* (Djakarta), January 3, 1958.

[27] *Ibid.*, January 6, 1958.

[28] *The Times of Indonesia* (Djakarta), May 24, 1958.

[29] 'Is Anti-Communism really the Issue?', *The Indonesian Spectator* (Djakarta), March 1, 1958.

[30] 'Soviet Loan to Sukarno', *PRRI Bulletin. Voice of Free Indonesia* (Macao?), January, 1959, p. 9–10; 'U.S. Aids Pro-Reds in Indonesia', *ibid.*, March 1959, pp. 8–10; 'Role of Bank China in Financing Indonesian Transactions', *ibid.*, April, 1959, pp. 18–19. Anti-Communist feeling among PRRI leaders often ran high. According to James Mossman, *Rebels in Paradise: Indonesia's Civil War* (London, 1961) pp. 63–64, Col. Dahlan Djambek, one of the principal PRRI military commanders, had been for some time active in organizing a popular anti-Communist movement which taught people to resist Communism in factories and villages. For other PRRI leaders the issue of regional autonomy was more important, however.

[31] *Indonesian Observer*, May 5, 1958. The edge of this PKI threat, which also lay in the implication that Communist-dominated trade unions might undertake actions against the Caltex and Stanvac petroleum establishments in Sumatra, was quickly dulled by Nasution's immediate announcement that any 'interference by any quarter whatsoever in the operations of the oil enterprises is forbidden'.

[32] Cf. Selo Soemardjan, 'Bureaucratic Organization in a Time of Revolution', *Administrative Science Quarterly*, vol. 2 (1957), pp. 194–196.

[33] In the regional elections of South Sumatra, results of which were announced on March 25, 1958, the PKI increased its votes by more than 46,000 or 26 per cent over what it had obtained in the parliamentary elections of 1955. The PKI thus became the second largest party in South Sumatra (behind Masjumi). In the regional election on Riau the party obtained 9,838 votes (out of a total of 79,170 voters), compared to 5,930 votes in the parliamentary elections of 1955. On Riau the party held third place. Cf. M. H. Lukman's report in *Harian Rakjat*, April 5, 1958. In the 1958 local elections held in Central Kalimantan (Borneo) the PKI nearly doubled its vote (from 7507 to 14,757 votes) but the party still lagged behind PNI, Masjumi and NU. The October 1958 elections in Central Kalimantan revealed great losses for Masjumi and NU, however, and significant gains not only for the PKI but also for the PNI. See *Review of Indonesia*, November, 1958, p. 19.

[34] *Indonesian Observer*, July 4, 1958.

[35] *Review of Indonesia*, October, 1958, pp. 13–14.

[36] On February 11, 1958, the East Java Branch of the PNI lashed out against the PKI, stating that it had become convinced that the PKI was seeking to make a Communist state out of the Indonesian Republic. See *Indonesian Observer*, February 17, 1958.

[37] The new *Partindo*, which had been dormant since 1936, based itself on 'marhaenism' or, as one of its spokesmen put it, on 'Marxism' adapted to the Indonesian 'situation' (*Times of Indonesia*, August 7, 1958). *Partindo* leaders, when still in the PNI, had been dissatisfied with the party's election losses in the recent regional elections and with the party's vacillating policies; they frankly cast their appeal in radical terms and made a bid for the support of smaller *marhaenist* groupings. The PKI's position toward *Partindo* became progressively warmer, though Communist leaders took care not to arouse PNI hostility. By 1963 *Partindo* radicalism and PKI infiltration had made *Partindo* into an informal Communist front organization.

[38] *Harian Rakjat*, April 5, 1958.

[39] D. N. Aidit, 'The New Phase and Bringing the Organization into Line with the Situation', esp. pp. 23, 44–47, in *Documents of the Sixth Plenum of the Central Committee of the Communist Party of Indonesia* (Djakarta, 1958). See also *D. N. Aidit. Pilihan Tulisan, op. cit.*, vol. 2, pp. 377–443.

[40] D. N. Aidit, 'The New Phase', *op. cit.*, pp. 60–64.

[41] *Ibid.*, pp. 71–73.

[42] 'C.P.I. Holds National Conference', *Review of Indonesia*, August, 1958, pp. 3–5.

[43] Dahono, 'Studying "On the Correct Handling of the Contradictions Among the People",' *Review of Indonesia*, September, 1958, pp. 31–32.

[44] Cf. Mao Tse-tung, *On the Correct Handling of Contradictions Among the People* (Peking, Foreign Languages Press, 1959), and *On Contradiction* (Peking, Foreign Languages Press, 1960).

[45] See, e.g., the interview of Njoto in *Far Eastern Economic Review* (Hong Kong), April 16, 1959, p. 530.

[46] *Harian Rakjat*, November 20, 1958; also D. N. Aidit, 'Bersatu Menumpuh Djalan Demokrasi Terpimpin Menudju Pelaksanaan Konsepsi Presiden Sukarno 100 per cent,' pp. 527–556, in *D. N. Aidit, Pilihan Tulisan, op. cit.*, vol. 2.

[47] 'Resolution of the Seventh Plenum of the CC C.P.I. on the Political Report', p. 19, in *Documents. Seventh Plenum of the Central Committee of the Communist Party of Indonesia. Jacarta, November 19–21, 1958.* Supplementary Issue to *Review of Indonesia*, 1958, No. 12.

[48] D. N. Aidit, 'Mari Kita Robek-Robek Terus. Itu Matjan Kertas', pp. 16–28, in *Menumpuh Tahun 1959* (Djakarta, 1959).

[49] *Indonesian Observer*, January 12, 1959.

[50] Sujono Atmo (a representative of the youth groups), Mohammad Munir (the delegate of SOBSI), and Henk Ngantung (representative of the artists) were all members of the 45-member National Advisory Council who leaned heavily toward the PKI, and Communist influence in all probability extended itself also toward two or three other council members. On the origin and function of the council see my articles 'Indonesia's "New Life" Movement', *Eastern World*, November, 1957, pp. 16–19, and 'The Changing Pattern of Indonesia's Representative Government', *Canadian Journal of Economics and Political Science*, vol. 26 (1960), pp. 215–240.

[51] *Indonesian Observer*, January 23, 1959.

[52] *Ibid.*, February 2, 1959.

[53] *Review of Indonesia*, March 1959, p. 10. For the manner in which functional group candidates would appear on lists of political party nominees in parliamentary elections, see premier Djuanda's statement to parliament, in *The Indonesian Spectator*, April 1, 1959, p. 21.

[54] *Indonesian Observer*, February 21, 1959.

[55] After the announcement of February 21, 1959, on the return to the 1945 Constitution, increasing pressure was put on the Constituent Assembly to accept the document. Thus shortly after his February 21 announcement, Sukarno declared, 'I believe if the members of the Constituent Assembly are true representatives of the people they will heed the people's voice and return to the 1945 Constitution'. Subsequent official pronouncements declared that the Assembly would be dissolved by the end of July after it had ratified the 1945 Constitution and intimated that there was really nothing more for the Assembly to do, in any case, except to ratify. By May 27 Djuanda in effect threatened the Assembly that 'situations as in our neighbor countries' might emerge if the Assembly rejected the 1945 Constitution, apparently intimating the possibility of some kind of dictatorship. See *The Indonesian Spectator*, March 1, 1959, p. 5, and *Indonesian Observer*, February 23, March 21, and May 28, 1959.

[56] *Indonesian Observer*, February 25, 1959.

[57] Njoto, 'Hold High the Spirit of 1945', *Review of Indonesia*, April-May, 1959, pp. 17–19.

[58] For details of this ordinance see J. D. Legge, *Central Authority and Regional Autonomy in Indonesia: A Study in Local Administration 1950–1960* (Ithaca, N.Y., 1961), pp. 209–229.

[59] 'Developments Around Presidential Ordinance Number 6', *Review of Indonesia*, November-December, 1959, pp. 14–15.

[60] *Harian Rakjat*, October 10, 1959.

[61] *Skets Masa* (Djakarta), February 15, 1960, pp. 3, 4, 5 and 9. A 'perfected version' of the ordinance gave local representative councils twice the opportunity to submit names of candidates of regional heads to the central government; the original version only gave them one opportunity to do so. Even so, among the first central government appointments of regional heads there were a number made directly by the President, after rejection of two lists of candidates submitted by the regional representative council. See Legge, *op. cit.*, pp. 211–212.

[62] *Indonesian Observer*, December 2, 1959. The People's Congress *(Madjelis Permusjawaratan Rakjat)* under the 1945 Constitution is the highest source of public power and consists of the members of parliament augmented by 'delegates from regional territories and groups' as provided by law. The Congress enacts the Constitution and must 'lay down the outlines' of national policy. The presently functioning Congress is considered provisional.

[63] *Indonesian Observer*, January 19, 1960.

[64] *Ibid.*, February 11, 1960.

[65] 'C.P.I. Representatives on State Budget for 1960', *Review of Indonesia*, February, 1960, pp. 10–11.

[66] *Review of Indonesia*, April 1960, p. 9. See also *Harian Rakjat*, March 9, 1960.

[67] *Review of Indonesia*, April 1960, p. 12.

[68] The 'Political Manifesto' was issued by Sukarno as his Independence Day address on August 17, 1959, and was declared to be 'the broad outlines of the State policy' by

decision of the Supreme Advisory Council on September 25, 1959. In essence the *Manipol* is a justification of the return to the 1945 Constitution and an excoriation of the political history preceding this return. Cf. *Political Manifesto. Republic of Indonesia of 17th August 1959* (Department of Information, Djakarta, 1959). Increasingly after 1959 *Manipol* became the basis of the new national effort under the 1945 Constitution. Aidit tied the principles of *Manipol* to the PKI's strategy of the two-stage revolution. See *Harian Rakjat*, March 18, 1960, and chapter IV below.

[69] On the Democratic League and resistance to the new parliament, see J. M. van der Kroef, 'Indonesia's New Parliament', *Eastern World*, September 1960, pp. 16–17. The League was a heterogeneous and rather informal organization, anti-Communist in character and supported by followers of IPKI (The Independence Upholders Party which has considerable backing from army officers), Masjumi and Socialist party leaders, and a scattering of NU and Christian confessional parties membership.

[70] After Sukarno promulgated the country's return to the 1945 Constitution on July 5, 1959, it was the army which feared abolition of parliament, according to one knowledgeable Dutch observer, lest Communists and fellow travellers would become dominant in the country. The structural change of parliament, so as to provide for inclusion of 'functional' group representatives—especially of representatives from the government and military services—was desired by the army. Sukarno and Nasution agreed at that time not to let Communist influence increase, according to this Dutch observer, who exchanged views with Nasution in connection with the West New Guinea issue. See F. J. F. M. Duynstee, *Nieuw-Guinea als Schakel tussen Nederland en Indonesië* (Amsterdam, 1961), p. 135.

[71] 'Settle the Question of the Overseas Chinese in the Spirit and Act of Indonesian-Chinese Friendship', *Review of Indonesia*, November-December, 1959, p. 3.

[72] *Review of Indonesia*, November-December, 1959, p. 5.

[73] *Indonesian Observer*, January 13, 1960.

[74] *Ibid.*, February 1, 1960.

[75] *Peking Review*, December 27, 1960, pp. 9–11, carries the complete text of the implementation agreement of December 15, 1960. See also *Indonesian Observer*, April 1, 1961.

[76] *Review of Indonesia*, June 1960, pp. 7–9.

[77] See Benjamin Higgins, *Indonesia's Economic Stabilization and Development* (New York, 1957); Douglas S. Paauw, *Financing Economic Development. The Indonesian Case* (Glencoe, Ill., 1960); Douglas S. Paauw, 'The High Cost of Political Instability in Indonesia 1957–1958', pp. 23–55, in B. H. M. Vlekke, ed., *Indonesia's Struggle 1957–1958* (The Hague, New York, 1959); also J. M. van der Kroef, 'Indonesia's Economic Future', *Pacific Affairs*, March 1959, pp. 46–72, and 'Indonesia's Economic Dilemma', *Far Eastern Survey*, April 1960, pp. 49–63.

[78] D. N. Aidit, 'Pembangunan Organisasi Penting, Tapi Lebih Penting Lagi Pembangunan Ideologi!', *Bintang Merah*, vol. 15 (1959), p. 240; and 'Back to the 1945 Constitution for a Change in Policies and Living Conditions', p. 5, in *Eighth Plenum of the Central Committee of the Communist Party of Indonesia. Political Report and Resolution. Review of Indonesia*, September-October, 1959, Supplement.

[79] D. N. Aidit, 'Back to the 1945 Constitution for a Change in Policies and Living Conditions', *op. cit.*, pp. 8–9.

[80] 'Consolidate Unity to Defend Democracy and Struggle for an Improvement in the Living Conditions of the People', *Review of Indonesia*, November-December, 1959, Supplement, p. 1.

[81] Interview with D. N. Aidit, in *Bintang Timur* (Djakarta), November 20, 1959, reprinted in *Review of Indonesia*, November-December, 1959, p. 7.

[82] 'Cancel the Rise in Petrol Price and the Increase in Taxes', *Review of Indonesia*, February 1960, p. 7.

[83] 'Statement of the Politbureau of the CC CPI on the Economic Situation', *Review of Indonesia*, March, 1960, pp. 3–4.

[84] See *Eighth Plenum of the Central Committee of the Communist Party of Indonesia. Political Report and Resolution, op. cit.*

[85] On this intervention see Justus M. van der Kroef, 'Indonesian Communist Policy and the Sixty Party Congress', *Pacific Affairs*, September 1960, p. 227.

[86] D. N. Aidit, 'Kongres Nasional Ke-VI PKI', *Bintang Merah*, vol. 15 (1959), p. 356.

[87] Jusuf Adjitorop, 'Kongres jang didukung Rakjat', *Bintang Merah*, vol. 15 (1959), p. 374.

[88] *40 Tahun PKI, op. cit.*, p. 52.

[89] Jusuf Adjitorop, 'Kongres jang didukung Rakjat', *op. cit.*, pp. 373–374.

[90] *Ibid.*

[91] D. N. Aidit, 'Kongres Nasional Ke-VI PKI,' *op. cit.*, p. 346.

[92] *Ibid.*, p. 350.

[93] *Ibid.*, p. 353. This statement embodies PKI policy to the government in a nutshell and again illustrates its 'support in principle, criticize the implementation' technique. The cabinet or government as such is usually supported (although, admittedly party criticism of the government's economic policy and of its policy toward the Chinese traders had been couched in such general terms as to create the impression that it extended to the entire cabinet); criticism of implementation of cabinet policies tends to be directed toward particular ministers in the cabinet.

[94] *Ibid.*, pp. 357–359.

CHAPTER IV

[1] J. Stalin, *Problems of Leninism* (Moscow, 1954, 11th edition), p. 792.

[2] *The China Quarterly*, January-March, 1961, p. 33; Lin Piao, 'The Victory of the Chinese People's Revolutionary War is the Victory of the Thought of Mao Tse-tung', *China Reconstructs*, December 1960, Supplement, p. 2

[3] *Program Partai Komunis Indonesia (PKI) disahkan oleh Kongres Nasional ke-VII (Luarbiasa) Partai Komunis Indonesia (25–30 April 1962)*, (Djakarta, 1962), p. 16. This phrase is a repetition of a similar provision in the PKI constitution adopted at the Sixth National Congress of the party in 1959. Cf. *Material for the Sixth Congress of the Communist Party of Indonesia* (Agitprop Department of the Central Committee of the Communist Party of Indonesia, s.a.e.l., 1959?), p. 97.

[4] Proof of Tan Malaka's interest in Marxist theoretical training was his effort to promote, along with others, the founding of 'Marx House' institutes throughout Java early in the Indonesian Revolution where training in Marxist and Leninist principles was given to Indonesian youth.

[5] D. N. Aidit, 'Lenin dan Indonesia', *Bintang Merah*, vol. 16 (1960), pp. 109–110.

[6] D. N. Aidit, *Peladjaran dari Sedjarah PKI* (Djakarta, 1960), p. 17.

[7] Cf. Aidit's essay 'Masjarakat Indonesia dan Revolusi Indonesia', pp. 296–300, in *D. N. Aidit. Pilihan Tulisan* (Djakarta, 1960), vol. 2. Because this essay will be frequently cited in this chapter it will hereafter be abbreviated as *MIRI*. It is to be noted that the scope and structure of this essay closely follows Mao Tse-tung's *The Chinese Revolution and the Chinese Communist Party* (Peking, 1960, 3rd edition), originally written in 1939. See also Aidit's address before the 'Assembly of the 1945 Generation', reprinted in *Harian Rakjat*, March 18, 1960.

[8] B. O. Hutapea, 'Beberapa Peladjaran dari Konferensi Nasional Tani Pertama PKI', *Bintang Merah*, vol. 15 (1959), p. 257.

[9] *Marx and Engels. Basic Writings on Politics and Philosophy*, Ed. by Lewis S. Feuer (New York, Doubleday, Anchor edition, 1959), pp. 17, 315, 419, and 451.

[10] V. I. Lenin, *Two Tactics of Social Democracy in the Democratic Revolution* (Library of Marxist-Leninist Classics, Moscow, 1950), pp. 64–65. Italics in original.

[11] *Ibid.*, pp. 67–68.

[12] Ruth T. McVey, *The Comintern and the Rise of Indonesian Communism* (Ph.D. Thesis, Cornell University, University Microfilms, Ann Arbor, 1961), p. 106.

[13] D. N. Aidit, 'Pembangunan Organisasi Penting, Tapi Lebih Penting Lagi Pembangunan Ideologi!', *Bintang Merah*, vol. 15 (1959), p. 244.

[14] *Political Manifesto Republic of Indonesia of 17th August 1959* (Department of Information, Republic of Indonesia, Djakarta, 1959), pp. 49–50; and *Harian Rakjat*, March 18, 1960.

[15] According to Soviet Communist doctrine today, there is first a 'national bourgeois' revolution, which brings freedom from colonialism and establishes the bourgeoisie in power; secondly, there is a 'bourgeois democratic' revolution, which leads to the formation of a coalition government in which Communists share power; third comes the stage of 'national democracy' during which the Communist party acquires dominance, and fourth, there is the 'people's democratic revolution' which leads to undivided Communist power. Cf. *Bulletin, Institute for the Study of the USSR*, August 1961, p. 8, citing *Malaya soveiskaya entsiklopedia* (Small Soviet Encyclopedia), 3rd. ed., vol. 2, 1958, p. 33. For Aidit Indonesia is in the 'bourgeois democratic' stage, which is his current 'first' stage. Though the PKI does not consider itself as having won complete dominance ('national democracy') Aidit has been wont to use the terms 'bourgeois democracy' (Indonesia's present stage) and 'national democracy' interchangeably, and recently has been particularly favoring the latter to the almost total exclusion of the former. Leaning heavily on Lenin and Mao, Aidit has also held that the 'bourgeois democratic' revolution in Indonesia is of a 'new type' and therefore is also called 'the new democratic revolution or the revolution of people's democracy'. *MIRI*, p. 297. The last term is synonymous, in effect, with 'people's democratic revolution' as used in Soviet doctrine, and mentioned above, so that this fourth stage of the road to Communist power (according to Soviet theory) for Aidit in fact becomes synonymous with the 'bourgeois democratic' struggle or the first stage! The bewildering variety with which terms like 'democracy' (or 'democratic'), 'people' (or 'people's), 'revolution' (or 'revolutionary') and 'government', singly or in combination, are used by Communist theoreticians, including Aidit, is perhaps of less importance for an appreciation of Communist strategy than the agreement on a phased development toward Socialism and Communism (whatever the terminology for the several phases).

The announced aim of the PKI, i.e. the creation of a 'People's Democratic Government' in Indonesia, should quite apart from its reference to *gotong royong* (see e.g. p. 191 *supra*) also be understood within the context of this phased development. 'People's Democratic Government' is the culmination of the first phase of the multi-phased revolution, i.e. it is the culmination of the bourgeois or national democratic revolution (see pp. 86, 166, 185). Until the end of the bourgeois or national democratic revolution, that is until the 'People's Democratic Government' has been established, there can be no meaningful effort toward completing the next phase of the revolution, the establishment of Socialism. In 'People's Democratic Government', the PKI as the vanguard of the working class and of 'the people' must be in a commanding position, but a spirit of *gotong royong* presumably animates PKI leadership and 'People's Democratic Society'. In practice this also means that 'People's Democratic Government' is a national coalition, government (led by the PKI) and that the concept of the latter shades into the former, particularly on the basis of *gotong royong*, making a conceptual and tactical difference between them—as experienced in the 1955 election, it will be recalled—unnecessary. However a national coalition can be achieved before a 'People's Democratic Government', i.e. Communists can enter the *gotong royong* cabinet and not, at first be dominant in it. When they do dominate a 'People's Democratic Government' may be said to have been established. Achieving both the national coalition and 'People's Democratic Government' must occur by peaceful means (on the basis of Presidential Decrees governing party activity—see pp. 190–191) and the 'revolution' of 'People's Democracy' which figures in party literature of the nineteen-fifties has, for the time being, at best a symbolic character. The concept of the 'August Revolution' as it has been developed by the PKI should be related to both the bourgeois or national democratic stage of the revolution, and to the revolution of 'People's Democracy'. In the mid-fifties PKI theory tended to think of the 'August revolution' as encompassing only the period up to the Madiun rebellion, i.e. up to 1948 (see again *supra* p. 42) and the failure of the 'August revolution' came to be seen as occasioned by the Madiun' 'provocation'. Subsequently the 'August revolution' has come to mean the entire national revolutionary period of struggle (1945–1949), and 'fulfilling' the 'August revolution' thus has come to be equated with fulfilling the bourgeois or national democratic revolution leading to the establishment of 'People's Democracy'.

[16] D. N. Aidit, *Peladjaran dari Sedjarah PKI, op. cit.*, p. 24. Cf. also, *MIRI*, pp. 299–300: 'Our Party has a double task in leading the Indonesian Revolution. First,

under the slogan "Complete the demands of the August Revolution in their entirety" we carry out to their completion the tasks of the bourgeois democratic revolution; secondly, *after the first task has been carried out*, we carry out to their completion the tasks of the revolution, which is proletarian and socialist in kind.' (My italics).

[17] *Marx and Engels. Basic Writings, op. cit.*, p. 44.

[18] V. I. Lenin, *'Left-Wing' Communism, An Infantile Disorder* (Library of Marxist-Leninist Classics, Moscow, 1952), pp. 45, 89, 90, 95.

[19] *Harian Rakjat*, March 18, 1960; *MIRI*, pp. 284–300.

[20] Mao Tse-tung, *On New Democracy* (Peking, 1954), pp. 10–12, 18.

[21] *MIRI*, p. 297.

[22] V. I. Lenin, *The National-Liberation Movement in the East* (Moscow, 1957), p. 43. Italics in original.

[23] *Ibid.*, pp. 44–47. It is well known that soon Lenin revised his views of Sun Yat-sen.

[24] *Ibid.*, p. 170, 266. Italics in original.

[25] See Justus M. van der Kroef, 'On "National Democracy",' *Survey*, April 1963, pp. 134–145.

[26] *World Marxist Review*, March 1963, p. 51.

[27] Cf. Mao Tse-tung, *Analysis of the Classes in Chinese Society* (Peking, 1960), p. 2, 5, and *MIRI*, pp. 290–292.

[28] J. Stalin, *Problems of Leninism, op. cit.*, pp. 39–41.

[29] See e.g. Shih Tung-hsiang, 'The Distinction and Link-Up between the Two Stages of the Chinese Revolution', *Peking Review*, January 20, 1961, pp. 9–18.

[30] Mao Tse-tung, *On New Democracy, op. cit.*, p. 12.

[31] Mao Tse-tung, *On the Correct Handling of Contradictions Among the People* (Peking, 1959), pp. 9, 23.

[32] Tan Malaka, *Naar de 'Republik Indonesia'* (Tokyo, 1925); also Harry J. Benda and Ruth T. McVey (eds.), *The Communist Uprisings of 1926–1927 in Indonesia: Key Documents* (Southeast Asia Program, Cornell University, Ithaca, 1960), pp. 129–134.

[33] See N. Bukharin, 'Perspektiven der Chinesischen Revolution', *Die Kommunistische Internationale*, 1927, pp. 669–671, and 'Theses on the Chinese Situation' by the Seventh Plenum of the Comintern's Executive Committee, in Xenia J. Eudin and Robert C. North, *Soviet Russia and the East, 1920–1927: A Documentary Survey* (Stanford, 1957), pp. 356, 359–362. B. Schrieke notes how Tan Malaka's socio-political analysis follows 'the prescriptions of Lenin'. Benda and McVey, *op. cit.*, p. 134.

[34] Benda and McVey, *op. cit.*, p. 134.

[35] The resolution went through various editions and revisions, the last probably being *Djalan Baru Untuk Republik Indonesia* (Djakarta, 1953, 7th ed.).

[36] Mao Tse-tung, *New-Democratic Constitutionalism* (Peking, 1960), pp. 1, 7, and *MIRI*, pp. 274–279.

[37] Mao Tse-tung, *On People's Democratic Dictatorship* (Peking, 1959), p. 17.

[38] Mao Tse-tung, *On Coalition Government* (Peking, 1960), p. 49.

[39] *MIRI*, pp. 297–300; *Program Partai Komunis Indonesia, op. cit.*, pp. 12, 18–19; *Material for the Sixth National Congress of the Communist Party of Indonesia*, op. cit., pp. 94, 99.

[40] *MIRI*, pp. 290–292. See also D. N. Aidit, *The Road to People's Democracy for Indonesia* (Djakarta, 1955), pp. 48–49.

[41] D. N. Aidit, *Peladjaran dari Sedjarah PKI, op. cit.*, p. 13, and 'Lenin dan Indonesia', *Bintang Merah*, vol. 16 (1960), pp. 102, 110.

[42] 'Consolidate Unity to Defend Democracy and Struggle for an Improvement in the Living Conditions of the People' (New Year's Message of the Politburo of the PKI, December 30, 1959, Djakarta, 1960), p. 3, and *C.P.I. National Economic Seminar. Documents. Review of Indonesia*, April-May, 1959, Supplement, p. 7.

[43] M. H. Lukman, *Adjaka PKI Kepada Kaum Pengusaha Nasional* (Djakarta, 1963), pp. 25–32.

[44] *Review of Indonesia*, March, 1960, p. 3; August, 1960, p. 9. See also *D. N. Aidit. Pihilan Tulisan, op. cit.*, vol. 2, pp. 554–555.

[45] See J. M. van der Kroef, 'Colonial Continuity in Indonesia's Economic Policy', *The Australian Outlook*, vol. 14 (1960), pp. 5–14.

[46] Mao Tse-tung, *On the Correct Handling of Contradictions Among the People* (Peking, 1959) pp. 10–11.

[47] Donald C. Hodges, 'The "Intermediate Classes" in Marxian Theory', *Social Research*, April, 1961, pp. 23–36; also *World Marxist Review*, May, 1961, pp. 71–84.

[48] V. I. Lenin, *Two Tactics of Social Democracy in the Democratic Revolution, op. cit.*, pp. 169–170; Mao Tse-tung, *On People's Democratic Dictatorship, op. cit.*, p. 11; *D. N. Aidit, Pilihan Tulisan, op. cit.*, vol. 2, pp. 294–295.

[49] *Material for the Sixth National Congress of the Communist Party of Indonesia, op. cit.*, p. 62, and D. N. Aidit, 'For Broad Unity of all National Forces in Indonesia', *For a Lasting Peace! For a People's Democracy!*, December 31, 1954.

[50] Mao Tse-tung, *On New Democracy, op. cit.*, p. 54.

[51] V. I. Lenin, *The Agrarian Programme of Social-Democracy in the First Russian Revolution 1905–1907* (Library of Marxist-Leninist Classics, Moscow, 1954), p. 343.

[52] V. I. Lenin, *Alliance of the Working Class and the Peasantry* (Moscow, 1959), p. 124.

[53] Cf. Karl A. Wittfogel, 'The Legend of "Maoism",' *The China Quarterly*, January–March, 1960, pp. 77–78.

[54] J. Stalin, *Marxism and the National and Colonial Question* (London, 1947, 4th ed.), p. 202.

[55] Mao Tse-tung, *On New Democracy, op. cit.*, p. 55.

[56] Mao Tse-tung, *On Contradiction* (Peking, 1960), p. 49.

[57] Mao Tse-Tung, *Analysis of the Classes in Chinese Society, op. cit.*, p. 2, 4, 8–9, 13–15; also *Selected Works* (London, 1954), vol. 1, pp. 138 ff.

[58] 'On the Question of the National Bourgeoisie and the Enlightened Gentry', in *Selected Works of Mao Tse-tung*, (Peking, 1961), vol. IV, p. 209.

[59] 'Speech at a Conference of Cadres in the Shansi-Suiyuan Liberated Area', in *Selected Works of Mao Tse-tung, op. cit.*, vol. IV, pp. 235–237.

[60] *MIRI*, pp. 292–293. See also *D. N. Aidit. Pilihan Tulisan, op. cit.*, vol. 2, pp. 542–543, and D. N. Aidit, 'Kibarkan Tinggi Pandji-Pandij "Tanah Untuk Petani" dan Rebut Kemenangan Satu Demi Satu', *Bintang Merah*, vol. 15 (1959), pp. 217–219.

[61] *Program Partai Komunis Indonesia, op. cit.*, p. 13. This clause is identical with one adopted at the Sixth National Congress in 1959. See *Material for the Sixth National Congress of the Communist Party of Indonesia, op. cit.*, p. 94.

Adoption of the Leninist and Maoist principle of outright individual land-ownership for the peasant did not come about until 1954. Between 1945 and 1953 the PKI advocated a form of 'sovietization' of the land, providing that though land should be redistributed, the land from the landlords should be vested in the village collectivity as a whole, to be re-allocated to the peasant's use as the village government decided. (Cf. *Bintang Merah*, November 17, 1945, and *Djalan Baru Untuk Republik Indonesia, op. cit.*, 1953, p. 29). This deference to traditional village communalism may have had behind it a policy of 'sovietizing' the land at once. In March 1954, Aidit, however, advocated that land be taken from the landlords and be given directly to the peasants 'as their own private property' and this principle the party adopted. D. N. Aidit, *The Road to People's Democracy for Indonesia* (General Report on the Political and Organizational Situation, delivered at the Fifth National Congress of the Communist Party of Indonesia, March, 1954, Djakarta, 1955), p. 32.

[62] Mao Tse-tung, *The Question of Independence within the United Front* (Peking, 1960), p. 1. It is of interest to note that in drawing a distinction between types of landlords, exempting some from confiscation, Aidit has trod in the footsteps of M. N. Roy, (the noted Indian ex-Communist, whose ideas influenced early Comintern directives to Asian Communists) and of the early Chinese Communists. At the Fifth Congress of the Chinese Communist Party in 1926 Roy counseled against immediate abolition of private property and Chinese cadres began to declare that the property of

left Kuomintang officers would not be confiscated; the Congress itself exempted from land confiscation the property of small owners and 'revolutionary' army officers. See Robert C. North, 'M.N. Roy and the Fifth Congress of the Chinese Communist Party', *The China Quarterly*, October-December, 1961, p. 193.

⁶³ *MIRI*, pp. 287–288.

⁶⁴ *Ibid.*, pp. 292–293.

⁶⁵ Cf. the remarks of PKI parliamentary deputy Nguntjik in *Review of Indonesia*, September-October, 1960, p. 20.

⁶⁶ Asmu, 'Masalah Landreform', *Bintang Merah*, vol. 16 (1960), pp. 14–28.

⁶⁷ 'Kesimpulan Mengenai Laporan Tentang Pekerdjaan Partai Dikalangan Kaum Tani', *Bintang Merah*, vol. 15 (1959), pp. 190–194; D. N. Aidit, Asmu, Mau Tje-tung, *Untuk Bekerdja Lebih Baik Dikalangan Kaum Tani* (Djakarta, 1958); *Undang Undang no. 2, tahun 1960 Tentang Perdjandjian Bagi Hasil* (Djakarta, 1960); *Suara Tani*, November, 1959, pp. 3–4; January, 1960, p. 3; *Kehidupan Partai*, June, 1960, pp. 97–100.

⁶⁸ *Madju Terus Menggempur Imperialisme dan Feodalisme (Sidang Pleno ke-II CC PKI, achir December 1960)* (Djakarta, 1961), pp. 12, 15, 16–17.

⁶⁹ By early 1964 the Indonesian peasantry was apparently ready to follow Aidit's advice and 'liberate' itself from the landlords. In Central Java land was reportedly being seized that would eventually have gone to the peasantry if land reform had been carried out. Landlords were no longer paid their shares of the crops. PKI cadres were quoted as saying that this 'arbitrary action' by the peasants was designed to help the government to speed implementation of the September 1960 'basic agrarian law' and subsequent land restrictive measures. At the present rate of implementation, *Harian Rakjat* complained that the government's land reform program would not have been implemented 'until one becomes old'. The PKI sharply accused local government officials of impeding the agrarian reform program.

⁷⁰ 'Kesimpulan Konferensi Nasional Tani PKI Tentang Masaalah Nelajan di Indonesia', *Bintang Merah*, vol. 15 (1959), pp. 196–200.

⁷¹ *MIRI*, pp. 294–295.

⁷² *Harian Rakjat*, April 5, 1958.

⁷³ Mao Tse-tung, *Problems of War and Strategy* (Peking, 1954), p. 6.

⁷⁴ Rahmat, 'Communist Party of Indonesia: Strengthen National Unity', *World Marxist Review*, August, 1961, p. 65. See also M. H. Lukman, *Tentang Front Persatuan Nasional* (Djakarta, 1960), and *Madju Terus Menggempur Imperialisme dan Feodalisme*, *op. cit.*, passim.

⁷⁵ D. N. Aidit, *The Road to People's Democracy*, *op. cit.*, p. 49.

⁷⁶ Mao Tse-tung, *The Question of Independence Within the United Front*, *op. cit.*, p. 4.

⁷⁷ *Antara Daily News Bulletin* (New York), August 10 and 21, 1961.

⁷⁸ See Edward Crankshaw, 'Khrushchev and China', *The Atlantic Monthly*, May 1961, pp. 43–47.

⁷⁹ Mao Tse-tung, *A Single Spark Can Start a Prairie Fire* (Peking, 1953), pp. 12–13.

⁸⁰ B. O. Hutapea, 'Kibarkan Tinggi Pandji Pandji Pembangunan Partai Dilapangan Ideologi', *Bintan Merah*, vol. 16 (1960), p. 229.

⁸¹ Jusuf Adjitorop, *Madjulah Inteligensia Indonesia Berkerumun Disekitar Manipol!* (Djakarta, 1962), pp. 15–20.

⁸² See e.g. D. N. Aidit, 'Lahirnja PKI dan Perkembangannja', in *D. N. Aidit. Pilihan Tulisan*, *op. cit.*, vol. 1, pp. 410, 412.

⁸³ B. O. Hutapea, 'Dua Sjarat Utama dari Partai Tipe Lenin: Sentralisme dan Disiplin', *Bintang Merah*, vol. 16 (1960), pp. 124–130.

⁸⁴ *MIRI*, pp. 293–295.

⁸⁵ B. O. Hutapea, 'Kibarkan Tinggi Pandji Pandji Pembangunan Partai Dilapangan Ideologi', *op. cit.*, pp. 228–229.

⁸⁶ D. N. Aidit, 'Lahirnja PKI dan Perkembangannja', pp. 421–422 in *D. N. Aidit, Pilihan Tulisan*, *op. cit.*, vol. 1.

[87] Lenin wrote in 'Struggle for Power and "Struggle for a Pittance"' (1906) that 'the mass struggle for freedom has passed through, and will always pass through, the most diverse and often unexpected stages: it cannot be otherwise, because of the immense difficulty of the struggle, the complexity of its problems and the changeable composition of those who are struggling' (*Lenin on the Revolutionary Proletarian Party of a New Type*, Peking 1960, pp. 10–11). In his essay 'Inflammable Material in World Politics' (1908) he wrote: 'The international revolutionary movement of the proletariat does not and cannot develop evenly and in identical forms in different countries . . . every country makes its own valuable contribution, adding new features to this common stream' (V. I. Lenin, *The National Liberation Movement in the East, op. cit.*, p. 18).

[88] *Indonesian Observer*, August 8, 1961.

[89] Njoto, 'Some Matters Concerning Yugoslavia and Indonesia Considered from the Philosophical Point of View', *Review of Indonesia*, October 1958, p. 31.

[90] D. N. Aidit, 'Kongres Nasional Ke-VI PKI', *Bintang Merah*, vol. 15 (1959), p. 354.

[91] Cf. Denis Warner, 'Will Indonesia become a Second Cuba?', *The Reporter* (New York), December 7, 1961, p. 46. The former Vice-Chairman of the Supreme Advisory Council, Ruslan Abdulgani, who has been the chief expositor of the ideology of 'guided democracy' in Indonesia in the past few years, has declared that the 'best pattern' of business management for Indonesia is probably the one in Yugoslavia, since Yugoslav enterprises are 'of a social nature'. *Antara Daily News Bulletin*, October 12, 1960.

[92] See editorial, 'Ambiguous Stand', *Indonesian Observer*, April 6, 1961.

[93] Foreign Broadcast Information Service, *The 22nd Congress of the Soviet Communist Party. Proceedings and Related Materials. Daily Report. Supplement. USSR and East Europe*, Monday, October 23, 1961, no. 18, 1961 (s.l., 1961), vol. 8, pp. 81–82.

[94] D. N. Aidit, 'Soalnja Bukan Siapa Akan Keluar Tapi Siapa Lagi Jang Akan Masuk Kubu Sosialis', pp. 112–114 in *Serba-Serbi Dokumen Partai 1961* (Djakarta, 1962).

[95] *Strengthen National Unity and Communist Unity. Documents of the Third Plenum of the Central Committee of the Communist Party of Indonesia, Djakarta, end December, 1961* (Djakarta, 1962), p. 24.

[96] D. N. Aidit, 'Solanja Bukan Siapa Akan Keluar Tapi Siapa Lagi Jang Akan Masuk Kubu Sosialis', *op. cit.*, pp. 114–115.

[97] *Indonesian Observer*, January 21, 1963.

[98] D. N. Aidit, 'Indonesian Communists March Forward for Full National Independence', *World Marxist Review*, June 1963, p. 16.

[99] D. N. Aidit, *Berani, Berani, Sekali Lagi Berani!* (Djakarta, 1963), p. 50.

[100] *Harian Rakjat*, April 19, 1963.

[101] Cf. '"Harian Rakjat" Refutes Yugoslav Revisionist Clique', *Peking Review*, May 17, 1963, pp. 13–15, and Njoto, 'Safeguarding the Unity of the International Communist Movement', *Peking Review*, July 19, 1963, pp. 21–22.

[102] Reuter despatch, Peking, September 6, 1963.

[103] Colina MacDougall, 'Aidit on the Fence', *Far Eastern Economic Review*, October 10, 1963, p. 49.

[104] *The Straits Times*, September 16, 1963.

[105] See the articles by Alex Josey in *The Straits Times*, September 20, 1963, and *Far Eastern Economic Review*, November 14, 1963, pp. 339–340.

[106] Justus M. van der Kroef, 'Communism and Chinese Communalism in Sarawak', *The China Quarterly*, October-December, 1964.

[107] For details on Peking's financing of the 'Games of the new Emerging Forces' in Djakarta, see *Malayan Times*, November 21, 1963.

[108] Richard Lowenthal, 'The World Scene Transformed', *Encounter*, October 1963, p. 8.

[109] The characterization of Gomulka appears in the original version of Aidit's report to the Fifth National Congress of the PKI in March, 1954. (See D. N. Aidit, *The Road to People's Democracy, op. cit.*, p. 17). The later version of this report (compare *D. N. Aidit, Pilihan Tulisan, op. cit.*, vol. 1, p. 219) omits all reference to Gomulka.

[110] Justus M. van der Kroef, 'An Indonesian Ideological Lexicon', *Asian Survey*, July, 1962, pp. 24–30.

[111] *Madju Terus Menggempur Imperialisme dan Feodalisme, op. cit.*, p. 10.

[112] See, e.g., D. N. Aidit, *Sosialisme Indonesia dan Sjarat-Sjarat Pelaksanaannja* (Djakarta, 1962), pp. 6–8, 25.

[113] Cf., e.g., D. N. Aidit, *Setudju Manipol Harus Setudju Nasakom!* (Depagitprop CC PKI, Djakarta, 1962) and A. Anwar Sanusi, et. al., *Patriotisme dan Internasionalisme* (Depagitprop CC PKI, Djakarta, 1962). Both of these volumes appear in the *Seri Kursus Rakjat*.

[114] D. N. Aidit, *Pengantar Etika dan Moral Komunis* (Djakarta, 1962), esp. pp. 21–32.

[115] D. N. Aidit, 'Indonesian Communists March Forward for Full National Independence', *World Marxist Review*, June, 1963, p. 11. See also Arnold Beichman, 'Vivere Pericoloso! Soekarno likes to Quote Il Duce', *The Bulletin* (Sydney), September 14, 1963, pp. 25–27.

[116] 'Strengthen National Unity and Avoid Provocations', *Review of Indonesia*, September-October, 1960, p. 4; italics in original. An interesting example of how Communist and fellow traveling publicists appropriate *Manipol* and fit it to Communist theory is the brochure by SOBSI vice-chairman Mohammad Munir, *Introduksi tentang Manifesto Politik Republik Indonesia* (Djakarta, 1960). For Munir, Sukarno's *Manipol* is 'aimed at imperialism in all forms', while the national aspects of Indonesia's revolution as outlined in *Manipol* can be likened to the 'Democratic Revolution' which seeks to obliterate 'feudalism' and dictatorship. The 'landlords' according to Munir, 'constitute the most important social basis for the forces of imperialism' and the peasant must therefore be liberated from them. *Manipol* sets the basis 'for uniting all anti-imperialist forces' and a socialist society is the long-range objective in *Manipol*, etc.

[117] *Harian Rakjat*, August 1, 11, 13, 1959; *Pedoman* (Djakarta), August 12, 1959; *Suluh Indonesia* (Djakarta), August 12, 1959.

[118] The extent to which *kiajih* collaborated with Communists in whipping up anti-Dutch agitation in West Java, especially in the nineteen-twenties, still awaits analysis. Around 1924 two Muslim clerics, Hadji Misbach in Java and Hadji Datuk Batuah in West Sumatra, propagated Communist doctrine in Islamic terms (J. Th. Petrus Blumberger, *De Communistische Beweging in Nederlandsch-Indië*, 2nd. ed., Haarlem, 1935), pp. 38, 41. After independence was attained, one of the oddities of the Indonesian political scene was the *Partai Komunis Indonesia Lokal Islamiet* (Indonesian Communist Local Muslim Party) on the West Coast of Sumatra. Cf. F. J. Goedhart, *Een Revolutie Op Drift* (Amsterdam, 1953), pp. 138–139.

[119] *Antara Daily News Bulletin*, June 30 and July 25, 1961.

[120] *Harian Rakjat*, March 18, 1960.

[121] *Ibid.*, January 12, 1960.

[122] *Ibid.*

[123] Cf. the views of SOBSI leader and parliamentary deputy F. Runturambi, 'Manipol, pembangunan dan pembeajaan', *Harian Rakjat*, August 29–30, 1960.

[124] See Sakirman, 'Lenin, Seorang Anli Strategi Revolusi dan Anli Pembangunan jang Briljan', *Bintang Merah*, vol. 16 (1960), pp. 112–123, and 'Apa arti sokongan PKI kepada UUD 1945 dan Demokrasi Terpimpin', *Bintang Merah*, vol. 16 (1960), pp. 194–219, 320–340. I have paraphrased Sakirman's argument regarding the establishment of 'Indonesian Socialism' above. The PKI's position that the establishment of socialism is not as yet possible suggests a possible conflict with Sukarno, who recently declared that 'we have swept away liberalism, capitalism, imperialism, fascism, and feudalism' and that the time had now arrived to change to 'a socialist society'. The period of transition to Socialism had already started, declared Sukarno. *Antara Daily News Bulletin*, January 15, 1962.

[125] Editorial, 'Lima Belas Tahun Revolusi Agustus', *Kehidupan Partai*, August 1960, pp. 163–166.

[126] Declared the Seventh Congress: 'The Communist Party's position is that only a Gotong Royong cabinet, i.e. a government based on representation of all parties (including the Communists), sincerely working for the ideals of the August revolution,

can rally all the national forces to cope with the difficulties facing the country and the people at the present time', *World Marxist Review*, August 1962, p. 65. During the latter half of 1962 and the first half of 1963 the party redoubled its efforts to enter the government. See e.g. *Antara Daily News Bulletin*, December 28, 1962, p. 4 and *Far Eastern Economic Review*, April 4, 1963, p. 8.

CHAPTER V

[1] M. H. Lukman, *Report on Changes in the Communist Party Constitution* (Djakarta, 1959; translated from the Indonesian by Joint Publications Research Service, no. 4411, Washington, D.C., 1961), p. 2.

[2] For the 1962 Constitution see *AD-ART (Konstitusi) Partai Komunis Indonesia (PKI)*, (Comité Central Partai Komunis Indonesia, Djakarta, 1962). Data for the 1959 Constitution are taken from *Material for the Sixth National Congress of the Communist Party of Indonesia* (Agitprop Department, CC. PKI, s.a.e.l; 1959?), pp. 107–137 and all data for the 1954 Constitution from *Kepartain dan Parlementaria Indonesia* (Kementerian Penerangan, Djakarta, 1954), pp. 492–512.

[3] Formal local government organization for the whole of Indonesia is still (in a process of development and has undergone a number of changes since independence was achieved. So-called 'first-level' regions correspond roughly to provinces (e.g. West, Central and East Java, the Greater Djakarta area, North West and South Sumatra, and so on), the 'second-level' regions correspond, at least in Java, to the former 're-gencies' (perhaps now best described as 'districts') and include towns of certain size, while the still largely undetermined 'third-level regions' may perhaps be seen as 'subdistricts' and are predominantly rural.

[4] M. H. Lukman, *Report on Changes, op. cit.*, p. 28.

[5] *Ibid.*, p. 33.

[6] *Ibid.*, pp. 23–24.

[7] Cf. e.g. Njoto, *Marxisme sebagai Ilmu* (Djakarta, 1959).

[8] M. H. Lukman, *Report on Changes, op. cit.*, p. 6.

[9] Editorial '40 Tahun PKI dan Pembangunan Ideologi', *Kehidupan Partai*, May 1960, pp. 81–83 and Untung, 'Peranan Diskusi Dalam Perdjuangan "Ideologi".' *Kehidupan Partai*, May 1960, pp. 87–90.

[10] Untung, 'Beberapa Pengalaman Dalam Melawan Subjektivisme', *Kehidupan Partai*, June 1960, pp. 102–105.

[11] M. T. Peleng, 'Pelaksanaan Plan 3-Tahun Kedua dan Kaum Tani di Kalimantan Tengah', *Kehidupan Partai*, June 1960, pp. 106–109.

[12] *Kehidupan Partai*, June-August, 1959.

[13] D. Amrin, 'Organisasi: Beberapa Peladjaran Tentang Pembangunan Partai Sedjak Revolusi Agustus', *Kehidupan Partai*, August 1960, pp. 166–168.

[14] *Kehidupan Partai*, January-February 1960, pp. 9–13.

[15] M. H. Lukman, *Report on Changes, op. cit.*, p. 32.

[16] *PKI dan Perwakilan* (Djakarta), vol. 5, no. 2–3, pp. 273–277.

[17] Cf. *Resolusi² Kongres Nasional ke-VII (Luarbiasa) Partai Komunis Indonesia* (Depagitprop CC PKI, Djakarta, 1962), p. 25.

[18] D. N. Aidit, *Untuk Demokrasi, Persatuan dan Mobilisasi (Laporan Umum atasnama CC PKI kepada Kongres Nasional ke-VII PKI 25 April 1962)*, Depagitprop CC PKI, Djakarta, 1962), pp. 76–85.

[19] D. N. Aidit, 'Party Building and Mass Work', *World Marxist Review*, September 1962, p. 33.

[20] D. N. Aidit, *Berani, Berani, Sekali Lagi Berani (Laporan Politik Ketua CC PKI Kepada Sidang Pleno 1 CC PKI, Disampaikan Pada Tanggal 10 Februari 1963)*, (Djakarta, 1963), pp. 61–66, and the same author's 'Indonesian Communists March Forward for Full National Independence', *World Marxist Review*, June 1963, p. 18.

[21] Rewang, 'From the Experience of the Communist Party in Indonesia', *World Marxist Review*, August 1963, pp. 59–60.

[22] M. H. Lukman, 'Laksanakan Plan 4 Tahun dengan Semangat Patriotisme dan Internasionalisme Proletar jang Tinggi', *Bintang Merah*, vol. 19 (November 1963), pp. 3–7 and H. Junus, 'Four Year Plan of the Communist Party of Indonesia', *World Marxist Review*, December 1963, pp. 53–55.

[23] D. N. Aidit, 'The Indonesian Revolution and the Immediate Tasks of the Communist Party of Indonesia', *Peking Review*, no. 37, September 13, 1963, p. 31.

[24] *World Marxist Review*, September 1961, p. 60.

[25] *Harian Rakjat*, January 16, 1961.

[26] *Ibid.*, January 30, February 2, and 22, 1961.

[27] *Ibid.*, January 17, 1961.

[28] *Ibid.*, January 18, 1961.

[29] *Indonesian Observer* (Djakarta), November 3, 1961.

[30] *Program Partai Komunis Indonesia, disahkan oleh Kongres Nasional ke-VII (Luarbiasa) Partai Komunis Indonesia (25–30 April 1962)*, (Depagitprop CC PKI, Djakarta, 1962), pp. 8–15.

The 1959 party program appears in *Material for the Sixth National Congress, op. cit.*, pp. 87–106.

[31] For this comparison see the 1954 PKI program in *Program of the Communist Party of Indonesia* (Agitprop Department of the Communist Party of Indonesia, Djakarta, 1954).

[32] *Madju Terus Menggempur Imperialisme dan Feodalisme (Sidang Pleno Ke II CC PKI Achir Desember 1960)*, Djakarta, 1961.

[33] *Ibid.*, pp. 5–6.

[34] *Ibid.*, pp. 37–38 and *Harian Rakjat*, January 3, 1961.

[35] *Madju Terus Menggempur Imperialisme dan Feodalisme! (Sidang Pleno ke-II CC PKI, Achir Desember 1960)*, (Djakarta, 1961), pp. 37–39.

[36] *Strengthen National Unity and Communist Unity. Documents of the Third Plenum of the Communist Party of Indonesia, Djakarta, end December, 1961* (Djakarta, 1962), pp. 40–41. See also the statement of the Politburo CC PKI, on August 23, 1961, in *Serba-serbi Dokumen Partai 1961* (Depagitprop, Djakarta, 1962), pp. 82–83.

[37] See, e.g. D. N. Aidit, 'The Indonesian Revolution and the Immediate Tasks of the Communist Party of Indonesia', *op. cit.* p. 33:

"There are certain differences between the Program of the Indonesian Communist Party and the Political Manifesto. The Program of the Indonesian Communist Party is the program of the working class to carry through the Indonesian Revolution, while the Political Manifesto is the common program of all the Indonesian people to carry through the Indonesian Revolution (a program for cooperation with other classes). From this it can be seen clearly that the most important difference lies in the question of the leadership of the revolution. The Program of the Indonesian Communist Party clearly points out that to achieve the aims of the Indonesian Revolution the revolutionary leadership must be in the hands of the working class. It is impossible to expect that the question of the leadership of the working class should be included in the Political Manifesto. The Political Manifesto only points out that the workers and the peasants are the supporters of the revolution and it says nothing about which class shoulders the task of leading the revolution."

[38] D. N. Aidit, 'Kibarkan Tinggi Pandji-Pandji "Tanah Untuk Petani" dan Rebut Kemenangan Satu Demi Satu' *Bintang Merah*, vol. 15 (1959), p. 216; and *Nieuwsgier* (Djakarta), May 31, 1955. As early as 1954 Aidit declared that 'work among the peasants is the most important sphere of party activity'. D. N. Aidit, 'For Broad Unity of all National Forces in Indonesia', *For a Lasting Peace! For a People's Democracy!* December 31, 1954.

[39] Soejono, 'Segi-segi pokok Sosial Ekonomi dari pada fungsi dan kedudukan desa dalam Pembangunan Nasional', *Ekonomi dan Keuangan Indonesia*, vol. 13 (1960), p. 407; Tjan Ping Tjwan, 'Population, Unemployment and Economic Development', *Ekonomi dan Keuangan Indonesia*, vol. 13 (1960), p. 459, and N. Keyfitz and Widjojo Nitisastro, *Soal Penduduk dan Pembangunan Indonesia* (Djakarta, 1955). See also Leon A. Mears, 'Economic Development in Indonesia through 1958', *Ekonomi dan Keuangan Indonesia*, vol. 14 (1961), p. 23: 'With the increase in population density on Java, the

size of individual holdings has declined to the point where approximately 90 percent of the farmers cultivate less than 1 hectare . . . of land. Almost 70 percent farm less than one-half hectare. Large holdings, excluding plantations, are the exception with less than one percent of the agricultural holdings exceeding 10 hectares.' A government survey of land tenure conditions in West Java revealed that in this province there were 2,026,771 landowners and a total area of 2,476,870 hectares in arable land. 1,461,189 of the landowners owned or held less than 0·5 hectare per head, 346,141 landowners held from 0·6 up to and including 1 hectare, 152,283 held from 1·1 up to and including 2 hectares, 55,355 held from 2·1 up to and including 5 hectares, 7,995 held from 5 up to and including 10 hectares, 1,436 held from 10·1 up to and including 20 hectares, and 372 held more than 20 hectares. *Indonesian Observer*, December 15, 1961.

[40] Tan Ping Tjwan, *op. cit.*, p. 455 and Stanislas Swianiewicz, 'Tendencies to development and stagnation in the Indonesian economy', *Ekonomi dan Keuangan Indonesia*, vol. 11 (1958), p. 96.

[41] From an unpublished work by Sarbini Sumawinata, cited in Ralph Anspach, 'Monetary Aspects of Indonesia's Economic Reorganization in 1959', *Ekonomi dan Keuangan Indonesia*, vol. 13 (1960), p. 17.

[42] M. A. Jaspan, *Social Stratification and Social Mobility in Indonesia* (Djakarta, 1960), p. 13.

[43] Cf. Raden A. Adiwilaga: *Land Tenure in the Village of Tjipagalo (Bandung Regency)* (Bandung, Kantor Perantjang Tata Bumi, 1954); and *Daerah Aliran Sungei Tjikapundung-Hulu* (Bandung, Kantor Perantjang Tata Bumi, 1954).

[44] See Raden A. Adiwilaga, *Ketjamatan Undjung Brung (Bandung Regency). An Agronomic Report* (Bandung, Kantor, Perantjang Tata Bumi, 1954), pp. 27–28.

[45] *Ibid.*, p. 29.

[46] *Indonesian Observer*, May 5, 1961.

[47] Pandam Goeritno, *Masjarakat Marangan: sebuah laporan sosiografi Ketjamatan Prambanan Daerah Istimewa Jogjakarta* (Jogjakarta, Panitya Social Research Universitas Gadjah Mada, 1958) and Jaspan, *op. cit.*, p. 37.

[48] *Indonesian Observer*, January 19, 1961.

[49] D. N. Aidit, 'Back to the 1945 Constitution for a Change in Policies and Living Conditions', p. 8 in *Eight Plenum of the Central Committee of the Communist Party of Indonesia. Political Report and Resolution. Review of Indonesia*, September-October, 1959 (Supplement).

[50] *Indonesian Observer*, December 22, 1959, January 8, 1960; *Bintang Timur* (Djakarta) November 20, 1959.

[51] *Material for the Sixth National Congress, op. cit.*, pp. 81–82.

[52] B. O. Hutapea, 'Beberapa Peladjaran dari Konferensi Nasional Tani Pertama PKI', *Bintang Merah*, vol. 15 (1959), p. 260.

[53] Aidit, 'Kibarkan Tinggi Pandji-Pandji "Tanah Untuk Petani" dan Rebut Kemenangan Satu demi Satu', *op. cit.*, p. 220.

[54] B. O. Hutapea, *op. cit.*, pp. 259–260, and 'Laporan Mengenai Masalah Koperasi', *Bintang Merah*, vol. 15 (1959), pp. 167–190. See also D. N. Aidit, *Peranan Koperasi Dewasa Ini* (Depagitprop CC PKI, Djakarta, 1963). On the Indonesian cooperative movement generally see Mohammad Hatta, *The Cooperative Movement in Indonesia* (Ithaca, N.Y., 1957).

[55] J. Kurdi, '15 Tahun Berdjuang mengabdi kepada Kaum Tani', *Harian Rakjat*, November 25, 26, 1960.

[56] Cf. *Konstitusi BTI—Barisan Tani Indonesia* (Dewan Pimpinan Pusat BTI, s.a.e.l.), pp. 7–22.

[57] *Suara Tani*, November 1959, pp. 3–4.

[58] *Ibid.*, January 1960, p. 3.

[59] D. N. Aidit, *Untuk Demokrasi, Persatuan dan Mobilisasi, op. cit.*, pp. 91–92.

[60] See *Pembangun Desa*, January-February, 1963, pp. 3–10 and *Suara Tani*, January 1963, p. 1.

[61] *Antara Daily News Bulletin*, February 20, 1963, and February 18, 1964.

[62] On the *klompok* see *Konfernas Tani ke-II PKI* (Djakarta, 1962), pp. 11–17 and Donald Hindley, 'The PKI and the Peasants', *Problems of Communism*, November-December, 1962, p. 34.

[63] *Review of Indonesia*, January 1959, p. 38. See also the article by the PKI's chief agricultural expert Asmu, 'Masalah Landreform', *Bintang Merah*, vol. 16 (1960), esp. pp. 21–22, which gives slightly different figures.

[64] *Kehidupan Partai*, April-May 1959, pp. 58–61.

[65] 'Landreform penting untuk menjelesaikan Revolusi', *Harian Rakjat*, August 4, 1960.

[66] Anwar Sanusi, 'Melalui turun sewa menudju perubahan Agraria', *Harian Rakjat*, November 28, 1960.

[67] *Ibid.*

[68] For details see Department of Information, *Land Reform in Indonesia* (Djakarta, 1961), *Asian Survey*, June 1961, p. 7; *Harian Rakjat*, November 10–12, 1960; *Indonesian Observer*, October 18 and 29, 1960; *Antara Daily News Bulletin*, January 6, 1961 and February 1, 1961, *Review of Indonesia*, September-October 1960, p. 20.

[69] Cf. Asmu, 'The Question of Land Reform', *Review of Indonesia*, July 1960, p. 31.

[70] *Indonesian Observer*, November 28, 1961.

[71] *Harian Rakjat*, March 2, 1961.

[72] Iskandar Tedjasukmana, *The Political Character of the Indonesian Trade Union Movement* (Southeast Asia Program, Cornell University, Ithaca, N.Y., 1958), pp. 21–23.

[73] *Ibid.*, pp. 31–32, and *Laporan Umum Dewan Nasional SOBSI Kepada Kongres Nasional ke-III SOBSI* (Djakarta, 1960), part 3.

[74] *Rentjana Perubahan Konstitusi SOBSI* (Djakarta, 1960), passim.

[75] Everett D. Hawkins, 'Labour Relations in Indonesia', *United Asia*, vol. 13 (1960), no. 3, p. 228.

[76] Philip Stephani, 'The Indonesian Economy', *Far Eastern Economic Review*, March 16, 1961, p. 459, and K. Krishna Moorthy, 'State of Indonesia's Economy', *Far Eastern Economic Review*, July 20, 1961, p. 143.

[77] Aidit's lecture before the *Himpunan Sardjana Indonesia* (Indonesian Scholars' Association) in *Harian Rakjat*, May 14–17, 20, 21, 1963.

[78] Cf. Nathan Keyfitz, 'On the Ecology of Indonesian Cities', *The American Journal of Sociology*, vol. 66 (1961), p. 352. On hunger oedema and malnutrition, see K. V. Bailey, 'Food Problems in Indonesia', *Australian Outlook*, vol. 14 (1960), pp. 299–305; M. Timmer, *Child Mortality and Population Pressure in the D. I. Jogjakarta, Java, Indonesia* (Rotterdam, 1961); and Justus M. van der Kroef, 'Cultural Aspects of Indonesia's Demographic Problem', *Population Review*, vol. 4 (1960), p. 29, and the literature therein cited.

[79] *Indonesian Observer*, October 31, 1961

[80] *Ibid.*, November 29, 1961.

[81] *Harian Rakjat*, November 19, 1963

[82] *Indonesian Observer*, February 23, 1963.

[83] See e.g. by Justus M. van der Kroef: 'Indonesia's Economic Difficulties', *Far Eastern Survey*, vol. 24 (1955), p. 17–24; 'Indonesia's Economic Future', *Pacific Affairs*, vol. 32 (1959), pp. 46–72; 'Indonesia's Economic Dilemma', *Far Eastern Survey*, vol. 29 (1960), pp. 49–63, and 'Indonesia's Economic Difficulties', *International Journal*, Autumn, 1962, pp. 399–413. See also Douglas S. Paauw, 'From Colonial to Guided Economy', pp. 155–243 in Ruth T. McVey, ed., *Indonesia* (New Haven, 1963).

[84] *Java Bode*, (Djakarta), March 20, 21, 23, 1957.

[85] *Nieuwsgier*, October 16, 1953.

[86] *Java Bode*, January 11, 1954.

[87] *Nieuwsgier*, September 16, 17, 1953.

[88] *Review of Indonesia*, April-May 1959, p. 35.

[89] *Ibid.*, May 1960, p. 27.

[90] *Ibid.*, August 1960, pp. 20–21.

[91] *Ibid.*, September-October 1960, pp. 22–23.

[92] *Nieuwsgier*, November 20, 1953.

[93] See J. Henry Richardson, 'Indonesian Labor Relations in their Political Setting', *Industrial and Labor Relations Review*, vol. 12 (1958), p. 68, table 4.

[94] *Indonesian Observer*, July 2, 1960.

[95] On Erningpradja's propagation of OPPI see *Indonesian Observer*, July 18, August 10 and 22, 1960.

[96] *Antara Daily News Bulletin*, September 14, 1960.

[97] Cf. *Laporan Umum Dewan Nasional SOBSI kepada Kongres Nasional ke-III SOBSI, op. cit.*, pp. 79 ff.

[98] *Harian Rakjat*, January 28, 1961.

[99] *Antara Daily News Bulletin*, January 28, 1964, p. 3.

[100] James Bruce Amstutz, *The Indonesian Youth Movement 1908–1955* (Unpublished Ph.D. Thesis, May 1958, Fletcher School of Law and Diplomacy, Medford, Mass.), pp. 328–331.

[101] Suroso in *World Marxist Review*, November 1961, pp. 66–69.

[102] Cora Vreede-De Stuers, *L'Emancipation de la Femme Indonésienne* (The Hague, 1959), p. 95.

[103] *Java Bode*, November 29, 1955.

[104] See *Seminar Nasional Wanita Tani* (Djakarta, 1962).

[105] *Harian Rakjat*, January 19, 1961.

[106] E.g. *Api Kartini* ('The Fire of Kartini') has been for several years, Gerwani's principal monthly, and virtually every issue features an article about Kartini.

[107] Though the Japanese established *rukun kampung* in other major cities, none showed the viability of those in Surabaya.

[108] Cf. *Nieuwsgier*, September 3, 1954.

[109] See the report of LEKRA activity at the national cultural congress in *Ibid.*, September 28, 1954.

[110] D. N. Aidit, 'Kongres Nasional ke-VI PKI', *Bintang Merah*, vol. 15 (1959), pp. 346–347.

[111] *Review of Indonesia*, February 1959, pp. 26–29.

[112] *Ibid.*

[113] Jusuf Adjitorop, *Madjulah Inteligensia Indonesia Berkerumun Disekitar Manipol!* (Djakarta, 1962), pp. 15–20.

[114] J. M. van der Kroef, 'Indonesian Communism's Cultural Offensive', *The Australian Outlook*, April 1964.

[115] See *Patriotisme dan Internasionalisme*, no. 3 in the series *Kursus Rakjat*, with contributions by Anwar Sanusi, Nursuhud, Aidit, *et. al.*

[116] J. H. A. Logemann, 'Indonesia's Terugkeer tot de Grondwet van 1945', *Bijdragen tot de Taal-Land-en Volkenkunde*, vol. 115 (1959), p. 213.

[117] I. Tedjasukmana, *op. cit.*, pp. 101–102.

[118] *Antara Daily News Bulletin*, September 19, 21, 1960.

[119] *Ibid.*, December 28, 1960.

[120] *Indonesian Observer*, March 16, 21, 1961.

[121] *Ibid.*, August 3, 1961.

[122] *Antara Daily News Bulletin*, November 7, and December 31, 1962.

CHAPTER VI

[1] *Review of Indonesia*, January 1960, pp. 20–21.

[2] *Ibid.*, February 1960, pp. 7–9.

[3] *Ibid.*, March 1960, pp. 3–4.

[4] *Harian Rakjat*, March 16, 1960.

[5] *Review of Indonesia*, May 1960, pp. 27–28.

[6] *Ibid.*, June 1960, pp. 28–29.

[7] *Indonesian Observer*, June 29, 1960.

[8] *Harian Rakjat*, July 8 and 13, 1960.

[9] Editorial, 'Keep Our Present Course', *Indonesian Observer*, July 11, 1960.

[10] *Indonesian Observer*, July 16, 1960.

[11] *Antara Daily News Bulletin*, August 5, 1960.

[12] Despite Yamin's denial, the PKI charge that he favored use of foreign capital investment in the financing of Indonesia's development plan is not without foundation. See Guy J. Pauker, *The Indonesian Eight-Year Over-All Development Plan* (Project Rand Research Memorandum, RM–2768, June 9, 1961, Santa Monica, California), p. 18.

[13] *Review of Indonesia*, August 1960, pp. 10–11.

[14] *Indonesian Observer*, July 28, 1960.

[15] *Antara Daily News Bulletin*, August 24, 1960.

[16] On the League, see Justus M. van der Kroef, 'Indonesia's New Parliament', *Eastern World*, September 1960, pp. 16–17, and Daniel S. Lev, 'The Political Role of the Army in Indonesia', *Pacific Affairs*, Winter, 1963–64, pp. 357–358.

[17] *Indonesian Observer*, August 26, 1960.

[18] *Ibid.*, August 30, 1960.

[19] *Ibid.*, August 29, 1960.

[20] *Antara Daily News Bulletin*, September 19, 1960.

[21] *Indonesian Observer*, July 26, 1960.

[22] *Antara Daily News Bulletin*, September 8, 1960.

[23] See press survey in *Indonesian Observer*, August 1, 1960.

[24] *Antara Daily News Bulletin*, September 15, 1960.

[25] *Indonesian Observer*, October 29, 1960.

[26] *Antara Daily News Bulletin*, April 17, 1961.

[27] *Ibid.*, May 4, 1961.

[28] *Indonesian Observer*, April 13, 1961.

[29] According to *Antara Daily News Bulletin*, August 16, 1961, the July-August, 1961 strikes on state plantations and on the Deli railroad both involved SOBSI-affiliated workers.

[30] *Antara Daily News Bulletin*, August 16, 1961,

[31] *Ibid.*, September 21, 1961.

[32] *Ibid.*, October 6, 1961.

[33] *Ibid.*

[34] *Ibid.*, October 3, 1961; and September 26 and 28, 1961.

[35] *Indonesian Observer*, March 23, 1961.

[36] This demonstration was an outgrowth of an anti-American demonstration on February 4, 1962 in Djakarta during which the U.S. embassy was attacked and the American flag was ripped and trampled. The reason for this demonstration was the permission originally given by U.S. officials (a permission withdrawn before the demonstration took place) to Dutch planes carrying military destined for West New Guinea. to land on U.S. territory. According to U.S. State Department spokesman Lincoln White, the attack on the U.S. embassy in Djakarta was inspired by Communist agitators.

[37] Information supplied by a high-ranking Indonesian military informant, whose name the author is not at liberty to divulge.

[38] *Indonesian Observer*, April 26, 1961.

[39] *Antara Daily News Bulletin*, October 31, 1961.

[40] Information supplied by a high-ranking Indonesian military informant.

[41] *Antara Daily News Bulletin*, May 16, 1961.

[42] *Nieuwsgier* (Djakarta), October 14, 1953.

[43] *Java Bode* (Djakarta), October 25, 1956.

[44] *Indonesian Observer*, February 11, 1959.

[45] *Ibid.*, July 3, 1961. The proposed bill established rigid educational and training requirements for journalists, allowed the government, if necessary, to establish its own newspapers, restricted foreign journalists and set many additional restrictions, especially on reporting and distribution.

[46] *Antara Daily News Bulletin*, February 15, 1962.

[47] Cf. *Second Indonesian National 'Peace Congress', Abridged Report and Resolutions, Review of Indonesia, March 1960, Supplement*, pp. 3, 13–14.

[48] *Antara Daily News Bulletin*, May 2, 1961.

[49] *Exchange of Opinions Between the Representatives of the Communist Party of Indonesia and Foreign Fraternal Delegations during the Sixth National Congress of the Communist Party of Indonesia, Review of Indonesia, September-October, 1959, Supplement*, p. 7.

[50] *Resolusi-Resolusi Kongres Nasional ke-VII (Luarbiasa) Partai Komunis Indonesia, Djakarta 25–20 April 1962* (Depagitprop CC PKI, Djakarta, 1962), pp. 64–65.

[51] *Antara Daily News Bulletin*, March 38, 1961.

[52] *Ibid.*, February 8, 1962.

[53] *To Build the World Anew. An Address by President Sukarno of the Republic of Indonesia at the Fifteenth General Assembly of the United Nations, Friday Afternoon, September 30, 1960* (Department of Foreign Affairs Republic of Indonesia, s.a.e.l.), pp. 31–32.

[54] *Indonesian Observer*, October 25, 1960.

[55] *Antara Daily News Bulletin*, October 17, 1960.

[56] Justus M. van der Kroef, 'Nasution, Sukarno and the West New Guinea Dispute', *Asian Survey*, August, 1961, pp. 20–24.

[57] See e.g. *Harian Rakjat*, September 29, 1960.

[58] See Justus M. van der Kroef, 'Nationalism and Politics in West New Guinea, *Pacific Affairs*, spring, 1961, pp. 38–53; 'Recent Developments in West New Guinea', *Pacific Affairs*, Fall, 1961, pp. 279–291; and 'Dutch Opinion on the West New Guinea Problem', *Australian Outlook*, December, 1960, pp. 269–298.

[59] *Antara Daily News Bulletin*, October 4, 1961.

[60] *Ibid.*, November 14, 1961.

[61] *World Marxist Review*, January 1962, p. 63.

[62] *Antara Daily News Bulletin*, February 20, 1962.

[63] On Nasution's attitude toward the West New Guinea crisis see J. M. van der Kroef, 'The Big Build Up', *Nation* (Sydney), February 11, 1961, pp. 10–13, and 'Nasution, Sukarno and the West New Guinea Dispute', *op. cit.*, pp. 20–24. See also Denis Warner, 'The Battle Lines in New Guinea', *The Reporter*, February 1, 1962, pp. 30–32.

[64] *Antara Daily News Bulletin*, January 29, 1962.

[65] *Indonesian Observer*, July 8, 1961.

[66] *Ibid.*, March 2, 1961.

[67] *Ibid.*, July 7, 1960 and *Antara Daily News Bulletin*, April 12, 1961.

[68] *Indonesian Observer*, May 2, 1962.

[69] See e.g. Leon A. Mears, 'Rice Marketing in the Republic of Indonesia', *Ekonomi dan Keuangan Indonesia*, vol. 11 (1958), pp. 45–61 and Leon A. Mears, et al., 'Rice Marketing in the Republic of Indonesia 1957–1958', *Ekonomi dan Keuangan Indonesia*, vol. 10 (1958), pp. 530–580.

[70] Zain Boor, 'How to Surmount the Present Economic Situation', *Indonesian Observer*, December 13, 1961.

[71] Herbert Feith and J. A. C. Mackie, 'The Pressures on President Sukarno', *Nation* (Sydney), January 27, 1962, pp. 6–7.

[72] *Antara Daily News Bulletin*, February 12, 19, and 28, 1962.

[73] Feith and Mackie, 'The Pressures on President Sukarno', *op. cit.*, p. 6.

[74] *Indonesian Observer*, April 4, 1962.

[75] *Foreign Commerce Weekly* (U.S. Department of Commerce, Washington D.C.), December 25, 1961, p. 26.

[76] Cited in *Economic Developments in Indonesia 1960* (Bureau of Foreign Commerce, U.S. Department of Foreign Commerce, Washington D.C., 1961), p. 3.

[77] For details see Justus M. van der Kroef, 'The West New Guinea Settlement: Its Origins and Implications', *Orbis*, Spring 1963, pp. 120–149.

CHAPTER VII

[1] *Malaysia* (Department of Information, Federation of Malaya, Kuala Lumpur), April 1962, no. 2, p. 6.

[2] *North Borneo News and Sabah Times* (Jesselton) November 19, 1962.

[3] *Strengthen National Unity and Communist Unity. Documents of the Third Plenum of the Central Committee of the Communist Party of Indonesia, end December 1961* (Djakarta, 1962), pp. 58–61.

[4] *The Straits Times* (Singapore and Kuala Lumpur), October 14, 1963.

[5] Information Division, Embassy of Indonesia, Washington D.C., *A Survey on the Controversial Problem of the Establishment of the Federation of Malaysia* (s.l., 1963), p. 2.

[6] *Resolusi-Resolusi Kongres Nasional ke-VII (Luarbiasa) Partai Komunis Indonesia* (Depagitprop, CC PKI, Djakarta, 1962), pp. 19, 60.

[7] *The Straits Times*, March 13, 1963.

[8] *Indonesian Observer*, February 1, 1962. Ibrahim Yaacob had been among the most prominent Malayan nationalist leaders before World War II and had been an early advocate of the union of Malaya and Indonesia in an independent state (Cf. Radin Soenarno, 'Malay Nationalism 1900–1945', *Journal of Southeast Asian History*, March 1960, pp. 20–25). In the past two years Ibrahim has notably participated in the anti-Malaysia campaign from Djakarta.

[9] *The Borneo Times* (Sandakan), December 24, 1962.

[10] *Indonesian Observer*, January 12, 1963.

[11] Information Division, Embassy of Indonesia, Washington D.C., *A Survey on the Controversial Problem of the Establishment of the Federation of Malaysia, op. cit.* p. 2.

[12] United States Economic Survey Team to Indonesia, *Indonesia. Perspective and Proposals For United States Economic Aid. A Report to the President of the United States* (New Haven, 1963).

[13] See e.g. Douglas S. Paauw, 'From Colonial to Guided Economy', pp. 155–243 in Ruth T. McVey, ed., *Indonesia* (New Haven, 1963) and Willard A. Hanna, 'Observations on U.S. Aid to Indonesia' *American Universities Field Staff*, *Reports Service, Southeast Asia Series*, vol. XI, no. 1, 1963.

[14] Benjamin Higgins, *Indonesia's Economic Stabilization and Development* (New York, 1957), p. 124.

[15] As late as October 17, 1963, Charles Baldwin, U.S. Ambassador to Malaysia declared that the U.S. 'would make sure that aid and loans would be used to boost its economy' and not on military ventures. In the wake of Congressional opposition to further U.S. assistance to Indonesia, U.S. Secretary of State Dean Rusk on March 24, 1964, declared that the U.S. would not give any *new* aid to Indonesia until the Malaysia dispute was settled, but officials of the U.S. Agency for International Development estimated at the same time that assistance to Indonesia already 'in the pipeline' would amount to from $30 to $40 million in food and $10 million for other activities. *The New York Times*, March 26, 1964.

[16] In the following two paragraphs I have drawn on my article 'Indonesia and the Confrontation', in *The Bulletin* (Sydney), December 14, 1963, pp. 23–26.

[17] Justus M. van der Kroef, 'Indonesia' Economic Dilemma', *Far Eastern Survey*, April 1960, p. 61 and Brig. Gen. Sokowati, *TNI dan Civic Mission: Suatu Aspek Pembinaan Wilajah* (Djakarta, 1963).

[18] *Indonesian Observer*, November 26, 1962.

[19] *Far Eastern Economic Review. 1964 Yearbook* (Hong Kong, 1963), p. 179.

[20] *The Straits Times*, September 27, 1962.

[21] On *Party Rakyat* relations with Azahari see *The Straits Times*, March 13, 1963; on *Barisan Sosialis* relations with the Brunei rebels see the government charge in *The Straits Times*, February 4, 1963.

[22] *Antara Daily News Bulletin*, December 19, 1962.

[23] *Indonesian Observer*, December 28, 1962.

[24] Justus M. van der Kroef, 'Communism and the Guerilla War in Sarawak', *The World Today*, February 1964, pp. 50–60.

[25] *The Sarawak Tribune* (Kuching), May 1 and June 10, 1963; *The Straits Times*, October 19 and November 29, 1963.

[26] *Sabah Times* (Jesselton), November 21, 1963, and January 8, 1964; *The Straits Times*, November 19 and December 19, 1963.

[27] *Antara Daily News Bulletin*, December 28, 1962.

[28] *Ibid.*, September 20, 1962.

[29] *Ibid.*, January 9, 1963 and *Indonesian Observer*, January 3, 1963.

[30] *Indonesian Observer*, January 4, 1963.

[31] *Antara Daily News Bulletin*, March 4, 1963.

[32] *Ibid.*, March 6, 1963.

[33] *Far Eastern Economic Review*, April 4, 1963.

[34] D. N. Aidit, 'Indonesian Communists March Forward for Full National Independence', *World Marxist Review*, June 1963, p. 14.

[35] *The Straits Times*, November 9, 1963.

[36] D. N. Aidit, *Berani, Berani, Sekali Lagi Berani! (Laporan Politik Ketua CC PKI Kepada Sidang Pleno 1 CC PKI, Disampaikan pada Tanggal 10 Februari 1963)*, (Djakarta, 1963), pp. 7–8.

[37] *Antara Daily News Bulletin*, May 17, 1963.

[38] *Indonesian Observer*, April 17, 1963.

[39] For details see Daniel Wolfstone, 'The Malays Move In', *Far Eastern Economic Review*, October 24, 1963, pp. 187–194.

[40] *Harian Rakjat*, August 7, 1963.

[41] *The Straits Times*, September 17, 1963.

[42] In this paragraph I have relied heavily on the insightful article by Alex Josey, 'Aidit andMalaysia', *Far Eastern Economic Review*, February 20, 1964, pp. 421–422.

[43] In September 1963, shortly after the first action against British enterprises Sukarno had issued a decree proscribing unauthorized seizures of foreign companies; similar measures had been issued and enforced by local army commanders since 1958 in a number of areas.

[44] See the article 'Indonesian Supervision of British Companies Stirs Fear of Seizure' by Norman Sklarewitz in *The Wall Street* Journal, February 2, 1964.

[45] *Antara Daily News Bulletin*, January 7, 1964.

[46] *Ibid.*, March 18, 1964.

[47] *Ibid.*, March 4, 1964.

[48] On October 17, 1963, in a speech in Pakanbaru, Central Sumatra, Subandrio accused Malaysian premier Rahman of wanting to annex, among other areas, Indonesian Kalimantan, and said that the Tunku was pursuing this aim by purposefully 'setting economic development in North Kalimantan(Sabah) at a greater pace than in Indonesian Kalimantan' so that Indonesian Kalimantan would secede and join Malaysia. Subsequently Subandrio declared that Indonesia, though poor, did not want the kind of prosperity Malaysia was enjoying since the prosperity of Malaysians 'is the remnant of huge profits made by capitalists and neo-colonialists in Southeast Asia'. *Far Eastern Economic Review*, October 31, 1963, p. 223, and November 21, 1963, p. 385.

[49] *The New York Times*, March 26, 1964.

[50] *Far Eastern Economic Review*, January 23, 1964, p. 164.

[51] *The Straits Times*, November 27, 1963.

[52] *Far Eastern Economic Review*, February 13, 1964, p. 339.

[53] *Ibid.*, May 2, 1963, p. 66 and October 17, 1963, p. 130.

[54] *Indonesian Observer*, June 20, 1963 and *Antara Daily News Bulletin*, March 17, 1964.

[55] *Review of Indonesia*, May 1960, p. 27; *Indonesian Observer*, January 5, 1963; D. N. Aidit, *Berani, Berani, sekali Berani!, op. cit.*, pp. 12–13.

[56] *Antara Daily News Bulletin*, February 26, 1964.

[57] *The Straits Times*, October 14, 1963.

[58] *Peking Review*, October 11, 1963, p. 18.

[59] See, e.g., the essay 'Gerakan Komunis Internasional dan Revolusi Asia Tenggara', pp. 24–40 in D. N. Aidit, *Langit Takkan Runtuh* (Djakarta, 1963), and *Far Eastern Economic Review*, January 30, 1964, p. 193.

[60] *Peking Review*, February 14, 1964, p. 22.

[61] See Bernard K. Gordon, 'The Potential for Indonesian Expansion', *Pacific Affairs*, Winter, 1963–64, p. 387.

[62] *Peking Review*, April 19, 1963, p. 9 and December 20, 1963, p. 25; *New China News Agency*, September 28, 1963; *North Borneo News and Sabah Times*, January 4, 1963.

[63] See 'A Journalist's Bandung', *United Asia* (Bombay), August 1963, pp. 589–590.

[64] *Malayan Times* (Petaling Jaya), November 21, 1963.

[65] *Peking Review*, November 15, 1963, pp. 21–22, and November 22, 1963, pp. 16–18.

[66] *Antara Daily News Bulletin*, March 10, 1964.

[67] *Indonesian Observer*, June 19, 1963 and *The Borneo Times*, November 29, 1963.

[68] *Antara Daily News Bulletin*, May 21, 1963.

[69] *Peking Review*, May 24, 1963, p. 20. See also *Far Eastern Economic Review*, May 30, 1963, pp. 463–464.

[70] *Antara Daily News Bulletin*, May 29, 1963.

[71] *Peking Review*, January 17, 1964, p. 32.

[72] On Indonesian repayments to the Soviet Union as affected by the economic 'confrontation' see *Indonesia, January 1964, Quarterly Economic Review. The Economist Intelligence Unit* (London), no. 47, pp. 6–9.

[73] *Peking Review*, January 31, 1964, p. 17.

CHAPTER VIII

[1] V. I. Lenin, *'Left-Wing' Communism, An Infantile Disorder* (Moscow, Foreign Languages Publishing House, 1952), p. 90.

[2] Donald Hindley, 'President Sukarno and the Communists: the Politics of Domestication', *The American Political Science Review*, vol. 56 (1962), pp. 915–926.

[3] *Antara Daily News Bulletin*, March 10, 1964.

[4] Cheng Hsueh-chia, *Wither Indonesia? PKI and CCP* (Taipei, Taiwan, June 1960; Asian People's Anti-Communist League, no. 45), pp. 107–108.

[5] Georg A. von Stackelberg, 'Renewed Attacks on the National Bourgeoisie', *Bulletin, Institute for the Study of the USSR*, August 1961, pp. 4–5.

[6] *World Marxist Review*, November 1963, pp. 59–61.

[7] These doctrinaire grounds of opposition were cogently formulated, for example, in the condemnation of Communism by the seventh congress of the Masjumi party in Surabaya in December, 1954. There Communism, because of its 'historical materialism', was held to be incompatible with Islam, and because it denies the existence of God. Communism was also described as regarding women as a 'communal possession', thus flouting Islamic family laws, as condemning private property, and as striving for the realization of its aims through dictatorship, instead of by the Islamic method of 'consultation'. Cf. Deliar Noer, *Masjumi. Its Organization, Ideology and Political Role in Indonesia* (Unpublished M.A. Thesis, Cornell University, February 1960, Ithaca, N.Y.), p. 193.

[8] G. W. J. Drewes, 'Indonesia: Mysticism and Activism', p. 286 in G. E. von Grünebaum (ed.), *Unity and Variety in Muslim Civilization* (Chicago, 1955).

[9] Cf. W. F. Wertheim in *Bijdragen tot- de Taal- Land- en Volkenkunde*, vol. 117 (1961), pp. 511–512.

[10] On this PKI identification see e.g. D. N. Aidit, *Tentang Marxisme* (Djakarta, 1963), esp. pp. 109–115, and Jusuf Adjitorop, *Peranan dan Tugas-Tugas Hukum Nasional dalam alam Manipol* (Djakarta, 1963).

[11] See e.g. Soekarno, *Marhaen and Proletarian* (Modern Indonesia Project, Southeast Asia Program, Cornell University, Ithaca, N.Y., 1960).

[12] Selosoemardjan, *Social Changes in Jogjakarta* (Ph.D. thesis, Cornell University, Ithaca, N.Y., September 1959), p. 279.

[13] *Ibid.*, p. 216.

[14] Justus M. van der Kroef, 'Land Tenure and Social Structure in Rural Java', *Rural Sociology*, vol. 25 (1960), pp. 414–430.

[15] I am grateful to a prominent Indonesian businessman, whom I am not at liberty to identify, for information upon this point.

[16] Cf. Donald R. Fagg, *Authority and Social Structure. A Study in Javanese Bureaucracy* (Unpublished Ph.D. Thesis, Harvard University, Cambridge, Mass., April 1958), p. 527.

INDEX